DON HASTINGS'

Month-By-Month Gardening in the South

DON HASTINGS'

Month-By-Month Gardening in the South

WHAT TO DO AND WHEN TO DO IT

DON HASTINGS *and*
CHRIS HASTINGS

LONGSTREET PRESS, INC.
Atlanta, Georgia

Published by LONGSTREET PRESS, INC.,
a subsidiary of Cox Newspapers,
a subsidiary of Cox Enterprises, Inc.
2140 Newmarket Parkway
Suite 122
Marietta, Georgia 30067

Printed in the United States of America

3rd printing, 1998

Library of Congress Catalog Number 96-76507

ISBN: 1-56352-551-8

Book and cover design by Jill Dible

CONTENTS

HOW TO USE THIS BOOK

What is a garden? Is it a formal terraced landscape kept by a professional staff, a small informal planting in a subdivision, a lawn, a vegetable plot, a group of fruits, pots on a patio, or plants growing indoors? It is any or all of these. Gardens are what we create for ourselves and our friends to enjoy.

Gardening isn't just a matter of doing things; it's a matter of doing things at the right time. If you prune Forsythia before it blooms, you will have few if any flowers in the spring. If you set out your tomato plants or Impatiens too early, frost kills them. If you fertilize boxwoods in September, they may be bleached or brown on the top in November as a result of the first hard freeze.

This book tells you what to do and when to do it to avoid making serious mistakes. There is nothing as disheartening as buying a plant and watching it die. It is even more discouraging to have a plant thrive for a year, and then suffer because of something you did or didn't do. Timing is a critical and necessary part of gardening.

But what happens if you prune your Forsythia at the right time and it still doesn't have as many beautiful blossoms as the one you saw on the way to work or to shop? This book also shows you the best way to grow plants. *When* to prune and fertilize is important; *how* to prune and fertilize is just as important. We have covered the basics of all the critical gardening activities so that you won't just be on time, you will be on target.

Everybody lives by the calendar, and though the calendar is great for planning our lives, it doesn't really fit gardening as well. The most important and pleasant times to garden are when plants grow, flower, and produce food. We call this time the growing season. Unfortunately, the growing season falls smack in the middle of a calendar year. The second most important gardening time, when we plant trees, shrubs, and fruits and prepare for spring plantings, comes outside the growing season. This period spans part of last year's calendar and part of this year's. When using this book, keep in mind that November and December are starting points for some plants, while others begin in March and April.

This book follows the real calendar: January through December. But we designed it so you can start any time you want. A pruning suggestion in the January activity list might be repeated in February and in December since you can prune in those months as well. Each "how to" article is placed in the most appropriate month for that activity but is also footnoted so you can refer to it whenever that subject comes up.

Just as the growing season does not follow the calendar, neither does the weather. In some years March may be warm and sunny; in others it may be cold and brutal. Since plants respond to weather, not the calendar, we have tied each month's gardening activity to the weather whenever possible. For instance, fertilize fruit trees when the buds begin to swell, put out pre-emergence weed killer when the Forsythia blooms, set out tomato plants after the danger of frost and when the ground begins to warm.

None of us have enough time to do all the things we want. Business, social activities, sports, and other activities go along with gardening. We hope this book will save you time by spreading gardening activities over the most suitable times rather than scheduling them for the third Tuesday of April.

We wrote this book as a gardening organizer and helper. We earnestly hope that at the same time, it heightens your interest in developing a love for plants.

DON HASTINGS'

Month-By-Month
Gardening in the South

January

IN THE SOUTHERN GARDEN

January might not seem like much of a month for gardening. After all, it is the dead of winter. The wonderful thing about the South, though, is that the dead of winter comes and goes through January and February like waves in the ocean. Cold fronts roar out of Canada and make it real winter, then warm air comes from the Gulf of Mexico and makes spring seem just around the corner. The good news is that outside gardening ceases for only short periods of time. The bad news is that there is a lot of cold weather ahead before spring arrives.

The South is never completely dormant, and when the cold wave goes back to Canada, winter flowers bloom. Pansies are bright, early spring bulbs show color, the last blossoms of Meratia (Chimonanthus) and early Winter Honeysuckle (Lonicera fragrantissima) perfume the garden. We see the last Camellia sasanquas blossom and the first mid-season Camellia japonicas. Yellow flowers of January Jasmine (Jasminum nudiflorum) peek out and perhaps the first Flowering Quince blossoms if the weather is mild. Even during terrible cold waves, the South's broadleaf evergreens provide gardens with rich green foliage, so our gardens are always alive and wonderful places.

Mild weather is the time to start gardening again, so use the coldest times to plan ahead and order new seeds and plants. On those miserably cold days, sit inside by the fire and prepare for spring. It will be here sooner than you think.

Some winters are colder, some are warmer. It may not be possible every year to finish dormant-season activities this month. Do as much as your weather permits, and then finish the rest in early February.

AT LEFT: *Leatherleaf Mahonia (Mahonia bealei)*

American Red Maple (Acer rubrum) in the winter

I. *Shade and Flowering Trees*

Look out the window at your trees. Their bare limbs look lifeless. Even magnolias and other evergreen trees seem asleep. Yet, deep in the soil there is life. Young feeder roots are inching out to start sending nutrients up the huge plant in readiness for warm weather and new leaves when spring finally arrives. Though it seems impossible, the Sugar Maple's rising sap is tapped even when there is snow on the ground and the tree seems without life.

Planting, fertilizing, and even pruning trees should be done when this first new effort by the tree begins. Plant when the ground is cold to give young trees ample time to develop many feeder roots before the demands of new top growth come as the weather warms. Fertilize established trees so that their feeder roots will have nutrients to send to their new leaves and growth. Prune while it is cold to allow time for the sap tubes to close and prevent precious nutrients from being lost through the wounds.

By February, some trees may even blossom, so January is a good time to start these important jobs even if they have to be continued into next month. Work outside while you can, for rain and snow and sleet may see the postman out, but not many of us gardeners.

PRUNING SHADE AND FLOWERING TREES

Trees come in a variety of shapes and forms. Consider the petite **Japanese Maple** and the giant **American Red Maple**: both are in the same family, yet by looking at them you would never imagine they are related. In addition to their different appearances, these two trees grow in completely different types of soil. While the **Japanese Maple** prefers soil with good drainage, the **Red Maple** will grow in swampy conditions. But the **maple** is just one of hundreds of families of trees! It is not hard to find a tree to fill a particular spot on your property or grow in a particular type of soil; it is just a matter of shopping around and asking knowledgeable people.

Despite the variety of trees available to plant in the South, there are people who insist on pruning trees so they will grow in unnatural ways. There are cases when growing a tree "unnaturally" proves beneficial, like the peach tree. Proper pruning not only increases the number of good peaches set on the tree, but also decreases the number lost due to brown rot. In this case, an increase in peach production compensates for the unnatural shape of the tree caused by the Open Head/Basket method of pruning. Another example is espalier, the art of pruning to make a tree grow flat against a wall. We can even say that the purpose of a bent-over Indian tree pointing the way toward water is beneficial enough to compensate for its unnatural appearance.

But I hope all this talk of beneficial pruning has not inspired you to go bend down all the trees in your yard so they point toward the nearest fire hydrant. A much more appealing sight is that of a beautiful, naturally growing **Kwanzan Cherry** tree or the magnificent **Gingko** in the fall. With the tremendous number of trees available for our use, why not create variety in your yard by planting different trees rather than trying to improve on nature by pruning the ones you have?

Newly Planted Trees

Newly planted shade trees should need very little pruning. The major structural cuts should have been made by the grower before you purchased the tree. If any limbs have been damaged in handling, however, they should be cleanly removed. Check also to see if there are any branches growing from the trunk at a very tight angle. These branches should be removed because they are weak and will likely break during a storm. This is especially important with the **Bradford Pear**, which has a natural tendency to develop this type of weak growth. Cut the branch at the trunk with a good, flush cut.

If you do feel the necessity to prune your newly planted tree, don't cut the main leader. Doing so will "top the tree," altering its growth pattern and ruining its natural shape.

Established Shade Trees

As a general rule, it is best to let established shade trees develop their natural shape with as little inter-ference from us as possible. Trees develop their own shapes, and our efforts to improve them seldom succeed. This does not mean that we cannot remove problem branches which are too close to the house or consistently in the way. This type of spot pruning is sometimes necessary. Once again, be careful not to prune the leader or central trunk because that will ruin the tree's natural shape.

If you must prune, it is best to do so when the sap is not flowing. Shade trees begin to "slow down" after they drop their leaves and enter a period of dormancy during the winter months. January is the best month for heavy pruning, although it is okay to do so with care between late November and February. It is best not to prune when the sap is frozen because the branches may "tear" rather than cut smoothly.

Even though the tree is dormant, prune carefully. Make clean cuts and try to prevent the bark from tearing along the branch. As you cut, it helps to saw through the underside of the limb first, and then finish cutting from the top. This will prevent the bark from tearing as the weight of the limb pulls the branch down. Also, try to cut immediately after a joint. If you cut at a spot one or two feet out from the trunk, the remaining stub will probably not survive. Since you'll have to remove the dead stub later, you may as well do it the first time.

It used to be common practice to treat fresh cuts with a sealant to prevent borers from entering the tree and also to prevent rot. New studies have shown, however, that these sealants tend to crack and allow water to seep underneath. The sealant then holds the water next to the cut and causes more rot than would normally have occurred. Keep an eye out, though, for new, improved sealant compounds at your local nurs-

Pruning a tree's leader alters its natural growth and may ruin its shape.

ery. In the meantime, we can rely on the tree's natural ability to heal itself by forming a callus over the newly cut area. In the long run, this callus is better than even the most improved sealant compound.

Finally, pruning to change the direction of a limb's growth should be done only on young one- or two-year-old wood. Old or heavily barked wood seldom sprouts new shoots.

Flowering Trees

Pruning a flowering tree is a little tricky because you must first determine if you are dealing with a spring or summer-flowering tree. Spring-flowering trees grow and set buds during the summer, and then become dormant in the winter. When spring arrives, the buds which have been waiting all winter begin to blossom. Summer-flowering trees are different in that they grow all summer long, but they go into the winter dormancy without setting buds. As spring arrives,

Crape Myrtle (Lagerstroema indica) pruned as a tree. Prune summer-flowering shrubs in the winter.

Crape Myrtle (Lagerstroema indica) blooms well after proper winter pruning.

the tree wakes up and begins work setting buds on its new shoots. This bud formation takes a while and holds up the blossoms until the summer.

Spring-flowering trees like **dogwoods, flowering cherries, flowering crabapples, flowering peaches,** and **flowering pears** should need very little pruning after their original structural pruning. Structural pruning of newly planted flowering trees is similar to that of shade trees in that you remove crossed branches, weak wood, or branches sprouting at tight angles. As with shade trees, it is better not to top a flowering tree. Once the original pruning of a newly planted tree is complete, you will need only to cut out damaged, diseased, dead, or troublesome branches.

Any structural pruning should be done during the winter dormant months to protect against the threat of pests and diseases. Remember that with spring-flowering trees, every branch you cut will most probably have buds on it. Pruning these will decrease the number of flowers the tree can produce this year. Minor pruning for shape should be done as soon after blossoming in the spring as possible so that the new growth will not be affected.

Summer-flowering trees require much heavier pruning. Heavily pruning **Crape Myrtle, Chaste Tree (Vitex),** and similar trees during the winter months will force new growth in spring. This new growth will set buds and ensure a beautifully flowering tree. Remember that the severity of your pruning should coincide with the shape you want your summer-flowering tree to take. **Crape Myrtles** and **Chaste Trees** can be heavily pruned to make a bush-like form, or pruned lightly to retain a taller tree-like form. **Southern Magnolias** are an exception to the summer-flowering tree rule and should largely be left alone. If you must prune, however, do so in the winter.

HOW TO FERTILIZE SHADE TREES

Everywhere I look these days I see young trees: in the supermarket parking lot, along the highway, and in new subdivisions. It seems to be a sign of our times that we clear undeveloped areas of pines, build new subdivisions, and then replant the front yards with a couple of trees. While these young trees may seem dwarfed by a sea of newly built houses, with proper attention they will attain maximum growth and the neighborhood children will soon have a tree to climb.

Of course, proper planting is of utmost importance for a tree not only to survive but to flourish. But after it is planted and has become established, it needs little help except for yearly fertilizing. Fertilizing established trees is just as important with a 15-year-old tree as it is with a five-year-old tree; both trees need nutrients as they grow. Fertilizing allows uniform and healthy development by providing the tree with the proper nutrients for growth.

So when does a tree become established? In the first three years after planting, a tree is much like a shrub. Its roots are shallow and should be fertilized just like a shrub. Use about 1/2 pound of 15-15-15 fertilizer per three feet of height. Spread the fertilizer evenly on the ground around the tree several feet from the trunk. About three years after planting, the tree's roots have grown deep and it has anchored itself in the soil. At this point the new tree is considered to be established.

Fertilizing an established tree with deep roots is different from fertilizing shrubs with shallow roots. Fertilizer for established trees must be placed in the ground near the roots, as opposed to fertilizer for shrubs which may be placed on top of the ground. If you fertilize a tree by spreading the fertilizer on top of the ground, the nutrients will most likely be absorbed by grass, weeds, shrubs, and other plants long before they sink down to the depth of the tree roots.

The amount of fertilizer a tree needs depends largely on the size and age of the tree. Measure the circumference of the trunk in inches at a point about three feet above the ground. If the tree has a fork, measure the circumference just below the fork. We can figure the amount of fertilizer by using one pound per inch of circumference.

Next, we need to determine where the tree's roots are so that we can properly place the fertilizer. A good rough measurement is to assume that the tree's roots grow underground in much the same direction and length as its limbs. By identifying a circle under the outer extremities (drip line) of the limbs, we hope to have located the outer, most active regions of the tree's roots. Fertilizing in these areas will encourage further growth.

Having found the drip line, bore or poke two rows of holes around this outer circle. The first row should be slightly outside the drip line and the second row slightly inside. The holes should be 18 inches apart in the row, and there should be 18 inches between the two rows. Use a soil auger or a two-inch steel pipe to make the holes 18 to 24 inches deep.

Now that we have determined the amount of fertilizer necessary and made the holes, we want to distribute the fertilizer evenly around the tree. Count the holes and divide the number into the amount of fertilizer required. This is the amount to put in each hole. It is helpful to use a large funnel (you can make one out of paper) to get the fertilizer in the holes.

It is important to use the correct fertilizer formula. A 15-15-15 fertilizer is all right, but check your local nursery to see if they have a special slow-release tree formula fertilizer.

TREE ACTIVITIES FOR JANUARY:

Plant

☛ Plant B&B, bare-root, and container-grown shade and flowering trees during the entire month when the ground is not frozen or likely to freeze soon. Make sure to plant trees at the correct depth in a well-prepared hole, and stake them to prevent swaying (especially bare-root trees). Never plant trees deeper than they were growing in the nursery. When planting B&B and container-grown trees, it is a good idea to leave the top of the root ball showing after planting. Plant bare-root trees with the soil level one inch above the top root.*

☛ Choose planting stock carefully. New shade trees should be straight with tight, smooth bark, a dominant central shoot or leader, and should not be loose in the ball or container. Choose flowering trees carefully also. They should be free from scars, which indicates they have been grown well.

☛ Plant shade trees dug from the wild only as a last resort and only if they are small. Their wide, sprangly roots are liable to be cut drastically during digging and then take forever to start growing vigorously again.*

☛ Do not plant **Southern Magnolia** and **Cherry Laurel** until late February or March.

* See "Planting Trees and Shrubs," p. 264

☛ When handling container-grown or B&B trees, never pick them up by the stem; if you do, you may break the roots in the ball of earth.

☛ It is best to plant trees when the soil is not too wet. However, if planting is necessary before the soil dries out, use dry peat moss as the soil amendment. It will absorb excess moisture and make it easier to prepare a good mixture for planting.

Prune

☛ Prune dormant, deciduous, and evergreen shade trees this month. Both light and heavy pruning are okay, but do not prune trees when the sap is frozen. Also, never remove the central shoot or leader of a shade tree; you will ruin its natural shape.†

☛ Prune spring-flowering trees like **Bradford Pear**, **flowering cherry**, **flowering peach**, and **flowering pear** but do so sparingly and selectively. Remove any crossed branches, damaged or diseased wood, and bad growth. Remember that buds for spring blossoms are already present on the branches and twigs grown last summer. Pruning them will reduce the number of flowers on the tree.†

☛ Summer-flowering trees like **Crape Myrtle** and **Chaste Tree (Vitex)** may be pruned severely to force new spring shoots on which the summer's blooms will develop. Prune selectively, however, to shape the tree and force new shoots in the direction you want them to grow.†

Fertilize

☛ Fertilize all newly planted trees with a 15-15-15 fertilizer. Spread the fertilizer in a circle at the edge of the hole you dug, using about 1/2 pound per three feet of the tree's height. Water thoroughly after fertilizing.

☛ Fertilize large deciduous and evergreen shade trees at the end of January. Use one pound of fertilizer per inch circumference of the tree, measured three feet above the ground. Use a 15-15-15 mix of fertilizer.

This is a once-a-year job.‡

☛ Fertilize summer-flowering trees after pruning with 5-10-15. Use one pound of fertilizer per inch circumference of the tree, measured three feet above the ground. This is also done once a year.

☛ Wait until March to fertilize **Magnolia** and **Cherry Laurel**.

Spray

☛ Control scale on all trees with Orthene or Cygon, except in the case of **hollies.** Use Orthene on **hollies.****

Water

☛ Water newly planted shade and flowering trees thoroughly, even if the ground is wet, in order to settle the soil around the roots.

Other

☛ Mulch newly planted and fertilized trees with pine straw or pine bark. Do not allow the mulch to pack against the tree's trunk.††

☛ Check mulch around older trees and replenish with fresh mulch if needed.

☛ Stake newly planted shade and flowering trees, especially if you purchased them bare root. Attach three wires to the trunk at about four to five feet off the ground and run them to wooden stakes driven at intervals around the tree. Make a collar of old watering hose to prevent the wire from cutting into the trunks.

---

† See "Pruning Shade and Flowering Trees," p. 4

‡ See "How to Fertilize Shade Trees," p. 6

** See "Controlling Insects and Diseases," p. 80

†† See "Mulching: A Lesson from Nature," p. 243

II. *Shrubs and Vines*

There is nothing as useless looking as a dormant flowering shrub or vine found in a nursery during January. It may hold vast potential for becoming an exquisite Hydrangea with huge summer flowers, a brilliantly colored Forsythia, or a spectacular Clematis but now it looks like a bunch of dead sticks, especially if it is in a package stacked into a nursery bin. Purchasing such a thing takes a bit of faith, but that is gardening. It really *is* best to plant while it *does* look like a bunch of dead sticks for the same reasons it is best to plant most deciduous plants while the ground is cold. They need to establish a heavy root system before the leaves come out.

Planting evergreen shrubs and vines while the ground is cold is done for the same reasons, but it doesn't take such a leap of faith. They look alive and look like something that has a chance to grow.

MAKING DORMANT CUTTINGS OF SHRUBS AND ROSES

Dormant cuttings are an easy way to increase the number of plants in your landscape at very little expense. A dormant cutting is made during the winter months while the plant is dormant. Unlike softwood cuttings made in the greenhouse or outside in the summer (see August, "Semi-Hardwood Cuttings" and October, "Propagating Herbaceous Houseplants and Garden Plants"), dormant cuttings require little care after the initial preparation. This makes the entire project possible as a weekend activity. Some of my favorite plants to propagate by dormant cuttings are **Althaea, Burford Holly, Otto Luyken Laurel, Oakleaf Hydrangea, Camellia japonica, Camellia sasanqua, Forsythia, roses,** and **bunch grapes.**

The first step in making dormant cuttings is to prepare a good rooting bed. Remember that cuttings made in January or February will need to sit undisturbed until they are well rooted in late March or early April. Try to find a spot for the rooting bed which won't conflict with other springtime activities. It should be located outside in a sheltered area (one that will not receive bitter cold winds) with light shade.

One of my biggest problems is deciding how big to build a new rooting bed. It always seems that I have loftier propagation goals than are humanly feasible. For instance, I once hastily built a rooting bed four feet by six feet which to this day is only half-filled. I also have a hard time setting cuttings in the back of the bed; my arms aren't long enough! A good way to decide on the size of your bed is to figure each cutting will probably take a 2-inch-by-2-inch square space (this is a generous amount). Every square foot then translates into 36 cuttings. As you can see by the numbers, my four-by-six rooting bed is capable of holding 864 cuttings. I would have a crowded landscape if I lived up to that goal!

As an alternative to a rooting bed, some people opt for using their cold frame. A cold frame is basically a 12-to-16-inch-high square frame and cover made out of treated lumber where plants can be acclimated to the cold, or spring vegetables can be started earlier than in the garden. This device can be used as a rooting bed by putting a four-to-six-inch layer of perlite in the rooting area.

Once you have decided on the size of your rooting bed, start by working the ground where the bed will be. Dig the soil out of the area of the bed at least twelve inches deep and remove it. I prefer to build a frame inside the excavated hole extending several inches above ground level using treated lumber. This prevents mud and surface water from flowing into

A simple rooting bed is easy to make. Winter cuttings are ready to set out next fall.

the bed. Next, place four inches of coarse bark in the bottom of the hole to improve drainage (gravel or small stones can be substituted for bark). On top of the bark, add about six inches of perlite. Some people prefer to use a two-inch sand base on top of the bark, followed by six inches of a peat-light soil mixture. Finally, provide a cover for the rooting bed made of clear plastic or glass. This will prevent pine straw and other debris from falling among the cuttings and it will also allow you to monitor the amount of water entering the rooting bed. Covers can range from a single weighted piece of plastic to an elaborate hinged window sash. I find it helpful to build the cover after you make your cuttings, when you have an idea of how tall they will be in the bed. The cover should be a good two inches above the tallest cutting.

Now that you have prepared your rooting bed, it is time to make some cuttings (as mentioned earlier, the best time to make dormant cuttings is in January or February). You will need a sharp knife or pruning shear, preferably a "knife-cut shear." Choose the young wood on the plant which was grown last season, but make sure it is at least as thick as a pencil. Tip-growth is usually the best and will root the fastest. Make cuttings between four and six inches long, with the initial cut (called the basal cut) about half an inch below a bud (sometimes called a "node" or leaf scar). Cutting below a bud is more important than staying in the four-to-six-inch range. When taking cuttings in the garden, you can cut larger sections which you can make into a number of four-to-six-inch cuttings in final preparation (make sure you know which is the top and which is the bottom). Make a number of cuttings from each shrub to help ensure success. Finally, if you are making many cuttings from different plants, be sure to label them so you won't mix them up. Dormant cuttings tend to look remarkably similar once they are off the mother plant!

Before you place the cuttings in your rooting bed, there are a few final steps of preparation. I like to re-cut the basal cut on a slant with the closest point to the bud about one-quarter of an inch. You might want to make this new "clean" cut with a sharp knife on a piece of wood. Some people prefer to shave a small portion of bark off instead, or you can do both. If you have not done so already, cut larger pieces into four-to-six-inch sections. The top cut should be slanting and just above a bud if the piece doesn't include the tip bud. With most cuttings, especially **roses** and **bunch grapes**, it is important to have at least two side buds per cutting: one just above the basal cut (from which roots will emerge), and one higher up (from which side shoots will sprout). I find that a helpful last step of preparation is to treat the basal cut with a rooting compound. Rootone and Hormodin are both excellent materials, and I find they increase the number of cuttings which root, as well as greatly speed up the rooting process and number of roots formed.

If you are working with evergreens, there is one extra step before placing the cuttings in the bed. Evergreen cuttings often die because without roots they cannot absorb as much water as is lost through evaporation from the leaves. If you remove all but two or three leaves from the cutting, you will decrease this evaporation to the point where the cutting absorbs at least as much water as is lost.

We are now ready to place our cuttings in the rooting bed. Keeping each group of cuttings identified, plant them one to two inches deep with about two inches between each cutting. I use one row per shrub so they are easier to label. Finally, water them using a hose-end water breaker to settle the rooting medium around the stem. Water covered beds using a water breaker about once a week over the coming months to keep the rooting medium moist. When the new buds come out, it's wise to mist them with a fog-mist nozzle several times a week.

Cuttings made in January should root by late March or early April. Carefully remove a cutting from a row to inspect the roots (I use an old teaspoon as a miniature trowel). Rooted cuttings are ready to pot when there are many roots at least an inch long. These young plants should be potted rather than planted directly in the ground. Use four-inch pots filled with a peat-light mixture and grow them initially in the same type of protected area as the rooting bed was in. These new plants will be ready to transplant into the garden when the weather cools next fall.

SHRUB AND VINE ACTIVITIES FOR JANUARY:

Plant

☞ Plant all dormant container-grown, B&B, and bare-root shrubs whenever the ground is not frozen. Prepare the holes as carefully as you do for shade trees.*

☞ Plant hardy woody vines like **Clematis, Carolina Jessamine,** and **Wisteria** during periods of mild weather, when the ground is not frozen.†

☞ Plant hardy ground covers like **English Ivy, Vinca minor, Liriope,** and **Spreading Juniper** whenever the ground is not frozen. These should be heavily rooted plants, not transplanted runners.*

☞ It is best to plant shrubs when the soil is not too wet. However, if planting is necessary before the soil dries out, use dry peat moss as the soil amendment. It will absorb excess moisture and make it easier to prepare a good mixture for planting.

Prune

☞ Heavy structural pruning of evergreen shrubs like **Burford Holly, Box Leaf Holly, boxwood,** and **cleyera** may be done this month. However, if most of the leaf area is to be removed, I prefer to wait until mid-February to mid-March so I don't have to look at stubby plants so long. Do not remove all the green leaves from **boxwoods** anytime you prune.

☞ Prune broadleaf evergreens like **hollies** and narrowleaf evergreens like **junipers** and **arborvitaes** to shape any time this month. Always prune so the top is narrower than the bottom in order to keep evergreens from becoming top-heavy and unsightly.

☞ Wait to prune cold-damaged stems until March or April when you can determine the true extent of winter damage.

☞ Prune deciduous summer-flowering shrubs (those which form their blossoms on the coming year's new growth) like **Hydrangea arborescens 'Grandiflora,' Hydrangea paniculata 'Grandiflora,'** and **Butterfly Bush (Buddleia)** any time this month when the wood isn't frozen.‡

☞ Do not prune deciduous spring-flowering shrubs (those which blossom on growth formed last year) like **deciduous azaleas, Forsythia, Spiraea,** and **Viburnum (Snowball)** until after they blossom.‡

☞ Wait to prune spring-flowering evergreen shrubs like **Camellia, azalea, Rhododendron,** and **Mountain Laurel** until after they have finished blooming.‡

☞ Prune **Blue/Pink Hydrangea** by removing the weak shoots at the ground and pruning the main shoots back one-third.‡

☞ Prune **Nandina, Mahonia** and **Aucuba** according to their specific methods.**

☞ Deciduous leafy shrubs like **barberry** and deciduous **Euonymus** can be pruned this month.

☞ Do not prune spring-flowering evergreen vines like **Carolina Jessamine** until after they bloom.‡

☞ Most giant hybrid **Clematis** can be pruned severely from now until new growth starts emerging in early spring since they blossom on new growth.†

☞ Other **Clematis** should only be thinned, leaving the main arms to develop shoots on which blossoms will form. Do this before shoots begin to emerge. Wait until after blossoming to prune **Clematis** like **Clematis montana** and **Clematis X 'Duchess of Edinburgh'** which bloom on last year's growth.†

☞ Prune other spring-flowering deciduous vines like **Wisteria** after they have finished blooming.‡

---

* See "Planting Trees and Shrubs," p. 264
† See "Growing Clematis and Other Southern Vines," p. 54

† See "Growing Clematis and Other Southern Vines," p. 54
‡ See "Pruning Flowering Shrubs and Vines," p. 31
** See "Pruning Aucuba, Mahonia, and Nandina," p. 33

☛ Other summer-flowering deciduous vines like **Silver Lace Vine (Polygonum aubertii)** and **Gold Flame Honeysuckle (Lonicera sempervirens)** should be pruned now before new growth starts.‡

☛ Cut back **Liriope** severely while the weather is cold and before new shoots begin emerging in early spring. If you wait too long, you will cut off new buds or emerging shoots and reduce the vigor of the clump.

Fertilize

☛ Do not begin fertilizing summer-flowering shrubs or vines until February.††

☛ Wait to fertilize evergreens until the new growth is just beginning. This is usually in early March, except in the lower South, where February is the right time.

☛ Wait to fertilize spring-flowering shrubs (those which blossom on growth formed last year) like **azalea**, **Forsythia**, **Spiraea**, and **Viburnum** until flowering has finished.††

Spray

☛ Inspect established evergreens for signs of scale. This insect is particularly bad on broadleaf evergreens. Control it with Cygon except on **hollies**; use Orthene on **hollies**. Dormant oil can also be used this month to control scale on broadleaf evergreens; however, do not apply dormant oil during periods when freezes are likely to occur before the material has dried on the leaves.‡‡

Water

☛ Soak newly planted shrubs and vines thoroughly after planting, even if the ground is wet, and mulch them to protect their roots from cold. Do not allow the mulch to crowd the trunks or lower stems.

☛ When a deep freeze is announced, water evergreens thoroughly, especially marginally hardy ones like **Loquat**, **Gardenia**, **Camellia japonica**, and **Fig Vine**. Wet soil protects the roots better than dry soil does. After the air temperature rises above freezing, water again to remove ice in the soil from around the roots.***

Other

☛ Check mulch around all plants. Be sure it is not crowding the trunks and stems of shrubs. Remove and replace mulch which contains a large number of leaves.†††

☛ During periods of extreme cold, protect broadleaf evergreens by erecting a wind and sun screen made of burlap. This will prevent damage to the leaves and stems when the ground is frozen.***

☛ Never cover plants with plastic to protect them from extreme cold. The plants will be damaged by heat build-up when the sun is out. Use an old sheet or blanket but do not leave it on too long, because an opaque material will stop photosynthesis in the leaves and make the plants more tender. ***

☛ During snowfalls, brush off accumulated snow from limber evergreens like **boxwood** with a broom to keep them from spreading and breaking.

☛ Leave snow on non-limber shrubs until it melts because it won't break them and actually insulates plants and helps prevent cold damage.

☛ January is an excellent time to make dormant cuttings of deciduous shrubs like **Hydrangea** and **Viburnum**. Root the cuttings in perlite or vermiculite beds in a cold frame or a protected place outside.‡‡‡

---

‡ See "Pruning Flowering Shrubs and Vines," p. 31

†† See "How to Fertilize Shrubs and Vines," p. 30

‡‡ See "Controlling Insects and Diseases," p. 80

*** See "Helping Plants Survive the Cold," p. 269

††† See "Mulching: A Lesson from Nature," p. 243

‡‡‡ See "Making Dormant Cuttings of Shrubs and Roses," p. 9

III. *Fruits*

We do many winter gardening activities despite the cold weather, but we do many fruit tree activities *because* it is cold. We humans can bundle up and work in the orchard while nature keeps insects and diseases inactive and protected from cold in their dormant stages. The cold weather is our best defense against pests as we undertake activities such as pruning, which initially expose the tree's underlying wood.

Spraying and fertilizing also become important activities in the fruit orchard this month. Flower and leaf buds are safely tucked in their sheaths and so are protected from strong spray materials we use to kill the dormant stages of those pesky insects and diseases which may later ruin good fruit.

We prune now to help the fruit trees, vines, or bushes grow in such a way that the maximum number of quality fruit can be set and the plants can develop and ripen them properly. Prune before dormant spraying to make it easier to concentrate the spray material on the areas of the plant where this year's fruits will form.

January is also an excellent time to plant new fruit trees, just as it is for most dormant deciduous trees and shrubs. Plant fruits while it is cold but when the ground is not frozen. There are two exceptions to this rule. In the mid and upper South, don't plant figs until March. Strawberries are also best planted in late February and March.

PRUNING FRUIT TREES

Unlike shade and flowering trees, pruning fruit trees improves their natural performance. Proper pruning will increase both the quantity and the quality of fruit production. It is an essential activity during the first two to three years of a fruit tree's growth, and a necessary one every following year if you hope to have a good harvest.

Fruit trees flower in the spring. That means they set their buds in the summer and blossom the following spring. Since we prune fruit trees every winter during their dormancy, logic tells us that we are taking off wood which contains buds. We are, in fact, decreasing the number of flowers which will blossom! This is perfectly okay. The purpose of pruning fruit trees for maintenance is to decrease the number of flowers so the tree will produce a sustainable number of fruits and to force new growth on which the following year's fruit will set.

As I mentioned, pruning is essential in the first two to three years you own the tree. During these first non-bearing years, you will prune using a specific method which will affect your tree's structure. After you have set the structure in these critical early years, your maintenance pruning will continue in that same method in order to retain the tree's structure. Just like later maintenance pruning to reduce flowers and force growth, initial structural pruning improves the natural shape of a tree. The method of structural pruning depends on the type of fruit tree and its natural way of growth.

The **Open Head** or **Basket** method is used on shorter-lived trees like **peaches**, **plums**, **nectarines**, and other fruits particularly susceptible to rot diseases. This pruning method spreads out the branches to allow more air flow, prevent disease problems (especially rot), and allow the sun to ripen the fruit. It also increases the growth of young wood on which the fruit is set.

The first step for most newly purchased **peach**, **plum**, and **nectarine** trees is to cut back the main stem to 18 to 24 inches. This will force the tree to branch out and leave an open space in the middle of

Open-head or basket pruning of peaches opens up the tree to produce better fruit.

1 – Maintenance pruning: Remove crossed branches.

2 – Maintenance pruning: Remove the weaker side of a "V" branch.

3 – Maintenance pruning: Remove water sprouts.

4 – Maintenance pruning: Do not remove fruiting spurs.

the tree. The tree you purchase may already have the stem cut and branches shooting outward. If so, determine whether its branches are in the 18-to-24-inch range. If they are, then they will become your scaffold branches. If not, you will need to cut the main trunk below the branches in the recommended range. The following year your fruit tree will have developed scaffold branches where you cut it back the year before. You will want to choose three or four strong, upward- and outward-growing branches to form the basic structure of the tree. Prune off the others. Also, cut back the strong scaffold branches to an outside bud. In following years during your maintenance pruning, cut back growth to an outward-facing bud, and thin out any growth which might grow inward and "fill up" the open head or basket.

The **Oval** or **Modified Leader** method is used on longer-lived trees with heavier fruit such as **apples** and **pears**. This pruning method allows you to keep the tree's natural shape while strengthening it to support the weight of the heavy fruit. Strengthening occurs by removing the tip or terminal bud of the main stem and main branches. This slows upward and outward growth causing the tree to increase the diameter of its trunk and branches. The first year, remove the tip of the leader. The following year you will remove the tip again, but several branches should have already formed. Remove their tips as well. Also, thin out the number of branches by removing those which have sprouted out at a tight angle from the trunk, crossed branches, and one side of all forked branches. Limbs should eventually be at least 18 inches apart. It is also necessary to remove water sprouts every year. These are rapid-growing shoots which grow directly up from branches, often up to three or four feet in one season.

Once you have spent the first several years training your fruit tree structurally, it will begin to bear fruit. At this point, you will begin maintenance

The modified leader method of pruning strengthens limbs and prevents breaking under the weight of heavy apples and pears.

pruning every winter to thin buds and force new growth. Stick with the prescribed method of pruning for your particular tree while removing crossed branches and spacing out your scaffold branches so they are about two feet apart. It is important to note that **apples**, **pears**, and **plums** set their buds on "trashy," sometimes wrinkled wood called fruiting spurs. Many people remove this wood thinking it is old, and they lose most of their crop! Be careful to investigate exactly where the buds are located on that particular type of tree before you begin pruning each winter.

When pruning, you might notice sprouts at the ground, shooting up from the base of your fruit tree. These sprouts are called "suckers" and should be removed every year. Remember that fruit trees like **apples**, **apricots**, **cherries**, **nectarines**, **peaches**, **pears**, **pecans**, and **plums** are all grafted. That is, a productive, high-quality cultivar is grafted or budded onto a strong seedling understock. The roots and the producing part of your tree are actually from different types of trees! Since the suckers are from the seedling understock, they produce poor-quality apples if you allow them to develop. They also detract from your regular fruit quality by stealing its energy. Remove these suckers by pulling them off with your hand. At the same time you will hopefully pull a small piece of wood from the trunk containing the sucker's bud. This will keep it from growing back again. If you cut them with shears, you may leave a bud and a new sucker will grow from the same spot next year.

FRUIT ACTIVITIES FOR JANUARY:

Plant

☞ Plant B&B, bare-root, and container-grown fruits all month. This includes fruit trees (**peaches**, **apples**, **cherries**, **pears**, etc.), bush fruits (**blueberries**), semi-bush fruits (**raspberries**, **blackberries**, etc.), and vine fruits (**grapes**, **muscadines**).*

☞ Do not plant **strawberries** or **figs** until February/March.

☞ Plant **Chinese Chestnut**, **pecan**, **walnut**, and other nut trees. (Always plant two or three **Chinese Chestnuts** so they can cross-pollinate. Otherwise, you will not have a good nut harvest.)

Prune

☞ Prune all fruit trees this month and in the first half of February. Use the Open Head or Basket method of pruning for **peaches**, **plums**, **apricots**, and **nectarines**. Use the Modified Leader method for pruning **apples**, **pears**, and **cherries**. Flower buds are already set on last summer's growth. Be sure to leave plenty of this growth for flowers and fruits. After pruning, fertilize your trees.†

☞ Be careful when pruning **apples**, **plums**, and **pears** not to remove the fruiting spurs.

☞ Continue to prune and train semi-bush fruits like **blackberries** and **raspberries**. Train last season's growth onto wires or trellises. You must keep these fruiting canes separate from the new growth which will grow this summer and bear fruit the following year.‡

☞ Prune **grapes** and **muscadines** and train them onto a one- or two-wire fence.

---

* See "Planting Trees and Shrubs," p. 264
† See "Pruning Fruit Trees," p. 13
‡ See "Secrets of the Berry Patch," p. 155

Fertilize

☞ Begin fertilizing fruit trees as their buds begin to swell. Use a 15-15-15 fertilizer at a rate of one-half pound per year of age of the tree. Use a maximum of 15 pounds on **apples** and **pears** and five pounds on **peaches, nectarines,** and **plums.** This is usually done once a year.**

☞ Fertilize **nut trees** at the end of the month. Use a 15-15-15 fertilizer, except on **pecans** which need a special pecan fertilizer containing zinc. This is done once a year.**

Spray

☞ Apply a recommended dormant spray on tree fruits, semi-bush fruits, and **grapes.** Spray only when the material will dry before it freezes.

☞ Wait until after you have pruned to spray fruits. It will save material and you won't be in contact with chemicals like lime sulfur as you make your cuts.

** See "How to Fertilize Fruit Trees," p. 37

Water

☞ Water newly planted fruit trees thoroughly, even if the ground is wet, in order to settle the soil around the roots.

Other

☞ Be careful when mowing in orchard areas not to hit the bark of fruit trees with the mower. Any damage to the bark will provide an entrance place for borers.

☞ Keep fruits mulched with pine straw to prevent weeds and grasses from competing for water and fertilizer. However, do not pile the mulch against the trunks of fruit trees.††

†† See "Mulching: A Lesson from Nature," p. 243

NOTES

IV. *Roses*

It takes a good deal of remembering to see much in your rose plant this month, or a lot of faith to believe a bunch of sticks received in the mail or brought home from the nursery will ever have the exquisite blossoms shown in pictures. Don't worry, though, last year's plantings will be better this year, and new plantings can be just what you expect. Merely follow the rules for rose growing in the South.

In the South, roses *are* handled differently than in places farther north. We plant more shallowly than where the ground freezes for long periods of time. We also plant more deeply than where the weather is mild all winter. A good rule is to plant with the graft union, or swollen area between stems and roots, right on top of the surface of the soil. Covering the graft invites many problems, so never plant roses too deeply.

Pruning roses in the South also breaks rules. Warm spells followed by severe freezes cause havoc among our roses. One moment they think it is time to start growing, then a cold wave arrives and kills the tender new growth. It is best to wait until early-mid February in the lower South and the end of February or the beginning of March in the upper South. Don't prune too early, even if new growth has started on the upper part of the plants. By doing so, you will encourage more new growth which is likely to be killed by a severe freeze.

There is an important job in January. Be sure to apply a dormant spray of lime sulfur when it won't freeze within 24 hours. This is one of the most important sprayings of the year to control a variety of diseases.

ROSE ACTIVITIES FOR JANUARY:

Plant

☛ Continue to plant bare-root roses whenever the ground is not frozen. Before planting, trim long or broken roots and cut stems back to a healthy bud. Try new varieties but keep old favorites as major plantings until new ones have proven themselves in your garden.*

☛ Container-grown roses can be planted now through April.†

Prune

☛ Do not prune roses until early-mid February in the lower South; late February/early March in the upper South.

Spray

☛ Apply lime sulfur as a dormant spray on roses during January, but only when the material will not freeze before it dries. Thoroughly spray the canes and the mulch around the plants. This application will control overwintering spores of major diseases.

Other

☛ Make dormant cuttings of roses this month. Cuttings should be five or six inches long and should be taken from canes about the size of your little finger which are clean and free from disease spots. Root cuttings in perlite or vermiculite beds.‡

☛ Keep roses well mulched but do not pile mulch against the crown or lower stems. Many problems like rose stem canker and botrytis can occur when mulch covers the lower stems.**

☛ Do not be concerned if new leaves which have emerged on the top of canes during the winter months are damaged by dormant sprayings or cold weather. You will be removing them during major structural pruning in February and March.

---

* See "Planting Bare-Root Roses," p. 250

† See "Planting Trees and Shrubs," p. 264

‡ See "Making Dormant Cuttings of Shrubs and Roses," p. 9

** See "Mulching: A Lesson from Nature," p. 243

V. *Flowers and Colorful Garden Plants*

Thank goodness for pansies, for how else could we have bright color in our January gardens? Their friendly faces smile at us when the rest of the garden is bleak and bare. Every freeze may take the smiles away, but wait, for within a few days of a Southern winter warm-up, the smiles are back again.

Flowers are an important part of creating a warm and cheerful home landscape. In January, we may find ourselves pulling out last year's pictures to remind us how beautiful our bleak annual bed will be. Most of us want flowers brightening the garden but fail to take advantage of opportunities for extending the season. This is largely due to the lack of a good selection of cool weather annuals in local nurseries. Why not grow these hardy and half-hardy plants from seeds by starting them inside this month? Seed catalogs are filled with wonderful possibilities. Choose things you like which are marked "Spring-flowering, HA or HHA or HP." These letters indicate a hardiness to cold, not as a seedling but as a plant growing in the garden. Careful planning can extend the garden flowering season by many months.

Sweet Peas seem to have passed out of style, but with little effort and by starting now, you can seed them directly into winter beds and have them in bloom long before summer annuals are ready to color your garden.

STARTING SEEDS INSIDE

Buying flower and vegetable plants from a nursery is not always the best way to start a garden. Nursery plants are often expensive, are sometimes contaminated with insects and diseases, and are seldom available in all the best varieties. One way to get around these problems is to grow the plants yourself from seed. Catalogs have a tremendous variety of different types of seeds, and they are much less expensive than those bought at a local nursery. Growing from seed is also an excellent way to start the year's gardening activity much earlier than waiting to plant until the danger of frost has passed.

January is a great time to order seeds through a cat-

Cell packs and seed trays with a humidity dome make starting seeds easy.

alog. One of our family's favorite activities is making a wish list around the kitchen table of all the different flowers and vegetables we want to grow in the coming year. It is the perfect way to cheer yourself up on a cold, damp January afternoon. Try to order as soon as possible because some varieties need to be planted in late January.

I like to start my hardy and semi-hardy flowers and vegetables in late January. This will give them plenty of time to develop before I set them out in March. Annuals and tender vegetables can be started later, as long as you allow six to eight weeks for them to grow before you set them out after the danger of frost has passed in April.

Growing flowers and vegetables from seed is not a difficult task. Just remember that not every seed will grow, and since seeds are relatively inexpensive, it is best to plant extra. I like to overseed and then remove the weaker sprouts, leaving the strongest plants to continue growing. This way I conserve space in the trays. If you have plenty of room to spare, you can spread out your seeds and plant more trays, but you will probably end up wasting valuable space.

The best way to grow seeds is to use cell trays or plastic seeding trays. These trays are convenient to label and do not require large amounts of soil. Use a peat-light soil mixture and moisten it before putting it in the trays. If you fill the tray with the dry, powdery soil mixture before wetting it, you'll have a real mess when you try to water it.

Plant two or three seeds per cell or, if you are using trays, plant them with the rows running from front to back. Since most flower and vegetable seeds are small, place them on the surface and cover with 1/4 to 1/6 inch of soil (a general rule is to plant seeds twice as deep as they are thick). It is easier to be consistent in covering if you add soil on top rather than burying the seeds. If you make tray furrows, press a ruler into the soil about 1/4 inch deep. Then drop the seed evenly in the furrow and pinch it closed with your fingers. Make sure to label each row. Trays are labeled front to back, left to right.

Since you have over-seeded to ensure germination, you may end up with too many seedlings per cell or row. Once you are able to identify the stronger seedlings, remove the weaker ones until there is one healthy plant per cell. Try not to let them grow too big before thinning them out or you might damage the roots of the healthy plants. If you started your seeds well in advance of planting them outside, you may need to transplant the seedlings from the tray to a small pot to continue growing inside. Pot them when they have formed their first true leaves. Leaving your seedlings too long in the confined area of a plastic seeding tray will cause them to grow tall and sprangly. While some flowers and vegetables will "bush out" after you eventually transplant them outside, others might retain their sprangly shape and never produce a very pretty plant.

Seed germination depends largely on moisture and temperature. Since soil in trays and cells dries out quickly, it is a good idea to cover the tray with a clear plastic tray dome. If you can't find one at the store which will fit your particular tray, you can make a tent using a plastic dry cleaning bag. This will slow down evaporation, helping to regulate the moisture and temperature. Keep the dome on the tray until the seeds have germinated and broken through the soil. Then open it a crack to allow extra ventilation until the seedlings are ready to pot.

Starting flowers and vegetables from seed will not only provide you with a better variety of plants but also save you money. Watch out though: seed propagation is addictive. Before you know it, you might find yourself in a seed swap club or advertising "100 **Catalpa Tree** seeds for one dollar with a self-addressed stamped envelope" in the local farmer's market bulletin!

FLOWER ACTIVITIES FOR JANUARY:

Plant

☛ Plant hardy biennial and perennial roots like **Chrysanthemum, Delphinium, Foxglove, Purple Cone-Flower, Rudbeckia,** and **Shasta Daisy** whenever the weather is mild. Plant in well-drained soil. Most perennials need a sweet soil. Check instructions and apply dolomitic limestone or bone meal if suggested. However, do not apply limestone in areas next to broadleaf evergreens, especially **hollies, azaleas, camellias,** and **rhododendrons.** Mulch biennnial and perennial roots heavily with pine straw to prevent their spewing out of the ground in a late freeze.

☛ Plant **peonies** and **Iris** whenever the weather is mild. Plant them shallowly with the roots close to the top of the soil. **Peonies** should be planted in morning sun with the pink buds just above the soil so they can freeze and produce better flowers. Use bone meal and mulch them heavily, but leave the crown open.

☛ Plant **pansies** and **English Daisies** in the garden whenever the weather is mild. Put newspapers or a light pine straw cover over them if there is a very severe freeze warning.

☛ Order mail-order seeds at the beginning of the month to have them on hand for planting at the end of the month. January is the rush season for seed companies, and it might take a while to receive your order.

☛ Start hardy annual, biennial, and perennial seed like **Foxglove, hollyhocks, Purple Cone-Flower, Rudbeckia, Shasta Daisy, stock, Stokesia,** and **Sweet William** inside or in a greenhouse in the second half of the month. They will be ready to plant in mid-March after the hardest freezes have passed.*

☛ Plant any unplanted spring-flowering bulbs as quickly as possible. You cannot carry them over to plant next fall.†

* See "Starting Seeds Inside," p. 18
† See "Southern Flowering Bulbs, Corms, Tubers, and Roots," p. 252

☛ Plant **sweet peas** in well-manured trenches whenever the weather is mild.

Prune

☛ Be sure to remove any remaining dead tops of last year's perennials or biennials.

Other

☛ Make cuttings from **Geranium, Begonia, Coleus,** and **Impatiens** stock plants which you have carried over from last fall. Cuttings taken now will make strong plants for setting in the garden after frost.‡

☛ Do not mulch bulbs to protect the new shoots from cold. These plants are hardy, and heavy mulching will keep the ground too warm, encouraging the flower stalk to emerge too soon. The flower buds are more tender than the leaves.†

☛ Keep **Canna** and **Dahlia** roots stored in a cool place. Do not set these in the garden until April when the ground is warm and the danger of frost has passed. Store **Caladium** and **Elephant Ear** tubers in a warmer spot than **Canna** and **Dahlia** roots.

‡ See "Propagating Herbaceous Houseplants and Garden Plants," p. 225

† See "Southern Flowering Bulbs, Corms, Tubers, and Roots," p. 252

NOTES

VI. *Vegetables*

A vegetable garden always promises to be productive in the future, but isn't it great to go into the garden and pull spring onions which you planted last fall? The future does become the present with a little planning. January is a good time to plant some more onion sets and hardy English Peas. It is also the time to start seeds inside of hardy vegetables like broccoli, cabbage, cauliflower, collards, and, for those of you who like such things, Brussels sprouts and kohlrabi. Many nurseries have very limited selections of vegetable seeds, so go through new seed catalogs where you will find newer varieties and better selections of old favorites.

Wouldn't it be great to cut fresh asparagus from your garden when it is selling for more than $3.00 per pound in the grocery store? January is a great time to start an asparagus bed, or rhubarb, or horseradish for better sauce than you get in a jar.

Take every opportunity to work vegetable gardens this month. February will probably be wetter than January, so get out the tiller and prepare the ground while you have a chance. Way back in the sixteenth century the English not only prepared their soil but made the beds at the same time. It's also a good idea here in the South. Raised beds dry faster than flat garden areas, and you won't have to delay planting early spring vegetables because the soil is too wet.

EARLY VEGETABLE GARDEN PREPARATION

Many of us do not use our vegetable gardens much during the winter. For one reason or another, we may have decided not to plant a green manure crop or some of the varieties of winter vegetables. Our dreams of vegetable gardening rest in the later plantings during springtime. Unfortunately, when the time rolls around for us to begin planting in late February or March, our gardens may be so water-logged from spring rains that we can't work up the soil enough to plant at the correct time.

The answer for people in this situation is to start preparing your soil whenever it is dry enough in January and February. Early vegetable garden preparation is basically the same initial process that you would undertake in preparing a vegetable garden in the spring. Consult "Planting a Vegetable Garden" in April for a more in depth discussion of this subject, especially if you are creating a new garden.

Early vegetable garden preparation consists of several steps. The first step is to work your soil thoroughly with a roto-tiller or a spade, if the area is small enough. Winter is a great time to rent a roto-tiller since it is "off-season." You might even qualify for an off-season discount. Whether you are working with an established garden or breaking in a new plot, it is always a good idea to "lighten" your soil content by adding humus. No matter how many years a South-ern garden has been under cultivation, it can always use more humus to improve the clay. Make sure that humus from a compost pile is completely broken down before you add it to the plot. Ideally, your soil will be light and airy without any large clods. This is a tall order with our Southern soils, and it may take many consecutive years to reach this ideal condition. You will also want to add dolomitic lime to sweeten the soil. Application is at a rate of 50 pounds per 1000 square feet.

Having worked the soil to a light composition, step two is to throw up the beds. Plan your garden as if you were planting tomorrow. The beds that you make during your winter preparations will be the same beds you plant later in the spring. Remember to

Apply dolomitic limestone several months before planting.

run beds north to south and never downhill. If, however, your north/south beds would run downhill, it is better to run them east to west to prevent erosion. When the rains begin to pick up in February and March, beds will shed water much quicker than flat ground. You may need to re-work the beds later if there is some minor erosion, but generally you will be able to plant more quickly and with less difficulty if you have prepared your soil ahead of time.

Although early vegetable garden preparation may seem like drudgery devised to meet the requirements of the old adage "Proper planning prevents poor performance," I enjoy it too much to consider it a chore. There is something about putting on my boots, cranking up the roto-tiller, and heading down to the garden that lifts my spirits on a gray January day. Working the ground and watching the soil churn up into a deep, rich color enlivens me more than any other wintertime activity. It gets me in the mood for spring, and reminds me that warm Saturday afternoons working in the garden are just around the corner. I recommend you try it!

VEGETABLE ACTIVITIES FOR JANUARY:

Plant

☛ Plant hardy, smooth-seeded **English peas** whenever the weather is mild. Plant them in trenches lined with cow manure and 15-15-15 fertilizer.*

☛ Plant **Asparagus, horseradish, Jerusalem Artichoke,** and **rhubarb** roots on beds. Mulch them heavily with compost and fertilize them.

☛ Start the following seeds inside during January: **broccoli, cabbage, cauliflower, collard, lettuce,** and **onion.** These can be planted outside in March after the danger of hard freezes are over.†

☛ Plant **garlic cloves** and **onion sets** on beds this month.

Fertilize

☛ Lime gardens with dolomitic limestone during January so the material will be effective by planting time. Application is at a rate of 50 pounds per 1000 square feet. Do not lime areas where you are going to plant **Irish potatoes**.

☛ Fertilize as you plant with 15-15-15. This fertilizer will be good for about six weeks. Application is at a rate of approximately one pound per 10 feet of row.*

Other

☛ Prepare garden areas for plantings later in the spring. February and March may be wet, so go ahead and prepare your beds, since they will dry faster than ground which is left flat.‡

☛ Turn under cover crops planted last fall in areas which will be used for vegetables in February and March.

---

* See "Planting a Vegetable Garden," p. 92
† See "Starting Seeds Inside," p. 18

* See "Planting a Vegetable Garden," p. 92
‡ See "Early Vegetable Garden Preparation," p. 21

VII. *Houseplants*

It is a real shame not to do something with the beautiful plants which helped make the holidays cheerful. Many of them can be saved for another day, but unfortunately, a few are best discarded when the blossoms fade. There is no way to save Paperwhite Narcissus so just take a deep breath and throw them out. Poinsettias last and last as a nice indoor plant, surviving under adverse conditions as long as they have good light. When you get tired of them, and they *do* get boring after spring really starts, give them the heave-ho because they won't bloom during the summer and getting them to rebloom next Christmas is difficult at best.

Blooming houseplants like azaleas and chrysanthemums are outdoor garden plants temporarily residing in a very hostile environment. Don't expect too much for too long. When the blossoms fade, put them on a protected porch with plenty of light where they can harden up and be planted in the garden later on.

Homes may be very comfortable to us humans, but they are almost exactly wrong for plants. We feel better when air is warm and humidity is low. Plants like warm conditions but high humidity. When they look sad, even sick, remember that the conditions aren't what they like. Mist them with clear water and see how quickly they look happier.

HOUSEPLANT ACTIVITIES FOR JANUARY:

Plant

☛ Houseplants, especially newly purchased ones, can be repotted at any time during the year. Use a pot at least two sizes larger so the plant will have plenty of room to grow. I prefer to grow most of my houseplants in a peat-light potting mixture.*

Prune

☛ Groom indoor plants whenever they need it. Remove any weak branches or stems as well as off-color leaves.

Fertilize

☛ Fertilize with a water-soluble fertilizer solution every time you water. Use half applications until the days become noticeably longer and new growth begins.†

Spray

☛ Check all indoor plants for insects such as spider mites, scale, and mealybug. I like to use a houseplant systemic insecticide to control them. It is easier and safer than spraying inside. If you do spray, remember to apply the insecticide to the undersides of the leaves. I like to spray houseplants when I can take them outside on a warm day. Bring them inside as soon as the spray material dries.‡

☛ Be careful when spraying **ferns**. Some insecticides are harmful to them. *Always read the label for warnings about **ferns** and other plants.*

Water

☛ Watch houseplants carefully during the winter. When they look limp, check for dry soil. If it is dry, water thoroughly in a sink or bathtub, letting the water drain completely, and don't water again until the surface is dry once more. Between waterings, mist with plain water on a regular basis. If the limp plants are in moist soil, do not water but allow the soil to dry a bit and mist frequently.†

☛ Tip-burn or edge-burn on leaves indicates that more water is being lost than is being absorbed by the roots. Check for dry soil, too much sunlight, or drafts from heater vents.†

* See "Repotting Houseplants," p. 67

† See "Houseplant Care and Maintenance," p. 232

‡ See "Common Houseplant Ailments," p. 280

† See "Houseplant Care and Maintenance," p. 232

☛ **Poinsettias** from Christmas survive well in the house if the plant is in a sunny location and if the soil is kept on the dry side. They may be planted outside in April, but they will not bloom all summer.

☛ Continue to watch **ferns** for signs of dead or dying foliage. Mist them frequently and remove any dead fronds as soon as they occur.

Other

☛ Houseplants which become lighter in color or have very long intervals between branches or stems (internodes) usually need more light and fertilizer.

☛ Place your **Christmas Chrysanthemum** in a cold but not freezing place. After it has hardened up, cut it back and plant the roots outside. Mulch heavily.**

☛ Forced **azaleas** should be in a cold but not freezing place. Keep the soil damp until planting time in the spring. Then plant outside.**

** See "Indoor Flowering Plants for the Holidays," p. 256

☛ **Giant Flowering Amaryllis (African Amaryllis)** may be carried over. After it flowers, remove the dead flower stalk, remove the plant from the small container and repot in a six- or eight-inch pot using a peat-light mixture. Grow until next September when you can begin the treatment for blossoms next Christmas.**

☛ Keep **ornamental peppers** growing inside. They may be planted outside in late April.**

☛ **Christmas Cactus** grows well indoors in a bright, sunny place with not too much water.

☛ **Kalanchoes** will also continue to blossom inside if they are in bright light.**

☛ **Paperwhite Narcissus** are useless after blossoming and cannot be carried over. Throw them in the compost pile.**

** See "Indoor Flowering Plants for the Holidays," p. 256

NOTES

VIII. *Lawns*

It is so nice not to have to mow. Even though lawns look rather dreary in the wintertime, we get a break from those weekly excursions on the lawn mower. Walking around evergreen lawns does bring on a bit of winter shame. During the summer, green grasses seem to mix in with green weeds enough to hide the fact that our lawns aren't quite up to par. But winter is much less forgiving. Even evergreen lawns like the fescues are littered with brown weed spots which make our lawns look disreputable. Since we don't have to mow, the least we can do is try to improve the quality of our lawns. Besides, it is nice to get out of the house.

February may be early to put out pre-emergence weed killer, but it is a good time to control winter weeds. Wander around the yard with your spray bottle and enjoy an hour of zapping these pesky plants. It is a wonderful winter tonic and you will be thankful next summer!

Control wild garlic (wild onion) in the winter before grasses start their spring growth.

LAWN ACTIVITIES FOR JANUARY:

Spray

☞ Control winter weeds like **wild garlic (wild onions)** and **chickweed** with a lawn formula broadleaf herbicide. Spray on a warm day and be patient because results are slow in the winter.*

Cut

☞ Cut evergreen lawns when the growth reaches the correct cutting height. Do not let newly seeded grasses become too tall before cutting.

EVERGREEN GRASSES	HEIGHT
Kentucky 31 Tall Fescue	3 to 3 1/2 inches
Turf-type Tall Fescues	3 inches
Fine Fescues	1 1/2 to 2 inches
Kentucky Bluegrass	2 to 2 1/2 inches

☞ If you have seeded **Ryegrass** over **Bermuda Grass**, keep the **Ryegrass** cut about an inch above the base lawn. If you let it grow tall in clumps, it will damage your permanent grass.

Other

☞ Keep falling oak leaves raked off your lawn. Heavy leaf fall can smother grasses, even those which are dormant.

* See "Fertilizing and Controlling Weeds in Lawns," p. 73

February

IN THE SOUTHERN GARDEN

Southern winters have the potential for many kinds of weather which affect gardening. Some years I have finished all winter and some spring jobs in February; in other years, I have watched snowflakes fall during much of the month. Happy is the gardener who accepts what the weather brings and does his gardening whenever possible.

February is both a catch-up month and a beginning month. Finish dormant pruning and spraying *before* buds begin to swell as the days get longer and cold waves are less severe and farther apart. When the weather is like spring and the snowflakes aren't falling, it is time really to start spring gardening. But don't let 70-degree weather fool you into planting tender annuals and perennials. There will be more cold! February gardening is centered around planting shrubs, trees, hardy flowers, and hardy vegetables, *after* you have finished January's jobs.

Do your time-sensitive garden activities by watching signals from plants rather than your calendar or even the five-day weather forecast. Nature seems to tell us things which weathermen can't. Some years it is fine to put out pre-emergence weed and weed grass controls in early February; in other years it may be too early. Watch the garden. Apply controls when the Forsythia blossoms (see picture, p. 48). Somehow Forsythia knows when to blossom and not be damaged. Those yellow masses seem to come about a week or so before weeds and crabgrass show up in warm, sunny areas.

By the end of the month, days are longer and weather is milder. Daffodils blossom, and we know that spring gardening is for real now— no more stops and starts.

AT LEFT: *Garden Pansies*

I. *Shade and Flowering Trees*

February is still a good month to plant new trees. Try to get them in the ground quickly while they are still dormant. This way, young trees will wake up from their winter dormancy all set in their new home. Then they can take root happily without being disturbed. You will be amazed how much better a tree planted this month will do than a tree planted later in the season. By April, your new tree will be developing its new root system and growing healthily. Trees planted in April will be several months behind and will have to be tended regularly to attain maximum growth.

Established trees are getting ready to emerge from dormancy as well. Make sure you fertilize to give them all the nutrients they need to start the season with strong growth.

If there is some pruning yet to do, try to finish it before the weather warms up late in the month. It is best to let the pruning scars heal well before the tree starts its growth.

TREE ACTIVITIES FOR FEBRUARY:

Plant

☞ Plant B&B, bare-root, and container-grown trees during the entire month when the ground is not frozen or likely to freeze soon. Make sure to plant trees at the correct depth in a well-prepared hole, and stake them to prevent swaying (especially bare-root trees). Never plant trees deeper than they were growing in the nursery. When planting B&B and container-grown trees, it is a good idea to leave the top of the root ball showing after planting. Plant bare-root trees with the soil level one inch above the top root.*

☞ Choose planting stock carefully. New shade trees should be straight with tight, smooth bark, dominant central shoot or leader, and should not be loose in the ball or container. Choose flowering trees carefully also. They should be free from scars to indicate they have been grown well.

☞ Plant shade trees dug from the wild only as a last resort and only if they are small. Their wide, sprangly roots are liable to be cut drastically during digging and then take forever to start growing vigorously again.

☞ Plant **Southern Magnolia** and **Cherry Laurel** toward the end of this month, or wait until March.*

☞ When handling container or B&B trees, never pick them up by the stem; if you do, you will break the roots in the ball of earth.

Prune

☞ Continue to prune all dormant, deciduous, and evergreen shade trees this month if needed. Both light and heavy pruning are okay, but do not prune trees when the sap is frozen. Also, never remove the central shoot or leader of a shade tree; you will ruin its natural shape.†

☞ Prune spring-flowering trees like **Bradford Pear**, **flowering cherry**, **flowering peach**, **flowering pear**, and **dogwood** but do so sparingly and selectively. Remove any crossed branches, damaged or diseased wood, and bad growth. Remember that buds for spring blossoms are already present on the branches and twigs grown last summer. Pruning them will reduce the number of flowers on the tree.†

☞ Summer-flowering trees like **Crape Myrtle** and **Chaste Tree** (**Vitex**) may be pruned severely to force new spring shoots on which the summer's blooms will develop. Prune selectively, however, to shape the tree and force new shoots in the direction you want them to grow.†

---

* See "Planting Trees and Shrubs," p. 264

† See "Pruning Shade and Flowering Trees," p. 4

Fertilize

☛ Fertilize all newly planted trees with a 15-15-15 fertilizer. Spread the fertilizer in a circle at the edge of the hole you dug, using about 1/2 pound per three feet of the tree's height. Water thoroughly after fertilizing.‡

☛ Fertilize large deciduous and evergreen shade trees at the beginning of the month if you have not already. Use one pound of fertilizer per inch circumference of the tree, measured three feet above the ground. Use a 15-15-15 mix of fertilizer. This is a once-a-year job.‡

☛ Finish fertilizing summer-flowering trees after pruning with 5-10-15 if you have not done it already. Use one pound of fertilizer per inch circumference of the tree, measured three feet above the ground. This is also done once a year.

☛ Wait until March to fertilize **Southern Magnolia** and **Cherry Laurel.**

Spray

☛ Control scale on all trees with Orthene or Cygon, except in the case of **hollies**. Use Orthene on **hollies.** **

‡ See "How to Fertilize Shade Trees," p. 6
** See "Controlling Insects and Diseases," p. 80

Water

☛ Water newly planted shade and flowering trees thoroughly, even if the ground is wet, in order to settle the soil around the roots.

Other

☛ Mulch newly planted and fertilized trees with pine straw or pine bark. Do not allow the mulch to pack against the tree trunk.††

☛ Check mulch around older trees and replenish with fresh mulch if needed.

☛ Stake newly planted shade and flowering trees, especially if you purchased them bare root. Attach three wires to the trunk at about four to five feet off the ground and run them to wooden stakes driven at intervals around the tree. Make a collar of old watering hose to prevent the wire from cutting into the trunks.

†† See "Mulching: A Lesson from Nature," p. 243

NOTES

II. *Shrubs and Vines*

Some spring-flowering shrubs may begin to bloom during February. If your January Jasmine didn't live up to its name, it will certainly show some color this month. Also, Forsythia in bloom will give us the truest sign that spring is almost here.

For best results, plant your shrubs and vines as soon as possible, before they begin their new growth. Try to choose a nice warm day to lay out a new garden or make additions to the old one. You will be amazed at how well a shrub or vine will grow in its first season if planted during dormancy.

Continue to fertilize shrubs and vines so they will have plenty of nutrients to absorb as they begin growing. Unlike trees, shrubs and vines can be fertilized by broadcasting on the surface. This is much quicker than boring holes, and you can probably fertilize all your shrubs in an hour or so.

Be careful with your pruning. In the rush of late winter, it is always a temptation to prune everything at once. Doing so can be hazardous to your plants' health! Take the time to determine whether it is a spring-flowering or summer-flowering shrub or vine and prune at the correct time (see below, "Pruning Flowering Shrubs and Vines").

Also watch out for scale on your evergreens, especially holly. These pests will be active soon and should be controlled as quickly as possible.

How to Fertilize Shrubs and Vines

Come February in the Southern garden, I always get gardening fever. Although we aren't really into spring, warm spells of 70-degree weather trick me into thinking spring has arrived. I rush out of the house on a warm Saturday afternoon just looking for a good garden activity. And that is where the trouble starts. I am thinking, "It is really too early to fertilize, but . . . ." If I'm not careful, I might end up fertilizing every shrub on the place and planting five rows of tomatoes as well! For that reason, February is always a time of garden education for me. While my impulsive side rationalizes that I could get away with fertilizing some shrubs a little early, my thinking side must provide a strong educated response. And there *is* a good reason to wait.

The first good reason not to fertilize shrubs too early is that it may be a waste of money. Fertilizer is designed to dissolve so that it can penetrate the soil. As it breaks up, rain water carries it deeper and deeper into the ground. The useful life of a fertilizer is the time before it dissipates so much that it is no longer available to the plant. The useful life of regular fertilizer (not a slow-release brand) has been determined to be about six weeks, and a much shorter time if there are heavy rains. Knowing this, we try to apply fertilizer so it will dissolve and penetrate the soil at the same time the plant is actively absorbing nutrients. If our timing is off, our money washes past the plant, unnoticed.

The second good reason to fertilize at the correct time is that fertilizer causes a distinct reaction in plants. I like to think of fertilizing my shrubs as giving candy to a child. There are times when that energy kick is not such a bad idea, like just before the big event on Field Day. But we all know better than to feed a child too much sugar on a rainy Saturday when there is no place to go. His ensuing activity will be downright counter-productive. In the same way, we have to learn the best time to "energize" our plants so they will react positively.

Productive fertilizing boils down to proper timing. Timing, in this case, is directly related to the growth cycle of the particular shrub or vine and whether it flowers in spring or in summer. Spring-flowering shrubs and vines grow vegetatively after they bloom, form their buds before fall, go into dormancy in the winter, and bloom again as spring arrives. Summer-flowering shrubs and vines grow vegetatively in the spring, set their buds by summer, blossom, and then go into dormancy in the winter. Our goal is to fertilize our plants just prior to their vegetative growth. A properly fertilized shrub or vine puts on a substantial number of new leaves, which in turn provide the necessary energy for bud formation through photosynthesis. This is why we need to fertilize summer-flowering shrubs and vines like **Hydrangea paniculata, Althaea,** and **Butterfly Bush** in late February or March and spring-flowering shrubs and vines like **azaleas, Rhododendron,** and **Viburnum** after they finish blooming.

With luck, we will be "feeding" our shrubs and vines their candy just before the big race. All that "sugar" will eventually go toward the productive goal of providing us beautiful flowers to decorate our landscape. But what happens if we fertilize them at the wrong time? Suppose we watch our spring-flowering shrubs and vines bloom, but forget to fertilize them afterwards. The plants will begin their vegetative growth as usual and eventually set their buds. Then suddenly, as new parents, we see the buds and decide to give them a little treat of fertilizer. The shrub gladly accepts the nourishment, but instead of packing all that food into a prize-winning flower bud, it thinks the time has come to grow vegetatively, and in a spurt of growth it might force the bud right off the plant! While this is an extreme example, it does illustrate the mess we can cause by fertilizing our shrubs and vines at the wrong time. As a rule, it is best not to fertilize spring-flowering shrubs and vines after June or we will disturb bud formation for the following year's bloom. The same sad story is true for spring-flowering shrubs and vines like **azaleas** if you fertilize them before they bloom in the spring. The plant might heed the call to grow vegetatively and force the buds off the plant before they bloom. This new vegetative growth may be doomed as well if a severe cold front moves through and kills the new shoots.

While there are circumstances where fertilizing a summer-flowering shrub or vine at the wrong time might force the buds off the plant (fertilizing, for instance, after bud formation in the summer), the most common occurrence is that we fertilize too early and the fertilizer dissipates before it is ever absorbed by the plant. This result is just as sad a story as ending up with a "messy house," and gets sadder when you have to reach deep into your pocket to buy another bag of fertilizer to apply at the right time. For this reason, we fertilize summer-flower shrubs and vines like **Butterfly Bush** in late February or March, as the ground begins to warm and the plant emerges from dormancy. We also fertilize evergreen shrubs

Althaea, Rose of Sharon (Hibiscus syriacus 'Diana') is one of our best summer-flowering shrubs.

and vines like **Box Leaf Holly, boxwoods,** and **cleyera** in late February or March as the plant emerges from dormancy.

There is no need to dig holes around your shrubs and vines when fertilizing, as we do with trees, because the roots are not deep enough to warrant it. It is important, though, to distribute the fertilizer evenly around the plants so that you will provide nourishment to all sides of the plant. Use a 15-15-15 fertilizer on deciduous shrubs and vines and an azalea/camellia acid fertilizer on broadleaf, narrowleaf, and flowering evergreen shrubs and vines. Use about 1/2 pound per three feet of height, but check the recommended level given for the particular fertilizer you buy. Remember that fertilizing more than the recommended level will not necessarily help. More than likely, this extra fertilizer will either wash away long before the plant has the chance to absorb it, or be so much as to damage the plant.

So as I sit in February, with my thoughtful side finally checking my impulsiveness, I am saved by one of the most redeeming features of gardening. While it might not be the right time to fertilize, it is always the right time to do *something* in the garden. Prune an apple tree, start some seeds in the greenhouse, or make dormant cuttings . . . the garden awaits me.

PRUNING FLOWERING SHRUBS AND VINES

The art of pruning goes way back as far as Biblical times. Remember the admonition in the New Testament about pruning grapes? The keepers of the vineyard knew the vines must be pruned properly to pro-

Flowering Quince (Chaenomeles speciosa) one of the South's earliest flowering shrubs, is pruned after blooming.

duce good fruit. Pruning flowering shrubs and ornamental vines is as important as pruning fruits. After all, the purpose is the same: to increase the quality and quantity of flowers each year.

An experienced gardener develops his own exacting techniques to accomplish the three functions of pruning: encouraging wood on which flower buds are formed, developing a pleasing plant structure, and removing any dead, diseased, damaged or unproductive growth. The new gardener who starts learning the techniques shouldn't worry too much about a few mistakes. A top surgeon once told me with a laugh that gardeners were luckier than doctors. "If *you* make a mistake, the plant will grow back. If *I* make a mistake, I'd rather not talk about it." Though plants will grow back, mistakes can hurt by costing your landscape a whole season of blossoms on fine shrubs or vines.

The art of pruning is as much knowing when to make proper cuts as how to make them. Winter is an excellent time to prune many trees, shrubs, and vines since plants are dormant and there is plenty of time for the remaining buds to force out and perform properly. However, *not all* flowering shrubs and vines should be pruned now. Determine first when your plants will bloom, to know what type of wood their buds are formed on. Some shrubs and vines blossom on "old wood" grown last summer. Others blossom on "new wood" produced after the plants begin growing this year. Plants which blossom before June 1 *generally* blossom on old wood, while plants which blossom after June 1 *generally* blossom on new wood.

Of course, gardens are filled with exceptions. Many roses blossom long before June 1 but the flowers are formed on new wood, while some **Rhododendron** blossom on old wood during June. You will soon learn the characteristics of plants in your garden and be able to adjust pruning practices to accommodate the exceptions.

Pruning Spring-Flowering Shrubs and Vines

Many of the South's most spectacular flowering shrubs and vines blossom from mid-winter until hot weather and are classed as spring-flowering. Such favorites as **azalea**, **Camellia**, early **Rhododendron**, **Flowering Quince**, **January Jasmine**, **Winter Honeysuckle**, **Forsythia**, **Spiraea**, and **Viburnum**, as well as vines like **Carolina Jessamine** and **Lady Banksia** rose, blossom on last year's growth, or old wood, so they must be pruned *after* they have finished blossoming to keep from removing this year's flowers.

The art of pruning flowering shrubs and vines is not nearly so precise as pruning fruits. You prune fruits to improve structure, remove bad wood, and maximize fruit size and quality; you prune flowering shrubs and vines to improve structure and maximize the growth which will set bloom buds for next year.

Young growth is the best for developing flower buds on most plants. However, flowering shrubs and vines need healthy trunks and branches to support this fresh young growth on which flowers are formed. You will soon be able to discover by observation the types of growth which you need for best flowering performance.

Prune spring-flowering shrubs and vines as soon as the last blossoms have fallen. Fertilize them at the

Camellia japonica buds were set last summer. Prune after flowers have finished.

same time to encourage growth for next year's flowers. You will need to prune evergreen spring-flowering shrubs like **azaleas** and **camellias** very little except for shaping. You may need to cut back bushy deciduous flowering shrubs like **Forsythia** and **Spiraea** and thin out the mass of twig growth from the ground. Flowering vines usually need little pruning except to shape and restrict their growth to an arbor or trellis.

Dormant Pruning Of Summer-Flowering Shrubs and Vines

Prune summer-flowering shrubs and vines while they are dormant in the winter. Normally you prune them more drastically than you do spring-flowering shrubs; you want to force heavy new growth on which flower buds *will* form. **Crape Myrtles, Chaste Tree (Vitex)**, and **summer hydrangeas** are spectacular when filled with their beautiful blossoms. Severely prune them both for structure and to force new growth. **Crape Myrtles** and **Hydrangea paniculata Cv. 'Grandiflora' (Peegee)** are easily trained into single, or multi-trunk small trees which have tops where abundant flowers are formed. Prune their tops heavily each year so that new growth develops above the main trunks, thus keeping their tree form. If you prefer, you can also prune **Crape Myrtles** and **summer hydrangeas** *as shrubs* by thinning out the weak shoots coming from the ground or lower stems and leaving three or more strong trunks which are cut back to three or four feet each year. This way, heavy bushy growth will develop and produce many flowers.

Unlike most other spring-flowering shrubs,

Summer-flowering Hydrangea (Hydrangea paniculata 'Grandiflora') should be pruned in the winter.

Blue/Pink Hydrangea and **hybrid roses** blossom before June 1 but on new growth. Each is pruned in a special way. Prune **Blue/Pink Hydrangea** by thinning out the weak basal growth to the strongest stems, then cutting each back one-third. The art of pruning **roses** is covered in detail in "Pruning Roses" later in the chapter.

Summer-flowering vines, like Lonicera heckrottii, also blossom on new growth. Prune to remove any weak, undesirable growth, and to train the vines to cover the structure in the way you want. New growth will develop and produce new flowers.

Common **Clematis** like **Sweet Autumn** and **Jackman** are pruned like other summer-flowering vines. However, giant hybrid **Clematis** must be pruned in a more special way. For a detailed description of growing and pruning Clematis, see "Growing Clematis and Other Southern Vines" in March.

PRUNING AUCUBA, MAHONIA, AND NANDINA

Most Southern broadleaf evergreens are pruned much like we prune deciduous shrubs. We force growth the way we want the plant to grow by pruning back to a young shoot, or latent bud on an older branch. New growth develops quickly in spring weather and can be shaped and trimmed as it develops during April, May, and early June. But there are a few Southern broadleaf evergreen shrubs like **Aucuba**, **Nandina**, and **Mahonia** which grow differently and must be dealt with in another way. They grow in a clump of many strong shoots from the base of the plant. The shoots do not seem to be coming from the main plant or from a central trunk like a **Burford Holly** does when it is drastically cut back close to the ground. Clump-type shrubs like **Aucuba**, **Nandina**, and **Mahonia** grow more like **bamboo** than **Burford Holly**. We speak of their shoots as canes like we speak of **bamboo** canes, as opposed to shoots of other broadleaf evergreens. Another distinctive feature of these clump-type evergreens is that new growth seldom (if ever) develops from side buds on the canes. If you prune below the leaf area you will have a dead cane. These distinctions between clump-type evergreens and other evergreens are important to know, especially when pruning them. Treat each cane as an individual plant which cannot be pruned back to make the plant bushy.

Nandina becomes leggy and unsightly when pruned improperly.

Nandina is a beautiful shrub when properly pruned.

We must consider the clump as a whole, in order to prevent a tall stalky plant with little or no leaf area except at the top. Since **Nandina** is usually grown as a foundation specimen plant, it looks bad when there is nothing but a group of visible stalks with bunches of leaves on top. **Mahonia** can be attractive because it is often grown among lower plants which hide its bare stalks. Unlike **Nandina** and **Mahonia, Aucuba** may occasionally develop side branches near the top which weep over and hide the unsightly stalks. All three of these clump plants develop more attractively when pruned correctly.

Before pruning, closely examine the plant from top to bottom. You will find some tall old shoots, some medium shoots, and some short new shoots. Avoid having an unsightly and stalky plant by removing some of the tall shoots and fertilizing the plant to force young new shoots to cover the base. Maintain the height you want by completely removing too-tall canes and leaving canes which are the height you

want. I prune one-third of the tall stalks of my **Nandina** at the ground each year and never prune back any stalks below the green area. The combination of tall, medium and short shoots keeps my plant bushy from top to bottom. The same combination keeps **Aucuba** and **Mahonia** attractive in the same way. Fertilizing is also an important part of keeping these clump plants beautiful because it forces new growth from the clump. Use an azalea-camellia fertilizer each spring to force new shoots from the base.

Mahonia and **Aucuba** are especially important to the landscape because they grow in more shade than most other broadleaf evergreens. **Nandina** is important because it makes a wonderful specimen plant with its colorful foliage all year and clusters of bright red berries in the fall. Prune all three correctly to maximize their beauty.

SHRUB AND VINE ACTIVITIES FOR FEBRUARY:

Plant

☛ Plant all dormant container-grown, B&B, and bare-root shrubs whenever the ground is not frozen. Prepare the holes as carefully as you do for shade trees.*

☛ Plant hardy woody vines like **Clematis, Carolina Jessamine,** and **Wisteria** during periods of mild weather, when the ground is not frozen.†

☛ Plant hardy ground covers like **English Ivy, Vinca, Liriope,** and **Spreading Juniper** whenever the ground is not frozen. These should be heavily rooted plants, not transplanted runners.*

☛ It is best to plant shrubs when the soil is not too wet. However, if planting is necessary before the soil dries out, use dry peat moss as the soil amendment. It will absorb excess moisture and make it easier to prepare a good mixture for planting.

* See "Planting Trees and Shrubs," p. 264
† See "Growing Clematis and Other Southern Vines," p. 54

Prune

☞ Heavy structural pruning of evergreen shrubs like **Burford Holly**, **Box Leaf Holly**, **boxwood**, and **cleyera** may be done this month. However, if most of the leaf area is to be removed, I prefer to wait until mid-February to mid-March so I don't have to look at stubby plants so long. Do not remove all the green leaves from **boxoods** anytime you prune.

☞ Prune broadleaf evergreens like **hollies** and narrowleaf evergreens like **junipers** and **arborvitaes** to shape any time this month. Always prune so the top is narrower than the bottom in order to keep evergreens from becoming top-heavy and unsightly.

☞ Wait to prune cold-damaged stems until March or April when you will be able to determine the true extent of cold damage.

☞ Prune summer-flowering shrubs (those which form their blossoms on the coming year's new growth) like **Hydrangea arborescens 'Grandiflora,'** **Hydrangea paniculata 'Grandiflora,'** and **Butterfly Bush (Buddleia)** any time this month before new growth emerges and when the wood isn't frozen.‡

☞ Prune deciduous spring-flowering shrubs (those which blossom on growth formed last year) like **January Jasmine**, **Flowering Quince**, and **Winter Honeysuckle** when they have finished blooming.‡

☞ Wait to prune flowering evergreen shrubs like **Camellia**, **azalea**, **Rhododendron**, and **Mountain Laurel** until after they have finished blooming.‡

☞ Prune **Blue/Pink Hydrangea** by removing the weak shoots at the ground and pruning the main shoots back one-third.‡

☞ Prune **Nandina**, **Mahonia** and **Aucuba** according to their specific methods.**

☞ Deciduous leafy shrubs like **barberry** and deciduous **Euonymus** can be pruned this month.

‡ See "Pruning Flowering Shrubs and Vines," p. 31

** See "Pruning Aucuba, Mahonia, and Nandina," p. 33

☞ Do not prune spring-flowering evergreen vines like **Carolina Jessamine** until after they bloom.‡

☞ Giant hybrid **Clematis** can be pruned severely from now until new growth starts emerging.†

☞ Other **Clematis** should only be thinned, leaving the main arms to develop shoots on which blossoms will form. Do this before shoots begin to emerge. Wait until after blossoming to prune **Clematis** like **Clematis montana** and **Clematis X 'Duchess of Edinburgh'** which bloom on last year's growth.†

☞ Prune other deciduous spring-flowering vines like **Wisteria** after they have finished blooming.‡

☞ Other summer flowering vines like **Silver Lace Vine (Polygonum aubertii)** and **Gold Flame Honeysuckle (Lonicera sempervirens)** should be pruned now before new growth starts.‡

Fertilize

☞ Begin fertilizing summer-flowering shrubs like **Hydrangea arborescens 'Grandiflora,'** **Hydrangea paniculata 'Grandiflora,'** and **Butterfly Bush (Buddleia)** with a 15-15-15 fertilizer as the weather warms and the danger of hard freezes passes. Use roughly 1/2 pound per three feet of the shrub's height (*the height before any pruning*). This is usually done once a year.††

☞ Fertilize summer-flowering vines like **Silver Lace Vine (Polygonum aubertii)** and **Gold Flame Honeysuckle (Lonicera sempervirens)** as the weather warms and the danger of hard freezes passes. Use 1/2 pound of 15-15-15 fertilizer on plants one to three years old. On older vines, add a pound of fertilizer per year of age up to a maximum of five pounds.††

☞ Fertilize established **Clematis** after pruning with half a pound of 5-10-15 fertilizer every six weeks. As an alternative, you can fertilize once with a slow release high nitrogen fertilizer. Do not fertilize

‡ See "Pruning Flowering Shrubs and Vines," p. 31

† See "Growing Clematis and Other Southern Vines," p. 54

†† See "How to Fertilize Shrubs and Vines," p. 30

Clematis like **Clematis montana** and **Clematis X 'Duchess of Edinburgh'** which bloom on last year's growth until after they finish blooming.

☛ Fertilize all spring-flowering shrubs and vines like **azalea, Camellia, Rhododendron, Forsythia, Flowering Quince, Spiraea, Viburnum** , and **Carolina Jessamine** after they bloom. Use a 15-15-15 fertilizer on deciduous shrubs and vines and an azalea/camellia acid fertilizer on evergreens. Use roughly 1/2 pound per three feet of the shrub's height (the height before any pruning). This is usually done once a year.††

☛ Begin fertilizing broadleaf evergreens like **hollies,** and narrowleaf evergreens like **junipers** with an acid azalea/camelia fertilizer as their new growth starts. Use roughly 1/2 pound per three feet of the shrub's height (the height before any pruning). This is usually done once a year.††

Spray

☛ Inspect established evergreens for signs of scale. This insect is particularly bad on evergreens. Control it with Cygon except on **hollies**; use Orthene on **hollies**.‡‡

☛ Inspect **azalea** and **Pyracantha** for signs of lacebugs. The upper sides of the leaves will have a silvery cast. The under sides will be covered with tiny balls of brown residue. Spray them with Orthene as the weather warms.‡‡

Water

☛ After planting, soak shrubs and vines thoroughly, even if the ground is wet, in order to settle the soil around the roots.

☛ Continue to watch extreme drops in temperature. Protect plants from cold by making sure that the ground is wet before cold weather arrives. When wet soil freezes, it helps to insulate the plants' roots.***

Other

☛ Keep evergreens well mulched but do not allow mulch to cover the lower stems or trunks.†††

☛ During periods of extreme cold, protect broadleaf evergreens especially **Banana Shrub, Gardenia, Loquat,** and **Aucuba** by erecting a wind and sun screen made of burlap. This will prevent damage to the leaves and stems when the ground is frozen.***

☛ Never cover plants with plastic to protect them from extreme cold; they would be damaged by heat build-up when the sun comes out. Use an old sheet or blanket but do not leave it on too long, because an opaque material will stop photosynthesis in the leaves and make the plants more tender.***

☛ During snowfalls, brush off accumulated snow from limber evergreens like **boxwoods** with a broom to keep them from spreading and breaking.

☛ Leave snow on non-limber shrubs until it melts because it won't break them and actually insulates plants and helps prevent cold damage.

☛ Continue to make dormant cuttings of deciduous shrubs like **Hydrangea** and **Viburnum**. Root the cuttings in perlite or vermiculite beds in a cold frame or a protected place outside.‡‡‡

---

†† See "How to Fertilize Shrubs and Vines," p. 30

‡‡ See "Controlling Insects and Diseases," p. 80

*** See "Helping Plants Survive the Cold," p. 269

††† See "Mulching: A Lesson from Nature," p. 243

*** See "Helping Plants Survive the Cold," p. 269

‡‡‡ See "Making Dormant Cuttings of Shrubs and Roses," p. 9

III. *Fruits*

February is the month of the fruit! By the end of the month, with our trees pruned, fertilized, mulched, and sprayed, we can feel confident that this year's crop will be a good one. We hoped to finish our pruning in January, but there is still a little time left. Try to get this job done as soon as possible so the pruning scars will heal before those dreaded pests start crawling and hopping around.

February is a great time to fertilize fruit trees. I like to fertilize and replace my pine straw mulch at the same time. It is a good feeling to tidy up around the trees and dream about all the wonderful apples I'll be chomping on in the summer and fall.

Remember to apply your dormant spray up until the time the buds begin to swell. After the buds begin to show color, it is too late for dormant spray.

HOW TO FERTILIZE FRUIT TREES

Of all the trees in their yards, gardeners probably remember to fertilize fruit trees more than any other tree. While it's hard to measure the new growth of a shade tree, it is not hard at all to notice whether your fruit trees have sumptuous fruit, ripe for plucking. As fruit and vegetable gardeners know, there is no greater motivator than the allure of homegrown produce. Whether last year's crop was less than you hoped, or this year's bountiful harvest is a special goal, fertilizing your fruit trees is probably on your checklist.

Fertilizing is a method of adding nutrients to the soil. The fruit tree then absorbs the nutrients and uses

A good time to fertilize fruit trees is when the buds swell and begin to show color.

them when producing its food through photosynthesis. Some people like to say they are feeding their tree when they fertilize, but the fruit tree feeds itself. It does need our help, though, in keeping the soil supplied with the necessary nutrients for it to manufacture its own food.

Fertilizing fruit trees can be as easy or difficult as you want it to be. The many different ways to apply fertilizer all have the same goal: to make nutrients available to the tree when it is actively absorbing them. Fruit trees begin growing — and absorbing nutrients — in late winter when the ground is warming and the danger of severe freezes has passed. Some application methods require you to apply a small amount of fertilizer every month from March through June. Others require you to continue fertilizing after that. I have found that for home fruit production, applying fertilizer every month does not increase your crop that much compared to one or two applications. Besides, we are likely to forget to continue it and then our tree will end up with only a small portion of the nutrients it needs.

A good time to fertilize fruit trees is in late winter when you notice the buds swelling. Depending on the year, this can vary from late February to late March. A swollen bud has cracked its brown shell so that you can see some green underneath. Use one-half to one pound of 15-15-15 fertilizer per year of age of the tree (a maximum of 15 pounds per tree for **apples**, five pounds per tree for **peaches/nectarines/plums**). This translates into about a pound for newly planted trees. Spread the fertilizer in a circle around the tree. For newly planted trees, this circle should be at the edge of the hole you dug when planting. For older trees, spread the fertilizer in a wider circle each year as the tree's roots expand. Remember not to place fertilizer against the trunk of the tree or in piles around the tree. *Too much fertilizer in one spot can damage the roots.*

As with most general rules, there are exceptions. **Peaches**, **nectarines**, and **plums** need an additional application of 15-15-15 in August. Use one-half pound per year of age of the tree up to a maximum of five pounds. **Apples** only need a second application if they are not growing well.

One fruit tree is such an exception that it has its own fertilizer! **Pecans** can be fertilized a month after planting with one-half pound of 15-15-15 (don't put

it in the hole; broadcast it around the tree) but later in their life they will need a special pecan fertilizer which contains zinc. Check the particular fertilizer for the recommended application rate.

Finally, most fruit trees like their soil to have a pH of at least 6.5. If you suspect your soil is acidic (perhaps from a nearby pine tree), or if you have had a soil test done showing acidity, you can sweeten the soil by applying limestone or dolomitic lime.

FRUIT ACTIVITIES FOR FEBRUARY:

Plant

☛ Plant B&B, bare-root, and container-grown fruits all month. This includes fruit trees (**peaches**, **apples**, **cherries**, **pears**, etc.), bush fruits (**blueberries**), semi-bush fruits (**raspberries**, **blackberries**, etc.), and vine fruits (**grapes**, **muscadines**).*

☛ Plant **Chinese Chestnut**, **pecan**, **walnut**, and other nut trees.

☛ Always plant two or three **Chinese Chestnuts** so they can cross-pollinate. Otherwise, you will not have a good nut harvest.

☛ Begin to plant **figs** and **strawberries** at the end of the month after the danger of hard freezes has passed.

Prune

☛ Finish pruning fruit trees as soon as possible this month. Use the Open Head or Basket method of pruning for **peaches**, **plums**, **apricots**, and **nectarines**. Use the Modified Leader method for pruning **apples**, **pears**, and **cherries**. Flower buds are already set on last summer's growth. Be sure to leave plenty of this growth for flowers and fruits. After pruning, fertilize your trees.†

☛ Continue to prune and train semi-bush fruits like **blackberries** and **raspberries**. Train last season's

* See "Planting Trees and Shrubs," p. 264

† See "Pruning Fruit Trees," p. 13

growth onto wires or trellises. You must keep these fruiting canes separate from the new growth which will grow this summer and bear fruit next year.‡

☞ Continue to prune **grapes** and **muscadines** and train them onto a one- or two-wire fence.

Fertilize

☞ Fertilize fruit trees as the buds begin to swell. Use a 15-15-15 fertilizer at a rate of one-half pound per year of age of the tree. Use a maximum of 15 pounds on **apples** and **pears** and five pounds on **peaches**, **nectarines**, and **plums**. This is usually done once a year.**

☞ Fertilize **nut trees** if you haven't already. Use a 15-15-15 fertilizer, except on **pecans** which need a special pecan fertilizer containing zinc. This is done once a year.**

☞ Begin fertilizing **grapes** and semi-bush fruits with 15-15-15. Use about two pounds per vine on established, producing grapes. Use one pound per plant on young (one to three years old) semi-bush fruits, and two pounds per plant for older semi-bush fruits. This is usually done once a year.

‡ See "Secrets of the Berry Patch," p. 155
** See "How to Fertilize Fruit Trees," p. 37

Spray

☞ Apply a recommended dormant spray on tree fruits, semi-bush fruits, and **grapes** if you haven't done so already. Spray only when the material will dry before it freezes and before the buds begin to swell.

☞ Wait until after you have pruned to spray fruits.

Water

☞ Water newly planted fruit trees thoroughly, even if the ground is wet, in order to settle the soil around the roots.

Other

☞ Be careful when mowing in orchard areas not to hit the bark of fruit trees with the mower. Any damage to the bark will provide an entrance place for borers.

☞ Keep fruits mulched with pine straw to prevent weeds and grasses from competing for water and fertilizer.††

†† See "Mulching: A Lesson from Nature," p. 243

NOTES

IV. *Roses*

It is not too late to buy some mail-order roses and get them in the ground before new growth begins. Container-grown roses can be planted through April, but you might find a better selection in the mail-order catalogs. Try out some new varieties this year.

Finish up your applications of lime sulfur by mid-February. It is okay if you burn some of the new tip growth because it will be pruned off anyway. This application is an important first step in your pest control program.

If you can't wait until early March, you can begin pruning your roses in late February. Wait until after you have pruned to fertilize.

PRUNING ROSES

In the South, we prune our roses in February and early March. There is an important reason for this timing, despite what successful rose growers are doing in other parts of the country. Since pruning stimulates growth, roses pruned earlier are liable to begin growing in one of the warm spells common to the South in January and February, only to be killed back when a cold front brings low temperatures, ice, or even snow. Even though they aren't pruned, bulbs are often tricked by warm spells into sprouting too soon, and some spring-flowering shrubs are tricked into blooming. For this reason, we must wait to prune roses until the end of the winter dormant season when chances of a frigid cold spell are minimal.

Severe structural pruning of **Hybrid Teas, Floribundas, Grandifloras,** and other "everblooming" bush roses takes place in early-mid February in the lower South and late February/early March in the upper South. Pruning encourages roses to grow healthy new canes on which many blossoms will form. Gardeners are sometimes shocked to see what "severe pruning" really means. Cutting a healthy three-foot-tall rose bush down to one foot takes a lot of confidence in yourself and the rose! Don't worry, though; roses have amazing regenerative abilities, and it is hard to do them substantial damage. No matter how you prune, your rose will probably grow back rapidly. But good pruning is a matter of cutting it back so it will grow with the desired strength, structure, and form. With a little practice, you can learn to prune like an expert.

As you may know, most purchased roses consist of the desired variety grafted onto an understock of a different rose which has a vigorous root system. If you look closely at your rose bush, you can still see the graft union, which is a calloused ball, sometimes as big as a golf ball, just above ground level. The rose canes growing from the graft union, or right above it are the desired variety, while everything below the graft union, including the roots, are of the understock. Never cut below the graft union. If you do, any rose canes which sprout will not be the rose you are interested in growing! The theory behind severe rose pruning is to choose the three to five best canes growing from above the graft union, cut them back so that each contains at least four healthy buds, and leave a rose bush 12 to 15 inches tall overall (from ground level).

Good rose pruning is the art of choosing the best canes to leave, cutting them back properly, and treating them so they will sprout healthy new growth. Let's start at the beginning. When choosing the three to five best canes to leave on the bush, try to find healthy canes which are a clean, green color (no brown or purple splotches), are one or two years old, are at least 1/4 to 1/2 an inch in diameter, and are currently at least a foot or two in length. Once you have determined which canes to leave on the bush, remove all the other weak, diseased, damaged, and older canes. If you didn't find at least three good canes, it is better to stick with two than to leave an old or damaged cane on the bush. In fact, I have seen roses with only one good cane develop into excellent plants.

Once you have thinned your rose bush down to the healthy canes which you intend to keep, you are ready to cut them back. Always use sharp, knife-cut pruning shears which will not tear or crush the cane

1 – A rose plant ready to prune.

2 – Choose three strong, well-spaced canes for good structure.

3 – Cut the remaining canes back to at least 6 to 8 inches.

4 – A well-pruned rose with its new growth

as they cut. If the canes are large, you might consider using a pair of loppers. The next step in good rose pruning is deciding where to make the cut. Make all cuts about a quarter of an inch above a dormant bud. Try to choose a bud at least six to eight inches above the graft union which is facing the outside of the bush so that new branches will grow outward rather than crowd the inside. Before you cut, be sure that the remaining cane will have at least four healthy buds. Make each cut on a slant, with the high side a half inch above the bud and the low side a quarter of an inch above the bud's level on the opposite side. Always cut with the blade side of the shears next to the bud to prevent tearing. The slanted cut will cause raindrops to run off the cut and prevent rotting. Finally, seal all the cuts with Elmer's Glue to prevent borers and other insects from entering the cane.

Climbing cultivars like 'Blaze,' 'New Dawn,' and the Climbing Hybrid Teas are pruned using a differ-

ent method. They should be pruned by thinning out the older canes leaving the long, young branches which produce the best blossoms.

Severe rose pruning sends a distinct message to your roses: "Grow!" It is therefore a good idea to fertilize them immediately after pruning, using a complete rose fertilizer with systemic insecticide. This way they will have plenty of nutrients and disease resistance to begin the rose season with healthy, abundant growth. When you prune, be sure to check that the soil has not packed up against the graft union, keeping it damp and causing problems. Another good idea is to mulch your newly pruned roses with pine straw. Mulch prevents weeds from growing up and competing with the rose for water and fertilizer. Mulch also prevents the ground underneath from drying out too quickly and keeps the rose roots cool during long, hot Southern summers.

ROSE ACTIVITIES FOR FEBRUARY:

Plant

☛ Continue to plant bare-root roses whenever the ground is not frozen. Before planting, trim long or broken roots and cut stems back to a healthy bud. Try new varieties but keep old favorites as major plantings until new ones have proven themselves in your garden.*

☛ Container-grown roses can be planted now through April.†

Prune

☛ Begin pruning roses in early-mid February in the lower South, late February/early March in the upper South. **Hybrid Tea**, **Floribunda**, **Grandiflora**, and other "everblooming" types should be pruned severely to force healthy new growth. Climbing cultivars like **'Blaze,'** **'New Dawn,'** and the **Climbing Hybrid Teas** should be pruned by thinning out the older canes leaving the long, young branches which produce the best blossoms.‡

* See "Planting Bare-Root Roses," p. 250
† See "Planting Trees and Shrubs," p. 264
‡ See "Pruning Roses," p. 40

Fertilize

☛ Do not fertilize established roses until after you have pruned.

Spray

☛ Apply lime sulfur as a dormant spray on roses in early February if you did not do so in January. Spray at a time when the material will not freeze before it dries. Thoroughly spray the canes and the mulch around the plants. This application will control over-wintering spores of major diseases.

Other

☛ Keep roses well mulched but do not pile mulch against the crown or lower stems. Many problems like rose stem canker and botrytis occur when mulch covers the lower stems.**

☛ Do not be concerned if new leaves which have emerged on the top of canes during the winter months are damaged by dormant sprayings or cold weather. You will be removing them during major structural pruning in early March.

** See "Mulching: A Lesson from Nature," p. 243

NOTES

V. *Flowers and Colorful Garden Plants*

There is nothing more fun than growing flowers from seeds. I love to start my spring garden this way because it gives me something to do on the dreary days of winter. If you started seeds inside during January, they have probably sprouted. Don't let them dry out in the harsh indoor environment. Mist them regularly with clear water and keep them in a sunny spot.

If you can't wait any longer to get outside, try planting some pansies or peonies. They are easy to grow and make a nice addition to the garden.

February is also a good time to repot your carried-over flowers like geraniums. This will give them added incentive to grow vigorously so you will have beautiful plants to set out once the weather is warm enough.

Over-wintered geraniums ready for spring potting.

Cut back and pot over-wintered geraniums to have heavy blooming plants to set in the garden after the danger of frost.

FLOWER ACTIVITIES FOR FEBRUARY:

Plant

☞ Plant hardy biennial and perennial roots like **Chrysanthemum, Delphinium, Foxglove, Purple Cone-Flower, Rudbeckia,** and **Shasta Daisy** whenever the weather is mild. Plant in well-drained soil. Most perennials need a sweet soil. Check instructions and apply dolomitic limestone or bone meal if suggested. However, do not apply limestone in areas next to broadleaf evergreens, especially **hollies, azaleas, camellias,** and **rhododendrons.** Mulch biennnial and perennial roots heavily with pine straw to prevent their spewing out of the ground in a late freeze.*

☞ Finish seeding hardy annuals, biennials, and perennials like **Foxglove, hollyhocks, Purple Cone-Flower, Rudbeckia, Shasta Daisy, stock, Stokesia,** and **Sweet William** inside or in a greenhouse as soon as possible.†

☞ Start seeds of tender annuals like **Ageratum, Begonia, Coleus, Impatiens, marigolds, petunias, Salvia,** and **Vinca** inside during the second half of the month. These will be ready for planting in the garden after frost.*

☞ Plant **pansies** and **English Daisies** in the garden all month whenever the weather is mild.

☞ **Sweet Peas** can still be planted in February. Plant them in trenches whenever the weather is mild.

* See "How to Plant a Flower Bed," p. 62

† See "Starting Seeds Inside," p. 18
* See "How to Plant a Flower Bed," p. 62

☛ Continue to plant **peonies** and **Iris** this month. Plant them shallowly with the roots close to the top of the soil. **Peonies** should be planted in morning sun with the pink buds just above the soil so the buds can freeze and produce better flowers. Use bone meal and mulch them heavily, but leave the crown open.

☛ Repot large **Geranium** and **Begonia** which are to be set outside on terraces and decks when the danger of frost is over. They need time to start growth and become beautiful before moving outside.‡

☛ Cut back and pot **geraniums** which were lifted from the garden and stored over winter in plastic bags. They will start growing almost immediately and be ready to set outside in late April or early May.

Fertilize

☛ Fertilize annuals, biennials, and perennials on the following schedule: Apply 15-15-15, which is a good starter fertilizer, on new and emerging plants. After six to eight weeks, switch to 5-10-15, which is a good fruit and flower fertilizer, and continue on that schedule for the rest of the season.

‡   See "Repotting Houseplants," p. 67
** See "Mulching: A Lesson from Nature," p. 243
†† See "Propagating Herbaceous Houseplants and Garden Plants," p. 225

Spray

☛ Spray the crowns and emerging shoots of **peonies** to control botrytis disease. Captan is a good recommended control.

Other

☛ Keep beds mulched with pine straw or grass clippings to protect newly emerging shoots from deep freezes and to keep beds free from winter weeds.**

☛ Protect **pansies** and **English Daisies** from extreme cold by placing several layers of newspaper over them. Be sure to remove it as soon as the cold wave has passed.

☛ Make cuttings of overwintered, tender plants like **Begonia, Coleus, Impatiens,** and **Geranium** as soon as possible to give them time to develop well before planting time in April.††

☛ Keep **Canna** and **Dahlia** roots stored in a cool place. Do not set them in the garden until April when the ground is warm and the danger of frost has passed. Keep **Caladium** and **Elephant Ear** tubers in a warmer spot than **Canna** and **Dahlia** roots.

** See "Mulching: A Lesson from Nature," p. 243
†† See "Propagating Herbaceous Houseplants and Garden Plants," p. 225

NOTES

VI. *Vegetables*

Despite the cold weather, there is plenty of vegetable gardening to do. Many cool weather crops like Asparagus and English peas can be planted regardless of the cold nights. Although most people think of vegetable gardening as a spring and summer activity, I encourage you to try some winter vegetables.

If your dreams do lie in later plantings, get ready by starting seeds of tomatoes, peppers, and eggplants inside. This is a great way to beat the high price of seedlings at the local nursery and also to enjoy watching the miracle of germination. These plants will grow into healthy young seedlings to be planted outdoors when the danger of frost has passed.

If you haven't done so already, lime your vegetable garden and turn under cover crops in areas where March plantings will be set out. You don't want to be caught unprepared when the weather finally warms up.

Start tomato seeds early to have strong plants ready to set in the garden after frost.

VEGETABLE ACTIVITIES FOR FEBRUARY:

Plant

☛ Plant **wrinkled English peas**, such as **snap peas**, as soon as the worst cold is over.*

☛ Plant **Irish potatoes** at the end of the month (when the threat of severe cold has passed). Be sure to plant on beds.*

☛ Plant hardy lettuce like **Black Seeded Simpson** as soon as the threat of severe cold has passed.*

☛ Plant **Asparagus**, **horseradish**, **Jerusalem Artichoke**, and **rhubarb** roots on beds whenever the ground is not frozen. Mulch them heavily with compost and fertilize them.*

☛ Continue to plant **garlic** cloves and **onion** sets this month. **Onion plants** (for growing large **onion bulbs**) can also be planted this month.*

☛ Start seeds of tender vegetables (**tomatoes**, **peppers**, **eggplant**) and tender annual herbs like **anise**, **coriander,** and **sweet basil** inside during the second half of the month. They will be ready to plant outside after the danger of frost has passed.†

* See "Planting a Vegetable Garden," p. 92

† See "Starting Seeds Inside," p. 18

☛ Start the following seeds inside as soon as possible in early February: **broccoli, cabbage, cauliflower, collard, lettuce,** and **onion.** These can be planted outside in March after the danger of hard freezes has passed.

Fertilize

☛ Lime gardens with dolomitic limestone if you didn't do so last month. Application is at a rate of 50 pounds per 1000 square feet. Do not lime areas where you are going to plant **Irish potatoes.***

☛ Fertilize as you plant with 15-15-15. Application is at a rate of approximately one pound per 10 feet of row. This application should be good for about six weeks.*

Spray

☛ Winter weeds which are growing in bare vegetable areas can be eradicated with Roundup. You must wait at least two weeks after application, however, before planting vegetables.

Other

☛ Turn under cover crops planted last fall in areas which will be used for vegetables in March.

* See "Planting a Vegetable Garden," p. 92

VII. *Houseplants*

The days are slowly getting longer, and your houseplants know it. Many will start a spurt of growth when they feel spring has officially arrived. When you see this growth, help them out by increasing your fertilizer applications to full strength.

February is also one of my favorite times to propagate plants. I like to take cuttings of plants like Piggyback and Hibiscus. The mother plant will rebound quickly and fill out wonderfully by spring. Cuttings also seem to have the will to grow and will take root in an amazingly brief time.

Despite the signs of spring to come, we are still running the furnace constantly during February. Watch out for leaf-burn as a sign that your houseplants are drying out too quickly. Mist them regularly to help your plants through the final months of winter.

HOUSEPLANT ACTIVITIES FOR FEBRUARY:

Plant

☛ While houseplants can be propagated all year long under the proper conditions, February and March are a good time to take cuttings of your existing stock. These cuttings should root fairly quickly and will have the whole summer to mature. This way you will have plenty of mature houseplants to drive away next year's winter blues.*

☛ Houseplants, especially newly purchased ones, can be repotted at any time during the year. Use a pot at least two sizes larger so the plant will have plenty of room to grow. I prefer to grow most of my houseplants in a peat-light potting mixture.†

Prune

☛ Groom indoor plants whenever they need it. Remove weak branches or stems as well as off-color leaves.

Fertilize

☛ Watch houseplants and tropical plants for evidence of new growth. As soon as you see plants beginning to grow, go to the full recommended strength of water-soluble fertilizer solution. Fertilize every time you water. You can also use fertilizer sticks or Osmocote fertilizer, both of which last for several months.‡

Spray

☛ Check indoor plants for insects like spider mites, scale, and mealybug. I like to use a houseplant systemic insecticide on the soil to control them. It is easier and safer than spraying indoors. If you do spray, remember to apply the insecticide to the undersides of the leaves. I like to spray houseplants when I can take them outside on a warm day. Bring them inside as soon as the spray material dries.**

☛ Be careful when spraying **ferns**. Some insecticides are harmful to them. *Always read the label for warnings about **ferns** and other plants.*

Water

☛ Watch houseplants carefully during the winter. When they look limp, check for dry soil. If it is dry, water thoroughly in a sink or bathtub, letting the water drain completely, and don't water again until the surface is dry once more. Between waterings, mist with plain water on a regular basis. If the limp plants are in moist soil, do not water but allow the soil to dry a bit and mist frequently.‡

* See "Propagating Herbaceous Houseplants and Garden Plants," p. 225
† See "Repotting Houseplants," p. 67
‡ See "Houseplant Care and Maintenance," p. 232
** See "Common Houseplant Ailments," p. 280

☛ Tip-burn or edge-burn on leaves indicates that more water is being lost than is being absorbed by the roots. Check for dry soil, too much sunlight, or drafts from heater vents.‡

☛ Keep watching **ferns** for signs of dead or dying foliage. Mist them frequently and remove any dead fronds as soon as they occur.

Other

☛ Keep **Poinsettia**, **Kalanchoe**, and **Christmas Cactus** barely moist and in a spot which receives bright outside light, but not direct sun.††

‡ See "Houseplant Care and Maintenance," p. 232
†† See "Indoor Flowering Plants for the Holidays," p. 256

☛ **Christmas chrysanthemums** and forced **azaleas** should be in a cold, but not freezing, place, and the soil should be kept moist. Let them harden up before planting outside.††

☛ **Amaryllis** and **ornamental peppers** grow best in bright light and should be watered the same as tropical houseplants.††

†† See "Indoor Flowering Plants for the Holidays," p. 256

NOTES

Many lawn activities need to be done when Forsythia blooms.

VIII. *Lawns*

Go buy your pre-emergence weed control! Every year I am a little late in applying mine. It is not because I don't wait until my Forsythia blooms; it just takes me too long to get around to going to the nursery to buy it. My New Year's resolution was to buy it *early* and have it ready when the time was right.

Besides applying pre-emergence, February is a month of tidying up the lawn. Make sure the final leaves of last fall are cleaned up and try to control winter weeds before they start growing rapidly as the ground warms. Keep evergreen lawns cut at the proper height if February is one of those warm times in the South.

LAWN ACTIVITIES FOR FEBRUARY:

Spray

☞ Apply pre-emergence weed and weed grass control in late February, or when the **Forsythia** blooms. Since pre-emergence controls are usually good for 160 days, be careful not to put them out too early or you will lose some effectiveness later on.*

☞ Do not use pre-emergence weed controls if you are planning to re-plant or reseed your lawn.

☞ Control winter weeds like **wild garlic (wild onions)** and **chickweed** with a lawn-formula broadleaf herbicide. During February they grow rapidly and can damage lawns. Spray on a warm day and be patient because results are slow in the winter.*

Cut

☞ Cut evergreen lawns whenever they need it. Do not let grass get too tall before cutting. Ideal heights:

* See "Fertilizing and Controlling Weeds in Lawns," p. 73

EVERGREEN GRASSES	HEIGHT
Kentucky 31 Tall Fescue	3 to 3 ½ inches
Turf-type Tall Fescues	3 inches
Fine Fescues	1 ½ to 2 inches
Kentucky Bluegrass	2 to 2 ½ inches

☞ If you have seeded **Ryegrass** over **Bermuda Grass**, keep the **Ryegrass** cut about an inch above the base lawn. If you let it grow tall in clumps, it will damage your permanent grass.

Other

☞ Dethatch summer lawns at the end of the month.

☞ Aerate evergreen lawns at the end of the month or in early March before fertilizing.

☞ Rake falling oak leaves off lawns.

NOTES

March

IN THE SOUTHERN GARDEN

Finally, March is here and spring begins to be a reality. We Southerners have been tempted with warm spells since January, only to have our hopes dashed on the edge of Arctic waves which chilled us again to the bone. The first part of March can be bad (remember the Great Blizzard of '93), but most years the month ends up like a lamb.

The first signs of the South's beautiful spring season are the early flowering trees like Bradford Pears and Oriental Magnolias, which suddenly break forth into gorgeous bloom after only a few warm days. Gradually, spring bulbs venture upward and burst into bloom. The wave of flowers starts in the lower South and along the coast and moves northward until it engulfs our whole region. March 20 or 21, the Vernal Equinox when night and day are equal, marks the official start of spring even though heavy frosts can occur into April in much of the South. By the end of March, there are so many beautiful plants in bloom that visitors flock to the South to be part of one of nature's most wonderful shows.

Confine your planting now to hardy and half-hardy types which could survive and prosper despite a possible heavy frost. It is still too early to set out tomatoes and zinnias except in the lower South, even though there is temptation to get a jump on the season. Play it safe! There is nothing more discouraging than seeing beautiful plants killed and facing the prospect of starting over again.

All winter we have planned our new plants and garden areas beside the fire, choosing from pictures in catalogs and books. In March we can dispense with the pictures and be inspired by the real blooming plants. Plan several visits to public gardens and good commercial plantings. March is still a great time to plant shrubs, trees, fruits, and flowers, and you'll find it far easier to choose what you like when you can see plants in full bloom. So give yourself the pleasure of some live research — see what shapes, varieties, and colors you can't live without, then go and buy and plant!

AT LEFT: *Star Magnolia (Magnolia stellata)*

I. *Shade and Flowering Trees*

As spring arrives, it is best not to work too much on your trees. It is too late to prune shade and flowering trees, and it's best to avoid any cutting since the danger of cutting off new growth is great. There are many planting activities we can do. March is the perfect time to plant Southern Magnolias and Cherry Laurels. Remember to fertilize them after planting to give them a good start.

Other shade and flowering trees should have been fertilized by now, but if you didn't have the chance, do it now. It is better to fertilize late than not at all. Don't plant bare-root trees after the leaves have come out; stick with container-grown plants to avoid the heartache of watching a newly planted tree suffer and die.

With the joys of warmer weather come worries of insects and disease. Just as leaves emerge from their buds, insects and diseases emerge from their dormant stages. In March we are likely to see leaf miners, dogwood petal blight, scale, worms, and a variety of other pests. Look for discoloration, deformed leaves, wilting, leaf scars, and other abnormalities as signs that these pests are active in your garden. Welcome to March!

The magnificent Southern Magnolia (Magnolia grandiflora) an evergreen tree with huge summer flowers.

TREE ACTIVITIES FOR MARCH:

Plant

☛ Now is the time to plant **Southern Magnolias** and **Cherry Laurels**. Make sure to plant in a well-prepared hole at the correct depth like you do with shade and flowering trees, and stake them to keep them from swaying.*

☛ B&B and container-grown trees may be planted this month with caution. It is not recommended, however, to plant bare-root deciduous trees after the leaves come out.*

☛ It is best to plant trees when the soil is not too wet. However, if planting is necessary before the soil dries out, use dry peat moss as the soil amendment. It will absorb excess moisture and make it easier to prepare a good soil mixture.

Prune

☛ Prune only dead, broken, or damaged tree limbs on shade and flowering trees.†

☛ If needed, spring-flowering trees like **Bradford Pear**, **flowering crabapples**, **flowering plums**, **flowering peaches**, and **flowering cherries** may be pruned after they finish blooming.†

* See "Planting Trees and Shrubs," p. 264   † See "Pruning Shade and Flowering Trees," p. 4

Fertilize

☞ Fertilize **Southern Magnolia** and **Cherry Laurel** with a slow-release nitrogen, evergreen formula. Use one pound of fertilizer per inch circumference of the tree measured three feet above the ground. This is done once a year.‡

☞ Though it's not the best time, fertilize shade trees if you have not done so already. Use one pound of fertilizer per inch circumference of the tree measured three feet above the ground. A 15-15-15 mix is recommended. This is done once a year.‡

☞ Fertilize spring-flowering trees like **Bradford Pear**, **flowering crabapples**, **flowering cherries**, **flowering peaches**, and **flowering plums** as the flower petals fall. Use one pound of 5-10-15 fertilizer per inch circumference of the tree measured three feet above the ground. This is done once a year.

Spray

☞ Control scale on all trees with Orthene or Cygon, except in the case of **hollies**. Use Orthene on **hollies**.**

☞ Watch out for worms and caterpillars eating the foliage of flowering forms of fruit trees. Spray with the Thuricide formulation of Bacillus thurengiensis (BT), or dust with the Dipel form of Bacillus thurengiensis (BT).**

☞ Protect **dogwood** buds from petal blight by spraying with Daconil or Dithane. Apply the spray when the bud cracks open, and every 10 days after until the petals have fallen. However, do not spray when flowers are at their peak.**

☞ Holly leaf miners are also a problem in the spring. This is a gnat-like insect which you will see flying around hollies, especially **American Hollies**. The insect lays eggs in the leaves which hatch into tiny worms. The worms tunnel inside the leaf, ruining its appearance and causing premature leaf drop. Use Orthene as a control when you first spot the gnats.**

☞ Watch out for the vole (pine mouse)! If your plant's bark has been chewed off near the ground, you might want to get a vole trap or a mean cat.

Water

☞ Water newly planted trees like **Southern Magnolias** and **Cherry Laurels** thoroughly, even if the ground is wet. This will settle the soil around the roots.

Other

☞ Mulch newly planted and fertilized trees with pine straw or pine bark. Do not allow the mulch to pack against the tree trunk.††

☞ Check mulch around older plants and replenish with fresh mulch if needed.

‡ See "How to Fertilize Shade Trees," p. 6
** See "Controlling Insects and Diseases," p. 80
†† See "Mulching: A Lesson from Nature," p. 243

II. *Shrubs and Vines*

Much like in February, it is important in March to determine whether your shrubs are spring-flowering or summer-flowering. All through spring we will need to know this information to determine the right time to prune and fertilize. If you haven't done so already, take a moment to wander around your garden and note whether or not your shrubs have buds on last year's growth. If they have, they are spring-flowering. On the other hand, summer-flowering shrubs are just now beginning to grow shoots on which buds will form later in the spring.

If terms like "spring-flowering" and "summer-flowering" make your garden sound too technical, remember what they really mean: your garden is about to burst forth with a myriad of wonderful colors! Blossoms are the blessing of every garden. If we keep this in mind, putting up with technical-sounding terms in order to help our gardens stay colorful is not such a tall order.

March is still a good time to plant container-grown shrubs and vines. Get them in the ground as soon as possible so that they will have a long season to grow and expand.

GROWING CLEMATIS AND OTHER SOUTHERN VINES

Mailboxes, fences, ugly posts, bird feeder poles, and downspouts are perfect places for the many excellent vines we have in the South, and March is a perfect time to plant them. Be careful, though, when choosing which vine to grow because a poorly growing vine seldom makes an unsightly structure look good. Also choose vines which wrap around as they climb (twine) rather than attach themselves, so as to prevent damage to permanent structures. When grown correctly, there is no addition to the landscape as attractive as a healthy vine.

Growing Hybrid Clematis

Our most spectacular vines are the hybrid **Clematis** which come in a range of colors and forms. Some varieties produce beautiful flowers over six inches across! These vines do well on trellises, posts, mailboxes, or fences but have to be grown well to perform up to expectations. With a few tips, though, you can grow hybrid **Clematis** which will outshine even the glorious exultations of catalogs and articles.

Clematis in the South grow best in cool, well-prepared soil which has good drainage, high humus, and a high pH (sweet soil). If possible, plant them in a location which receives plenty of morning sun up to about noon but is not exposed to the hot afternoon rays. I have found several such spots on the east side of our house where the house itself blocks the afternoon sun.

March is an excellent time to plant your **Clematis**. You can plant bare-root or packaged plants in the early part of the month; after mid-March it is best to use container-grown **Clematis**. Once you have found a good location, dig a wide, deep hole several times larger than the root system or ball of earth in the container. Place about four inches of pea gravel or gravel chips in the bottom of the hole for drainage. Marble chips are also excellent since they are alkaline and contribute to the high pH we are looking for. Next, make a soil mixture using one-third soil, one-third peat moss or ground bark, and one-third vermiculite. You can use perlite instead of vermiculite if you are using peat moss. Add to the mixture two double

Giant flowering Clematis ('Lanuginosa Candida')

handfuls of dolomitic limestone like you use on the lawn. Limestone is "basic," meaning it will raise the pH level.

Now that the hole is ready, partially fill it with the mixture and plant the **Clematis** shallowly with the top roots at the surface of the ground. You might need to adjust the height by adding some soil underneath the ball of earth. Then pack the mixed soil around the roots or ball of earth, and water thoroughly to settle the soil. Add more soil if necessary, but do not cover the top roots too deeply. Finally, keep your new **Clematis** mulched with pine straw or pine bark chunks to keep the roots cool and also prevent weeds from competing for nutrients.

Many years ago, I learned a helpful method the English use to keep **Clematis** roots cool in their gardens. Knock the bottom out of a six- or eight-inch clay pot and invert the pot over the newly planted **Clematis**. Press the lip of the pot about an inch into the freshly prepared soil. Pull the vine through the large, knocked-out hole and allow the plant to grow normally. I have a beautiful **Ramona Clematis** which was planted many years ago in this manner. It has survived well and still produces enormous numbers of flowers most of the summer.

After the second growing season, hybrid **Clematis** are established and should be pruned heavily each winter. I alternate my pruning on a two-year cycle. The first year, I cut back the twigs and branches to the main stems and laterals, leaving a main vine with several strong branches. The second year, I drastically prune all the way to the top of the inverted pot. This method helps to force new growth which will produce an abundance of flowers on vigorous healthy plants.

It is important to fertilize **Clematis** during the growing season to force heavy growth on which new buds and flowers will be formed. I use a double handful of 5-10-15 fertilizer every six weeks for this purpose. An easier method is to fertilize once in the spring with a slow-release, high-nitrogen fertilizer. Try to find one high in potassium and phosphate which will stimulate flower production. Since **Clematis** like soil with a high pH, apply bone meal or limestone every spring to help sweeten the soil. Watch out if you have dogs; they love the smell of bone meal and will dig up your clematis trying to find it! Dog owners should stick with limestone.

Clematis do best when there is plenty of moisture, as long as the spot is well-drained. Soak them thoroughly during dry spells in the summer. Clip off seed formations as soon as the petals fall to help future flower formation. As with most Southern plants, there is the danger that some insects will decide to make a meal out of your clematis. This happens only occasionally, but keep an eye out for thrips, Japanese beetles, and Clematis Blister Beetle. These pests can be controlled relatively easily with prompt applications of a recommended control. Sevin is good for beetles and Orthene for thrips.

CLEMATIS FOR THE SOUTH:

CULTIVAR	DESCRIPTION
Lanuginosa Candida	Large white with darker stamens in the center
Henryi	Large white with yellow stamens in the center
Nelly Mosser	Pink with deeper pink bars on the petals
Ramona	Deep purple with lighter reverse
Mrs. N. Thompson	Deep violet with red bar and red stamens

Use an inverted flower pot to keep Clematis roots cool during the hot summer.

There are a number of new hybrid **Clematis**, but I would suggest trying them on a limited basis. Be careful when choosing the doubles; they are highly susceptible to thrip attack and should be avoided unless they are regularly sprayed.

Other Excellent Twining And Support-Needing Vines

Although hybrid **Clematis** are my personal favorite, many other vines can be grown with ease in the South. Since few of these plants are native to our area, it is important to choose one that can withstand our winter cold spells. Remember that "wind-chill" is one of the most deadly killers of plants. A plant on one side of the house might easily survive the winter, while the same variety on the windy, unprotected side might perish. Keep this in mind when you choose a location for a new vine. But remember, our summers can be just as deadly as winter! Protection from the powerful July sun is just as important for some vines, if not more so. Here are other vines for you to try:

PERMANENT VINES	DESCRIPTION
Lady Banksia rose	Deciduous, Semi-hardy
Carolina Jessamine	Mostly Evergreen, Hardy
Confederate Jasmine	Evergreen, Semi-hardy
Gold Flame Honeysuckle	Deciduous, Hardy
Silverlace Vine	Deciduous, Hardy
Climbing Fern	Top dies during winter, Hardy
Fruiting Grapes	Deciduous, Hardy

The native Carolina jessamine (Gelsemium sempervirens) covers an area rapidly and is covered with bright yellow flowers each spring.

ANNUAL VINES	DESCRIPTION
Moonflower	Large white flowers open in the evening.
Morning Glory	Red, white, and blue varieties. My favorite is 'Heavenly Blue.'
Scarlet Runner Bean	Colorful red ornamental flowers. The beans are edible!
Passion Vine	Commonly called May-pop. Beautiful flowers can cover entire walls.
Thunbergia or **Black-Eyed Susan Vine**	Orange flowers with black center bloom all summer.
Luffa Gourd	Attractive flowers, but grow them for their bath "sponges."
Ornamental Gourds	There are numerous varieties, all with useful end products.

SHRUB AND VINE ACTIVITIES FOR MARCH:

Plant

☛ Plant dormant container-grown, B&B, and bare-root shrubs this month. Prepare the holes as carefully as you do for shade trees. *Don't plant* bare-root shrubs or vines after they have leafed out.*

☛ Plant hardy woody vines like **Clematis** and **Gold Flame Honeysuckle** any time this month.†

☛ Continue to plant hardy ground covers like **English Ivy**, **Vinca**, **Liriope**, and **Spreading Juniper**. Plant only heavily rooted plants, not runners.*

☛ It is best to plant shrubs when the soil is not too wet. However, if planting is necessary before the soil dries out, use dry peat moss as the soil amendment. It will absorb excess moisture and make it easier to prepare a good soil mixture.

Prune

☛ Heavy structural pruning of evergreen shrubs may be done this month. However, try not to remove all the leaf area on broadleaf evergreens like **Burford Holly**, **Box Leaf Holly**, or **cleyera**, and do not prune narrowleaf evergreens like **junipers** and **arborvitaes** too severely.

☛ Prune broadleaf and narrowleaf evergreens to shape any time this month. Always prune so the top is narrower than the bottom to keep evergreens from becoming top-heavy and unsightly.

☛ Check plants, especially **Gardenia**, **Loquat**, and **Banana Shrub**, for cold-damaged stems and remove them before spring growth begins.

☛ Finish pruning deciduous summer-flowering shrubs like **Hydrangea arborescens 'Grandiflora,'** **Hydrangea paniculata 'Grandiflora,'** and **Butterfly Bush (Buddleia)** (those which form their blossoms on the coming year's new growth) any time this month before new growth appears.‡

☛ Prune deciduous spring-flowering shrubs (those which blossom on growth formed last year) like **deciduous azalea**, **Forsythia**, **Flowering Quince**, **Spiraea**, and **Viburnum** after they finish blooming.‡

☛ Wait to prune flowering evergreen shrubs like **Camellia**, **azalea**, **Rhododendron**, and **Mountain Laurel** until after they have finished blooming.‡

---

* See "Planting Trees and Shrubs," p. 264
† See "Growing Clematis and Other Southern Vines," p. 54

* See "Planting Trees and Shrubs," p. 264
‡ See "Pruning Flowering Shrubs and Vines," p. 31

☞ Prune **Blue/Pink Hydrangea** by removing the weak shoots at the ground and pruning the main shoots back one-third.‡

☞ Prune **Nandina**, **Mahonia**, and **Aucuba** according to their specific methods.**

☞ Deciduous leafy shrubs like **barberry** and deciduous **Euonymus** can be pruned this month before new shoots appear.

☞ Do not prune spring-flowering evergreen vines until after they bloom.‡

☞ Prune other spring-flowering deciduous vines including **Clematis X 'Duchess of Edinburgh'** and **Clematis montana** after they have finished blooming.†

☞ Other summer-flowering deciduous vines like **Gold Flame Honeysuckle** should be pruned now before new growth starts.‡

☞ Cut back **Liriope** with care if you have not done so already. Make sure not to cut emerging shoots and buds because doing so will reduce the vigor of the clump.

Fertilize

☞ Finish fertilizing summer-flowering shrubs like the **summer hydrangeas** with a 15-15-15 fertilizer. Use roughly 1/2 pound per three feet of the shrub's height (*the height before any pruning*). This is usually done once a year.††

☞ Fertilize all spring-flowering shrubs and vines like **Forsythia**, **Flowering Quince**, **Spiraea**, **Viburnum**, and **Carolina Jessamine** after they bloom. Use a 15-15-15 fertilizer on deciduous shrubs and vines and an azalea/camellia acid fertilizer on evergreens. Use roughly 1/2 pound per three feet of the shrub's height (the height before any pruning). This is usually done once a year.††

☞ Fertilize summer-flowering vines like **Gold Flame**

Honeysuckle after pruning. Use half a pound of 15-15-15 fertilizer on plants one to three years old. On older vines, add a pound of fertilizer per year of age up to a maximum of five pounds.††

☞ Fertilize established **Clematis** with a double handful (one cup or 1/2 pound) of 5-10-15 fertilizer every six weeks. As an alternative, you can fertilize once with a slow-release, high-nitrogen fertilizer.

☞ Fertilize broadleaf and narrowleaf evergreens like **boxwood**, **Box Leaf Holly**, **Burford Holly**, **cleyera**, **junipers,** and **arborvitae** with an acid azalea/camellia fertilizer. Use roughly 1/2 pound per three feet of the shrub's height (the height before any pruning). This is usually done once a year.††

Spray

☞ Inspect established evergreens for signs of scale. This insect is particularly bad on evergreens. Control it with Cygon except on **hollies**; use Orthene on **hollies**.‡‡

☞ **Boxwoods** and **hollies** may show signs of leaf damage from the leaf miner. At first, the damage appears as tiny pin pricks in the foliage. Later, as the miner develops, the leaf will be discolored. Spray with Orthene when you first see it.‡‡

☞ Inspect **azalea** and **Pyracantha** for signs of lacebugs. The upper sides of the leaves will have a silvery cast. The undersides will be covered with balls of brown residue. Spray them with Orthene as the weather warms.‡‡

Water

☞ After planting, soak shrubs and vines thoroughly, even if the ground is wet, in order to settle the soil around the roots.

Other

☞ Keep evergreens well mulched but do not allow mulch to crowd the trunk or cover the lower stems.***

‡ See "Pruning Flowering Shrubs and Vines," p. 31
** See "Pruning Aucuba, Mahonia, and Nandina," p. 33
† See "Growing Clematis and Other Southern Vines," p. 54
†† See "How to Fertilize Shrubs and Vines," p. 30

†† See "How to Fertilize Shrubs and Vines," p. 30
‡‡ See "Controlling Insects and Diseases," p. 80
*** See "Mulching: A Lesson from Nature," p. 243

Strawberries are an excellent home fruit since they produce heavily and last for years.

III. *Fruits*

While it is still fine to plant container-grown fruit trees, I like to spend March concentrating on figs and strawberries. This is the best month to plant these fruits, and I especially enjoy working with strawberries since they require less digging than planting fruit trees. Try them out!

March is a good time to fertilize your figs and blueberries. Before you fertilize your figs, check them for cold damage and cut them back if there is any. Blueberries don't usually have any cold damage and should be fertilized lightly with an azalea/camellia fertilizer. They like acidic soil.

As the weather warms, insects will begin emerging which could damage your fruit trees. Begin your home orchard spray program as soon as you see color on the flower buds. This is a job that you will be continuing throughout the season, so go ahead and buy any safety equipment you need as soon as possible. It is not worth jeopardizing your health just for a good apple.

FRUIT ACTIVITIES FOR MARCH:

Plant

☛ March is an ideal time to plant bare-root and container-grown **figs**.

☛ March is the best time of the year to set **strawberries**. Plant them on beds in well-prepared soil which has good drainage.

☛ Plant only B&B and container-grown fruits this month.*

Prune

☛ Check **figs** for winter cold damage. Prune away any damaged wood, even if it means cutting them almost to the ground.

☛ March is considered too late to prune fruit trees except in the mountains.

Fertilize

☛ Fertilize **figs** with a 15-15-15 fertilizer and apply lime. Use about 1/2 pound of 15-15-15 per three feet of height. This application will be repeated in July.

☛ Fertilize **blueberries** lightly with an azalea-camellia fertilizer, but do not lime them. Watch out, **blueberries** can be damaged by over-fertilizing.

☛ Finish fertilizing fruit trees. Use a 15-15-15 fertilizer at a rate of 1/2 pound per year of age of the tree. Use a maximum of 15 pounds on **apples** and **pears** and five pounds on **peaches**, **nectarines**, and **plums**. This is usually done once a year.†

☛ Finish fertilizing **grapes** and semi-bush fruits with 15-15-15. Use about two pounds per vine on established, producing **grapes**. Use one pound per plant on young (one to three years old) semi-bush fruits, and two pounds per plant for older semi-bush fruits. This is usually done once a year.

Spray

☛ Begin an insect and disease control program on fruits as the flower buds begin to show color. A complete home orchard spray is the most practical method of control. Continue applications at recommended intervals until the fruit ripens. Do not spray, however, when the flowers are open.

☛ There is a very exacting spray control program for fire blight on **pears**, but it is not practical for most homeowners.

Other

☛ Replace old mulch around semi-bush berries like **blackberries** and **raspberries** with fresh pine straw before new leaves appear. This helps to remove emerging mites and other damaging insects.

☛ Mulch **figs** with well-rotted compost or cow manure.

☛ Be careful when mowing in orchard areas not to hit the bark of fruit trees with the mower. Any damage to the bark will provide an entrance place for borers.

☛ Keep fruits mulched with pine straw to prevent weeds and grasses from competing for water and fertilizer, but do not pile the mulch against the trunks of fruit trees.‡

* See "Planting Trees and Shrubs," p. 264

† See "How to Fertilize Fruit Trees," p. 37

‡ See "Mulching: A Lesson from Nature," p. 243

IV. *Roses*

March is the true start of the rose season. After you finish your rose pruning in early March, plants should begin to grow rapidly. Warm spells can cause as much as five inches of growth in a week! Remember to fertilize on a regular schedule to sustain this heavy growth.

As new leaves appear, begin a complete rose spray program to protect your flowers from the insects and diseases which love to munch on our roses. Remember to spray the mulch as well as the canes.

ROSE ACTIVITIES FOR MARCH:

Plant

☛ Continue planting dormant bare-root roses through mid-March. Before planting, trim long or broken roots and cut stems back to a healthy bud. Try new varieties but keep old favorites as major plantings until new ones have proven themselves in your garden.*

☛ Container-grown roses can be planted now through April.†

Prune

☛ Finish pruning roses in early March if you have not done so already. **Hybrid Teas, Floribundas, Grandifloras**, and other "everblooming" types should be pruned severely to force healthy new growth. Climbing cultivars like '**Blaze**,' '**New Dawn**,' and the **Climbing Hybrid Teas** should be pruned by thinning out the older canes leaving the long, young branches which produce the best blossoms.‡

Fertilize

☛ Fertilize immediately after pruning. Use a complete rose fertilizer with systemic insecticide. Continue to fertilize every six to eight weeks throughout the season.

Spray

☛ Begin a complete rose spray program as soon as new leaves appear. Use a combination insecticide and fungicide spray. Spray every 10 to 14 days according to the directions and continue applications through September.

☛ Spray the top of the mulch and canes, as well as the leaves, whenever you spray.

Water

☛ Water newly planted roses thoroughly, even if the ground is wet, in order to settle the soil around the roots.

Other

☛ Remove old mulch after pruning to get rid of insects and disease which have overwintered in the bed. Replace with clean pine straw, but do not pile mulch against the crown or lower stems. Many problems like rose stem canker and botrytis occur when mulch covers the lower stems.**

☛ After pruning, work established beds and add cow manure.

* See "Planting Bare-Root Roses," p. 250
† See "Planting Trees and Shrubs," p. 264
‡ See "Pruning Roses," p. 40
** See "Mulching: A Lesson from Nature," p. 243

V. *Flowers and Colorful Garden Plants*

Watch them grow! Perennials are cautiously poking their heads out and so are gardeners all over the South. Is it true? Has spring really arrived? Neighborhood nurseries are stocking trays of annuals, shrubs are blooming everywhere, and it is almost time for the summer flower bed.

Hopefully, the tender annuals which we have been growing inside since late winter have filled out and are ready to be planted when the danger of freezes has passed. Perennials, hardy annuals, and half-hardy annuals can be planted outside in March and are a good way to start the flower bed.

How to Plant a Flower Bed

The South is famous for its beautiful spring. **Dogwoods, camellias, azaleas, flowering cherries**, and other spectacular flowering plants in March and April make our spring gardens the envy of gardeners everywhere. Once spring is over, Southern gardeners used to rest on their laurels while their landscapes lapsed into a sea of green. Now we are interested in having our landscapes as colorful in the summer and fall as they are in the spring.

Colorful flower beds are the answer. Combinations of annuals, perennials, and biennials planted together will give bright color from the last frost of spring until the first frost of fall, making summer gardens as bright and colorful as our famous spring gardens.

These herbaceous, summer-flowering plants are easy to grow provided you develop the growing area as carefully as you plant a vegetable garden, an **azalea** bed, or a foundation shrub planting. The soil is the key element. Flower beds need rich, well-drained soil whether they are in sun or shade. Wet, sticky soil is as difficult for flowers as it is for vegetables or shrubs. Since hardy perennial plants will remain in the same place for many years, you must prepare perennial beds especially well. Annual flower beds or parts of perennial beds where annuals are grown must be worked each year.

Spray weed-covered areas with Roundup at least two weeks before preparing the bed to keep residual chemicals from damaging new plants. If you kill these

March is the time to prepare flower beds for bright summer color.

weeds before you work the soil, you'll save the time and effort during the growing season trying to keep weeds from competing with your flowers.

Work the soil deeply and thoroughly by tilling back and forth a number of times or working the ground with a forked spade. Unlike vegetable areas, flower beds are seldom wide enough to till across, so till them back and forth, letting the tines go deeper and deeper. After the soil is thoroughly worked, take a handful of the soil and look at it carefully, then squeeze it in the palm of your hand. If it looks light red or yellowish and if the ball of soil is hard to break up with your thumb, you need to add humus. In addition, think about what you have observed in the past about the area. Did water stand there or was slow to drain away after a heavy rain? This indicates poor drainage and will lead to poor growth of most flowers. Correct poor drainage by adding perlite along with humus.

Most flowers do best in soils with a medium range pH between 6.0 and 6.5. Most Southern soil has a lower pH, so add dolomitic limestone. Flowers need nutrients to perform well. I like to use a 15-15-15 fertilizer at planting time and switch to 5-10-15 fertilizer after six weeks for the rest of the growing season.

Most garden soil in the South will need all of the following amendments to produce good results. Measure the area of your bed and use this guide to determine how much of each kind you should work into the bed:

1) Sphagnum Peat Moss:	1 five-cubic-foot bale per 100 sq. ft.
or Finely Ground Bark:	3 three-cubic-foot bags per 100 sq. ft.
or Compost:	Add as you till until the soil is soft and crumbles easily when you squeeze it in your hand
2) Dolomitic Limestone:	10 lbs. per 100 sq. ft.
3) 5-10-15 fertilizer:	10 lbs. per 100 sq. ft.
4) and, if needed, Perlite for drainage	1 or more four-cubic-foot bags per 100 sq. ft.

After you have tilled the bed several times, apply the humus material and perlite. Work them in while tilling as deeply as possible. Then broadcast the limestone and work it into the top four or five inches of the bed. Rake the bed, removing any clods or rocks, and then broadcast the 15-15-15 fertilizer and rake it into the top two to three inches.

Now you are ready to plant. Mark where each group of plants will be planted. New plants seem awfully small but you will have to resist the temptation to plant them too close together. Take into consideration the ultimate height and breadth of each type and space your plants accordingly. Now it is time to get on your hands and knees. Plant one group at a time, starting at the back of the bed and planting forward. Most plants come in cell packs or pots. Remove them as you plant. If their roots are heavily matted against the ball, loosen them by carefully pulling them away from the ball. Sometimes squeezing the ball will accomplish this quite well.

I open the hole with my fingers since the soil is now loose, but others may prefer using a trowel. Set herbaceous plants slightly deeper than they were growing in the cell or pot, but don't bury them too deeply.

After planting is finished, water the bed well to settle the soil around the roots and to drive out any air pockets. Water thoroughly every four or five days unless it rains. Continue this until you notice new growth starting.

Make a map of your garden so that you know exactly which type and variety you have put in each part of the bed. No matter how careful you are, there is a possibility that you will lose one or more plants, and you will need to replace them with the same cultivar which you originally planted.

FLOWER ACTIVITIES FOR MARCH:

Plant

☛ Start seeds of tender plants like **marigolds**, **petunias**, **Salvia**, and **Zinnia** inside as soon as possible so they will be ready to plant after the danger of frost has passed.*

☛ Keep germinated seedlings of tender plants growing in a sunny spot inside.

* See "Starting Seeds Inside," p. 18

☛ After the danger of heavy freezes (below 28-32 degrees for many hours), set out hardy annuals, biennials, and perennials like **Foxglove**, **pinks**, **stock**, **Sweet William**, and **Shasta Daisy** which were started inside or purchased as plants.†

☛ Dig, separate, and reset perennials like **chrysanthemums** at the beginning of March before the new tops become too large and are easily broken.

☛ Replant perennials in well-prepared soil which drains well.

☛ There is still time to plant **peonies** and **Iris**. Plant them shallowly with the roots close to the top of the soil. **Peonies** should be planted in morning sun with the pink buds just above the soil so the buds can freeze. Use bone meal and mulch them heavily, but leave the crown open.

☛ Get a jump on the season by potting **Caladium** and **Elephant Ear** tubers inside at the end of March. Starting them inside will ensure better early color when you set them out in late April when the ground is warm. Pot them shallowly.

☛ Cut back and pot **geraniums** which were lifted from the garden and stored over winter in plastic bags. They will start growing almost immediately and be ready to set outside in late April or early May.

Prune

☛ Cut back and fertilize tropical flowering plants like **Hibiscus**, **Ixora**, and **Allamanda** so they will be growing well by late April (after the night temperatures are warm) when you put them out.

Fertilize

☛ Apply a liquid or soluble houseplant fertilizer like Rapid-Gro or Peters to carried-over tender and semi-hardy garden plants which have been growing inside. This will force new growth and get them ready for planting outside.

☛ Fertilize annuals, biennials, and perennials on the following schedule: Apply 15-15-15, which is a good starter fertilizer, on new and emerging plants. After six to eight weeks, switch to 5-10-15, which is a good fruit and flower fertilizer, and continue on that schedule for the rest of the season.

Spray

☛ Watch for slugs and snails on emerging perennials, especially **Hosta**. Use a snail bait to control.‡

☛ Spray the crowns and emerging shoots of **peonies** for botrytis. Captan is a good recommended control.‡

☛ Use Orthene to control the spider mites, thrips, mealybugs, and spittlebugs which will attack at the end of the month.‡

Other

☛ Make cuttings of overwintered, tender plants like **Begonia**, **Coleus**, **Geranium**, and **Impatiens** as soon as possible to give them time to develop well before planting time after the night temperatures have warmed in late April.**

☛ Remove pine straw mulch early in the month to give sprouting biennials and perennials plenty of light and air.††

☛ Keep **Canna** and **Dahlia** roots in a cool place. Do not set them in the garden until the ground is warm after the danger of frost. Store **Caladium** and **Elephant Ear** tubers in a warmer spot than **Canna** and **Dahlia** roots.

† See "How to Plant a Flower Bed," p. 62

‡ See "Controlling Insects and Diseases," p. 80
** See "Propagating Herbaceous Houseplants and Garden Plants," p. 225
†† See "Mulching: A Lesson from Nature," p. 243

VI. *Vegetables*

March is often a wet month. Some gardeners are raring to get out in the garden and plant semi-hardy vegetables like cabbage, cauliflower, lettuce, and Asparagus. Unfortunately, the ground may be too wet. If you did prepare your garden early during the drier months of January and February, you can probably plant as soon as you rework the beds which eroded in heavy rains. Otherwise, there is nothing to do but wait for the ground to dry. Working wet ground can cause the soil to stick in large clumps which will be tough to work with, even in drier periods. It is better just to wait it out.

If you are planning to wait until after the danger of frost has passed, don't forget to turn under any remaining cover crops, especially before they bloom and go to seed. Also, keep an eye out for your tender vegetable seedlings which are growing inside. With warmer days, they are likely to dry out quickly. Keep them well watered and mist them every now and then.

VEGETABLE ACTIVITIES FOR MARCH:

Plant

☞ After the danger of hard freezes (below 28-32 degrees for many hours), plant **broccoli**, **Brussels sprouts**, **cabbage**, **cauliflower**, **collard**, **kale**, **kohlrabi**, **lettuce**, and **onion** plants. These may have been started inside during January.*

☞ After the danger of hard freezes, you can plant **beet**, **carrot**, **turnip**, **mustard green**, **rapegreen**, **spinach**, **Swiss chard**, and **lettuce** seeds outside.*

☞ You can still plant **Asparagus**, **horseradish**, **Jerusalem Artichoke**, and **rhubarb** roots on beds in early March while the ground is still cold. Mulch them with compost and fertilize.*

☞ Finish planting **Irish potatoes** and hardy **lettuce** (like **Black-Seeded Simpson**) as soon as possible this month. They need plenty of time to grow before hot weather arrives.*

☞ **Garlic** cloves, **onion** sets, and **onion** plants can be planted on beds any time this month.*

☞ Finish seeding tender vegetables like **tomatoes**, **peppers**, and **eggplant** and tender annual herbs like

anise, **coriander**, and **sweet basil** inside as soon as possible so that they will be ready to plant outside after the danger of frost has passed and the ground warms.†

☞ Plant roots or plants of hardy perennial herbs like **Lemon Balm**, **mint**, **lavender**, and **oregano** during March and early April while the ground is cool. They need plenty of time to grow before hot weather arrives.

☞ Start gourd seeds (**Luffa**, **Martin**, **ornamental**, **Dipper**) indoors at the end of the month. These will be ready to plant outside after the danger of frost has passed and the ground warms.†

Fertilize

☞ Fertilize as you plant with 15-15-15. Application is at a rate of approximately one pound per 10 feet of row. This application should be good for about six weeks.*

☞ Continue to fertilize growing vegetables with 5-10-15 about every six weeks for the rest of the season. Application is at a rate of approximately one pound per 10 feet of row. ‡

☞ If you haven't limed your garden, it is better to do it now than not at all. This lime may not break down

† See "Starting Seeds Inside" p. 18

* See "Planting a Vegetable Garden" p. 92

‡ See "Fertilizing, Spraying, and Watering Vegetables" p. 115

* See "Planting a Vegetable Garden," p. 92

in time to help tender plants as they begin to grow, but it will help them later on. Application is at a rate of 50 pounds per 1000 square feet.*

Spray

☞ Watch out for aphids on all your vegetables. Malathion is a good recommended control.**

---

* See "Planting a Vegetable Garden," p. 92

** See "Controlling Insects and Diseases," p. 80

Other

☞ Prepare your garden for April planting whenever the soil is dry. Go ahead and prepare your beds since they will dry faster than ground which is left flat.††

☞ Turn under all remaining cover crops before they bloom.

---

†† See "Early Vegetable Garden Preparation," p. 21

NOTES

VII. *Houseplants*

By March many of our houseplants are looking pretty bad. Ferns which we moved inside last fall are tired and sparse. The winter months inside have been tough on them. Piggyback plants might look thin and viney as their new offshoots hang down out of the pot. Even Pothos and Philodendron are looking the worse for wear.

March is a great time to cut these plants back. I do this every year to give my plants a new lease on life and my spirits a lift. When cutting back ferns, make sure not to chop off any of the new fiddlesticks sprouting up from the crown. Cut Piggybacks back to the edge of the pot so they will bush out.

Sunny March days are also a good time to let your plants have a breather. Take them out onto a warm porch or deck for a taste of freedom. Be careful, though, that they don't get caught by a late freeze.

REPOTTING HOUSEPLANTS

One of the necessities of growing houseplants is repotting them when they outgrow their present pot. People usually repot in the spring or fall when the houseplant growth cycle is changing, due to shortened or lengthened daylight hours. In spring, plants which have been growing inside all winter should be checked for the need to repot so they will have plenty of room to grow and expand over the summer months. In fall, houseplants should be checked again to see if they have outgrown their pots over the summer months.

There is always the temptation to let plants continue to grow in their present condition, especially with houseplants. We often use houseplants as part of our interior decorating scheme, so using a larger pot might force us to move them and redecorate, too! Unfortunately, the status quo doesn't work for a living and growing plant. Leaving a fern in the same small pot will not mysteriously keep it from growing. Instead, its roots will continue to grow and soon will start competing with one another for the remaining water and nutrients in the pot. Not finding enough, they will not be able to supply leaves properly and the plant's overall appearance will be affected. Leaves might brown or fall off or a whole side of the plant might die. The best plan is to repot when the plant needs it to keep both you and your houseplant happy.

Repot houseplants whenever their roots become matted against the inside of the pot. In some cases, houseplants will become so pot-bound that their roots will be visible on the surface of the soil or growing through the drain holes. It is best not to let them go that long without repotting. Every spring and fall, carefully slide the plant and ball of earth from the pot.

You can usually do this by laying the pot sideways, tapping the pot to loosen the ball of earth, turning the pot upside down, and gently pulling the plant out. A healthy plant should have plenty of white growth roots throughout the soil. A pot-bound plant will have roots winding laterally around the outside of the ball of earth, and they may be darker in color.

In repotting a pot-bound plant, choose a pot at least two sizes larger than the old one. Place a broken piece of an old clay pot over the drain hole to keep the soil from coming out. Fill the new pot about one-third with a peat-light mixture. Work the soil up the sides of the pot, coating the sides with a half-inch layer of soil. Before you put your plant in the new pot, loosen the roots by working your fingers into the mat of roots. Roots which are woven together should be worked free so they will be able to grow in the new pot. Next, place the plant in the new pot and check the surface level. The surface of the soil should be about an inch below the lip of the pot so that you can water without it running over. The plant should sit at the same level as it was in the old pot, with the crown at the surface. After you have adjusted the height, slowly fill in the sides, packing the soil with your fingers. Try not to leave any large air pockets. After you are satisfied with your plant's placement in the new pot, water it thoroughly to settle the soil around the roots and remove any small air pockets.

Repotting is also a good time to check for insects. Sowbugs and pillbugs, insects which feed on roots, are two of the most common pests on houseplants. While the plant is out of the pot, check the roots for signs of insect activity. If you find some, treat the soil with Diazinon according to the instructions before you put the plant in its new pot. Make sure to treat the bottom of the pot and the saucer as well. Apply some material

1 – Repot when roots become matted around the ball of soil.

2 – Work the matted roots loose with your fingers.

3 – Loosened roots are free to grow actively in the new pot.

4 – The new pot should be two sizes larger than the current one.

also to the surface of the soil and water it in.

As we discussed before, repotting a houseplant sometimes forces us to move it to a location more suitable to the plant. In this case, it is important to remember how sensitive plants are to changes in light. Potted plants can be shocked by exposing them to more or less light. One way to compare the light conditions of a new spot to the old spot is to use a light meter (the light meter on your camera will do just fine). Check the plant's old resting place at the brightest time of day. Then find a spot with roughly the same conditions. An exception to this rule is a plant which is light in color due to lack of sunlight. In that case, find a spot with slightly more light. Don't make too drastic a change, though, even with a light-starved houseplant.

After repotting, make sure to fertilize your plant. Soluble fertilizers work best with indoor plants. Fertilize every time you water with a full-strength solution during the indoor plant's growing season (March-October), and cut back to a half-strength solution over the winter

months. As an alternative, you might want to use plant spikes. You can place these two-inch sticks of fertilizer in the soil at intervals around the pot, and they will fertilize your plant for about two months. Osmocote is another slow-release fertilizer which will last several months.

Repotting can be a blessing for both you and your houseplant. From the standpoint of the plant, it will continue to have adequate room to grow and expand. From the owner's standpoint, repotting allows you to grow a large, impressive plant from the starter sizes available at local nurseries. The problem sometimes arises, however, that with continued repottings our houseplant stock consists of too many large plants.

A nice way to deal with this situation is with propagation, the process of creating new plants from an established "mother" plant. In many situations, propagation is the perfect answer to keeping a variety of different sizes of houseplants around your house. Propagation is covered in October's "Propagating Herbaceous Houseplants and Garden Plants."

HOUSEPLANT ACTIVITIES FOR MARCH:

Plant

☞ While under the proper conditions houseplants can be propagated all year long, I prefer to make cuttings of my existing stock in February and March. These cuttings should root quickly and will have the whole summer to mature. By fall, I should have plenty of mature plants to beautify the house.*

☞ Carefully remove each plant from its container and check the roots for the need to repot. Repot when the roots have massed against the edge of the ball of soil and are dark in color. Repot in a container which is at least two sizes larger. Check for sowbugs and pillbugs while the plants are out of the pot.†

☞ **Christmas chrysanthemums** and forced **azaleas** can now be planted outside.

Prune

☞ Cut back **ferns** and fertilize. Repot if necessary, using a peat-light mixture.

☞ Check all hanging basket plants. Cut them back, fertilize, and repot if necessary.

Fertilize

☞ Fertilize with a full-strength, water-soluble liquid fertilizer like Peters every time you water. As an alternative, I like to use fertilizer spikes or Osmocote, both of which last several months.‡

Spray

☞ Check all indoor plants for insects such as spider mites, scale, and mealybug. I like to use a houseplant systemic insecticide to control them. It is easier and safer than spraying inside. If you do spray, take your plant outside and remember to apply the insecticide to the undersides of the leaves.**

☞ When repotting houseplants, check for aphids, scale, mites, and mealybugs. Take the plants outside and spray with Orthene if you find any.**

☞ When repotting, also check for sowbugs and pillbugs. If you find any, dust the surface of the soil in the pot with Diazinon and water it in.

☞ Be careful when spraying **ferns**. Some insecticides are harmful to them. *Always read the label for warnings about **ferns** and other plants.*

Water

☞ Watch houseplants carefully as they begin their spring growth. Plant growth usually requires extra water. When houseplants look limp, check for dry soil. If it is dry, water thoroughly in a sink or bathtub, letting the water drain completely, and don't water again until the surface is dry again. Between waterings, mist with plain water on a regular basis. If the limp plants are in moist soil, do not water but allow the soil to dry a bit and mist frequently.‡

☞ Tip-burn or edge-burn on leaves indicates that more water is being lost than is being absorbed by the roots. Check for dry soil, too much sunlight, drafts from heater vents, or overwatering.‡

Other

☞ Keep all porch and patio plants in a warm, sunny place until all danger of frost has passed.

☞ March 20/21 marks the Spring Equinox, the official end of winter. On this day, the number of light and dark hours are equal. After March 20/21, the daylight hours will increase until the Summer Solstice on June 20. Remember to check your houseplants periodically as the sun's position in the sky changes. Windows which may have received plenty of light in the winter may no longer receive adequate light.

* See "Propagating Herbaceous Houseplants and Garden Plants," p. 225

† See "Repotting Houseplants," p. 67

‡ See "Houseplant Care and Maintenance," p. 232

** See "Common Houseplant Ailments," p. 280

‡ See "Houseplant Care and Maintenance," p. 232

Fescue makes our best evergreen lawn.

VIII. *Lawns*

March is our first taste of spring, and we are bound to start thinking about baseball, soccer, barbeques, and various other outdoor fun (minus the mosquitoes). Luckily (and unluckily), most of these activities take place on our lawn — luckily because there is nothing nicer than standing outside on a beautiful, well-groomed lawn; unluckily because it gives friends and neighbors a chance to notice the bare spots, weeds, and poor growth in our lawns. This is the cross we bear when dealing with a lawn.

For many of us, March will be the first month of the season to crank up the lawn mower. A few Tylenols and a stubbed toe later (from kicking the mower), we hope it will be off and running. If not, here are some quick tips. Check to see if the engine is getting fuel. Check the fuel line, which could have air in it from sitting so long. Check the spark plug for a spark. You might want to file down the connector. Check to see if the air filter is clogged. And finally, check the throttle and choke. I have a push mower which has to be hand-choked only one time a year, in March. Good luck!

PLANTING OR RESEEDING EVERGREEN LAWNS

Bare ground is the curse of Southern homes. Here comes mud and dirt onto beautiful carpets or kitchen tiles, brought inside by old and young *and* pets. Where does all the dirt come from? It comes from where every homeowner wants a lush, thick carpet of grass. New homes, old homes, and all those in between are candidates for changing their field of mud into a lush carpet of green grass.

Despite all the advertisements, growing a beautiful lawn is not that difficult and also not that simple. Don't opt for throwing some seed out every now and then, rebelling against the effort it takes to prepare the ground properly. Short cuts seldom work. Do it right the first time because once a lawn area is well-prepared and the grass is growing beautifully, you won't have to remake it each year as you do an annual border or vegetable garden. Lawns, like trees and shrubs, should do well for years and years with only regular maintenance. In the case of lawns, this means cutting, fertilizing, watering, and preventing weeds.

Deciding what to do is easy when you have bare ground. You have to start a new lawn from scratch. The decision is harder, though, when the lawn you have is growing poorly. Is it worth trying to save or should you start over?

Grass is like any other garden plant. It needs well-prepared soil, humus, fertilizer, and the right pH. Choose the right type for a given location, then plant it correctly.

The right type of grass to plant depends on many factors. Every homeowner wants a lush, thick, fine-textured carpet of green. But there are other factors which may affect your ability to grow the perfect grass. The type and cultivar of grass which you should use depends on conditions like sun and shade, the amount of traffic the lawn will get, and the amount of time you want to spend on lawn work.

In the South, there are two general categories of lawn grasses: those which grow and are green year-round, and those which are green only from the last frost in the spring until the first frost in the fall. It seems the choice should be easy. Everybody wants a lush, green lawn twelve months of the year. Unfortunately, it is not as easy as it seems. Summer lawns grow best when we use them the most, while evergreen lawns grow best in cool weather during the spring and fall when children are in school and foot traffic is reduced. Though still green in the summer, evergreens grow poorly at a time when lawns are used the most. Southern summer lawns generally do best in warm sunny areas, while evergreen grasses generally do best in cooler places with some shade.

March is a good time to begin planting evergreen grasses. **Kentucky 31 Fescue**, the turf-type fescues like **Rebel**, fine-leaf fescues like **Creeping Red** and **Chewing**, and various **bluegrasses** are grown in the mid and upper South and need to be planted as soon as the danger of hard freezes has passed. This is extremely time-sensitive; evergreen grasses must be planted so that maximum top growth and root development occurs well ahead of hot weather.

Planting a New Evergreen Grass Lawn

Choose the type of grass carefully. The following chart should help you:

GRASS NAME	CONDITIONS	TEXTURE	CUTTING HEIGHT
Kentucky 31 Fescue	Sun to light shade	Coarse	3 1/2 inches
Turf-type Fescues	Sun to light shade	Medium	3 1/2 inches
Fine-leaf Fescues	Light to moderate shade	Fine	1-1 1/2 inches
Kentucky Bluegrass	Light to moderate shade	Medium	2-2 1/2 inches

When growing grass near trees, remember that shade is not the only problem. Many shade trees, especially **oaks**, have heavy roots which grow from near the surface to deep in the ground. Competition from these roots may cause serious problems when trying to grow grass over them. The larger the tree, the more difficult it is to establish a lawn under its canopy. There are some trees like **Sugar Maples** whose feeder roots are deeper in the ground, allowing grass to grow up to the trunk of the tree.

Getting Ready To Plant

Measure the new lawn area to find the actual square feet to be seeded. Amounts of seed, humus, fertilizer, and lime are figured in pounds per thousand square feet. It is very important to use the correct amounts for the area sown. You will need the following amendments *per 1000 square feet* of new lawn area:

- 5 to 8 pounds of seed for any type of fescue grass
- 1 or 2 five-cubic-foot bales of sphagnum peat moss or, 4 to 5 three-cubic-foot bags of ground bark
- 50 pounds of Dolomitic Limestone
- Lawn fertilizer (recommended rate per 1000 square feet for the particular brand you use)

Planting

Next, work the soil thoroughly and deeply. Rototilling is the only way I know for a homeowner to do this properly. Till the area several times both lengthwise and crosswise until the soil is thoroughly pulverized.

Apply the peat moss or ground bark evenly over the area. Till it in.

Broadcast the limestone and fertilizer over the area and till again. This time till across the fall of the land.

Rake the area to prepare a good seed bed. Split the seed into two even parts. Sow 1/2 lengthwise and 1/2 crosswise to get even distribution. Rake the seed into the soil's surface.

Thoroughly water the area with a sprinkler. I prefer the pulsating types. If the weather is dry or there is a potential washing problem, lightly cover the area with clean wheat straw, then water the area.

Apply at least one inch of water per week if there is no rain.

Mowing After Germination

Most of us have a tendency to allow newly-seeded lawns to grow too tall before the initial cutting. This can be very bad, especially in the spring when the grass is tender and rapidly growing.

Set your mower at the prescribed cutting height, then always keep the lawn cut at that height. This helps the grass to spread and become tough. Until the grass has been cut several times, however, be sure neither the ground nor grass is wet when you cut the lawn. Mower wheels tend to make ruts in soft ground and wet grass will also mat under the mower wheels. Both events can damage lawns.

Reseeding an Evergreen Grass Lawn

Not all poorly growing lawns must be completely redone to be beautiful. Many homeowners do not properly cut, fertilize, water, and lime lawns; they therefore allow grasses to die out and become unsightly. A good way to determine if a lawn can be rejuvenated is to choose a representative square foot spot. Count the number of the desired lawn grass plants in that square foot area. If there is at least one good plant, rejuvenation will probably be successful. If not, it is probably best to work the ground and start over. Lawns which are weak, have bare spots, and are weed infested but which have a good population of a desirable grass are candidates for reseeding.

Measure the square feet in your lawn to determine how much of each ingredient you will need. Use the same amount of dolomitic limestone and fertilizer

One good grass plant in a square foot of lawn can expand and produce a thick turf.

The new turf-type fescues produce a beautiful thick year-round lawn.

needed to plant a new lawn. You will need only enough peat moss or ground bark to amend the bare spots which must be worked. Do not top dress evergreen grasses with these materials; you may damage them. Purchase about 1/2 the seed recommended for new plantings.

Take a sample of the grass which seems to predominate in your yard to a nursery or garden center for identification. If it is a type which does well under your conditions, purchase more of that same type.

First, rake the lawn with a garden rake (a sharp-tooth rake, not a leaf rake) and remove as much dead grass as possible. Then work the soil in any completely bare areas. Now apply the limestone and fertilizer and rake it in. Finally, reseed the lawn, planting half of the seed lengthwise and then the other half crosswise. Lightly rake the lawn one more time to help cover the seed. Now water the lawn thoroughly, using a pulsating sprinkler. Apply at least 1/2 inch of water. Keep the lawn well watered during dry periods and cut at the proper height for the type of grass you have planted.

Do not apply pre-emergence grass and weed preventers to any area which you reseed or spray newly germinating grass with broadleaf weed killers.

FERTILIZING AND CONTROLLING WEEDS IN LAWNS

Green grows the grass, or does it? The lawn serves as the landscape's welcome mat, existing to tie together all the various components of a home design. Lawns take people from flower beds to shrub borders and from fruit orchards to vegetable gardens and offer visitors a warm invitation to your home.

Unfortunately, established lawns are not always the welcoming sight we want them to be. Poor growth, light color, and weeds make them less than inviting. As I drive around, I look at lawns and wonder why some are so beautiful and some are not. Sometimes when I see gardeners working on their lawns, the reason is clear. Some day, temptation is going to make me stop and tell the homeowner sitting on his front

Weeds and weed grasses die out leaving discolored areas and an unattractive lawn.

steps haphazardly watering the lawn with a spray nozzle that he is doing more harm than good (I'll tell you why next month). I'll probably get punched in the nose and told to mind my own business despite my good intentions. Spraying designs on the yard with a hose is too relaxing and too much fun to be stopped by dire warnings from a complete stranger!

Good lawns are more often the result of knowing how to grow grass properly than the result of continuous hard work. Initially, they do take your hard work or a lot of money paid to an installer, but after a lawn starts growing, what keeps it doing well is knowing what to do and when to do it.

An established lawn needs four things: (1) fertilizer, (2) water, (3) proper cutting, and (4) weed control measures. Thin, weak lawns cannot be turned magically into lush green areas by throwing out seeds every few months. Like spraying with a hose, reseeding *seems* to be the magic elixir which will bring about the lawn we want. Unfortunately, reseeding is seldom a permanent answer.

Lawns with thinning grass, an intrusion of weeds, and, I hate to say it, plain ugliness result from natural conditions, not some lawn monster who has it in for *your* lawn. Grasses die because the soil compacts and cannot support healthy growth. Weeds enter and gradually spread, choking out what grass is left.

Take a look at your poorly growing lawn. If you have at least one good grass plant in a square foot area, you can bring your lawn back to life and beauty with fertilizer and, perhaps, with better cutting practices. Most grasses are killed out by cutting too closely, so watch your cutting height.

Modern science has come to the aid of lawn owners. Fertilizers are better than ever before, and there are remarkable weed preventers which kill sprouting annual weed grasses and annual broadleaf weeds. Use them both to improve and maintain a beautiful lawn. There are also sprays and dry materials which can be applied to weedy lawns to kill the perennial invaders.

Early March is a great time to start the year's lawn

work. Established evergreen lawns containing **fescues** or **bluegrasses** will really begin to grow this month, and it is a great time to fertilize and apply weed controls. Kill winter weeds like chickweed with a special chickweed spray in both evergreen and summer grass lawns.

As for your pre-emergence weed grass and broadleaf weed controls, a good time to apply this material is when you see the **Forsythia** in bloom. *Do not* apply this material when you need to reseed the lawn this spring; it will also prevent new grass seeds from sprouting. Apply these materials on both evergreen grasses and summer grasses.

A good way to apply both fertilizer and pre-emergence materials is to spread 1/2 lengthwise and 1/2 crosswise to prevent skips of light and dark growth and have a lawn which is evenly green. Concentrations of the active ingredients in pre-emergence controls and the formulas of fertilizers vary with the brand. Always follow application instructions for best results.

LAWN ACTIVITIES FOR MARCH:

Plant

☛ Begin planting evergreen grasses (all **fescues** and **bluegrasses**) as soon as possible after the danger of hard freezes has passed. They need plenty of cool weather to establish themselves before summer arrives. This includes installation of new lawns as well as reseeding of established ones.*

Fertilize

☛ Fertilize evergreen grasses with a complete lawn fertilizer which contains a slow-release form of nitrogen.†

☛ Fertilize summer grasses like **Bermuda Grass**, **Centipede**, **St. Augustine**, and **Zoysia** with a high-nitrogen, slow-release fertilizer as soon as the danger of frost has passed. (For **Centipede** lawns, use a fertilizer designated for that type of grass.) This application will be good for about 90 days.†

☛ Apply pre-emergence weed and weed grass controls at the beginning of the month or when the **Forsythia** blooms. Do not apply this material if you plan to reseed.*

☛ Apply dolomitic lime on evergreen lawns at a rate of 50 pounds per 1000 square feet if it hasn't been done within a year.

Spray

☛ Keep lawns free of chickweed and other winter weeds with a spray or dry application. Don't use these controls on newly seeded lawns.†

Cut

☛ Cut grasses at the proper height:

SUMMER GRASSES	HEIGHT
Common Bermuda Grass	2 inches
Hybrid Bermuda Grass	1 to 1 $\frac{1}{2}$ inches
Centipede	1 $\frac{1}{2}$ to 2 inches
St. Augustine	2 to 2 $\frac{1}{2}$ inches
Zoysia	1 to 2 inches

EVERGREEN GRASSES	HEIGHT
Kentucky 31 Tall Fescue	3 to 3 $\frac{1}{2}$ inches
Turf-type Tall Fescues	3 inches
Fine Fescues	1 $\frac{1}{2}$ to 2 inches
Kentucky Bluegrass	2 to 2 $\frac{1}{2}$ inches

Other

☛ Begin aerating and dethatching summer lawns. Be sure to do this before fertilizing and before grasses green up.

* See "Planting or Reseeding Evergreen Lawns," p. 71

† See "Fertilizing and Controlling Weeds in Lawns," p. 73

April

IN THE SOUTHERN GARDEN

April in the South is the visual definition of spring. Flowering trees and shrubs fill gardens, landscapes, parks, and woodlands. Everything seems to be a blaze of color. Visitors from other parts of the country and from overseas simply cannot believe the beauty found in the South at this time of the year. There are more camellias, azaleas, and dogwoods here than in any place in the world. Southern gardeners need no further inspiration to get outdoors and start bringing January dreams to fruition.

So much beauty at the beginning of the growing season may be a hard act to follow, but with such an auspicious start, it is not hard to try. We have six to seven months now before frost next fall over which to extend the beauty of spring with a whole new class of plants, colorful summer flowers. And there is a huge potential in the vegetable garden. Gardening is fun in April because the weather is ideal, there is plenty to do, and there is no lack of motivation.

Nurseries and garden centers are as busy as the malls at Christmas. Gardeners taking home carloads of trees, shrubs, roses, fruit trees, bedding plants, and vegetable seeds are full of high hopes and happy smiles. I am like them. I love spring, especially April.

Though this is our most beautiful time of the year, summers can also be spectacular. Summertime visitors extol the rich beauty of our Crape Myrtles and summer hydrangeas. Plant some this year to extend your landscape's spring-type beauty through the summer.

Remember that bunch of dead sticks somebody said was a snowball plant? Look how beautiful it is now! Spring flowers may be awesome to behold, but gardeners know that the deepest beauty of spring is in the way Nature brings our plants and us back to life.

AT LEFT: *Azaleas blooming mean it's spring in the South.*

I. *Shade and Flowering Trees*

Flowering trees are one of the greatest gifts of spring. The fluffy pink blossoms of the Kwanzan Cherry seem almost out of place against the lush, green backdrop of emerging leaves. How could such a vivid color ever find its way into nature?

With flowering trees like Kwanzan Cherry inspiring us, we might feel obliged to dress up our landscapes with some new colors. When choosing trees this time of year, stick to the container-grown or B&B types. If you do plant, give your new tree special attention. Water it frequently and keep it well mulched to prevent the roots from getting dry during the growing season. I recently heard a woman at a nursery complaining that the deciduous Magnolia she bought the year before lost all its blossoms right after she planted it. She was blaming the nursery for selling her a bad tree. Since the tree had kept its petals at the nursery after handling and transportation, it is more likely that she either damaged the tree herself or did not water it after planting. A tree in shock will quickly drop its petals.

Try to plant trees carefully and water them frequently this late in the season. Extra care this year will pay off generously when your tree blooms next spring.

The deep rose 'Kwanzan' flowering cherry is one of our spectacular spring flowering trees.

TREE ACTIVITIES FOR APRIL:

Plant

☛ B&B and container-grown shade and flowering trees may be planted with caution this month; however, it is not recommended to plant bare-root trees after the new leaves have come out.*

Prune

☛ Prune dead, broken, crossed, or damaged tree limbs of spring-flowering trees as soon as the flower petals have fallen.†

☛ It is not the best time to prune shade trees. Unless there is a real problem like a limb badly damaging your roof, wait until the tree is dormant next winter before pruning.†

---

* See "Planting Trees and Shrubs," p. 264

† See "Pruning Shade and Flowering Trees," p. 4

Fertilize

☞ Fertilize **Magnolia** and **Cherry Laurel** if you have not already done so. Use a slow-release nitrogen, evergreen formula at a rate of one pound of fertilizer per inch circumference of the tree, measured three feet above the ground. This is done once a year.

☞ It is too late to fertilize large shade trees. Remember, it takes a long time for nutrients to reach the leaf area of a large tree. The reason you fertilize in January or February is so that the nutrients will be in the upper part of the tree when growth starts.

☞ Small one- or two-year-old trees may still be fertilized since nutrients quickly reach the growth areas. Use 15-15-15 at a rate of 1/2 pound per three feet of height.‡

☞ Fertilize spring-flowering trees as the flower petals fall. Use one pound of 5-10-15 fertilizer per inch circumference of the tree measured three feet above the ground. This is done once a year.

Spray

☞ Control scale on all trees with Orthene or Cygon, except in the case of **hollies**. Use Orthene on **hollies**.**

☞ Watch out for worms and caterpillars eating the foliage of flowering forms of fruit trees like **flowering peaches, flowering plums, flowering cherries, flowering crabapples,** and **Bradford Pear**. Spray with the Thuricide formulation of Bacillus thurengiensis (BT), or dust with the Dipel form of BT.**

☞ Protect **dogwood** buds from petal blight by spraying with Daconil or Dithane. Apply the spray when the bud cracks open, and every ten days after until the petals have fallen. However, do not spray when the flowers are at their peak. Spray new foliage with the same material to prevent leaf spots.

☞ Another leaf disease, Cedar-Apple Rust, may cause yellow spotting of **crabapple**, **apple**, and **pear** leaves. The alternate host of the disease is **Red Cedar**. Large, gelatinous, orange bodies will form on the cedar. Try to find and remove those found on cedars growing close to **crabapples** and **apples**. Spray the foliage of **crabapples, apples,** and **pears** with Maneb or a complete home orchard spray.**

☞ Holly leaf miners are also a problem in the spring. This is a gnat-like insect which may be seen flying around **hollies**, especially **American Hollies** and their hybrids. The insect lays eggs in the leaves which hatch into tiny worms. The worms tunnel inside the leaf, ruining its appearance and causing premature leaf drop. Use Orthene as a control when you first spot the gnats.**

Water

☞ Newly planted trees should be soaked once a week when there is no significant rainfall.††

Other

☞ Mulch newly planted and fertilized trees with pine straw or pine bark. Do not allow the mulch to pack against the tree's trunk.**

☞ Check mulch around older plants and replenish with fresh mulch if needed.

☞ Be extremely careful when mowing or using a power trimmer around old and new trees. *Do not hit or damage the bark.* Even the slightest damage may make an entrance for borers or other damaging insects. This is true for all trees in the landscape or a natural area, including planted and natural trees.

‡ See "How to Fertilize Shade Trees," p. 6
** See "Controlling Insects and Diseases," p. 80

** See "Controlling Insects and Diseases," p. 80
†† See "Does Your Tree Have Enough Water?," p. 150
‡‡ See "Mulching: A Lesson from Nature," p. 243

Boxwood leaf miners burrow inside the leaves causing discoloration and leaf fall.

II. *Shrubs and Vines*

Many shrubs will be finishing up their bloom during April. This is the time to encourage new growth by fertilizing. You will be amazed at how much bigger a shrub can get in a given year.

Boxwoods and hollies may be attacked by leaf miners this month. Although these bugs are bad for the shrub, I cannot help but feel a little excited when I find them. It is like finding a hidden pot of gold. I usually notice that something is wrong when I look across the yard at my boxwoods. They don't have their normal deep, rich green color. When I walk over to investigate, the off-color leaves are much more visible. Some leaves have brown areas with an almost reddish halo. This is where the fun starts. When I pluck off a leaf, it appears to have a bubble in it. Cracking the leaf in half reveals the inside of the bubble. There it is! A little worm happily eating away. He has made a nice little home for himself.

Of course, finding such a pot of gold is only fun for the first three leaves you crack open. After that, you start feeling sorry for your boxwood. With no young children in the house this year, I decide to spray with Orthene. The spray is systemic, which means that the boxwood absorbs the insecticide into its leaves. The worms then eat the inside of the leaf and die. So much for my pot of gold.

CONTROLLING INSECTS AND DISEASES

Word spreads rapidly when fall Armyworms enter a neighborhood and start to devour beautiful lawns, or when spider mites and thrips attack the flowers next door. War is declared.

The goal of every gardener is to produce beautiful, or fruitful, or useful plants. We encourage growth with good soil, nutrients, water when needed, and insect and disease control. When plants begin to perform well, insects and diseases become our greatest concern. Hot and humid Southern summers are just what many insects and diseases like. They multiply and spread through the garden, often causing havoc in flower beds, vegetable gardens, fruits, roses, shrubs, and lawns. The battle begins and the outcome depends mainly on you.

We use specific materials to control insects and diseases. A spray for blackspot on roses does no good for leafhoppers on **hostas.** One of the best ways to be successful with plants is to be a good detective. I like to walk in the garden every day and observe what's going on. Suddenly I see gnats flying around **boxwoods** or a silvery cast on my **raspberry** leaves. What is happening? Large vegetable and flower farming operations have teams of scouts who walk the fields daily to spot any insects or diseases which might damage crops. It saves crops and money on spray material if they can find the problems before their plants are seriously damaged. Gardeners must also become good detectives and be their own scouts. The discovery process centers on whether the problem is an insect, disease, or merely a growth condition.

Identification is the key to good pest control. Which insect or disease is causing the problem? Most gardeners learn insect and disease identification by taking a sample to a nursery which can identify it and suggest a control. Your County Extension Service is also willing to help. Once you find the answer, put it permanently into your mental data bank to use every time this problem occurs in the future.

Watch for sudden changes in the appearance of your plants since many insects and diseases can be identified by symptoms. Unfortunately, symptoms can be confusing. Some insects, like lacebug on **Pyracantha** and **azalea,** cause leaf discoloration which may be confused with yellowing from chlorosis. A good

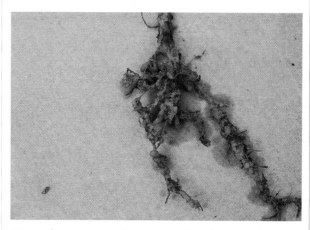

Golden and other aphids attack in huge numbers, sucking the life out of garden plants.

Nematodes attack roots of many plants. Since they are underground, diagnosis comes from symptoms.

detective must search diligently for the real cause. In the case of lacebugs, simply turn over the leaf and look for residue from the lacebug or perhaps the insect itself. Chlorosis is treated by spraying with an iron compound, while lacebugs are controlled with an insecticide spray.

There are dozens of potentially damaging insects to contend with: aphids, thrips, spider mites, mealybugs, leafhoppers, Japanese Beetles, and all sorts of worms, to name just a few. Some, like slugs or snails, chew away plant parts, making them easier to identify from the symptom; others, like spider mites and lacebugs, pierce the surface and insert their mouths into the cells to suck the plant's juices. They are harder to identify directly since many are very small, and the symptom is not as obvious as a chewed leaf. Discoloration or sudden changes in a plant's color is a good cause for suspicion and a search for the cul-

Lacebug attacks a number of Southern evergreen shrubs. They feed on the underside of the leaves and will cause severe damage.

prit in the damaged area of the plant.

Some diseases have very clear symptoms: Blackspot causes a distinctive spot on roses; powdery mildew looks like the plant has been dusted with powder; rust looks like common metal rust beads; and rots, especially on fruits, are familiar to everyone.

The hardest insects and diseases to identify are those which attack the roots because you can't see the cause of the problem without damaging the plant. The only way to start this discovery process is from the symptoms. A plant is wilting in the afternoon. The cause can be nematodes (a microscopic insect on the roots), pythium or fusarium, diseases of the lower stems and roots, or even a stem borer which is above the ground but inside the stem of the plant and therefore invisible. The tip-wilting problem can also be the result of bad soil conditions which prevent good moisture-holding capacity, or poor root development, or even drought.

Being a good detective may seem overwhelming, but it really isn't. In the case of the tip-wilting plant, begin with the process of elimination. If there are many plants in the row but only one is tip-wilting, you can usually eliminate soil conditions, nematodes, pythium, and fusarium. It is then a good bet that a borer in the stem may be the problem. Carefully slit open the stem where it seems to be a bit enlarged. Perhaps there is a worm inside. If not, check at the lower stem right above the ground for soil fungi, like pythium and fusarium, which may dry out the stem as it comes from the ground. If the stem looks healthy, carefully take up the plant and inspect its roots. Swollen club-shaped roots indicate the presence of nematodes. If the roots are clean, the most likely problem is the soil's condition or extremely dry conditions. This process of discovery and elimination is the best way to find the cause of your plant's problem. The key is to watch your plants constantly for changes.

Fortunately, your nursery experts and your county's Cooperative Extension Service agents keep up with problems which affect plants in your area. Call on them to help after you have made a tentative diagnosis.

Once you've identified the cause of a problem, how do you overcome it in the best and safest way? Insects and diseases can quickly damage or kill plants, so most gardeners must decide how to control or prevent their attacks. Start control measures with good garden hygiene *before* the growing season ever begins. The fall

activities list reminds you to remove dead vegetable and flower parts where insect eggs and disease spores overwinter until they come out with warm weather in the spring. There is an old saying that "one aphid killed in the fall is a thousand killed in the spring." Remove their habitats and you greatly reduce next year's pest population. If neighbors also practice garden hygiene, their insects and diseases cannot quickly move to your garden.

Hygiene is a good start, but no matter how hard we try, insects and diseases come from open land and forests on wind currents, from neighbors' yards, and from places on your own property which may not seem to be good overwintering spots, but are. When pests appear during the spring, control them quickly to prevent rapid buildup and extensive plant damage.

Once the attacks begin, a gardener can take several approaches: (1) Do nothing and let plants endure the attacks, (2) let natural predators and insect cycles reduce populations, (3) plant more disease- and insect-resistant types and cultivars next time, (4) introduce biological control measures which may be slow but are effective on some insects, (5) use traps to catch insects before they damage plants, and (6) resort to chemical sprays which are effective but must be used with caution because when improperly used, they can be dangerous to families, pets, and wildlife.

Consider the first two approaches carefully, for they may keep your plants from performing the way you want. I have found the third approach extremely important when deciding what to plant, especially when choosing vegetable cultivars. Plant breeders spend years developing successful types and cultivars of vegetables and flowers which are resistant to many diseases and some insects.

A number of biological controls, like Bacillus thurengiensis, are effective in controlling insects, particularly soft worms. More will be developed from the extensive scientific research now going on. Traps are a type of biological control which I use for several insects. Japanese Beetle traps are efficient when properly placed. Sticky yellow strips attract white fly successfully, especially when placed among vegetables like **tomatoes**.

There are also a number of chemicals which can be very effective. Whenever possible, I prefer to use natural substances, like the insecticide Pyrethrum, which are less toxic to humans and animals than many man-made chemicals. The repellent Neem, Sabadilla Dust

Wood borer worms cause great damage to many trees including peaches, cherries, and dogwoods.

(for Mexican Bean Beetles), and simple deterrents like soaps (which can be used for Whitefly) can also be effective in the garden.

Whenever conditions require the use of man-made chemical insecticides and fungicides, I use them only with extreme caution. Read the entire label before using any chemical, whether it is natural or man-made, since even the natural substances can be toxic to humans, animals, and plants.

For more information, be sure to read "Fertilizing, Spraying, and Watering Vegetables" in the May chapter.

SHRUB AND VINE ACTIVITIES FOR APRIL:

Plant

☛ B&B and container-grown deciduous and ever-green shrubs and vines may be planted with caution this month; however, it is not recommended to plant bare-root shrubs and vines after the new leaves have come out.*

* See "Planting Trees and Shrubs," p. 264

☛ Plant container-grown hardy woody vines like **Clematis** and **Gold Flame Honeysuckle** any time this month.†

☛ Continue to plant container-grown hardy ground covers like **English Ivy**, **Vinca**, and **Liriope**. Use well-rooted plants, rather than runners, for best results.*

☛ It is best to plant shrubs and vines when the soil is not too wet. If planting is necessary before the soil dries out, however, use dry peat moss as the soil amendment. It will absorb excess moisture and make it easier to prepare a good planting mixture.

☛ Plant seeds or seedlings of annual vines like **Morning Glory**, **Moonflower**, **Scarlet Runner Beans**, and **Passion Flower** after the danger of frost in your area.

† See "Growing Clematis and Other Southern Vines," p. 54
* See "Planting Trees and Shrubs," p. 264

Prune

☞ Wait to prune spring-flowering evergreen shrubs like **Camellia**, **azalea**, **Rhododendron**, and **Mountain Laurel** until after they have finished blooming.‡

☞ Do not prune summer-flowering shrubs like **Hydrangea arborescens 'Grandiflora,'** **Hydrangea paniculata 'Grandiflora,'** and **Butterfly Bush** (**Buddleia**) after their leaves have emerged.

☞ Do not prune spring-flowering evergreen vines like **Carolina Jessamine** until after they bloom.‡

☞ Prune other spring-flowering deciduous vines like **Wisteria** and **Lady Banksia rose** after they have finished blooming.‡

Fertilize

☞ Finish fertilizing summer-flowering shrubs with a 15-15-15 fertilizer. Use roughly 1/2 pound per three feet of the shrub's height (the height before any pruning). This is usually done once a year.**

☞ Finish fertilizing summer-flowering vines after pruning. Use half a pound of 15-15-15 fertilizer on plants one to three years old. On older vines, use a pound of fertilizer per year of age up to a maximum of five pounds on large woody vines like **Wisteria**.**

☞ Fertilize established **Clematis** with a double handful (one cup or 1/2 pound) of 5-10-15 fertilizer every six weeks. As an alternative, you can fertilize once with a slow-release, high-nitrogen fertilizer.

☞ Fertilize all spring-flowering shrubs and vines after they bloom. Use a 15-15-15 fertilizer on deciduous shrubs and vines and an azalea/camellia acid fertilizer on evergreens. Use roughly 1/2 pound per three feet of the shrub's height (the height before any pruning). This is usually done once a year.**

Spray

☞ Inspect established evergreens for signs of scale, which is particularly bad on evergreens. Control it with Cygon except on **hollies**; use Orthene on **hollies**.††

☞ **Boxwoods** and **hollies** may show signs of leaf damage from the leaf miner. At first, the damage appears as tiny pin pricks in the foliage. Later, as the miner develops, the leaf will be discolored. Spray with Cygon or Orthene on **boxwoods** and Orthene on **hollies** when you first see the signs.††

☞ Inspect **azalea** and **Pyracantha** for signs of lacebugs. The upper sides of leaves will have a silvery cast. The undersides will be covered with balls of brown residue. Spray them with Orthene as the weather warms.††

☞ Aphids may attack the new shoots of many evergreens like **Red Tip Photinia**. Watch for them and if you see them, spray with Orthene.††

Water

☞ Water newly planted shrubs and vines thoroughly, even if the ground is wet, in order to settle the soil around the roots.

Other

☞ Clean old mulch from around **azaleas**, **camellias**, **boxwoods**, **hollies**, and other broadleaf evergreens. Replace with fresh pine straw or pine bark.‡‡

---

‡ See "Pruning Flowering Shrubs and Vines," p. 31
** See "How to Fertilize Shrubs and Vines," p. 30

†† See "Controlling Insects and Diseases," p. 80
‡‡ See "Mulching: A Lesson from Nature," p. 243

Apple blossoms form on the fruiting spurs.

III. *Fruits*

Fruit planting season has basically passed. The strawberries you planted last month should be establishing themselves and will do best if you keep them mulched. Otherwise the weeds will take over your beds.

The main worry for fruit growers during April is insect and disease control. Since there are no visible apples, pears, or peaches on our trees, it is a temptation to skip a spraying or two. *Don't be fooled!* If you let the insect and disease populations get ahead of you, there will be no stopping them later in the season when your fruit *is* visible.

FRUIT ACTIVITIES FOR APRIL:

Plant

☞ Continue to plant container-grown fruits but do so with caution.*

Fertilize

☞ Lightly fertilize **blueberries** a second time when they bloom. Use an azalea-camellia fertilizer, but do so very sparingly. **Blueberries** are sensitive to excess fertilizer.

Spray

☞ Continue your insect and disease control program on fruits as the flowers open. A complete home orchard spray is the most practical method of control. Continue applications at recommended intervals until the fruit ripens.

☞ Fire blight may attack **pears** and **apples** this month. You can identify it as a problem when tip growth turns black and hangs on the tree like it has been scorched or when a twig dies back (the bark will appear shrunken). Eradication of the twig is the only practical control. Examine the dying twig and notice any shriveling bark below the dead leaves. Cut the twig several inches below this area. **Sterilize the blades of your shears between cuts by dipping them in alcohol or a bleach solution.** (There is a very exacting antibiotic spray control program for fire blight, but it is not practical for most homeowners.)†

---

* See "Planting Trees and Shrubs," p. 264
† See "Controlling Insects and Diseases," p. 80

☞ Watch for spider mites on **raspberries** and other semi-bush berries. Their presence is evident when the foliage has a silvery gray appearance. Spray with Kelthane to control this serious pest.†

☞ Spray **bunch grapes** with a complete home orchard spray to prevent brown rot and control leaf worms.†

Water

☞ Newly planted fruits should be soaked once a week when there is no significant rainfall.‡

Other

☞ Keep **strawberries** mulched with pine straw to prevent weeds from taking over the bed.

☞ Mulch fruit trees to prevent weeds and grass from growing up around the trunks and competing for water and fertilizer. Pine straw is excellent for this purpose. However, do not pile the mulch against the trunks.**

☞ Be careful when mowing in orchard areas not to hit the bark of fruit trees with the mower. Any damage to the bark will provide an entrance place for borers.

---

† See "Controlling Insects and Diseases," p. 80
‡ See "Does Your Tree Have Enough Water?" p. 150
** See "Mulching: A Lesson from Nature," p. 243

NOTES

The first buds on roses foretell beautiful flowers will soon grace your plants.

IV. *Roses*

As you watch your roses spring into action with an abundance of growth, you might decide to plant a few more. It is best to stick to the container-grown varieties in April. You might find some bare-root roses in local nurseries, but chances are they are left over from February or March. These poor roses are not the ones you want to add to your collection.

Cut back any dead stubs or canes which might be left over from your severe pruning a month ago. Cleanly pruned roses will grow better and produce more flowers.

While the first big rose bloom usually comes in May, you may get a few early risers in late April. Remember to cut these flowers at a joint where a five-leaflet originates. This will force a strong new shoot for more blossoms.

ROSE ACTIVITIES FOR APRIL:

Plant

☞ For best results, plant only container-grown roses this month.*

☞ Plant bare-root roses with extreme caution.†

Prune

☞ Check recently pruned plants for dead stubs or canes. Immediately cut them back to a live bud.

☞ It is too late to undertake any structural pruning beyond the removal of dead wood.

☞ Inspect new growth. Weak, yellow leaves may indicate problems on a cane. Check the cane from which the shoot arises. If it is dying, remove the cane back to healthy wood. Seal all cuts into old wood with Elmer's Glue.

☞ Remove spent flowers immediately. Seed formation retards stem growth and the production of new blossoms.‡

Fertilize

☞ Continue fertilizing with a complete rose fertilizer on your six-to-eight-week program.

* See "Planting Trees and Shrubs," p. 264
† See "Planting Bare-Root Roses," p. 250
‡ See "Grooming Roses," p. 110

Spray

☞ Continue with your complete rose spray program every 10-14 days according to the directions. Use a combination insecticide and fungicide spray and continue applications through September.

☞ Don't let diseases get started. It is easier to control them now than during hot weather. Blackspot causes the most damage on roses, so don't let it get ahead of you. Use Funginex on a regular 10-12 day program.

Other

☞ Keep roses well mulched but do not pile mulch against the crown or lower stems. Many problems like cankers and botrytis occur when mulch covers the lower stems.**

☞ Remember to cut flowers correctly. Always make the cut above a joint where a five-leaflet originates. Cutting at this point encourages a strong new shoot and a healthy blossom to form.‡

☞ Many **Hybrid Tea** and **Grandiflora** roses have several flowers in a cluster (called a candelabra) which may not all bloom at the same time. Remove each spent flower in the cluster as it finishes blooming. When all the flowers are done, cut the whole cluster stalk back to a five leaflet set.‡

** See "Mulching: A Lesson from Nature," p. 243
‡ See "Grooming Roses," p. 110

NOTES

V. *Flowers and Colorful Garden Plants*

After frost danger has passed, it's time to plant summer flowers like Periwinkle which blooms all summer.

April is finally here and it is time to plant our annual bed. As soon as the danger of frost has passed, we can arrange and plant the tender annuals and perennials we have been growing inside since late winter. Those of us who didn't start our plants from seeds will be visiting nurseries and farmer's markets to buy trays of young seedlings. Planting an annual bed is one of my favorite projects of the year!

We like to plant our annual bed as a family. There is nothing like getting everyone involved in the design, arrangement, planting, and reminiscing involved in planting an annual bed. Imagine a warm Saturday afternoon with the fresh smell of spring in the air. Everyone is busy; pulling the hose up to the bed, bringing down the seedlings from the greenhouse, cranking up the roto-tiller, carrying a few trowels and a shovel. What will look best where? Are the salvias too close? Should we extend the herbs? Do we have enough Impatiens? Everyone is chattering at once.

Later that evening we usually cook hamburgers on the grill. No one wants to go inside; it's too much fun standing around admiring the work we have accomplished. These annuals will bush out and fill the bed to become a part of our summer garden. Bumblebees will hum around the flowers and joust with the hummingbirds for the sweet flower nectar. Summer is on its way.

ANALYZING SOIL WITH A PAIR OF RUBBER BOOTS

There is something deep within the human psyche that knows good soil. All it takes is slogging through wet Southern soil on a rainy day. As the clay sticks to the soles of your rubber boots and weighs down your feet, a grimace works its way onto your face from somewhere deep inside. Yuck. There is no disputing it; Southern soil is not the best.

If knowing good soil is instinctive, then it should be easy to define. I'm sure you will agree that rich, dark, loamy soil is preferable — the kind of soil that doesn't cling to your boots. It feels light and airy when you pick it up in your hand. It falls through your fingers and doesn't stain your clothes. If you were a seed, this is the kind of soil you would want to call home.

As Southern gardeners, one of our gardening activities is to fix our soil. Changing soil from bad to good can be a very technical endeavor or you can go by instinct. The technical approach would be to have a soil analysis performed by your Cooperative Extension Service or a local laboratory. These analyses show deficiencies in your soil which need to be corrected. In my experience, having a soil sample analyzed every year is overkill for the average gardener. Most soils all over the South have the same problems, and we can raise the quality of our particular soil dramatically with a few basic steps.

A good first step in soil conditioning is applying limestone. Soil is naturally either acidic, basic, or neutral as measured on a pH scale. Most plants grow best in a 6.0 - 6.5 pH range. Some plants, like **azaleas,** prefer acidic soils. Other plants, like **peonies,** prefer a more alkaline soil. With time, as soil naturally becomes more acidic, it becomes necessary to sweeten the soil in order to grow certain crops. Applying limestone is the easiest, safest, and cheapest way to sweeten your soil. Just like soil content, the exact amount of change needed can be determined by a soil analysis. Without a test, however, we can assume that some areas of the garden will need sweetening every year while others will not. The general rule is to lime garden areas like the vegetable garden and annual bed which you prepare every year. In addition, you should lime evergreen lawns once a year. Watch out, though. There are exceptions like the **Irish potato** area in the vegetable garden, and areas of the annual bed which are close to broadleaf evergreens. The best way to be specific is to get to know your individual plants.

The second basic step of soil conditioning is getting the correct soil mix. Soil is made up of two major components: solid matter and the space between it. The solid matter is made up of organic and inorganic components which contain the nutrients our plants need. The empty space is filled with water and air. An ideal soil is composed of 50% solid matter, up to 25% water, and at least 25% air. Soil which is sticky probably doesn't have enough air in it. Working the soil and cultivating are methods of breaking up the solid components and putting more air into the soil.

Unfortunately, the type of solid matter determines how long that air will remain in the soil. In the mid-South, where our solid matter contains a lot of clay (to say the least), air in the soil lasts for about 10 seconds. Seriously, though, clay compacts easily, holds water, and forms large particles which reduce the percentage of air and water per unit volume. It is our foremost job to reduce the amount of clay in the solid matter component of the soil. By doing so, we will create a soil which holds air longer and drains excess water more quickly so that our soil percentages stay closer to the "up to 25% water and at least 25% air" mix.

One of the best ways to conquer the clay is by adding humus. Humus is decomposed organic material and can be bought in bags at a nursery. A better way is to make your own humus by composting organic material at home. If you use compost, make sure the material is thoroughly decomposed before adding it to your garden. Another way to add humus is to grow green manure cover crops in your garden in the off-season. When these crops are turned under, they will decompose quickly into humus (see September, "Growing Cover Crops").

Humus improves the quality of the soil by breaking up the clay particles and contributing to the percentage of solid matter in the soil. Adding humus to sticky soil will increase the amount of air in the soil and the drainage. As an added bonus, humus is full of raw materials needed for normal plant growth.

In addition to humus, you can add drainage-improving natural materials like perlite, vermiculite, and sand to lighten your soil mix. Like humus, they help break up the clay particles. While these amendments are great materials to increase the air percentage and drainage in the soil, they do not contain any of the nutrients required for plant growth. My favorite method is to add both humus and perlite when amending my soil.

In the lower South, there is a different problem: soils tend to have higher quantities of sand. Sandy soils are those which consist of 45% or more sand. While sand is great for drainage, sandy soils do not retain the soil-water content needed for proper plant growth. In addition, sand does not have many of the needed plant nutrients. The answer is to add humus to hold together sand particles, help the soil retain the proper level of moisture, and to provide many essential nutrients.

While all this talk of percentages and soil components might seem overwhelming, it boils down to the fact that Southern soil could use more humus. In the areas of the South with sticky clay soils, you might want to throw in some perlite for good measure. While having a soil analysis is the best way to find out exactly how much humus or perlite to add, you will probably know instinctively. Just walk around your garden on a rainy day in a pair of rubber boots. If "yuck" doesn't automatically pop into your head, your analysis is favorable.

FLOWER ACTIVITIES FOR APRIL:

Plant

☛ Plan flower beds carefully. Consider the mature heights of various plantings so you can see and enjoy each group. Color combinations are also important. Plant pleasing blends as well as suitable contrasts. Do not plant too close. Take into consideration the ultimate width of each plant so that plants do not end up too crowded. Try new types and cultivars to add interest to your plantings.

☛ Prepare flower beds carefully. Good drainage is necessary to have beautiful flowers. Work beds thoroughly and deeply. Incorporate organic matter, limestone, and fertilizer into flower beds and borders. If beds are sticky, add perlite to improve the drainage.*

☛ Remember to protect established roots and sprouts of perennials growing in flowers beds which will also be planted with annuals. Either work around perennials or lift them, work the bed, and reset them.

☛ Continue planting newly purchased or home-grown hardy annuals, biennials, and perennials like **Foxglove**, **pinks**, **stock**, **Sweet William**, and **Shasta Daisy** while there is *still* a danger of frost.

☛ Plant newly purchased or home-grown hardy, long-lasting aromatic and culinary herbs like **Lemon Balm**, **catnip**, **horehound**, **lavender**, **oregano**, **peppermint**, **sage**, and **thyme** while there is *still* a danger of frost.

☛ *After* the danger of frost has passed and the ground begins to warm, plant all tender flowering plants like **Ageratum**, **Begonia**, **Coleus**, **Geranium**, **Impatiens**, **marigold**, **Petunia**, **Vinca**, and **Zinnia** which were started from seed in February/March, grown from cuttings, or purchased at a nursery.*

☛ *After* the danger of frost has passed and the ground begins to warm, plant tender annual aromatic and culinary herbs like **anise**, **sweet basil**, **coriander**, **dill**, **sweet marjoram**, and **fennel** purchased at the nursery or grown from seeds.*

☛ Plant tender annual vines like **Moonflower**, **Morning Glory**, and **Scarlet Runner Bean** *after* the danger of frost has passed and the ground begins to warm.

☛ Begin planting **Canna**, **Caladium**, **Elephant Ear**, **Dahlia**, **Ginger Lily**, **Tuberose** and other tender bulbous, tuberous, and rhizome plants when the night temperatures are above 55 degrees.

☛ Carefully separate and reset perennial clumps which you did not take care of earlier. Don't do this if the plants have heavy tops or have started to bloom.

☛ Get a jump on the season by potting **Caladium** and **Elephant Ear** tubers inside as soon as possible in April. Starting them inside will ensure larger leaves and better early color when you set them out in late April or early May after the ground is warm. Pot them shallowly.

☛ Cut back and pot **geraniums** which were lifted from the garden and stored over winter in plastic bags. They will start growing almost immediately and be ready to set out in late April or early May when the ground is warm.

Prune

☛ Cut back and fertilize tropical flowering plants like **Hibiscus**, **Ixora**, and **Allamanda** as soon as possible so they will be growing well by late April or early May when you put them out on decks, patios, or terraces for the summer.

Fertilize

☛ Fertilize annuals, biennials, and perennials on the following schedule: Apply 15-15-15, which is a good starter fertilizer, on new and emerging plants. After six to eight weeks, switch to 5-10-15, which is a good fruit and flower fertilizer, and continue on that schedule for the rest of the season.

Spray

☛ Watch carefully for insects and diseases on sprouting plants. Insects are the greatest problem. Fast succulent growth is highly susceptible to aphid, spider mite, leafhopper, thrip, and worm damage. Orthene is an excellent all-around control.†

Other

☛ Mulch young plants with dried grass clippings or pine straw to protect them from heavy rains, dry spells, and weeds.‡

* See "How to Plant a Flower Bed," p. 62

† See "Controlling Insects and Diseases," p. 80

‡ See "Mulching: A Lesson from Nature," p. 243

VI. *Vegetables*

While some vegetables may have their heyday at other times of the year, April represents the single most active vegetable gardening month.

If you haven't started preparing your soil, begin as early in the month as possible. Take your time with it; a well prepared vegetable garden is one of the most important steps of the entire growing process. Those of you who prepared your gardens early might want to check for erosion and correct any problems which might have popped up.

Besides planting and starting your insect and disease control program, there are some other great April vegetable garden activities. Get started on your scarecrow! Old winter clothes are great for scarecrows because the material is thicker and will last longer outside. You connoisseurs of the pest-scare world can inflate your blow-up barn owls and hang them from nearby trees. Those who have no fear of their neighbors can hang pie pans on lines criss-crossing the garden to scare away the crows. Have fun!

PLANTING A VEGETABLE GARDEN

Brilliant summer flowers and ornamental plants are beautiful enough in the home landscape. Imagine a bouquet of them in the center of a dinner table with bowls of steaming **sweet corn**, **snap beans**, and **squash** *plus* a huge salad made with **sweet peppers**, **onions**, and **Bibb Lettuce** from your very own garden. That is really the good life!

Growing your own groceries is a Southern tradition born of economic necessity but adopted by gardeners who delight in having the best. Vegetable gardens not only save grocery money but provide far better quality than is possible from a supermarket which must depend on distant production areas for its vegetables.

The taste of home grown vegetables, especially **tomatoes**, is so superior to supermarket kinds that they can hardly be compared. Growing them is no more difficult than growing the bouquet of flowers used on the same table. Vegetable plants have special needs in order to produce well; six hours of full sun per day and well-drained soil are the two most important. They also need rich soil which is not too acid, but most soils do not fit this requirement and can easily be amended to provide what is needed. Choose an open area which doesn't lie in a low, poorly-drained spot. Soggy soil and standing water after heavy rains are the nemesis of vegetable plants and they will not do well in such a place.

How large should your vegetable garden be? That's like asking how long should a string be. The size depends on you: what you want to grow, how much harvest you can handle, how much time and effort you want to spend, and what kind of equipment you have available. Small, well-planned gardens can produce plenty for the table. A friend of mine once used a 25 ft. x 25 ft. spot to produce plenty of fresh vegetables for a family of three.

The next step is to decide what you want to grow. Everybody includes **tomatoes** since garden **tomatoes** are *so* much better than supermarket **tomatoes** even in season. It is wise to divide your plantings into those which produce over a long period of time like **tomatoes**, **peppers**, **eggplant**, **pole beans**, **summer squash**, and **okra**, and those which are harvested in a week or so like **sweet corn**, **snap beans**, and **melons**.

Lay out your garden on paper. This enables you to buy the right items and plant them in the garden correctly. Put short-harvest vegetables together so you can remove and replace them when they are finished. Plant tall crops like **corn**, **okra**, and **pole beans** on the edge of the garden so as not to shade lower growing plants.

After choosing the site of your garden, work the ground deeply and thoroughly. Use a roto-tiller for best results. Till back and forth deeper and deeper until you have prepared a good seed bed at least eight inches deep. Observe and feel the tilled soil. Pick up some soil, squeeze it into a ball in the palm of your hand, and try to break up the ball with your thumb. If it crumbles easily, the soil is fine and you can lay out your rows. If not, you will need to till some more and add humus to the soil. Finely-ground bark, peat moss, and well-rotted compost are excellent materials to add organic matter to your soil. Till in the material thoroughly. After the final tilling, broadcast dolomitic limestone over the area, using 50 pounds per 1000 square feet. Now rake this into the surface as you smooth the area.

There are many ways to lay out a garden and prepare it for planting. *Try* to make the rows run north and south, allowing the sun to shine more evenly over the entire area. However, if north-south rows would run up and down an incline, adjust your rows to run across the incline, to prevent washing down the middles.

The two general types of planting are flat planting, which is opening a row in the prepared soil, and bed planting, which is pulling soil into a ridge down the row. These ridges should be at least 28 inches across and eight to 10 inches above the level between the rows (called the middle). Flat planting is fine if the soil drains well and remains loose. Bed planting is essential for all root crops like **potatoes**, **beets**, **carrots**, **onions**, and **turnips** so they have loose soil in which to develop their underground edible parts. I prefer bed planting for all vegetables here in the South. We have large amounts of rain during the summer followed by hot dry spells which bake the soil. If planted flat, plants are first inundated by rain, then baked dry. On the other hand, beds allow excess water to drain away and the middles are easily irrigated in dry weather. Whichever method you use, make your rows at least four feet apart. Wider rows are especially advisable if cultivation is done with a tiller.

There are two essential tools for vegetable gardening: a garden rake (the sharp-tooth bow type) and a pointed hoe. The rake is for smoothing prepared soil, and the pointed hoe is for opening rows in which to plant.

Open a four-inch-deep furrow down the middle of the bed or on the flat ground, using the pointed hoe. You should have in mind, before you open your rows, which seeds or plants will be in each row because large seeded vegetables are planted deeper than small ones. When growing things flat, use a string to mark the furrow and keep rows straight. After all furrows are opened, apply a 15-15-15 fertilizer in the bottom at a rate of approximately one pound per 10 feet of row. For this purpose, I use an eight-inch flower pot with a single drain hole. Put one finger under the drain hole, fill the pot with fertilizer, and remove

Open a garden furrow with a pointed hoe.

An eight-inch pot with a single drain hole makes a wonderful and accurate fertilizer distributor.

your finger when you reach the start of the furrow. Walk down the row at a quick pace, allowing the fertilizer to meter out the drain hole as you go. At the end of the row, replace your finger, move to the next row and fertilize it the same way. Repeat until all the furrows have fertilizer. Use the pointed hoe to work

Seed leaves (cotyledons) on a tomato seedling.

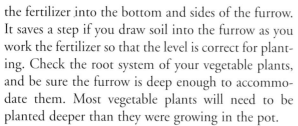

Plant tomatoes deeper than they are growing in the pot or cell to make them tough and strong. Plant up to the seed leaves (cotyledons).

When seeding, drop seeds evenly in the furrow. Prevent skips in the row by overseeding and thinning out.

the fertilizer into the bottom and sides of the furrow. It saves a step if you draw soil into the furrow as you work the fertilizer so that the level is correct for planting. Check the root system of your vegetable plants, and be sure the furrow is deep enough to accommodate them. Most vegetable plants will need to be planted deeper than they were growing in the pot.

When you are seeding, drop seeds evenly in the furrow. I prefer to overseed than underseed. No matter how careful you are, not all seeds will germinate. It is easier to thin the plants later to the proper spacing than have to reseed skips in a row.

After the garden is up, the art of vegetable growing consists of: cultivation (or mulching) to prevent weeds from taking fertilizer and water which your plants need, fertilizing alongside the row of plants (side-dressing), watering in dry times with at least an inch of water per week (irrigation), and keeping pests from damaging or ruining your plants (insect and disease control).

Remember that vegetables are grown to eat and many chemicals used on flowers and ornamentals are toxic to humans. I prefer to use biological controls like Bacillus thuringiensis (BT) on vegetable plants whenever possible, even though they are slow, not always 100% effective, and not as broad spectrum as many garden chemicals. For instance, BT *only* controls soft worms, not aphids, thrips, or mites. It is best to start using biological controls when you anticipate problems, not after insect populations build up.

There are also safe chemicals to use. Sevin is a good general vegetable insect control. Always read the label to find the number of days prior to harvesting that these chemicals can safely be used.

The principles of vegetable gardening may seem a bit strict compared to flower and shrub growing, but they really are not. Good planting and growing procedures improve every type of gardening. Vegetables may seem harder to grow than flowers, but the same good growing techniques used on them will make any type of gardening a lot better. Besides, vegetable gardening produces far better quality food than you can possibly buy at the supermarket.

VEGETABLE ACTIVITIES FOR APRIL:

Plant

☛ Select a bright, sunny, well-drained area for your garden. Vegetables need at least six hours of sun to do well.*

☛ Make your rows running north to south whenever possible. This will allow sunlight to shine evenly over the entire garden. Do not, however, make rows running up and down an incline because rain will erode the incline.*

☛ **Beets, carrots, celery, collards, lettuce, mustard greens, parsley, radish, rapegreens, spinach, Swiss chard,** and **turnips** can be planted from seed in April while there is *still* a danger of frost and the ground is cool.*

☛ *After* the danger of frost and the ground is warm, you can plant seeds of **lima beans, pole beans, snap beans, cantaloupe, cucumber, gourds, okra, cow peas, pumpkins, summer squash, baking squash, sweet corn, watermelons,** and **zucchini.** *

☛ The following can be planted as seedlings/plants *after* the danger of frost and the ground is warm: **tomatoes, pepper** (sweet and hot), **eggplant, sweet potatoes, annual herbs,** and **gourds.** *

☛ Continue to plant roots and plants of hardy perennial herbs while there is *still* a danger of frost and the ground is cool.

☛ Plant **tomatoes, eggplant,** and **peppers** deeper than they are growing in the pot. Place the stake or support before you set the plant so you will not damage the roots putting it in.

* See "Planting a Vegetable Garden," p. 92

Fertilize

☛ Fertilize as you plant with 15-15-15. Application is at a rate of approximately one pound per 10 feet of row. This application should be good for about six weeks.*

☛ Continue to fertilize vegetables with 5-10-15 about every six weeks for the rest of the season. Application is at a rate of approximately one pound per 10 feet of row.†

☛ If you haven't limed your garden, it is better to do it now than never. Application is at a rate of 50 pounds per 1000 square feet.*

Spray

☛ Numerous insects and diseases will be feeding on our vegetables gardens throughout the season. The first step to contolling them is detecting the pests before they have damaged your crop extensively. Once you spot a problem, take an infected leaf, flower, or fruit to your local nurseryman or Cooperative Extension Agent for identification. There are a wide variety of organic and inorganic materials to control most garden pests.†

☛ **Broccoli, cabbage, cauliflower,** and similar crops may be attacked this month by green worms (loopers), particularly in the lower South. Spray with Bacillus thuringiensis for safe biological control.†

☛ Watch out for aphids on all vegetables. Malathion or Sevin are recommended controls.†

Other

☛ Mulch plants heavily with grass clippings or hay to prevent weeds and conserve moisture. Dethatched lawn material is also an excellent mulch.‡

☛ Turn over all remaining cover crops before they bloom and go to seed.

* See "Planting a Vegetable Garden," p. 92
† See "Fertilizing, Spraying, and Watering Vegetables," p. 115
‡ See "Mulching: A Lesson from Nature," p. 243

VII. *Houseplants*

As the danger of frost passes, it is finally time to set our patio plants outside. Wait until the day and night temperatures are both above 55 degrees. Most patio plants don't like chilly weather at all.

Moving tropical plants and houseplants to a new location can be hard on them. We like to think that with plants, more sunlight is always better, but this is not the case! Moving even a sun-loving plant from shade to sun can be disastrous. Just like people trying to get a tan, a plant needs to be slowly acclimated to the sun.

Some houseplants don't like much sun at all. Spathiphyllum (Peace Lily) is a shade-loving plant. I recently had one growing near a window which was plainly unhappy. It had a few yellow leaves and seemed drained of energy. I checked for everything — water, fertilizer, insects, and diseases. The antidote turned out to be moving it to a much shadier location.

HOUSEPLANT ACTIVITIES FOR APRIL:

Plant

☛ Check plants for the need to repot if you haven't done so already. Carefully remove the ball of earth and check the roots. If they are dark and heavily matted, repot in a larger pot. If the roots are sparse and light, the plant will grow all summer in the present pot.*

☛ After danger of frost, **Poinsettia** and **ornamental peppers** may be planted in the garden. **Poinsettia**, however, does not set new flower buds during our long summer days.

Prune

☛ Porch and patio plants like **Hibiscus**, **Allamanda**, and **Ixora** should be cut back, repotted, and fertilized.

☛ If needed, **ferns** can still be cut back but watch out for new, emerging fiddlesticks. Also check to see if they should be repotted and fertilize them to stimulate new growth.

Fertilize

☛ Fertilize with a full-strength water-soluble fertilizer solution every time you water. As an alternative, you can use fertilizer spikes or Osmocote, both of which last several months.†

Spray

☛ Check all indoor plants for insects like spider mites, scale, and mealybug. I like to use a houseplant systemic insecticide in the soil to control them. It is easier and safer than spraying inside. If you do spray, remember to apply the insecticide to the undersides of the leaves. I prefer to take houseplants outside to spray.‡

☛ Be careful when spraying **ferns**. Some insecticides are harmful to them. *Always read the label for warnings about **ferns** and other plants.*

Water

☛ Continue to watch houseplants. When they look limp, check for dry soil. If it is dry, water thoroughly in a sink or bathtub, letting the water drain completely, and don't water again until the surface is dry once more. Between waterings, mist with plain water on a regular basis. If the limp plants are in moist soil, do not water but allow the soil to dry a bit, and mist frequently.†

☛ Tip-burn or edge-burn on leaves indicates more water is being lost than is being absorbed by the roots. Check for dry soil, too much sunlight, or drafts from vents.†

* See "Repotting Houseplants," p. 67 .
† See "Houseplant Care and Maintenance," p. 232

‡ See "Common Houseplant Ailments," p. 280
† See "Houseplant Care and Maintenance," p. 232

Other

☛ Plants are very sensitive to the amount of light they receive. When moving houseplants outside for the summer, try to place them initially in the same light conditions they were in while inside. One way to test light conditions is to use the light meter on your camera. Before moving the plant, test the spot inside. Then try to find a suitable place outside with approximately the same light meter reading. Houseplants and overwintered tropical plants which are taken outside during the summer should not be placed in direct sunlight for several weeks until they become acclimated.

NOTES

VIII. *Lawns*

April lawn cutting is kind of fun. This early in the season it is more like a new hobby than a tired old chore. It is also fun to have a machine to tinker with after being cooped up all winter.

Back in the 1960s, loud music was cool. Rock stars and their fans would crowd up against giant concert speakers in order to "feel the music." These days those same rock stars are wearing ear plugs at their reunion concerts. Half of them are deaf from exposing themselves to so many decibels.

I wear ear protection while I mow the lawn. I don't know the exact decibel comparison between a Snapper lawn mower and a rock concert, but I can imagine it is pretty close. I use the headset ear protection instead of the plugs because my hands usually get dirty while I'm working and I don't want to handle the plugs. My ear protection is actually a headset designed for wearing when shooting guns, and it's pretty comfortable too. While it may be cool for old rock stars to say they are deaf from too many concerts, I doubt anyone would give me credit years from now for being deaf from too many lawn cuttings.

PLANTING AND RESEEDING SUMMER LAWNS

In the South, we have two major groups of lawn grasses. The first group, *evergreen grasses*, consists of four types: (1) the very popular **Kentucky 31 Fescue**, (2) the new improved **turf-type fescues** which are thicker, greener, and more compact growing than **Kentucky 31 Fescue**, (3) the fine-leaf fescues like **Creeping Red Fescue** and **Chewing Fescue**, and (4) **Kentucky Bluegrass**. All of these grow best during the cooler months of the year and should be planted in September and early October or after severe freezes are over in late February and March. I discussed how to plant these in March's "Planting or Reseeding Evergreen Lawns."

The second group, called *Southern summer grasses*, contains types which are green in spring, summer, and fall until frost causes them to become dormant and turn brown until the following spring. **Bermuda Grass, Zoysia, Centipede**, and **St. Augustine (Charleston Grass)** make up this group. They are tough grasses and make some of the most beautiful lawns in the South. Many of their hybrids are well known to golfers and athletes. Some of the finest golf courses around the world have greens and fairways of hybrid **Bermuda Grass** cultivars developed by Dr. Glen Burton at Tifton, Georgia. The well-known hybrid **Emerald Zoysia** is found in many of the most beautiful Southern lawns. Though coarser in texture, **Centipede** and **St. Augustine** are ideal in the Coastal Plain region. They are also grown in the Piedmont region in high traffic areas, as well as in part-shade where **Bermuda Grass** and **Zoysia** don't do well.

Why grow a grass which is not green all the time? The reason is that Southern summer grasses are stronger, tougher, and make better turf than the evergreen grasses. You will need to make a type-to-grow decision based on your lawn's use. When does it get the most use? Is it sunny or shady? Is it essential to your landscape to have an evergreen lawn?

If you decide that a summer grass lawn fits your needs, the time to plant is after frost danger has passed and the ground begins to warm in March or April. You can plant Southern summer grasses from that time until about the first of August, even later if you want to solid-sod the entire area. It is best to finish solid-sodding a month before frost danger in your area to allow the grass time to develop good roots in the underlying soil before it goes dormant. Otherwise, the grass may not survive the following winter.

Summer grasses like Centipede are dormant and brown all winter but start greening up in the spring.

Exposure Requirements For Southern Grasses

GRASS	EXPOSURE
Bermuda Grass	Full sun
Bluegrass	Medium Shade
Centipede	Full Sun to Light Shade
Chewing Fescue	Light to Medium Shade
Creeping Red Fescue	Light to Medium Shade
St. Augustine	Full Sun to Light Shade
Kentucky 31 and Turf-Type Fescues	Full Sun to Light Shade
Zoysia	Full Sun to Light Shade

Soil Preparation

Lawns are long-lasting, like permanent foundation shrub plantings, perennial beds, and home fruit orchards. Prepare the soil for your new lawn as carefully as for any other permanent plantings. Soil preparation for summer lawns is similar to preparation for evergreen lawns described in the article "Planting or Reseeding Evergreen Grasses" in the March Chapter. There is one important difference for areas growing summer grass lawns, however; *do not* apply lime when growing **Centipede, Zoysia**, and **St. Augustine** grasses. These plants need soils with a lower pH than evergreen grasses. It helps to lime common and hybrid **Bermuda Grass** lawn areas at planting time, but not each year as you do on evergreen grasses.

Centipede lawns turn green in the spring and remain thick and beautiful until frost next fall.

Seeding, Sodding, and Solid Sodding Summer Grasses

Summer grasses are planted from seed, sod or sprigs, or using blocks laid solid over prepared ground. You can buy seed of common **Bermuda Grass** and **Centipede**. But, you *must* sod the hybrid **Bermuda Grasses, Emerald Zoysia**, and **St. Augustine (Charleston Grass)**. I also prefer to sod **Centipede** because the seeds are extremely small, expensive, and difficult to germinate in bare ground unless it is prepared almost perfectly.

Sow common **Bermuda Grass** seed carefully since they are small. Use 2 lbs. of seed per 1000 sq. ft. of lawn area. Mix seed with an equal amount of dry sand to make seeding easier and more uniform. Divide the mixture in half and seed one-half walking lengthwise and one-half crosswise. Cover the seed by raking *very* lightly to prevent covering the tiny seed too deeply.

Sod can be planted by either cutting the blocks into four-inch plugs and planting one plug per one or two square feet or, in the case of **Bermuda Grass** or **Centipede** and **St. Augustine**, by pulling the block apart and planting the sprigs. I prefer planting four-inch plugs. **Zoysia** is best planted as plugs.

Solid-sodding is popular since it provides an instant lawn. Well-laid sod on well-prepared soil will quickly provide a beautiful lawn. Plugging or sprigging a lawn takes several months to cover an area completely.

Reseeding or Renovating an Old Lawn

Summer grass lawns may eventually weaken and thin. Weeds and weed grasses indicate that the soil may be compacted and depleted. Renovation starts with determining how much good grass is left in the lawn. If you have at least one good plant per square foot, renovation is possible. In the winter before your grass greens up, kill the weeds and weed grasses with a weed killer which is recommended for your base grass. After weeds and weed grasses are dead, wait three or four weeks to reseed or plug the bare or thin areas. Aerate the area with a plug-type machine which can be rented at most garden rental shops. Fertilize with slow-release, high-nitrogen lawn fertilizer. Work the bare areas with a potato hook, mixing in peat moss if possible. Broadcast a seed and sand mix (the same as when planting a new lawn) over the bare or thin areas.

Plugging sod into bare areas is a good way to renovate an old lawn. Work thin or bare areas with a potato hook and mix in peat moss or compost. Use a trowel or bulb planter to make the hole, then set the sod plug.

Watering a New or Renovated Lawn

Summer grasses grow rapidly as the new seeds or plugs begin to grow and need plenty of rain. If there is no significant rainfall for one week, water your lawn with a sprinkler. I prefer the pulsating types which give an even distribution of water over an entire area. Place a straight-sided can or glass halfway between the sprinkler and the outer fall of water. Run the sprinkler until water puddles on the ground. Measure the amount of water in the glass. If there is less than one-half inch in the container, let the puddles soak in, then start watering again until there is at least one-half inch in the container. It is best to apply one inch at a time, but if water keeps puddling or begins to run off, move your sprinkler after one-half inch has accumulated in the container. Water again after a week of no rain if you applied an inch, or again after three days if you applied one-half inch. Shallow watering can be very damaging to a lawn by causing roots to remain near the surface. These roots dry out quickly when it is hot. Proper watering helps roots develop downward, where they can find moisture.

Cutting a New or Renovated Lawn

Cut newly reseeded lawns as soon as all grasses, new and old, reach the proper cutting height for the type. Newly plugged lawns must be cut much higher since the wheels of the mower will be lower in relation to the plug than when a lawn is covered with grass. The plugs need to be cut enough to make them spread, but cutting too much will damage the clump.

SUMMER LAWN CUTTING HEIGHTS*

Common Bermuda Grass	2 inches
Hybrid Bermuda Grass	1 to 1 $1/2$ inches
Centipede Grass	1 $1/2$ to 2 inches
St. Augustine Grass	2 to 2 $1/2$ inches
Zoysia (all types)	1 to 2 inches

* The number of inches above a hard surface like a driveway that you set the blade on.

LAWN ACTIVITIES FOR APRIL:

Plant

☛ Continue planting evergreen grasses (all **fescues** and **bluegrasses**) as soon as possible. They need plenty of cool weather to establish themselves before summer arrives. This includes installation of new lawns as well as reseeding of established ones.*

☛ After the danger of frost is over and the ground begins to warm, begin seeding or sodding all summer lawn grasses like **Bermuda Grass**, **Centipede**, **St. Augustine**, and **Zoysia**.†

Fertilize

☛ Fertilize evergreen grasses with a complete lawn fertilizer containing a slow-release form of nitrogen if it wasn't done previously this spring.‡

☛ Fertilize summer grasses like **Bermuda Grass**, **Centipede**, **St. Augustine**, and **Zoysia** with a high nitrogen, slow-release fertilizer as soon as the danger of frost has passed, if it wasn't done last month. (For **Centipede** lawns, use a fertilizer designated for that type of grass.) This application will be good for about 90 days.‡

* See "Planting or Reseeding Evergreen Lawns," p. 71

† See "Planting and Reseeding Summer Lawns," p. 98

‡ See "Fertilizing and Controlling Weeds in Lawns," p. 73

Spray

☛ Spray weed-filled areas where you want to plant a new summer grass lawn. Use Round-up to kill all weeds, weed grasses, and undesirable grasses. Wait at least two weeks before preparing the ground and seeding or sodding.

Cut

☛ As summer lawns begin to green, start cutting them on a regular basis.

☛ Cut grasses at the proper height:

SUMMER GRASSES	HEIGHT
Common Bermuda Grass	2 inches
Hybrid Bermuda Grass	1 to 1 $^1/_2$ inches
Centipede	1 $^1/_2$ to 2 inches
St. Augustine	2 to 2 $^1/_2$ inches
Zoysia (all types)	1 to 2 inches

EVERGREEN GRASSES	HEIGHT
Kentucky 31 Tall Fescue	3 to 3 $^1/_2$ inches
Turf-type Tall Fescues	3 inches
Fine Fescues	1 $^1/_2$ to 2 inches
Kentucky Bluegrass	2 to 2 $^1/_2$ inches

Water

☛ Water newly planted summer grass lawns with at least one inch of water per week when there has been no significant rainfall.†

Other

☛ Before fertilizing your summer lawn, be sure to aerate and dethatch it. This is done once a year.

† See "Planting and Reseeding Summer Lawns," p. 98

NOTES

May

IN THE SOUTHERN GARDEN

May is one of my favorite gardening times. Spring-flowering shrubs and bulbs and summer annuals in bloom give me inspiration to work in the garden until dark. As dusk arrives, the Chuck-Will's-Widow (Southern Whippoorwill) calls its mate, and the sweet smell of honeysuckle permeates the air. The weather is warmer now but not hot and muggy like summer. Since I never seem to finish all my April plans, it is pleasant in May to finish summer flower and vegetable plantings as well as spring jobs like fertilizing and trimming new growth on my shrubs.

In most of the South, May has two parts. The first is like a warmer April and the second is like a cooler June. It starts with planting and ends with harvesting. Suddenly our winter efforts pay off with vegetables to gather, early fruits to harvest, and bouquets of flowers to cut for the house.

By the end of the month, the weather is summer-like, with hotter days and warmer nights. May is also our second-driest month of the year, which means you'd better check your water hose for leaks and find your best nozzle and sprinkler, since new plantings will need some help when it doesn't rain for a week. This kind of weather also brings insects and diseases in abundance. We cringe and look frantically for our Japanese Beetle traps when we discover the first of these insidious creatures devouring the grape leaves. This is the time to become a good detective as we work in the garden or take a cool evening stroll. Watch for any sudden change in a plant's appearance and let your curiosity discover the cause. Quick action before problems multiply will save a lot of work trying to overcome them later on.

Since January, gardeners have been planning, planting, and dreaming of success. May is the first month this year's efforts pay off. In March and April, past years' plantings produced the splendor which makes the Southern spring world famous. In May, this year's dreams begin to make our gardens more beautiful and fruitful. Now is the time to relish every moment in the garden as you cut a rose, pick a mess of greens, or just enjoy the delicious air of late spring.

AT LEFT: *Oakleaf Hydrangea (Hydrangea quercifolia)*

American Red Maple (Acer rubrum) one of our finest shade trees

I. *Shade and Flowering Trees*

After the glorious spring blooms we have witnessed for the past couple of months, May can be somewhat of a letdown. The Bradford Pears have come and gone, the flowering cherries are finished, and even the dogwoods are concentrating on growing leaves. But on the other hand, with perfect timing nature calls forth the tree leaves just as the sun begins to threaten a little too much. Summer is definitely on its way.

If you don't already have a hammock, May is the month to hang one. Summer gardening means hoeing and mowing, and it is great to collapse afterwards into a hammock and enjoy the maintenance-free shade of a beautiful Red Maple.

Since May is usually a dry month, I don't even consider planting a new tree. It would mean regular watering and nursing to help the young tree through the dry month and then the blazing hot summer. Georgia summers are more suited to sitting under a big shade tree than worrying about a small newly planted one.

TREE ACTIVITIES FOR MAY:

Plant

☛ B&B and container-grown deciduous and evergreen trees may still be planted, but do so with *extreme* caution. Soak trees thoroughly after planting and then once a week until they are growing well.*

Prune

☛ Summer is not the time to prune tree limbs unless absolutely necessary. If there is a broken branch, however, remove the limb (including the jagged break or split) with a clean cut.†

Spray

☛ Look for damaging insects on evergreen trees like **magnolias** and **hollies**. Scale, spider mite, lacebug, leaf miner, spittlebug, and leaf hopper are the most prevalent in May. Use Cygon or Orthene to control. Do not use Cygon on **hollies**.‡

☛ Another leaf disease, Cedar-Apple Rust, may cause yellow spotting of **crabapple** and **apple** leaves. The alternate host of the disease is **Red Cedar**. Large gelatinous orange bodies will form on the cedar. Try to find and remove those found on **cedars** growing close to **crabapples** and **apples**. Spray the foliage of the **crabapples** and **apples** with Maneb or a complete home orchard spray.‡

☛ Watch for tiny gnat-like insects flying around **holly** trees. These are the adult form of leaf miners. As soon as you see them, spray the tree with Orthene to prevent further leaf damage.‡

☛ Protect flowering trees, like **flowering peaches** and **flowering plums**, from Japanese Beetle damage by spraying with Sevin or putting traps downwind from the tree.‡

☛ On occasion, insects and diseases may show up on trees. If you can't identify them, take a branch containing some of the infected area to your local nurseryman or Cooperative Extension Service agent for identification and recommended control measures.‡

Water

☛ Newly planted trees should be soaked once a week when there is no significant rainfall.**

Other

☛ Keep newly planted trees mulched to conserve moisture when it is hot and dry.††

☛ Be extremely careful when mowing or using a power trimmer around old and new trees. Do not hit or damage the bark. Even the slightest damage may make an entrance for borers or other damaging insects. This is true for all trees in landscaped or natural areas, including planted and native trees. **Dogwoods**, **flowering peaches**, **flowering plums**, and **flowering cherries** are particularly prone to borer damage.

* See "Planting Trees and Shrubs," p. 264
† See "Pruning Shade and Flowering Trees," p. 4
‡ See "Controlling Insects and Diseases," p. 80

‡ See "Controlling Insects and Diseases," p. 80
** See "Does Your Tree Have Enough Water?" p. 150
†† See "Mulching: A Lesson from Nature," p. 243

May-blooming Rhododendron

II. *Shrubs and Vines*

By May, most of the flowering shrubs like azaleas have finished blooming, but there are some Rhododendron and Mountain Laurel cultivars which have yet to bloom. They are the last in the succession of spring-flowering trees and shrubs. These shrubs could use a good fertilizing after they have finished blooming.

May is also the first month of the summer battle against insects and diseases. At the end of May we see the first Japanese Beetles. It is a little sad that we Southerners recognize Japanese Beetle bait as one of the scents of summer. That sweet smell brings to mind visions of clumsy Japanese Beetles smacking into the side of the trap and falling down through the yellow funnel into the bag below. Ah, summer.

SHRUB AND VINE ACTIVITIES FOR MAY:

Plant

☛ B&B and container-grown deciduous and evergreen shrubs may be planted now, but do so with *extreme* caution. Soak shrubs thoroughly after planting and once a week until they are growing well (be prepared to water all summer).*

☛ Container-grown woody vines like **Clematis**, **Carolina Jessamine**, and **Wisteria** can be planted with *extreme* care. Soak them thoroughly after planting and once a week until they are growing well.†

☛ Plant seeds or seedlings of annual vines like **Morning Glory**, **Moonflower**, **Scarlet Runner Beans**, and **Passion Flower** any time this month.

* See "Planting Trees and Shrubs," p. 264

† See "Growing Clematis and Other Southern Vines," p. 54

Prune

☛ Wait to prune spring-flowering evergreen shrubs like **Camellia, azalea, Rhododendron**, and **Mountain Laurel** until after they have finished blooming.‡

☛ Do not prune spring-flowering evergreen vines like **Carolina Jessamine** and **Confederate Jasmine** until after they finish blooming.‡

☛ Prune other spring-flowering deciduous shrubs like **Weigela** and **Oakleaf Hydrangea** after they have finished blooming.‡

☛ Evergreen shrubs like **Buford Holly** may be shaped by trimming new growth, but avoid removing all of the new shoots and cutting into last year's growth.

☛ Pruning summer-flowering shrubs like **Butterfly Bush** and **Althaea** this month can disturb their growth and bloom.

Fertilize

☛ Fertilize all spring-flowering shrubs and vines after they bloom. Use a 15-15-15 fertilizer on deciduous shrubs and vines and an azalea/camellia acid fertilizer on evergreens. Use roughly 1/2 pound per three feet of the shrub's height (the height before any pruning). This is usually done once a year.**

☛ **Rhododendrons** which bloom in April and May should be fertilized after they bloom with an azalea/camellia acid fertilizer. Use roughly 1/2 pound per three feet of the shrub's height, but check the directions of your specific brand. This is usually done once a year.**

☛ Fertilize **Rhododendron** cultivars which blossom in June after they finish blooming. Use roughly 1/2 pound per three feet of the shrub's height, but check the directions of your specific brand. This is usually done once a year.**

Spray

☛ Watch out for damaging insects on evergreens. Scale, aphids, spider mites, lacebug, leaf miner, spittlebug, and leaf hopper are the most prevalent in May. Use Cygon or Orthene to control them. Do not use Cygon on **hollies**.††

☛ **Azaleas** and **camellias** may develop grotesque swollen leaves. This condition is caused by a fungus called Azalea or Camellia Leaf Gall and is controlled by removing and disposing of affected leaves. Sprays are ineffective once the disease is in the leaf. It may be unsightly, but it is not harmful to the plant.††

☛ Inspect established shrubs for signs of scale. This insect is particularly bad on evergreens, especially **Euonymus**. Control it with Cygon except on **hollies**; use Orthene on **hollies**.††

☛ **Boxwoods** and **hollies** may show signs of leaf damage due to the leaf miner. At first, the damage appears as tiny pin pricks in the foliage. Later, as the miner develops, the leaf will be discolored. Spray when first seen with Cygon except on **hollies**; use Orthene on **hollies**. Both are systemic insecticides and can kill the young miner inside the leaf. ††

☛ Check **Red Tip Photinias** frequently for signs of leaf spot. When you see it, immediately spray affected and adjacent plants with Daconil.††

Water

☛ Slowly soak shrubs and vines if there has been no significant rain in a week, especially if they were planted this year.‡‡

Other

☛ Mulch shrubs to conserve moisture during the summer. Do not allow the mulch to crowd or pack against the lower stems and trunks. This can be damaging during the summer.***

---

‡ See "Pruning Flowering Shrubs and Vines," p. 31

** See "How to Fertilize Shrubs and Vines," p. 30

†† See "Controlling Insects and Diseases," p. 80

‡‡ See "Proper Watering," p. 130

*** See "Mulching: A Lesson from Nature," p. 243

III. *Fruits*

In the cold of winter when we planted a new fruit tree, I didn't pay as much attention to the label as I wish I had. Here we are in May and the early summer cultivars of peaches and plums are beginning to ripen. Back in January, early summer and mid-summer didn't seem so far apart. For many years to come, though, I will have to watch neighbors harvest early cultivars while I continue the battle against insects and diseases on my later-ripening ones.

Depending on the year, there might be some blackberries by the end of the month. I have a special plastic pail that I use during the summer for blackberries, raspberries, and blueberries. It is a 1970s orange color with a metal handle. I keep it on the porch as a reminder to leave the house on warm summer evenings and walk down to check on the berries. While in May and early June, I might return with only a few blackberries to top my ice cream (I eat most before they reach the pail), by August I am returning with a pail full of blueberries worthy of several pies.

FRUIT ACTIVITIES FOR MAY:

Plant

☞ Plant container-grown fruits with *extreme* caution. If you do, soak them thoroughly after planting and once a week until they are growing well.*

Fertilize

☞ Fertilize **blueberries** lightly for the second time this season when they bloom (most will have done this last month). Use an azalea/camellia acid fertilizer but do it sparingly. **Blueberries** can be damaged by over-fertilizing.

Spray

☞ Continue a regular control program for fruit insects and diseases. A complete home orchard spray is the most practical method of control. Continue applications at recommended intervals until the fruit ripens. Brown rot on **peaches, plums, cherries,** and **nectarines** is bad this month now that fruits are becoming soft prior to ripening.†

☞ Fire blight may attack **pears** and **apples** this month. You can identify it as a problem when tip growth turns black and hangs on the tree or when a twig dies back (the bark will appear shrunken). Eradication is the only practical control. Examine the dying twig and notice any shriveling bark below the dead leaves. Cut the twig several inches below this area. *Sterilize the blades of your shears between cuts by dipping them in alcohol or a bleach solution.* (There is an extremely exacting antibiotic spray control program for fire blight, but it is not practical for most homeowners.)

☞ Another leaf disease, Cedar-Apple Rust, may cause yellow spotting of **crabapple** and **apple** leaves. The alternate host of the disease is **Red Cedar**. Large gelatinous orange bodies will form on the **cedar**. Try to find and remove any found on **cedars** close to **crabapples** and **apples**. Spray the foliage of the **crabapples** and **apples** with Maneb or a complete home orchard spray. This disease is not a fatal one but can reduce the vigor of your fruit tree.†

☞ Watch for spider mites on **raspberries** and other semi-bush berries. You'll know they're there when the foliage has a silvery gray appearance. Spray with Kelthane to control this serious pest.†

☞ Spray **bunch grapes** with a complete home orchard spray to prevent brown rot and to control leaf worms.†

* See "Planting Trees and Shrubs," p. 264

† See "Controlling Insects and Diseases," p. 80

† See "Controlling Insects and Diseases," p. 80

Water

☛ May can be a dry month. Soak newly planted fruit trees thoroughly when there has been no significant rain in the past week.‡

Other

☛ **Peaches** and **plums** often shed small fruits. This may indicate that too many were set for the tree to support. Don't worry about it, though; it is a perfectly natural process and the remaining fruits should mature well.

☛ Be careful when mowing in orchard areas not to hit the bark of fruit trees with the mower. Any damage to the bark will provide an entrance place for borers.

☛ Keep fruits mulched with pine straw to prevent weeds and grasses from competing for water and fertilizer.**

‡ See "Proper Watering," p. 130

** See "Mulching: A Lesson from Nature," p. 243

NOTES

IV. *Roses*

'Harry G. Hastings' rose blooms well in hot weather.

In May we see the first big rose bloom. What a joy! Ever since severe pruning in early March, roses have been steadily growing new, robust canes ready to sustain the amazingly long summer bloom. This big bloom is not the end of the story but the beginning. All summer our plants will be blessing our mornings with new buds and our evenings with fully opened masterpieces.

Don't fall into the trap, however, of thinking that untended roses will bloom happily all summer. Grooming, proper cutting, fertilizing, insect and disease control, and watering are all necessary steps to keeping your roses beautiful throughout the season.

GROOMING ROSES

Roses are amazing plants. Not only do they produce beautiful flowers to decorate our gardens and homes, but they *keep* producing. Roses have one of the longest blooming seasons of all Southern woody plants. With a little encouragement, we can help them bloom productively throughout the summer.

In late February or early March we severely pruned our roses back to about 12 inches in height. The remaining canes represented old growth. From that 12-inch-tall plant, the leaf buds broke and sprouted new canes which grew rapidly in March and April. Probably by April, some of those canes were ready to support a few flowers. If not last month, however, there will definitely be some rose blooms in May.

As the bloom season begins, the rose grooming season begins as well. Luckily, rose grooming is not very complicated. Rose canes have different types of leaves: three-leaflet sets and five-leaflet sets. As you cut a rose or remove a spent flower, always cut the cane just above where a five-leaflet set originates. These sets lie beside a bud which will send up a shoot bearing a healthy flower. Three-leaflet sets lie beside a bud which will not produce as good a flower. By cutting back to just above a five-leaflet set, you will be removing unnecessary growth and forcing growth

into the most productive area of the plant.

You may notice that there is more than one five-leaflet set coming from any given cane and thus many different spots to which we could cut back. Our first instinct is to cut back to the first five-leaflet set we come to as we remove a flower. This is not always the best method. You should consider the overall structure of the plant whenever you cut. I remember one rose bush I let grow rather haphazardly. By the end of the season, it had one large cane jutting out three feet to one side, making it one of the most awkward, top-heavy roses I have ever seen.

A good rose plant is well-balanced, has at least three or four healthy main canes, and is somewhat

Cut rose flowers slightly above a five-leaflet group.

Prune to a bud facing outward for a wider growing plant.

bud opens before the lateral buds, and it will die before the others. Prune out this flower by cutting the flower stem at the point it arises from the candelabra. When the *whole* cluster has finished blooming, then cut the cluster's stem back to where a five-leaflet set originates.

Besides cutting back to a five-leaflet set, the good groomer also removes weak, spindly, dead, and diseased canes as they occur. Unfortunately, it is hard to make it through the season without encountering some die-back or stem disease. If you remove these canes immediately, you can minimize the extent of their damage. Leaving a diseased cane on a rose will enable the disease to spread and infect other areas of the plant.

Some people prefer to leave roses on the plant to bloom rather than cutting them. Try to cut back these flowers as soon as they have dropped their petals. Dead flowers are an enticement to insects and diseases. It is also important to remove them before the plant sends its growing energy into seed formation.

One final thing to watch for is suckers. Suckers are especially common on young two- or three-year-old roses, though they may occur at any time. Remember that roses are grafted onto an understock. The understock has vigorous roots but not the kind of flowers you would like growing in your garden. All growth above the graft union (the swollen area below the limbs) is from the desired rose. A sucker is part of the understock which is growing from below the graft union. If you let the sucker develop, it will steal nutrients from your roses and never produce any desirable flowers itself. Try to catch suckers early. Dig down to the spot where they are growing from the plant. If possible, remove the sucker by pulling it off with your hand. At the same time you might manage to pull a small piece of wood from the base containing the sucker's bud. This will keep it from growing back again. If you can't pull it off, cut it as close as possible to the point where it originates.

Rose grooming is about a five-minute process. The five minutes you take to cut back canes and remove others could be the most economical use of time in your rose garden. Let the sight of a fresh new rose bud on a summer morning provide the impetus you need to spend that little extra time working on your roses.

open in the middle to allow light and air to reach all the developing buds. When we cut back to a five-leaflet set, we can manipulate the future growth of the plant so that it continues to grow into a well-structured plant. If you think a higher-up set might eventually grow into the middle and fill the open space, you might choose instead to cut back to an outward facing set. If your plant is lopsided, you might cut back to a set which will grow the other way and balance the structure of the plant.

To a large extent, grooming is just like the severe rose pruning done at the beginning of spring, except it is performed on new wood rather than old. That is your only limitation. It is best not to groom a rose by cutting back into the old growth. Also, leave at least two buds when you prune back this year's new wood. If you do prune a cane back to the last bud (probably an inch or two from the old growth), you have no recourse if that bud dies or fails to produce a healthy cane.

Grandiflora and some **Hybrid Tea** roses will have a cluster of flowers called a candelabra. The center

ROSE ACTIVITIES FOR MAY:

Plant

☛ Container-grown roses may still be planted but do so with *extreme* care and be prepared to water often. It is too late to plant bare-root roses.*

Prune

☛ Groom roses constantly. Never leave a dead or dying stem on the plant because the disease will spread to healthy canes. Also remove weak, broken, or spindly shoots.†

☛ Remove spent flowers immediately. Seed formation retards stem growth and the production of new blossoms.†

Fertilize

☛ Continue fertilizing with a complete rose fertilizer on your six-to-eight-week program. I use a combination fertilizer and systemic insecticide to give my roses the nutrients they need as well as to control many insects.

Spray

☛ Continue with your complete rose spray program every 10 to 14 days according to the directions. Use a combination insecticide and fungicide spray and continue applications through September.

☛ Watch out for Japanese Beetles. Normal spray programs will not control these pests. Use Japanese Beetle traps or supplement your spray program with Sevin.‡

☛ Blackspot is the most serious disease of summer. Consistent applications of your regular spray should prevent heavy damage.‡

☛ During hot, dry weather, thrips may become a problem. Rose blossoms with thrip damage will first turn brown on the petal edges. Check for these pests by pulling one of the discolored flowers apart. Rod-shaped thrips will be at the base of the petal. Thrips are controlled with Orthene.‡

Water

☛ Use a soaker hose to water rose beds. It will keep foliage dry and help prevent the spread of diseases.**

Other

☛ Keep roses well mulched with pine straw during the summer but do not pile mulch against the crown or lower stems. Many problems like cankers and botrytis occur when mulch covers the lower stems.††

☛ Remember to cut flowers and flower clusters correctly. Always make the cut above a joint where a five-leaflet originates. Cutting at this point encourages a strong new shoot and blossom to form.†

☛ Many **Hybrid Tea** and **Grandiflora** roses have several flowers in a cluster (called a candelabra) which may not all bloom at the same time. Remove each spent flower in the cluster as it finishes blooming. When all the flowers are done, cut the whole cluster stalk back to a five-leaflet set.†

---

* See "Planting Trees and Shrubs," p. 264

† See "Grooming Roses," p. 110

‡ See "Controlling Insects and Diseases," p. 80

‡ See "Controlling Insects and Diseases," p. 80

** See "Proper Watering," p. 130

†† See "Mulching: A Lesson from Nature," p. 243

† See "Grooming Roses," p. 110

Foxglove (Digitalis purpurea) has tall spikes of colorful flowers.

V. *Flowers and Colorful Garden Plants*

The month of May is dichotomous. The first half is still spring and the second half is summer. Cool weather flowers will still be blooming this month, and warm weather plants will be beginning to bloom. The result is an amazing month of beautiful flowers.

Columbine, snapdragons, hollyhocks, and Foxglove continue to bloom in May. These flowers like a little cool weather, though, and once the heat of late May and June arrives they are ready to retire. Others like daisies, Purple Cone-Flower, Rudbeckia, and Astilbe don't mind the heat and will keep us company throughout the summer.

Our newly planted annuals like Salvia, Zinnia, Vinca, Impatiens, Geranium, and Begonia will also add to the month's bloom despite their fledgling size. They will continue to grow and flower throughout the summer, keeping our gardens colorful all the way to frost.

FLOWER ACTIVITIES FOR MAY:

Plant

☛ You can still plant tender flowering annuals like **Ageratum**, **Begonia**, **Coleus**, **Geranium**, **Impatiens**, and **Salvia** with excellent success. Also plant perennials like **Astilbe**, **Shasta Daisy**, **Purple Cone-Flower**, and **Rudbeckia**. These plants will bloom and be beautiful from now until frost if you care for them properly.*

☛ Continue to plant tender annual aromatic and culinary herbs like **anise**, **sweet basil**, **coriander**, **dill**, **sweet marjoram**, and **fennel** purchased at the nursery or grown from seeds.

☛ Annual vines like **Moonflower**, **Morning Glory**, and **Scarlet Runner Bean** can be planted all month.

☛ **Cannas**, **dahlias**, and other tender bulbous and root plants should be planted outside as soon as possible.

☛ **Elephant Ears**, **Caladiums**, and other tender tuberous plants started inside can now be planted outside.

☛ Choose carefully the right type of plant for each situation. Sunny, semi-sunny, and shady spots should have plants which take that particular exposure.

☛ Flowers seldom do well in damp, sticky soil. Correct any drainage problems before you plant. Perlite is an excellent soil amendment for this purpose.*

Prune

☛ Pinch **Chrysanthemum** and **Dahlia** shoots when they are four to six inches long to make the plants bushy and strong. Well-pinched plants will have more flowers than unpinched plants.†

☛ Do not prune **Chrysanthemum** or **Dahlia** with shears. Pinch the terminal bud out of the main shoot as well as the laterals. Improper pruning will cause crown flower buds which never flower as well as flower buds from the shoots.†

☛ Cut back foliage of spring-flowering bulbs like **daffodils**, **hyacinths**, and **tulips** *after* it has started turning yellow. Cutting back green foliage will reduce the bulb's stored food and result in smaller flowers next year.

Fertilize

☛ Fertilize annuals, biennials, and perennials on the following schedule: apply a good starter fertilizer like 15-15-15 on new and emerging plants. After six to eight weeks, switch to a good fruit and flower fertilizer like 5-10-15, and fertilizer every six to eight weeks for the rest of the season.

Spray

☛ Watch carefully for insects and diseases on flowers. Insects are the greatest problem. Fast, succulent growth is highly susceptible to aphids, spider mites, leaf hoppers, thrips, and worm damage. Orthene is an excellent all-around control.‡

☛ **Geraniums** may be attacked by worms. When you first see them, dust your plants with Dipel or spray with Thuricide (both are forms of BT, an excellent biological control).‡

Water

☛ Water plants thoroughly with about one inch of water per week if there has been no significant rainfall.**

Other

☛ Mulch flower beds to control weeds and conserve moisture. I like to use grass clippings as a flower bed mulch. Let clippings dry on the lawn and then pack them around plants and on areas of bare ground.††

☛ Dig and separate spring-flowering bulbs like **Narcissus, tulips,** and **hyacinths** after the foliage has died. This is necessary if the clumps are crowded and this year's flowers were small. Store in a cool place until you set them out in the fall after the first frost.

---

* See "How to Plant a Flower Bed," p. 62

† See "Grooming and Pinching Flowers," p. 137

‡ See "Controlling Insects and Diseases," p. 80

** See "Proper Watering," p. 130

†† See "Mulching: A Lesson from Nature," p. 243

VI. *Vegetables*

May is usually thought of as a time to finish planting warm season crops, but for those of us who planted cool weather crops, it's also harvest time! Broccoli, cabbage, cauliflower, Brussels sprouts, and green onions should all be about ready to eat. I especially love these crops because they motivate me. Heading down to the garden in May to hoe, spray, train, and water doesn't seem like quite as much work if I can return to the house with a few vegetables to stock the refrigerator.

The first harvest of the season brings that inevitable encounter with non-gardeners. Each year I plant more vegetables than my family will need so that I can give some away. It always seems like such a good idea to give my produce to non-gardeners so they will be impressed by the wonderful taste of homegrown vegetables. In the back of my head is the thought that they will be so impressed as to rush out, rent a roto-tiller, and become vegetable gardeners themselves. To my dismay, non-gardeners often act like you had unexpectedly gone grocery shopping for them. They seem confused that you would show up on their doorstep with a basket of broccoli. Someday I'll learn that vegetable gardening is an experience that can't be summed up with one clump of broccoli. Half the reason a homegrown broccoli tastes so good is that it is filled with the memories of happy afternoons in the garden. Those memories are much harder to give away.

FERTILIZING, SPRAYING, AND WATERING VEGETABLES

Vegetable seeds have sprouted, and the strong plants you so carefully set out some time ago seem to double in size right before your eyes. Vegetables are growing well, but it takes careful tending to have the harvests you dreamed about. Since vegetables grow rapidly and quickly produce large numbers of edible parts, their needs and problems are different from other annuals in the garden. Besides sunlight, vegetables need nutrients (fertilizer), water, and good growing conditions to develop and produce abundantly. Unfortunately, the conditions which help vegetables do well also make weeds and competing plants develop rapidly. Also, rapid growth makes growing vegetables highly susceptible to insect and disease attacks. But despite all obstacles, growing vegetables is an easily realized dream.

Fertilizing

In April ("Planting a Vegetable Garden"), I discussed how to prepare and plant in order to obtain the best results. I stressed the need to properly prepare the soil, apply dolomitic limestone, and fertilize with a 15-15-15 fertilizer. Now that vegetables are up, it is time to keep them growing with a continuous fertilizing program.

Gardeners do not "feed" vegetable plants, despite what we are told by fertilizer advertisements and the directions on the bag. Fertilizers provide the basic nutrients which plants must have to feed themselves through the process of photosynthesis. Vegetables need large amounts of all three major nutrients: nitrogen, phosphorous, and potash, plus small amounts of minor nutrients like calcium, zinc, magnesium, boron, and sulfur. Soils usually have enough of the minor nutrients, except for magnesium. That is why I recommend using dolomitic limestone, which contains magnesium, when preparing the garden instead of plain limestone, which does not. However, some vegetable fertilizers contain a complete range of minor nutrients which give even better results.

Fertilizers are identified by their nutrient content in a precise way. The most important information a gardener needs are the three numbers found on every bag, like 15-15-15. This tells you that this bag of fertilizer contains 15% nitrogen, 15% phosphorous, and 15% potash. The analysis table on the bag also tells you which materials each of the major nutrients is derived from, as well as which minor element is in the mixture and how much of it is included.

There are other ways to provide these nutrients to plants. Many organic substances like manures contain one or more of the major nutrients, though usually in small amounts. The plant does not care whether the nitrogen, phosphorous, or potash come from a plant or animal source or a 15-15-15 inorganic fertilizer, so if you prefer to use organic fertilizers as a nutrient source as well as soil-building humus, do so; but use higher amounts since they contain less of the needed nutrients. Organic fertilizers must also list the nutrient percentages on the bag. Carefully note these percentages and use the right amount of organic fertilizer to provide the correct amounts of each nutrient the plant needs. You may find that one organic fertilizer does not contain *all* the necessary nutrients and you will need to purchase additional ones to provide the total nutrient requirements for the plant.

Nutrients in organic fertilizers become available more slowly than those in inorganic fertilizers; therefore you must apply them well before planting time so nutrients are available when vegetable plants need them. Organic fertilizers usually last longer than inorganic fertilizers.

No matter what the source of the essential nutrients, vegetables must have them to produce well. I use organic matter derived from compost, from commercial organics, and from cover crops for soil building purposes, and then I use inorganic fertilizers to help my vegetables grow and produce well. Inorganic fertilizers cost less per unit of nutrient and also give a more even release of the nutrients in the soil so that each stage of the vegetable plant's development has the correct amounts when needed.

Vegetables need different nutrients for various stages of their development. With the exception of **sweet corn** and vegetables grown for greens, they need all three nutrients when they begin to grow, and more phosphate and potash as they set fruits. Therefore, I start with an even number fertilizer like 15-15-15 at planting time and follow with a 5-10-15 fertilizer about six weeks later. A good rate for both these applications is one pound per ten feet of row. **Sweet corn** and vegetables for greens need a different schedule. I use 15-15-15 at planting time for both, and on **sweet corn**, I apply only ammonium nitrate at the rate of 1/2 pound per 10 feet of row when the plants are knee high. On greens, I use another one pound of 15-15-15 per 10 feet of row about six weeks after planting. If **sweet corn** is not a dark green when it tassles, I apply an additional 1/2 pound of 15-15-15 per 10 feet of row. Continue to fertilize long-standing crops like **tomatoes, pepper, eggplant, cucumber,** and **okra** with 5-10-15 every six weeks through their

Use a flower pot filled with fertilizer to side dress easily.

producing season at a rate of one pound per 10 feet of row.

Applying fertilizers after the initial application at planting time is easy. Cultivate to make the soil loose, then with a pointed hoe, open a small, shallow trench at the edge of the bed or about one foot from the row of plants when they are planted flat. After fertilizing, pull soil into the small trench to prevent the fertilizer from washing away from the plants' roots. This is called side-dressing. Use the eight-inch-pot method of distribution described in April's "Planting a Vegetable Garden."

Controlling Insects and Diseases

As vegetables grow rapidly, insects and diseases love to feed on their tender foliage. Good insect and disease control is essential to have clean, healthy harvests. It is so discouraging to shuck a beautiful ear of **sweet corn** and find a large earworm having it for dinner before you do.

Diseases are generally less of a problem than insects. Plant breeders have been very successful in developing cultivars with resistance or immunity to many plant diseases. It is essential for gardeners in the South, where hot, humid conditions are perfect for many diseases, to use disease resistance as a criteria when choosing vegetable cultivars to grow. When I was growing up, if **tomatoes** were planted for two years in the same part of the garden, nematodes, fusarium wilt, or verticillium wilt would ruin the second year's crops. Now the best **tomato** cultivars (VFN resistant varieties) have resistance to all three of these problems, plus resistance to other major diseases like leaf spot. Many other vegetable types and cultivars also have disease resistance. *Be sure the vegetables you select have the highest disease resistance ratings.*

I would rather not spray or dust any vegetable. It makes me queasy to think that I might possibly eat some chemical used for killing insects or controlling diseases. Over the years I have learned that planting time is extremely important in keeping destructive insects off my vegetables. If you plant **sweet corn** as soon as frost danger has past, it will mature before earworms become a serious problem, whereas **sweet corn** planted a month later matures after earworm and stalk borer populations become serious problems. If you plant **cabbage, broccoli,** and **cauliflower** as soon as danger of hard freezes is over, they will mature before the onslaught of cabbage loopers. **Peppers, eggplant,** and **tomatoes** planted too early (while the nights are still very cool) are growing in the garden when flea beetles are bad, so wait to plant them until the nights warm up.

No matter how hard you try to plant at the right time, insects can be a problem, especially on crops which grow for many weeks or months. Some type of insect and disease control program is necessary. Watch vegetables for the first signs of any insect problems. If you catch them early, you won't need to spray or dust as often.

There are safe biological materials which can be used with no concern to your own health. Bacillus thuringiensis (BT) is an excellent control for soft worms but *most* effective when sprayed or dusted before they get too large and tough. Spray or dust crops with BT as soon as you see the first worms on

Dusting with BT (Bacillus thuringienses) prevents green worms from ruining broccoli.

your vegetables. Spray or dust **sweet corn** with BT as soon as the tassel peeks out of the whorl. Then dust again when the tiny ear appears and once a week until the silks are brown and corn is ready to harvest. Aphids, flea beetles, squash bugs, and a myriad of other insects are more persistent, but Sevin will control most of them.

Diseases may be a problem, especially during periods of excess rain and high temperatures. Some are hard to identify because the fungi cannot be seen with the naked eye. If you suspect a disease is attacking your vegetables, take an affected leaf to a nursery, garden center, or your Cooperative Extension Service for identification and suggested control measures.

Insect and disease control materials which are not specifically meant for vegetables should not be used. Read the label carefully to see if it is appropriate for the produce you are growing. Also, strictly follow the guidelines for the number of days you must wait after a specific chemical's last application before you can harvest.

Not all disease-like problems are caused by bacteria or fungi. Some, like blossom end rot on **tomatoes** and **peppers**, are caused by a calcium deficiency in the soil. If you lime the soil before planting, you will help prevent this physiological disease, and if you spray with a calcium spray when you find fruits with the tell-tale corky black bottom, you will prevent future fruits from being affected.

Your Cooperative Extension Service is as concerned about safety in the vegetable garden as you are. Get them to send you their vegetable insect and disease control guide to be sure you are using the safest materials possible on the vegetables you grow and eat.

Watering Vegetables

Vegetables require a great deal of water to support their rapid growth and fruit development. Since droughts reduce growth, yields, size, and quality of crops, water your vegetables with at least an inch of water per week, either as rainfall or irrigation. Most gardeners water vegetables with the same sprinkler they use for lawns and flower beds, which is fine, especially if it is a impulse sprinkler. Always measure the amount of water applied with a sprinkler. This is described in detail in the June chapter ("Proper Watering").

Water vegetables in the morning or early afternoon up to about 2:00 p.m. so the foliage will be dry before the cool, still evening. Insects and diseases multiply rapidly under cool, moist conditions and can cause extensive damage.

Weeds Cause Problems

Weed-free vegetable gardens produce the best crops and harvests. Weeds rob plants of fertilizer and water, make excellent harbors for insects, and serve as hosts for many diseases. Hoeing, cultivating with a tiller, and mulching reduce weed infestations and keep gardens healthier and more productive. These are not glamorous jobs, but your reward will be a clean, neat, and productive garden. It is hot work, so try to do it in the cooler parts of the day.

Training Vegetables off the Ground

Pole beans and **cucumbers** are up and growing, and **tomatoes, peppers,** and **eggplants** seem to double in size when you blink your eyes. Now gardeners are faced with a decision: whether to allow the plants to grow on the ground or provide some sort of support to train and hold them off the ground.

We have a few facts to guide us: **pole beans** must have support; **cucumbers** growing on the ground become spotted in rainy weather and often rot; **tomatoes** grow all over everywhere, and limbs break or lean on the ground; and **pepper** and **eggplant** limbs break easily under the weight of the fruits. All of these vegetables do best with some sort of support. The type of support varies not only with the type of vegetable, but also with the size of the garden and the gardener's wishes. I have used many different types. Following are the descriptions, advantages, and disadvantages of the types of supports most often used.

Pole Beans

Teepee supports are widely used in small gardens where only a few bean plants are grown and only when they are planted flat (not in beds). Gardens must be planned for their use since you use several plants per teepee and they don't naturally fall in a straight row. Place three poles in the ground at an

Train pole beans on a teepee made of 8-foot stakes.

angle so their tops come together like an Indian teepee. Place the base of the poles three feet apart, which is an ideal distance for **pole bean** plants. Tie the three together where they meet at the top. I prefer to plant the beans *after* setting the poles. Plant two to three seeds at the foot of every pole and let them grow up the poles. **Beans** are easily harvested when using this method.

Pole and Ridge training is excellent for larger gardens because it covers two rows of **pole beans** at a time, whether they are planted flat or on beds. With this method, you can seed *before* or *after* setting the poles. To begin with, set a pole in each row so they angle up and meet over the middle between the two rows. Use poles which are long enough for you to walk under when they are tied together. Continue to set poles at each hill of beans. If you haven't planted yet, set the poles three feet apart in the row and sow seeds at the foot of the poles. After all the poles are set and tied, place and tie a ridge pole in the "v" formed by the joining of the two poles over the middle. Lastly, tie heavy cords or flexible wires from the last two poles on either end to a secure stake. This prevents wind from blowing along the row and toppling the whole system like dominos. I have experienced this personally. One year I had the most beautiful **pole beans** ever, using the "pole and ridge" system. Rain drenched the heavily laden vines, then a strong wind blew along the row, pulling my support stakes out of the ground and pulling down my beautiful structure along with all its beans. My advice is to drive the stakes deeply into the ground and secure them *firmly* at both ends of the row.

Tall bamboo stakes make excellent poles for staking crops.

The *Tall Stake* method is commonly used and simple to construct. Plant **pole beans** three feet apart in rows on beds or in flat ground. After they sprout, drive an eight-foot pole two to three feet into the ground at each group of sprouting beans so they will quickly climb the poles. The disadvantage of this system is that the beans grow taller than the poles and get all over everything. Gardeners use several variations of the basic system to try to overcome this disadvantage. You can tie strings between the poles for the vines to run on, or you can tie ridge poles at the top of the poles on which the vines can run.

No matter which system you decide to use, I find the best poles are bamboo. They are strong, light, and easy to work with.

Cucumbers

The *Stake and String* method of training **cucumbers** is widely used in private gardens and on commercial farms. Plant **cucumbers** two to three feet apart on a bed or in a flat row. When they sprout, drive an eight-foot 1" x 1" stake at least two feet in the ground at the beginning of the row. Skip two plants, then drive the second stake, continuing to set stakes with two plants between. Always set the last stake at the end of the row, even if there is only one plant between the last two stakes. Now tie a heavy cord between the stakes two feet off the ground, securely tying to the two end stakes. Then tie a second string two feet higher in the same way. Continue until you reach the top of the stakes.

When the **cucumber** plants are two feet long, fasten them with a twist'em-type plant tie or string to the first string down the row of stakes. The **cucumber** runners have tendrils which wrap around the strings, allowing them to climb up the ladder of strings until they cover the system.

Fence Systems are sold in many garden centers. These consist of a heavy poly-vinyl mesh fence which can be attached to poles set at various distances in the row. Once the vine attaches to the mesh fence, they climb easily and cover the area.

Tomatoes

Everyone has their own pet method of training tomatoes. I much prefer a stake and string system similar to the one described above for **cucumbers**, even though I have used many others. Woe be to the writer who interferes with someone's successful way of training **tomatoes**. It is better to disagree on politics! With that said, I throw myself on your good will and describe several methods which I have used, showing the advantages and disadvantages of each.

The *Stake-and-String* method is basically the same as the **cucumber** method above. I like it because it keeps more air moving through the row of **tomatoes**, which reduces the amount of leaf disease, makes spraying or dusting for worms much easier, and makes harvesting fruits a simple matter since you can easily walk down the middles. You can plant *before* or *after* setting your stakes.

I have also used a variation of this method which is basically a type of fencing. Heavy posts are set at the end of each row and a #10 wire is attached at the top to a turnbuckle, which is used to tighten the wire. Plants are set every three feet under the wire. As they

Stake-and-String method of training reduces diseases on plants.

Set wire cages immediately after planting.

Wire Cages have become popular because they are easy to set over the plant. There are two main types of cages: (1) inverted cone, and (2) straight side. I prefer the inverted cone since it allows the top of the plant to develop more naturally. The disadvantage of wire cages is that heavy growing plants are held tightly and are subject to more disease than when they are open, as with the stake-and-string method. They are also more difficult to spray and harvest. The cages are placed *after* the plants are set in the garden.

Single Stakes are used by many gardeners. This is the easiest method if you have only a few plants. Since the stakes are set next to each plant, you must drive them into the ground when you plant. If you wait, you may severely damage the plants' roots when you drive the stake through them. The disadvantage of this system is that it takes a lot of work to keep tying the plant to a single stake as it grows taller.

Peppers and Eggplants

Peppers and **eggplants** differ from the viney crops above since they naturally grow into large bushes. However, I give them some support to prevent breaking of limbs and loss of fruit.

Single Stakes provide an easy way to handle a few plants. Use a large enough stake to hold up each heavy plant. I use loops of string around the limbs and tied to the stake to hold the branches and fruit upright.

Multiple Stakes are used in most large plantings, especially in commercial production. Set the plants three feet apart in the row, then drive five- or six-foot stakes two feet into the ground at the edge of the bed on each side of the row. Attach a wire to the top of each stake, starting at an end stake and each stake down the row. Securely fasten it to the top of the stake at the other end. You do not need to tie the two rows of stakes together across the row of plants. The advantage of this system is that fewer stakes are needed and no additional tying after setup is required. The disadvantage is that you must use a heavy mulch over the bed since cultivating is almost impossible.

grow, tie a string from the main plant and the branches up to the wire. The advantage of this system is that it is permanent. Once you till the area and set the plants, you are ready to grow **tomatoes**. However, there are several disadvantages to this system: (1) yearly rotation is not possible, so you must use VFN resistant varieties; (2) some hand suckering is required; and (3) since it is impossible to work the bed after the plants are mature, you must overcome this difficulty by heavy mulching.

VEGETABLE ACTIVITIES FOR MAY:

Plant

☞ Continue April's post-frost plantings of **snap beans**, **pole beans**, **sweet corn**, **cucumber**, **cantaloupe**, **water-melon**, **squash**, **zucchini**, **pumpkins**, **tomatoes**, **pepper** (sweet and hot), **eggplant**, **sweet potatoes**, **annual herbs**, and **gourds** until the weather gets hot and dry. This usually occurs about a month after the last frost.*

Prune

☞ Train and support **tomatoes**, **cucumbers**, **pole beans**, **peppers**, and **eggplant** on a regular basis.†

Fertilize

☞ Fertilize as you plant with 15-15-15. Application is at a rate of approximately one pound per 10 feet of row. This application should be good for about six weeks.

☞ When **sweet corn** is knee high, side-dress with ammonium nitrate at the rate of 1/2 pound per 10 feet of row.‡

☞ Vegetables grown for their greens, like **turnips**, **mustard**, **rapegreens**, and **Swiss chard**, should be side-dressed with 15-15-15 fertilizer six weeks after planting. Application is at a rate of approximately one pound per 10 feet of row.‡

☞ **Tomatoes**, **peppers**, **eggplant**, **cucumber**, and **okra** should be fertilized with 5-10-15 every six weeks throughout their growing season. Application is at a rate of approximately one pound per 10 feet of row.‡

☞ Continue to fertilize other growing vegetables with 5-10-15 about every six weeks for the rest of the season. Application is at a rate of approximately one pound per 10 feet of row. ‡

Spray

☞ There are numerous insects and diseases which feed on vegetables in our gardens throughout the season. The first step to effective control is detecting the pest before it has damaged your crop extensively. Once you spot an unfamiliar problem, take an infected leaf, flower, or fruit to your local nursery-man or Cooperative Extension Service agent for identification and control measures. There is a wide variety of organic and inorganic materials to control most garden pests.‡

Water

☞ Water vegetables thoroughly with about one inch of water if there has been no significant rainfall for a week.‡

Other

☞ Keep vegetables free of weeds by tilling, hoeing or mulching. Weeds harbor damaging insects and compete with vegetables for essential nutrients.

☞ Harvest frequently, correctly, and at the proper time. Vegetables left too long on the plant lose taste and quality.**

☞ Harvest **broccoli** and **cauliflower** before any yellow flowers appear in the heads.

* See "Planting a Vegetable Garden," p. 92
† See "Training Vegetables off the Ground," p. 118
‡ See "Fertilizing, Spraying, and Watering Vegetables," p. 115

‡ See "Fertilizing, Spraying, and Watering Vegetables," p. 115
** See "Harvesting Vegetables and Keeping Them Tasty," p. 140

The tender tropical Hibiscus (Hibiscus rosa-sinensis) is a beautiful summer potted plant with extraordinary blossoms.

VII. *Houseplants*

The days continue to lengthen in May, and houseplants should be growing well by now. Though the furnace has been quieted for the year, we may be turning on the air conditioner this month. Air conditioners dry the air just like furnaces, so our indoor plants have little reprieve. Don't forget to keep plants misted.

Some of our carried-over plants like Geranium and Hibiscus will have made the switch from being indoor plants to being patio plants. Ferns, Ficus, Rubber Plants, and Piggybacks can be put out as well if you have a nicely shaded porch or patio.

The wrens are happy whenever I put out my ferns because they love to nest in these hanging baskets during the summer months. They don't hurt the plants, but they give me quite a fright if I try to water when they are napping.

HOUSEPLANT ACTIVITIES FOR MAY:

Plant

☞ Houseplants, especially newly purchased ones, can be repotted at any time during the year. Use a pot at least two sizes larger so the plant will have plenty of room to grow. I prefer to grow most of my houseplants in a peat-light potting mixture.*

Prune

☞ Groom indoor plants whenever they need it. Remove weak branches or stems as well as off-color leaves.

Fertilize

☞ Fertilize with a full-strength, water-soluble fertilizer solution every time you water. As an alternative, I also like to use fertilizer spikes or Osmocote, which lasts several months.†

☞ Remember to keep patio and porch plants like **Hibiscus**, **Allamanda**, and **Ixora** well fertilized.

Spray

☞ Check all indoor plants for insects like spider mites, scale, and mealybug. I like to use a houseplant systemic insecticide to control them. It is easier and safer than spraying inside. When I do spray, I prefer to take the plants outside. Remember to apply the insecticide to both the top and the undersides of the leaves.‡

☞ Be careful when spraying **ferns**. Some insecticides are harmful to them. *Always read the label for warnings about **ferns** and other plants.* **Ferns** are very susceptible to scale, but the systemic insecticides work very well in controlling this serious pest.

Water

☞ Continue to watch houseplants. When they look limp, check for dry soil. If it is dry, water thoroughly in a sink or bathtub, letting the water drain completely, and don't water again until the surface is dry once more. Between waterings, mist with plain water on a regular basis. If the limp plants are in moist soil, do not water but allow the soil to dry a bit and mist frequently.†

☞ Tip-burn or edge-burn on leaves indicates that more water is being lost than is being absorbed by the roots. Check for dry soil, too much sunlight, or drafts from air-conditioning vents.†

Other

☞ Many people turn on their air-conditioners this month. Remember the following tips: Never place houseplants in front of an air-conditioner vent; mist them frequently when the air-conditioner is running; use a cold-air vaporizer to increase the humidity if you need to.†

☞ With proper care, houseplants can be propagated at any time during the year. Since May is a dry month, mist cuttings frequently so they don't dry out.**

---

* See "Repotting Houseplants," p. 67
† See "Houseplant Care and Maintenance," p. 232
‡ See "Controlling Insects and Diseases," p. 80

† See "Houseplant Care and Maintenance," p. 232
** See "Propagating Herbaceous Houseplants and Garden Plants," p. 225

VIII. *Lawns*

Summer grasses should be gearing up in May. The ground has warmed to the temperature they like, and they will begin to grow furiously. I like to watch my Centipede come to life and form a beautiful thick mat of grass. Remember to keep summer grasses well fertilized so they will have plenty of nutrients and grow as much as possible.

While summer grasses may seem like new arrivals on the scene, evergreen grasses are old hands by now. Mowing them has become a weekly routine. Evergreen grasses don't need to be fertilized again because their major growth spurt has passed.

LAWN ACTIVITIES FOR MAY:

Plant

☛ Continue to plant or reseed summer grasses like **Bermuda Grass**, **Centipede**, **St. Augustine**, and **Zoysia**. May is too late to successfully plant evergreen grasses. They need cool weather to grow and establish themselves *before* the summer heat arrives.*

Fertilize

☛ Continue fertilizing summer grasses with a high-nitrogen, slow-release fertilizer if you didn't in April. (For **Centipede** lawns, use a fertilizer designated for that type of grass.) This application will be good for about 90 days. *Do not over-fertilize **Centipede** lawns.*†

☛ Do not fertilize evergreen grasses like the **fescues** unless they are light green or yellow.

Spray

☛ Watch for insect and disease problems. Insects cause irregular dead areas while diseases cause well-defined dead areas. Take a plug of grass which has both dying and healthy grass to your local nurseryman or Cooperative Extension Service agent for identification and suggestions for controlling the problem.

☛ As the ground warms, Japanese Beetle grubs move close enough to the surface to be controlled. Their presence can be determined by signs of weak grass growth, the presence of moles (which feed on the grubs), or large adult populations the year before. Grubs are controlled by chemicals like Diazinon or organic controls like Milky Spore.

☛ If the weather becomes hot and dry this month, chinch bugs might appear. They cause brown patches in **Centipede** and **St. Augustine** lawns. Remove a plug of sod with a bulb planter. Slowly immerse the plug in a bucket of water. Look for small insects to rise. Apply a soil insecticide like Diazinon to the whole area where you find chinch bugs.

Cut

☛ Cut summer grasses like **Bermuda Grass** often to prevent them from browning. Cutting grass after it is very tall removes the green part, leaving only brown stems. This condition will remain until new green leaves grow.

☛ **Hybrid Bermuda Grass** may need cutting twice a week.

* See "Planting and Reseeding Summer Lawns," p. 98
† See "Fertilizing and Controlling Weeds in Lawns," p. 73

☞ Cut grasses at the proper height:

SUMMER GRASSES	HEIGHT
Common Bermuda Grass	2 inches
Hybrid Bermuda Grass	1 to 1 ¹/₂ inches
Centipede	1 ¹/₂ to 2 inches
St. Augustine	2 to 2 ¹/₂ inches
Zoysia	1 to 2 inches

EVERGREEN GRASSES	HEIGHT
Kentucky 31 Tall Fescue	3 to 3 ¹/₂ inches
Turf-type Tall Fescues	3 inches
Fine Fescues	1 ¹/₂ to 2 inches
Kentucky Bluegrass	2 to 2 ¹/₂ inches

Water

☞ Keep lawns watered during dry spells. Place a one-pound coffee or similar straight-sided can halfway between the sprinkler and the end of the fall of water. Allow the sprinkler to run until there is one inch of water in the can. If water starts puddling on the surface of the lawn, turn off the water and check the amount in the can. If there is one-half inch, do not water again for three or four days. If there is an inch, do not water for a week. If it puddles when there is less than one-half inch, let it soak in and then continue watering until there is at least one-half inch in the can.‡

‡ See "Proper Watering," P. 130

NOTES

June

IN THE SOUTHERN GARDEN

June is the first true *summer* month in the South. The days are hot and muggy, and the nights are still and cool. With children on summer vacation, it is a good time to cultivate the gardening interests of our future gardeners. With vegetables coming in, flowers blooming, and lawns growing, it is a fun time to teach children about nature and how plants interact with the environment. Being a good detective in the garden whets the interest of all gardeners, especially the budding scientists in a family. Discovering the cause of some plant difficulty can expand the horizons of a gardening family.

The most exciting activities occur in the vegetable garden. Irish potatoes and onions finish their cycle as their tops begin to die. Suddenly there are cracks around the mother plant, indicating there are delights hidden in the ground underneath. Beets, carrots, and turnips are also ready to harvest when the surface cracks around the plants. The first tomatoes, peppers, and eggplants are ready to harvest. Those prolific zucchini plants and summer squash seem to have fruit ready every night, and beans, corn, and okra may be ready, depending on when you planted them. Vegetable harvests are a gardener's dream come true, but we'll have to become good garden detectives to deal with the inevitable problems which arise on the way to harvest. Observe the garden carefully and search for answers when plants suddenly look different.

Don't neglect your fruiting plants this month. Insects and diseases love fruits as much as they do vegetables, especially now that peaches, plums, cherries, and nectarines are ripening. Annual summer flowers grow well in this hot weather, and June finds them blooming their heads off. Give them a pinch or two to help them branch out and produce even more flowers.

Summer weather is unpredictable. Every year it seems that plants either drown or parch. I really prefer having a good afternoon thundershower a couple of times a week over a hurricane-induced flood. But in the drought years, I long for either. A great part of the challenge of gardening is knowing how to deal with too much or too little rain and how to make plants produce with either.

I grew up with fickle summer weather. I always enjoy (and sometimes believe) the old-time sayings like "Thunder before seven (a.m.) brings rain before eleven" or "You can make it rain by hanging a dead snake over a tree limb." If a dead snake isn't handy, keep an eye on your dogs. We have never had a dog who didn't get under our feet whenever the barometric pressure was dropping before an approaching storm.

Even trees planted in January, like this Yoshino Cherry (Prunus yedoensis), cast very little shade in June.

I. *Shade and Flowering Trees*

As the summer heat arrives, we are apt to see landscapers rushing around neighborhoods trying to drum up new work. In late April and May, they "installed" many new flower beds and borders, but by June that type of work is trailing off. No doubt there will be a few landscapers who offer to "install" a new tree for us.

June is hot. Our bodies aren't used to the heat, and it can feel sweltering. With the electricity bill on the rise as well, a landscaper's offer of a beautiful *shade* tree can be enticing. Don't listen to him! June is a terrible time to plant a tree. Besides, a young tree will do little to shade you this summer. So if it is shade you're after, you might as well wait until next winter to plant so that your new tree will grow to its best ability.

TREE ACTIVITIES FOR JUNE:

Plant

☛ It is too late to plant B&B and container-grown trees successfully unless *extreme* care is taken.

Prune

☛ Summer is not the time to prune tree limbs. If there is a broken branch, however, remove the limb (including the jagged break or split) with a clean cut.*

Spray

☛ Look for damaging insects on evergreen trees like **magnolias** and **hollies**. Scale, spider mite, lacebug, leaf miner, spittlebug, and leaf hopper are the most prevalent in May. Use Cygon or Orthene to control them. Do not use Cygon on **hollies**.†

☛ Protect flowering trees, like **flowering peaches** and **flowering plums,** from Japanese Beetle damage by spraying with liquid Sevin or putting traps downwind from the tree.†

☛ On occasion, insects and diseases which you can't identify may show up on trees. When discovered, take a branch containing some of the infected area to your local nurseryman or Cooperative Extension Service agent for identification and suggested controls.†

* See "Pruning Shade and Flowering Trees," p. 4
† See "Controlling Insects and Diseases," p. 80

Water

☛ Newly planted trees should be soaked once a week when there is no significant rainfall. ‡

☛ During periods of extreme drought, large trees may need watering. Watch for discoloration, drying, die-back, and premature leaf-fall as signs that the tree is being affected. Use a watering spike placed intermittently around the perimeter of the tree's roots, approximately under the edge of the farthest reaching limbs. Soak thoroughly.‡

Other

☛ Keep newly planted trees mulched well to conserve moisture when it is hot and dry, but do not pile mulch against the trunk.**

☛ Be extremely careful when mowing or using a power trimmer around old and new trees. *Do not hit or damage the bark.* Even the slightest damage may make an entrance for borers or other damaging insects. This is true for all trees in the landscape or natural area, including trees you have planted as well as native trees. **Dogwood, flowering peach, flowering cherry,** and **flowering plum** are highly susceptible to borer attacks. Shade trees like **pines** are also attacked by various borers and bark beetles.

‡ See "Does Your Tree Have Enough Water?" p. 150
** See "Mulching: A Lesson from Nature," p. 243

NOTES

II. *Shrubs and Vines*

Moonflower is an easy-to-grow annual vine which blossoms in the evening.

By June, most of our spring-flowering shrubs like camellias and azaleas are growing vegetatively. Their blossoms have finished and they are settling in for the green months of summer. Luckily, there are summer-flowering shrubs and vines which will color our gardens over the summer months. Moonflower, an annual herbaceous vine, is one of my favorites and blooms in late afternoon and in the light of the moon. Its large white flowers are quite a sight against the black backdrop of night.

Another group of summer friends are the summer-flowering cultivars of Rhododendron. Their blooms seem a cool reminder of spring as they rest easily in a shady spot. One tradition of summer for many gardeners is that of "deadheading" Rhododendron. This is the practice of removing spent blossoms to encourage next year's bloom. There seems to be quite a cult of those who swear by this activity. It can't be all bad if it means standing in a cool Rhododendron bed for an hour or two.

PROPER WATERING

Watering the garden is a Southern tradition — it has to be. Without supplemental watering, Southern gardens would not live up to the glory we have come to expect. Just like planting, pruning, and fertilizing, watering is a garden activity Southerners must get used to.

In discussing the components of soil in April ("Analyzing Soil with a Pair of Rubber Boots"), we discovered that up to 25% of the ideal soil mix is water. Fortunately for non-technical gardeners, the best way to measure this percentage is to pick up a handful of soil. If you can squeeze the soil into a nice, firm ball, the percentage is correct. If the soil crumbles and falls apart, there is not enough water. If your soil is more like a mud pie than a firm ball, get out of the rain!

Generally, an inch of water per week will give soil the proper amount of moisture. This is a *very* general rule, though, and there are exceptions. Well-mulched garden areas will retain moisture better than areas left un-mulched. Sandy soils tend to drain quickly and will not hold moisture. Shady spots don't dry out as quickly as sunny ones. The list goes on. The best way to be sure is to feel the soil and determine for yourself if you need to water.

All plants should be watered in the same way: slowly and thoroughly. If you water too much too fast, the water will probably run off before it has a chance to completely penetrate the soil's surface. A good slow soaking allows the water to work deeply into the ground and reach the areas of the soil where the plant's roots are located.

It is possible to water slowly and thoroughly in many different ways. The most basic is barely turning on the hose so that water trickles out over a period of several hours. For trees, we use a watering spike so that the water penetrates more deeply into the root area. Other watering techniques include using fan sprinklers, impulse sprinklers, water breakers, self-watering pots, and soaker hoses. There are home-made watering tools as well. One is a one-gallon milk jug with several tiny holes poked in the bottom placed next to a plant. The gallon of water seeps out in about 45 minutes, depending on the size of the holes you poked. This is a great way to water plants that are out of your hose's reach. I have also buried quart cans with holes in the bottom around my tomato plants. After they are filled, the water seeps out slowly at the level of the tomato's roots. A final method is to bottom-soak potted plants by filling up their saucers with water. The dry soil in the pot sucks

Measure sprinkler water falling on your garden. You need one inch of water per week from sprinkling or rain.

the water right up into the pot. But don't leave pots sitting in a saucer filled with water for too long, the pot will become water-logged, resulting in serious root damage.

Of all these techniques, the most commonly used is a sprinkler. Impulse sprinklers are better than fan sprinklers because they distribute water evenly over an entire area. Fan sprinklers apply more water to the middle area than the edges. When using a sprinkler, place an empty straight-sided glass or container half-way between the sprinkler and the farthest reach of the water. The container will measure the amount of water applied to any given area. Allow the sprinkler to run until there is one inch of water in the can. If water starts puddling on the surface of the ground, turn off the water and check the amount in the can. If there is one-half inch, do not water again for three or four days. If there is an inch, do not water for a week. If it puddles when there is less than one-half inch, let it soak in and then continue watering until there is at least one-half inch in the can. While this may seem like overkill, watering shallowly can be detrimental because it draws the plant's roots to the surface. Since surface soil dries out quickly, the roots will dry out and might die.

Whichever technique you choose, remember to water your plants before the mid-afternoon so the foliage will dry before evening. Wet foliage in the cool of the evening makes a perfect breeding ground for fungus and disease (especially on **roses**). The simple step of watering early in the afternoon is a major preventative treatment for insects and diseases.

If watering were as easy as turning on the sprinkler,

none of us would have suffered at the sight of a dried-up plant. Unfortunately, watering is not as easy as keeping the soil moist to the touch. Many plants don't like moist soil! The obvious examples are cacti and succulents. These plants have adapted to dry conditions and do not appreciate over-watering. There are many other plants which don't like to get their feet wet. The best approach is to get to know your particular plant. By realizing that too much moisture can be a detriment, we can learn the particular preferences of our plants.

One sign of an over-watered plant is wilting. Believe it or not, wilting is a common reaction to both under-watering and over-watering. If you find yourself saying, "I watered it yesterday and it's still wilted," try helping your plant by *not* watering. Let it dry out so that the surface of the soil is dry to the touch. Then water it thoroughly and wait until the soil is dry before watering again (see December, "Common Houseplant Ailments").

Another way to get to know a plant's preferences is to determine its native environment. **Rhododendron** grow naturally along the cool banks of mountain streams. It is no wonder they won't survive out in the middle of your yard! Picturing a mountain stream, I can deduce that **Rhododendron** will grow in well-drained (because they grow on banks), moist (because mountain areas get a lot of rain), cool soil (because it's shady). All that is left is to go out and check my **Rhododendron** for these conditions. If the soil dries often, I might add a soaker hose. If the soil is too warm, I can mulch and maybe even place some rocks (to keep the roots cool) on the surface of the ground. If there is too much water, I might dig a shallow trench to drain excess water away.

Rhododendrons need cool spots and moist but well drained soil.

While it is a good general rule to properly apply one inch of water a week, there is no better rule than getting to know the plants around your house. Not only will you find it easier to care for plants you know; you will probably find that it makes caring for them much more a joy than a burden.

SHRUB AND VINE ACTIVITIES FOR JUNE:

Plant

☞ It is too late to successfully plant B&B and container-grown shrubs or vines unless *extreme* care is taken.

Prune

☞ Wait to prune flowering evergreen shrubs like **Rhododendron** and **Mountain Laurel** until after they have finished blooming, but before their new growth darkens in color.*

☞ Evergreen shrubs like **Buford Holly** may be shaped by trimming new growth. However, avoid removing all of the new shoots and cutting into last year's growth.

Fertilize

☞ **Rhododendron** and **Mountain Laurel** should be fertilized after they finish blooming. Those which bloom in June and July should be given a lighter application of fertilizer since their roots are closer to the surface and could be damaged by the fertilizer. During hot, dry weather, use an acid azalea/camellia fertilizer at roughly 1/4 a pound per three feet of the shrub's height, but check the directions of your specific brand. This is usually done once a year.†

Spray

☞ Watch out for damaging insects on evergreens, especially **Euonymus, azalea, Camellia, Pyracantha, Gardenia,** and **Photinia.** Scale, spider mites, lacebug, leaf miner, spittlebug, and leaf hopper are the most prevalent. Use Cygon or Orthene as a control. Do not use Cygon on **hollies.**‡

☞ The grotesque swollen leaves which you saw on **azaleas** and **camellias** in May will now be hard and corky. This condition is caused by a fungus called Azalea or Camellia Leaf Gall and is controlled by removing and disposing of affected leaves. It is important to remove them now to prevent infection next year. This is not a fatal disease.‡

☞ Check **Red Tip Photinias** frequently for signs of leaf spot. When seen, immediately spray affected and adjacent plants with Daconil.‡

Water

☞ Slowly soak shrubs and vines if there has been no significant rain in a week. This is especially important for this year's plantings.**

Other

☞ Mulch all shrubs and vines to conserve moisture during the summer. Do not allow the mulch to crowd or pack against the lower stems and trunks.††

* See "Pruning Flowering Shrubs and Vines," p. 31
† See "How to Fertilize Shrubs and Vines," p. 30
‡ See "Controlling Insects and Diseases," p. 80
** See "Proper Watering," p. 130
†† See "Mulching: A Lesson from Nature," p. 243

Prune young peach trees to make this shape.

III. *Fruits*

In June we can expect the first big soft fruit harvest. Peaches, plums, nectarines, and cherries will all be ripening. We will also see the first strawberries of the year and maybe some figs on everbearing bushes. Raspberries and blackberries will also be producing nicely by the end of the month.

Not altogether coincidently, June is also a big month for insects and diseases. These pests explode at this time of year with the purpose of eating our fruit before we can. Watch out!

While it is discouraging to lose fruit to insects and diseases, I find it much more an insult when birds feast on my harvest. They seem so confident chattering away on a high branch, waiting until I leave to light on my fruit bushes and devour my berries. I have tried everything — nets, fake owls, rubber snakes, scarecrows, and rattling pie pans. Unfortunately, none of these methods seems to be sure-fire. I think the best long-term solution is to overplant. That way the birds are full and I am, too.

FRUIT ACTIVITIES FOR JUNE:

Plant

☞ June is not a good time to successfully plant B&B and container-grown fruits.

Prune

☞ Remove all canes of semi-bush fruits like **blackberries** when they finish fruiting. This will encourage new shoots from the crown on which next year's berries will be set.*

Spray

☞ Continue a regular control program for fruit insects and diseases. A complete home orchard spray is the most practical method of control. Continue applications at recommended intervals until the fruit ripens. Read the directions and do not spray fruits too close to harvest.†

☞ Brown rot is a serious disease on many ripening fruits like **cherries**, **peaches**, and **plums**. You must control it if you are to harvest good fruit. Remain diligent with your complete home orchard spray program to control this disease.†

☞ Japanese Beetles are often a serious problem this month. They attack **grapes**, **plums**, and other fruits. Those which have finished fruiting should be sprayed or dusted with Sevin to prevent defoliation. Beetle traps work as well, but remember to place the traps downwind from your fruits.†

☞ **Bunch grapes** will be expanding in size for ripening in July. Keep them sprayed with your complete home orchard to control Japanese Beetles, brown rot, and leaf worms.†

☞ Watch for spider mites on **raspberries** and other semi-bush berries. Their presence is evident when the foliage has a silvery gray appearance. Spray with Kelthane to control this serious pest.†

Water

☞ Slowly soak fruit trees and bushes if there has been no significant rain in a week. This is especially important for this year's plantings.‡

Other

☞ Some **strawberries** may ripen in June. Keep fruit picked regularly to discourage birds and other animals from getting more than you do.

☞ Keep **strawberries** well mulched to prevent the fruit from being covered with soil and sand.

☞ Be careful when mowing or using a power trimmer in orchard areas not to hit the bark of fruit trees with the mower. Any damage to the bark will provide an entrance place for borers.

☞ Keep fruits mulched with pine straw to prevent weeds and grasses from competing for water and fertilizer. However, do not pile the mulch against the trunks of fruit trees which may soften the bark and give borers an easy entrance.**

☞ Keep fruit harvested as it ripens. If you leave fruit hanging on the tree after your spray program is completed, you are issuing an invitation for insects and diseases.

☞ Remove all undeveloped fruit which failed to ripen for whatever reason. Never leave it on the tree.

---

* See "Secrets of the Berry Patch," p. 155
† See "Controlling Insects and Diseases," p. 80

‡ See "Proper Watering," p. 130
** See "Mulching: A Lesson from Nature," p. 243

In the South, Blackspot is our worst disease on roses.

IV. *Roses*

In June, roses are enjoying the warm weather, and so is the Blackspot. This fungus disease is worst at this time of year and can be controlled by your regular spray program. Another way to control Blackspot is to encourage your roses to grow vigorously. Quickly growing leaves are not as susceptible to fungus. Help your roses by fertilizing them on a consistent schedule.

Since June can be a dry month, many of us will decide to water our roses for the first time. Remember not to wet the foliage, especially if you water in the evening when it will not dry for a while. Fungus will quickly take hold on wet foliage in the cool of a summer evening.

ROSE ACTIVITIES FOR JUNE:

Plant

☛ June is not a good time to plant bare-root and container-grown roses.

Prune

☛ Groom roses constantly. Never leave a dead or dying stem on the plant because the disease will spread to healthy canes. Also remove weak, broken, or spindly shoots.*

* See "Grooming Roses," p. 110

☞ Remove spent flowers immediately. Seed formation retards stem growth and the production of new blossoms.*

Fertilize

☞ Continue fertilizing with a complete rose fertilizer on your six-to-eight-week program. I use a combination fertilizer and systemic insecticide to give my roses the nutrients they need as well as to control many insects.

Spray

☞ Continue with your complete rose spray program every 10 to 14 days according to the directions. Use a combination insecticide and fungicide spray, and continue applications through September.

☞ Watch out for Japanese Beetles. Your normal spray program will not control these pests. Use Japanese Beetle traps or supplement your spray program with Sevin.†

☞ Blackspot is the most serious disease of summer. Consistent applications of your regular spray should prevent serious damage.†

☞ During hot, dry weather, thrips may become a problem. Infected rose blossoms will turn brown on the petal edges. Check for these pests by pulling one of the discolored flowers apart. You will see rod-shaped thrips at the base of the petal. Control thrips with Orthene.†

☞ Bud worms eat holes in maturing rose buds. They are usually controlled by your regular complete spray program, but applying Bacillus thuringiensis (BT) is a good supplemental control method.†

Water

☞ Water when there has been no significant rain for a week. A soaker hose is a good way to prevent wetting the foliage and thereby encouraging diseases.

Soak the bed thoroughly. Shallow watering does more harm than good.‡

Other

☞ Remember to cut flowers correctly. Always make the cut above a joint where a five-leaflet originates. Cutting at this point encourages a strong new shoot and blossom to form.*

☞ Remove all dead flowers by clipping above a five-leaflet set, as if you were cutting the flower to take inside.*

☞ Many **Hybrid Tea** and **Grandiflora** roses have several flowers in a cluster (called a candelabra) which may not all bloom at the same time. Remove each spent flower in the cluster as it finishes blooming. When all the flowers are done, cut the whole cluster stalk back to a five-leaflet set.*

☞ Keep roses well mulched with pine straw during the summer. Add fresh mulch when you can see bare ground around the plants, but do not pile mulch against the crown or lower stems. Many problems like cankers and botrytis occur when mulch covers the lower stems.**

☞ Cut roses will last longer in an arrangement when stems are recut underwater before placing in the vase. This allows water, not air, to travel up the stem.

* See "Grooming Roses," p. 110
† See "Controlling Insects and Diseases," p. 80

‡ See "Proper Watering," p. 130
* See "Grooming Roses," p. 110
** See "Mulching: A Lesson from Nature," p. 243

V. Flowers and Colorful Garden Plants

It is a wonder to watch our annuals grow to fill out a flower bed or border. They seem to be growing so quickly this time of year that it speeds up the passing of the days. Everywhere things are growing with a passion, especially the grass. One way to cope with all the grass clippings is to let them dry and then use them as mulch on flower beds. Mulched flowers are much happier, and tests have shown that they produce up to three times as many flowers.

Another important way to keep flowers happy is by watering them thoroughly when needed. While the best way to water is to use an impulse sprinkler and to measure the amount of water with a container, many of us like to drag the hose around the yard and hand water. This is not a bad method as long as you don't grow impatient and rush the job. Since it is harder to measure the amount of water applied by hand, apply as much water as the ground will hold. Wait a few minutes and return to the same spot. If the water runs off again, you have probably saturated the soil and can move on.

GROOMING AND PINCHING FLOWERS

Grooming herbaceous plants like **Impatiens**, **Begonia**, and **Salvia** is an important summer job. Grooming simply means minor pruning to encourage the best growth for more blooms and the plant's desired characteristics. While some herbaceous plants like **snapdragons** respond if you cut them back severely, most remain productive if you merely remove spent flowers, any seed pods, yellow leaves, and improper growth.

Plants have a limited amount of nutrients and food to spread among stems, leaves, flowers, and roots. During certain parts of their growth cycle, their effort is concentrated on certain areas and activities. For instance, in the spring most herbaceous plants focus their effort into vegetative growth. This means that they try to grow as large as possible and put on as many leaves as possible. Later on, when they begin to blossom, their effort is diverted into reproductive activities: forming buds, blossoming, and producing seed.

For centuries, plant growers have been practicing methods of forcing a plant's effort into certain desired areas of activity. One simple method is to remove spent flowers. In the normal growth cycle of a plant, flowers begin to die after they are pollinated. The plant then turns its attention to forming seeds, which take precedence over other growth. When you remove the spent flower, you are also removing the unformed seeds and thwarting seed formation. The plant responds by diverting its effort to other growth patterns, most likely the formation of more beautiful flowers.

In the same way, removing yellow or deformed leaves allows nutrients to be dedicated to healthy

Groom New Guinea Impatiens frequently to encourage fresh blossoms.

White Nicotiana blossoms permeate the garden with sweet fragrance.

Easy-to-grow dwarf dahlias bloom all summer.

areas of the plant. Be careful with this method, however. I once knew a man who used this technique to groom his okra. His thought was that if he removed all the branches and leaves that did not have any flowers or developing okra, all the plant's nutrients and food would flow into his okra and he would have a bumper crop. Unfortunately, he forgot that leaves are themselves the major source of the plant's food. Those were some of the sickest okra plants I have ever seen.

A very specific type of grooming is called pinching. Two of the plants we most commonly pinch are **Dahlia** and **Chrysanthemum**. These plants, not normally bushy, can be forced into a bushier shape which will produce many more flowers. The method of pinching is simple. When the plant reaches six inches high, firmly pinch and remove the bud at the top of the main shoot (the terminal bud) just above the highest mature leaf. Normally, the terminal bud's growth takes precedence over side shoots, thus producing a taller plant. When you remove the terminal bud, the plant will start growing side shoots outward and upward from the pinched area (you might be reminded of the Open Head/Basket method of pruning peaches). Continue to pinch these side shoots when they become four to six inches long, causing more and more lateral growth. Stop pinching after July 1 so that you will not disrupt the bud formation and future bloom. Do not substitute cutting back with shears for pinching. Heavy pruning with shears will cause flower buds to develop from the lower stems which never flower as well as flower buds from the side shoots.

The most severe summer grooming can be carried out on cool-weather herbaceous plants like **snapdragons**, **hollyhocks**, **stock**, and perennials which may not be blooming well due to the long, hot summer. You can cut back these plants severely in August when their blooms have begun to slow down and the plants have lost much of their beauty. After cutting back, fertilize them with a 5-10-15 fertilizer and give them a good watering. If the weather cooperates, you are likely to have a strong fall bloom.

While it is not the most common thing to do, you can groom your vegetative flowers so they put their effort into herbaceous growth. Most people would be shocked at the sight, but in some cases I remove buds and flowers long before I have had the chance to enjoy their bloom. One such case is in growing newly potted plants from cuttings. I want all of the plant's effort to go toward filling out into a mature-sized plant before I set them in the garden. Removing the flowers prematurely focuses the plant's effort on vegetative growth and provides me with a bigger and better plant in less time!

FLOWER ACTIVITIES FOR JUNE:

Plant

☞ Most herbaceous garden plants and annual vines can still be planted with success in June. If you plant them carefully and don't let them dry out, they will perform well the rest of the season.*

☞ Continue planting summer-flowering bulbs, corms, tubers, and roots like **Gladiolus**, **Dahlia**, and **Canna**.

☞ Don't leave empty spaces in beds or borders. Fill them in with summer-flowering annuals like **Ageratum**, **Begonia**, **Coleus**, **Geranium**, **Impatiens**, and **Salvia** which will bloom until frost. Hot-weather perennials like **Astilbe**, **Shasta Daisy**, **Purple Cone-Flower**, and **Rudbeckia** can also be planted with success.*

* See "How to Plant a Flower Bed," p. 62

Prune

☛ Groom herbaceous flowering plants like **Impatiens**, **Begonia**, and **Salvia** by removing spent flowers, seed pods, yellow leaves, and improper growth.†

☛ Continue pinching **chrysanthemums** and **dahlias** to encourage lateral growth.†

☛ Do not cut back **chrysanthemums** or **dahlias** with shears. Pinch the terminal bud out of the main shoot as well as the laterals. Heavy pruning with shears will cause flower buds to develop from the lower stems (which never flower) as well as flower buds from the side shoots.†

☛ Cut back foliage of spring-flowering bulbs like **daffodils**, **hyacinths**, and **tulips** now that it has turned yellow. Cutting back green foliage reduces the bulb's stored food and will result in smaller flowers next year.

Fertilize

☛ Continue fertilizing plants with 5-10-15 on a six-to-eight-week schedule through the end of the season.

☛ Fertilize **chrysanthemums** and **dahlias** with a 5-10-15 formula every four to six weeks.

☛ During dry weather, spray a water-soluble fertilizer solution like Peters on foliage to keep plants growing well when roots are not as active and fertilizer is not taken from the soil.

Spray

☛ Watch carefully for insects and diseases on flowers and control them as soon as you see them. Insects are the greatest problem. Fast succulent growth is highly susceptible to aphid, spider mite, leaf hopper, thrip, and worm damage. Orthene is an excellent all-around control. ‡

☛ Large attacks of worms on a particular plant, like **Geranium**, can be controlled by Dipel dust or Thuri-cide spray which contain Bacillus thuringiensis (BT), an excellent biological control.‡

☛ Slugs and snails will be bad this month on **Hosta**, **Caladium**, **Elephant Ear**, **Coleus**, and other succulent summer flowers. Use a snail bait or shallow pans of stale beer to kill them.‡

☛ As in other areas of the garden, Japanese Beetles are often a serious problem this month. Plants can be sprayed or dusted with Sevin to prevent damage. Beetle traps work as well but remember to place the traps downwind from your garden.‡

Water

☛ Water plants thoroughly with about one inch of water per week if there has been no significant rainfall.**

☛ Hanging baskets will need more water during the hot summer months, but do not overwater them. Soak them thoroughly, then soak them again only when the surface is dry. I like to set hanging baskets out on our garden bench during a good rain. This natural water washes the foliage and keeps the plants more attractive.

Other

☛ Dig and separate spring-flowering bulbs like **Narcissus**, **tulips**, and **hyacinths** after the foliage has died. This is necessary if the clumps are crowded and this year's flowers were small. Store in a cool place until you set them out in the fall.

☛ Keep beds and borders free from weeds which compete with good plants for water and fertilizer.

☛ Mulch beds with dry grass clippings or pine straw to reduce weed problems and to conserve moisture.††

☛ Some flowering plants may have grown top-heavy and fallen over. Stake them with small green bamboo stakes which do not show.

† See "Grooming and Pinching Flowers," p. 137

‡ See "Controlling Insects and Diseases," p. 80

‡ See "Controlling Insects and Diseases," p. 80

** See "Proper Watering," p. 130

†† See "Mulching: A Lesson from Nature," p. 243

VI. *Vegetables*

By June, we can expect our Irish potatoes and maybe our bulb onions to be ready by the end of the month. These are the last of our cool-weather crops. Our post-frost crops like squash, beans, and even a few early tomatoes will begin ripening by mid-month as well, giving us a glimpse of the rest of the summer.

Digging potatoes has long been one of our family's favorite activities. There is nothing quite like the allure of an underground harvest. It takes a lot of confidence to dig into your garden with a shovel, assured only by the telltale sign of a cracked surface. But once the first potato is unearthed, the hunt is on and everyone is happily scampering around looking for anything even slightly resembling a crack in the ground.

Harvesting Vegetables and Keeping Them Tasty

Every gardener dreams of walking into the vegetable garden, plucking a ripe **tomato** or an ear of **sweet corn**, and having it for dinner. Vegetables from the supermarket or even the farmer's market just can't compare with the delights of your own vegetable garden, just a few yards from the kitchen.

However, vegetables from your own garden are better *only* if they are harvested at their prime and handled properly before eating. Commercially produced vegetables might be just as good as your own if the fields were next door and you could walk out and pluck the ripe fruit. The enemies of great taste in vegetables, however produced, are: degree of ripeness at harvest, time since harvest, temperature, and water loss.

Sweet corn plucked and cooked immediately is far better than that left on the porch a day or two before cooking. Tests show that without immediate cooling, sweet corn may lose 50% of its sugar in 24 hours.

Eggplant ready to harvest

Tomatoes harvested when still a bit green and placed in the refrigerator never taste as good as if they are fully ripened on a window sill before refrigerating. Be sure to harvest and handle homegrown vegetables carefully in order to overcome the enemies of vegetable quality and taste.

Each vegetable has its own characteristics. **Squash** and **cucumber** mature very quickly and will become tough and tasteless when left on the plant too long before harvesting. **Beans** become leathery if left too long on the plant; **lettuce** loses its crispness; **beets**, **carrots**, and **turnips** become pithy. Some vegetables like **tomatoes** and **okra** cannot be kept too cold after harvesting or they lose taste and quality. Others like **sweet corn** and **melons** must be kept very cold to prevent loss of sugar and taste.

After harvesting, handle vegetables with great care. Hot summer weather quickly ruins many vegetables after you remove them from the plant. **Sweet corn, lettuce,** and **melons** continue to mature after harvesting. **Asparagus, okra,** and **beans** lose moisture quickly and become tough. This won't happen to your vegetables if you follow good harvesting rules: (1) harvest at the best stage of maturity, (2) never leave freshly harvested vegetables in the sun (I prefer to harvest in the evening), (3) quickly cook or prepare for the table whatever you are going to eat the same day that you harvest, (4) correctly handle surpluses which will be eaten later. In addition, thoroughly wash all vegetables to remove soil particles, insects, and chemical residues and help reduce spores of rots and other organisms which cause post-harvest decay.

The following chart shows when to harvest and how to handle vegetables to keep that "homegrown" quality and taste:

VEGETABLE	WHEN TO HARVEST	POST-HARVEST TREATMENT
Asparagus	Cut fast-growing spears when young and tender	Plunge in cold water, then refrigerate.
Bibb Lettuce	When butterheads form	Plunge in cold water, then refrigerate.
Broccoli	While beads are green	Plunge in cold water, then refrigerate.
Cabbage	When heads are firm	Wash and refrigerate.
Cantaloupe	When stem slips off fruit	Plunge in cold water, then refrigerate.
Cauliflower	When "curds" are white	Plunge in cold water, then refrigerate.
Cucumber	When firm and shiny	Wash and refrigerate.
Eggplant	When a slick shiny purple	Wash and refrigerate.
English Pea (for peas)	When pods are easy to crack open	Wash and refrigerate.
Garlic	When tops break over	Hang in mesh bags in a cool place.
Greens	When young and tender	Wash and refrigerate.
Head Lettuce	When heads are firm	Plunge in cold water, then refrigerate.
Irish Potato	When tops begin to die and soil cracks around mother plant	Let them dry and toughen. Do not wash until preparing to cook.
Lima Bean	When pods crack open easily	Wash and refrigerate.
Okra	When 3 to 4 inches long	Refrigerate. Do not wash.
Onion Bulbs	When tops break over	Hang in mesh bags in a cool place.
Green Onions	Whenever large enough	Plunge in cold water, then refrigerate.
Pepper, Bell types	When large and well colored	Wash and refrigerate.
Pepper, Hot types	When pods are still slick	Wash and refrigerate.
Root Crops	When soil cracks around mother plant	Wash and store in a cool place.
Snap Pea	While still flat with no peas bulging	Wash and refrigerate.
Snap and Pole Beans	While smooth and before beans enlarge	Wash and refrigerate.
Sweet Corn	After silks turn brown to the nose of the ear	Plunge in cold water, then refrigerate.
Sweet Potato	In the fall before frost and after soil cracks around the mother plant	Dig and cure for several days in the sun. After skin is tough, gently wash and dry. Store in a cool place.
Tomato	When two-thirds pink	Finish ripening on a sunny window ledge or counter until full red, then refrigerate.
Yellow Squash	While young and still slick	Wash and refrigerate.
Zucchini	While young and firm	Wash and refrigerate.

A tub filled with ice and water removes heat from many vegetables and slows ripening after harvest.

Cantaloupes continue to ripen after harvest because the growth pocket is insulated by the flesh.

Many fruits and vegetables continue to metabolize after harvest. **Corn** cobs, **melon** seed cavities, and **lettuce** centers are insulated from a refrigerator's cooling so they must be treated differently. I have found that a sink filled with ice cubes and water duplicates the hydro-cooling process used by commercial growers. Plunge vegetables needing a cold treatment into this very cold water for twenty minutes before refrigerating. This action takes out most of the heat deep within the vegetable or fruit and stops further ripening. This is extremely important to prevent **sweet corn** from losing sweetness and becoming tough and **melons** from becoming mushy inside. **Lettuce** will begin to rot in the center when this interior growth-point is not sufficiently chilled.

Wash vegetables, except those noted, before refrigerating to remove soil, chemical residue, and maybe a nice worm or two. Refrigerate vegetables in the crisper or in tightly closed plastic bags, which prevent dehydration. There are very good new zipper bags designed especially for vegetables.

Tomatoes are an exception to most rules. The last few days of ripening in the hot sun are critical times when bruising, cracking, and worm damage can be bad, so I always harvest **tomatoes** before they are fully ripe. However, do not refrigerate **tomatoes** before they are fully ripe. Place them on a counter top or a bright window sill to finish fully ripening. Then refrigerate.

Eating vegetables immediately is the best answer to post-harvest vegetable problems. That's when garden-fresh vegetables are better than all the others.

VEGETABLE ACTIVITIES FOR JUNE:

Plant

☞ Plant cowpeas like **Lady Peas**, **Black-Eyed Peas**, and **Crowder Peas** in bare garden areas. All cowpeas are a good green manure cover crop (plow them under while the stems are still succulent). They can also be left to maturity for their excellent edible peas. Both methods help to build the soil and prevent bare ground from washing.*

☞ All summer vegetables can be planted with caution, but insect problems will be much greater with late or repeat plantings.†

Prune

☞ Train and support **tomatoes**, **cucumbers**, **pole beans**, and **peppers** on a regular basis.‡

Fertilize

☞ When **sweet corn** is knee high, side dress with ammonium nitrate at the rate of 1/2 pound per 10 feet of row.**

☞ If **sweet corn** is not dark green when it tassles, apply 15-15-15 fertilizer at the rate of 1/2 pound per 10 feet of row.**

---

 * See "Planting Cover Crops," p. 205

 † See "Planting a Vegetable Garden," p. 92

 ‡ See "Training Vegetables off the Ground," p. 118

** See "Fertilizing, Spraying, and Watering Vegetables," p. 115

☛ **Tomatoes**, **peppers**, **eggplant**, **cucumber**, and **okra** should be fertilized with 5-10-15 every six weeks throughout their growing season. Application is at a rate of approximately one pound per 10 feet of row.**

☛ Continue to fertilize other growing vegetables with 5-10-15 about every six weeks for the rest of the season. Application is at a rate of approximately one pound per 10 feet of row. **

Spray

☛ There are numerous insects and diseases which feed on vegetables in our gardens throughout the season. The first step to effective control is detecting the pest before it has damaged your crop extensively. Once you spot a problem, take an affected leaf, flower, or fruit to your local nurseryman or Cooperative Extension Service agent for identification. There is a wide variety of organic and inorganic materials to control most garden pests.**

☛ **Cabbage**, **collards**, **cauliflower**, and **broccoli** will be suffering from attacks of a small green worm called a looper. Sevin will not control this pest, so use Dipel dust or Thuricide spray which contain Bacillus thuringiensis (BT).**

☛ Spray or dust frequently to control fruit worms, blights, and other diseases, especially on **tomatoes**. I like to use BT for worms and a home vegetable spray or dust for the diseases.**

☛ Black corking of the bottom (blossom end) of **tomatoes**, **peppers**, and **eggplants** is caused by a calcium deficiency aggravated by improper watering (too much or too little). Apply a calcium solution to the foliage and correct the watering problem. Liming during the winter will also help correct this problem for the next season.**

☛ Japanese Beetles are often a serious problem this month. Dust or spray vegetables with Sevin. Beetle traps work as well, but remember to place the traps downwind from your garden.**

Water

☛ Water vegetables thoroughly with about one inch of water if there has been no significant rainfall for a week.**

☛ Cracking of **tomato** fruit is generally caused by uneven watering, whether from rain or irrigation. If cracking occurs, use a soaker hose and let water run for several hours. Do not use again for three or four days. If you keep tomatoes evenly watered, they will not crack after a heavy rain.**

Other

☛ Suckering **tomatoes** (removing the fast growing shoots between the leaf and the stem) will reduce the number of fruit, even though what is left will be larger. Some gardeners partially sucker their plants to strike a happy medium. It is up to the gardener to decide which he/she prefers.‡

☛ Remove all finished crops as soon as possible and plant the bare areas with a cover crop. Old dying plants are perfect breeding grounds for insects and diseases.*

☛ Keep vegetables free of weeds by hoeing or mulching. Weeds compete with vegetables for essential nutrients and harbor damaging insects.

☛ Harvest frequently and correctly. Vegetables left too long on the plant will lose taste and quality.††

** See "Fertilizing, Spraying, and Watering Vegetables," p. 115
‡ See "Training Vegetables off the Ground," p. 118
* See "Planting Cover Crops," p. 205
†† See "Harvesting Vegetables and Keeping Them Tasty," p. 140

** See "Fertilizing, Spraying, and Watering Vegetables," p. 115

Give houseplants a frequent shower to remove dust, raise the humidity, and control some insects like thrips.

VII. *Houseplants*

With the official start of summer on June 21, most of us will have our air conditioners running on a regular basis. The house will be drying out and our houseplants will probably not be very happy. I like to take mine out on the porch and water them down thoroughly every now and then to give them a little treat. The nights are warm enough so that there is plenty of time for them to dry before returning them to their spot inside.

While a good washing down is a treat for houseplants, setting them out in direct sunlight can be torture. Don't fall into the trap of thinking that more sunlight is always a good thing. Plants are very light sensitive and unlike humans do not necessarily enjoy "lying out" on a sunny weekend.

HOUSEPLANT ACTIVITIES FOR JUNE:

Plant

☛ Houseplants, especially newly purchased ones, can be repotted at any time during the year. Use a pot at least two sizes larger so the plant will have plenty of room to grow. I prefer to grow most of my houseplants in a peat-light potting mixture.*

Prune

☛ Groom indoor plants whenever they need it. Remove weak branches or stems as well as off-color leaves.

Fertilize

☛ Fertilize with a full-strength, water-soluble fertilizer solution every time you water. As an alternative, I also like to use fertilizer spikes or Osmocote slow-release fertilizer, which lasts several months.†

Spray

☛ Check all indoor plants for insects such as spider mites, scale, and mealybug. I like to use a houseplant systemic insecticide to control them. It is easier and safer than spraying inside. Remember to apply the insecticide to the undersides of the leaves as well as the top.‡

☛ Be careful when spraying **ferns**. Some insecticides are harmful to them. *Always read the label for warnings about **ferns** and other plants.*

Water

☛ Keep an eye on houseplants during the summer. When they look limp, check for dry soil. If it is dry, water thoroughly in a sink or bathtub, letting the water drain completely, and don't water again until the surface is dry once more. Between waterings, mist with plain water on a regular basis. If the limp plants are in moist soil, do not water but allow the soil to dry a bit and mist frequently.†

☛ Tip-burn or edge-burn on leaves indicates that more water is being lost than is being absorbed by the roots. Check for dry soil, too much sunlight, or drafts from air-conditioning vents. Overwatering can also cause this condition.†

Other

☛ June 21 marks the Summer Solstice, the official beginning of summer — and the longest day of the year. After June 21, the daylight hours slowly decrease until the Winter Solstice on December 21. Remember to check your houseplants periodically as the sun's position in the sky changes. Windows which currently receive enough light may lose some as the sun's position lowers in the sky.

☛ With proper care, houseplants can be propagated at any time during the year. Since June is a hot month, keep cuttings out of direct sunlight and mist them frequently so they don't dry out.**

---

* See "Repotting Houseplants," p. 67
† See "Houseplant Care and Maintenance," p. 232
‡ See "Common Houseplant Ailments," p. 280

† See "Houseplant Care and Maintenance," p. 232
** See "Propagating Herbaceous Houseplants and Garden Plants," p. 225

Fescue "stools" when cut too closely.

VIII. *Lawns*

While June is a month of growth and expansion for summer grasses like Centipede, evergreen grasses like the fescues are at their weakest point of the year. These grasses produce seeds in the early summer and are not concentrating their major efforts on growing faster than we can keep them cut.

Be careful not to cut evergreen grasses too low in June. While summer grasses might be able to respond, the effect could be disastrous on the weakened evergreen lawns. Fertilizing is of no use, because the grass is not actively absorbing nutrients. The best way to help your evergreen lawn through this period is to keep it well watered and properly cut.

LAWN ACTIVITIES FOR JUNE:

Plant

☞ Continue planting or reseeding summer grasses like **Bermuda Grass, Centipede, St. Augustine,** and **Zoysia.***

☞ It is too late to successfully plant evergreen grasses. They need cool weather to grow and establish themselves.

Fertilize

☞ Keep summer grasses like **Bermuda Grass, St. Augustine,** and **Zoysia** well fertilized with a high-nitrogen lawn fertilizer. (**Centipede** usually does not need fertilizing unless it is light green or yellow, at which time it should be fertilized with a Centipede-specific fertilizer.) This application will be good for another 90 days.†

☞ Do not fertilize evergreen grasses unless the color is light green or yellow. Then fertilize with a high-nitrogen lawn fertilizer at one-half the recommended rate.†

Spray

☞ Watch for chinch bugs. They cause brown patches in **Centipede** and **St. Augustine** lawns. Remove a plug of sod with a bulb planter. Slowly immerse the plug in a bucket of water. Look for small insects to rise. Apply a soil insecticide like Diazinon to the whole area where you find chinch bugs.†

☞ Spray weeds to keep them from crowding out your grass.

☞ Watch for insect and disease problems. Insects cause irregular dead areas while diseases cause well-defined dead areas. Take a plug of grass which has both dying and healthy grass to your local nurseryman or Cooperative Extension Service agent for identification and suggested controls.†

Cut

☞ Cut summer grasses often to prevent browning. If you cut grass after it is very tall, you remove the green part, leaving brown stems. This condition will remain until new green leaves grow.

☞ **Hybrid Bermuda Grass** may need cutting twice a week.

☞ In the summer months, cut evergreen grasses at the highest level for the type. See chart below.

☞ Cut grasses at the proper height:

SUMMER GRASSES	HEIGHT
Common Bermuda Grass	2 inches
Hybrid Bermuda Grass	1 to 1 $\frac{1}{2}$ inches
Centipede	1 $\frac{1}{2}$ to 2 inches
St. Augustine	2 to 2 $\frac{1}{2}$ inches
Zoysia	1 to 2 inches

EVERGREEN GRASSES	HEIGHT
Kentucky 31 Tall Fescue	3 to 3 $\frac{1}{2}$ inches
Turf-type Tall Fescues	3 inches
Fine Fescues	1 $\frac{1}{2}$ to 2 inches
Kentucky Bluegrass	2 to 2 $\frac{1}{2}$ inches

Water

☞ Keep lawns watered during dry spells. Place a one-pound coffee or other straight-sided container halfway between the sprinkler and the end of the fall of water. Allow the sprinkler to run until there is one inch of water in the can. If water starts puddling on the surface of the lawn, turn off the water and check the amount in the can. If there is one-half inch, do not water again for three or four days. If there is an inch, do not water for a week. If it puddles when there is less than one-half inch, let it soak in and then continue watering until there is one-half inch in the can.‡

* See "Planting and Reseeding Summer Lawns," p. 98

† See "Fertilizing and Controlling Weeds in Lawns," p. 73

‡ See "Proper Watering," p. 130

July

IN THE SOUTHERN GARDEN

Mid-summer in the South (July and August) is called a variety of names by the old-timers: Dog Days, black gnat and mosquito time, and the doldrums. Our thinking has been changed by air-conditioned houses and cars, riding lawn mowers, and mechanized roto-tillers. Mid-summer may still be unpleasant when we work in the garden under the mid-day sun, but unlike our forebears, we can take refuge inside where it is cool and be thankful there are no "mules to plow" or 50-acre fields of cotton to hoe. We have more pleasant ways to keep in shape than tossing heavy bales of hay onto a wagon. That is why so many people like gardening: It provides as much exercise as working out in a gym or jogging a mile, and it's a lot more productive.

This time of year, I prefer to work in the garden during the late afternoon and early evening when it is cooler. The extra evening hour Daylight Savings Time adds is a bonus for gardeners who wait for more pleasant conditions to pull weeds in the flower bed, harvest vegetables, or cut the lawn. Early morning is when I stroll through the garden observing changes which indicate a possible plant problem; the late afternoon and evening are when I attack the problem with fertilizer, spray, hoe, or tiller.

July is not much of a planting month, so we concentrate on tending what we planted many months ago. Now is the time to hone your detective skills by observing changes, discovering causes, and overcoming problems. A basket of freshly harvested vegetables or fruit, a well-manicured lawn, and the sight of a colorful flower bed are ample rewards for a garden detective's skills.

"The blueberries are ripe," one of our family's vigilant sleuths reports excitedly. Everyone finds a harvest pail and rushes to the garden with visions of fresh blueberries on ice cream or breakfast cereal. Mid-summer in the South has its rewards.

AT LEFT: *Red Crape Myrtle (Lagerstroemia indica)*

I. *Shade and Flowering Trees*

The smooth attractive bark of Crape Myrtle

As if in a world of their own, Crape Myrtles all around the South are blooming. As the spring beauty of Bradford Pears, dogwoods, and Yoshino Cherries is fading in our memory, Crape Myrtles rush onto the scene to steal the show. Their blossoms range from red to purple with some handsome white ones thrown in for good measure.

With all eyes on the Crape Myrtle, I will make my pitch for this tree. Tree? you say. Why, Crape Myrtle is a shrub! Not so. Crape Myrtles are trees which can be pruned severely each year to force them into a bushier shape. And by doing so, we miss out on one of the most wonderful aspects of a Crape Myrtle — its beautiful slick bark. Those of you who have seen a thirty-year-old specimen will know that this tree is magnificent even in winter. It is almost impossible not to want to run your hand over the smooth tan trunk. There are even new cultivars with red and tan bark.

The Atlanta Botanical Garden has a walkway lined with Crape Myrtle trees which give an air of graceful elegance. So next time you head out to chop your Crape Myrtle into a bush, take a look at its bark and imagine how beautiful it would be if you let it grow tall enough to have an eight-inch diameter trunk.

DOES YOUR TREE HAVE ENOUGH WATER?

Georgia summers can be devastating — unbearably hot and dangerously dry. Vegetables, flowers, shrubs, and trees all need special attention during the relentless summer months, especially if hot weather comes with little rain. A general garden rule is to give plants about one inch of water per week if there has been no significant rainfall. The effects of this irrigation can be dramatic. **Impatiens** which begin to wilt in the noonday heat jump back to life within an hour after the sprinkler comes on. But what about our trees?

When it comes to watering, trees have special needs. More than any other plant on your property, every tree is an investment. Not only is the initial cost of the tree greater than other landscape additions, but the length of time a tree takes to mature makes it very valuable. A thirty-year-old tree cannot be replaced overnight, regardless of how much money you are willing to spend. For this reason, it is very important to keep an eye on your trees during the hot summers and blistering droughts common in the South, when trees are losing tremendous amounts of water due to evaporation.

Because of a tree's unique needs, there is a special watering device commonly known as a watering spike. The watering spike fits on the end of your garden hose just like any other hose-end attachment. The spike is about three feet long, usually made of metal or a very strong plastic. When turned on, the water travels down the inside of the spike and seeps out of one or two holes at the bottom end. Just like fertilizer, water applied on the surface of the ground under a tree is likely to be absorbed by grass, weeds,

A watering spike places water deeply near a tree's active roots.

or other plants long before it soaks down to the level of the tree roots. By using the watering spike, you can penetrate the first two feet of soil, bypass the roots of other plants, and water the tree closer to its roots. In my opinion, a watering spike is one of the most valuable tools a gardener can have.

Knowing when to begin watering a tree with a watering spike isn't easy. The roots of an established tree run deep (it is sometimes estimated that they are 1/3 as deep as the height of the tree), and they absorb water mainly from the sub-surface. Unlike vegetables and flowers, it is impossible to look at the ground and tell if a tree has enough water 10 feet below. One of the best indicators I know is the rainfall deficit announced on the news. Do not be fooled, however, by the monthly rainfall total. Underground water is regulated much more by the year-to-date figure. For instance, a winter of heavy rains will increase the water table enough to compensate for one dry summer month. But an average rainfall in July might not significantly affect a year-to-date deficit of five to six inches. If you are unable to keep up with the rainfall totals, you know your tree is really thirsty when it drops green leaves (premature leaf drop) or loses a whole limb.

One of the worst methods of determining when to start watering a tree is to wait until drought damage is apparent. Unlike the **Impatiens** in your annual bed, a tree will not wilt one day and spring back to life the next. It takes time for water to seep down to the roots and then be taken up to the leaf area of a 50-foot tree. Large shade trees are often lost because of this "lag time." Imagine what happens to a beautiful 50-foot **Sugar Maple** during a period of drought.

A Sugar Maple killed by drought

Feeder roots are damaged and new ones must grow. By the time the tree starts showing the effects of the dry weather, it has been suffering for a while. The homeowner then reacts to the sight of a dying limb by watering. Even when applied properly, the water will not seep into the ground, be absorbed by the roots, and reach the top of the tree overnight. By the time the water does reach the top of the tree, it is likely that more than one limb has died. The moral is to use preventive care, rather than curative care, when watering a valued tree, no matter how unaffected the tree appears.

When to use the watering spike on established trees is a decision which has to be made with a careful, conservative eye for the well-being of your tree. When it comes to newly planted trees, though, the answer is much easier. A newly planted tree's roots have not become established and are not much deeper than a shrub's roots. For this reason, newly planted trees should be watered with a tree-watering spike and surface soaked with a regular water breaker. This method will keep the root ball moist and provide water deeper down toward which the roots will grow. Newly planted trees should be watered every week that has no significant rainfall for at least the first year after planting.

Watering with a watering spike is relatively easy. Attach the hose and pull the spike out to your tree. Choose a spot and stand underneath the edge of the farthest reaching branches. This is the "drip line." Insert the spike into the ground as far as you can push it. It helps to turn on the water as you insert the spike to help loosen the soil and make the job a little easier. Once the spike is completely in the ground, adjust the water flow to the maximum possible without water bubbling up around the insertion point. If water does flow up around the insertion hole, reduce the water flow a little. Don't worry if a mere trickle is flowing down the hose; that is the best way to water underground.

Remember to check your watch when you start the first watering and leave the spike in that spot for at least an hour. Next, move the spike eight to ten feet around the drip-line of the tree and begin watering again. I like to water consistently clockwise or counter-clockwise so I don't forget which way I'm moving. A large tree might require five or six moves.

Now suppose the weather does catch up with you and a dead limb appears on one of your trees. For whatever reason, that side of the tree is not getting as much water as the others. While it is very important to water the dying side of the tree to prevent further damage, don't neglect the healthy side. Without watering, the healthy side might die in a matter of weeks as well.

While the thought of watering all the trees in your yard might seem overwhelming, I can tell you from experience that it is not nearly as overwhelming as the sight of a dead 30-year-old shade tree in your yard. Another way to look at it is one born out of pure selfishness. Regardless of the value of the tree, I would rather spend several hours over the summer moving a three-pound watering spike and hose around the yard than several hours chain-sawing and lugging 80-pound logs out of the yard the next winter!

TREE ACTIVITIES FOR JULY:

Plant

☛ July is *not* a good time to plant B&B and container-grown trees. Wait until late fall/winter when your money will be well spent.

Prune

☛ Summer is *not* the time to prune tree limbs. If there is a broken branch, however, remove the limb (including the jagged break or split) with a clean cut.

Spray

☛ Look for damaging insects on evergreen trees like **magnolias** and **hollies**. Scale, spider mite, lacebug, leaf miner, spittlebug, and leaf hopper are bad in July. Use Cygon or Orthene to control them. Do not use Cygon on **hollies**.*

☛ Protect flowering trees, like **flowering peaches** and **flowering plums,** from Japanese Beetle damage by spraying with Sevin or putting traps downwind from the tree.*

☛ On occasion, insects and diseases which you can't identify may show up on trees. When this happens, take a branch containing some of the affected areas to your local nurseryman or Cooperative Extension Service agent for identification and suggested controls.*

Water

☛ Newly planted trees should be soaked each week throughout the month if there is no significant·rainfall.†

☛ During periods of extreme drought, large trees may need watering. Watch for discoloration, drying, die-back, and premature leaf-fall as signs that the tree is being affected. Use a watering spike placed intermittently around the perimeter of the tree's roots, approximately under the edge of the farthest reaching limbs. Water thoroughly.†

Other

☛ Keep newly planted trees well mulched to conserve moisture when it is hot and dry. However, do not let the mulch pack against the trunks of your trees.‡

☛ Be extremely careful when mowing or using a power trimmer around old and new trees. *Do not hit or damage the bark.* Even the slightest damage may make an entrance for borers or other damaging insects. This is true for all trees in the landscape or natural area, including trees you have planted as well as native trees. **Dogwood, flowering peach, flowering cherry,** and **flowering plum** are highly susceptible to borer attacks. Shade trees like **pines** are also attacked by various borers and bark beetles.

---

* See "Controlling Insects and Diseases," p. 80
† See "Does Your Tree Have Enough Water?" p. 150
‡ See "Mulching: A Lesson from Nature," p. 243

---

* See "Controlling Insects and Diseases," p. 80

Summer-flowering Butterfly Bush (Buddleia davidii) gives bright summer color and attracts butterflies.

II. *Shrubs and Vines*

July is filled with splashes of whites, yellows, reds, pinks, and purples amid the luscious dark green of summer leaves. There are summer hydrangeas showing off their huge white snowballs, and the many colorful varieties of giant hybrid Clematis unfolding their large blossoms with patient grace.

Sometimes we forget that the colorful flowers in our garden aren't meant for us. With all of our hard work and careful tending, we would like to believe that flowering trees, shrubs, and plants are repaying us for all the attention we show them. In July, the folly of these thoughts is apparent when the Butterfly Bush blooms in spectacular white, pink, purple, or red. The butterflies float in to feast on the nectar and the bush happily supplies it in exchange for a little help in pollinating all its flowers. Watching the wonderful symbiotic relationship of butterfly and bush makes us realize we are just bystanders fortunate to behold the glory of nature.

SHRUB AND VINE ACTIVITIES FOR JULY:

Plant

☛ July is *not* the best time to plant B&B and container-grown shrubs or vines. Wait until the late fall/winter when you won't shock the plant as much.

Prune

☛ Do not prune spring-flowering evergreens like azalea, **Camellia**, and early-flowering cultivars of **Rhododendron** (those which bloomed in April and May). They have started setting flower buds for next spring's blossoms. Pruning will reduce or remove next year's flowering potential. *

☛ Late-flowering cultivars of **Rhododendron** and **Mountain Laurel** (both of which bloom in June and early July) can be pruned after they have finished blooming, but before new growth darkens.*

* See "Pruning Flowering Shrubs and Vines," p. 31

☞ Evergreen shrubs like **Burford Holly, Red Tip Photinia, Box Leaf Holly,** and **Otto Luyken Laurel** may be shaped by trimming new growth. However, avoid removing all of the new shoots and cutting into last year's growth.

☞ It is best not to prune summer-flowering shrubs like **Althaea, Butterfly Bush,** and **Hydrangea** in the summer unless absolutely necessary. Wait until next winter.

Fertilize

☞ Late flowering cultivars of **Rhododendron** and **Mountain Laurel** should be fertilized after they finish blooming. Those which bloom in June and July should be given a lighter application of fertilizer since their roots are close to the surface and could be damaged by the fertilizer in hot, dry weather. Use an acid azalea/camellia fertilizer at roughly 1/4 pound per three feet of the shrub's height, but check the directions of your specific brand. If you apply the fertilizer on top of the mulch, there is less chance of burn. This is usually done once a year.†

☞ Do not fertilize spring-flowering shrubs like **azalea, Camellia,** and **Viburnum** (you will disturb bud formation) or broadleaf evergreens like **Burford Holly** and **Box Leaf Hollies** in July.

☞ Do not fertilize summer-flowering shrubs like **Althaea, Butterfly Bush,** or **Hydrangea** because you might disturb the bloom. Summer-flowering shrubs are fertilized in the early spring before their growth spurt begins. However, you may fertilize any which are off-color and showing signs of fertilizer deficiency.

Spray

☞ Watch out for damaging insects on evergreens, especially **Euonymus, azalea, Camellia, Pyracantha, Gardenia,** and **Photinia.** Scale, spider mites, lacebug, leaf miner, spittlebug, and leaf hopper are very active in July. Use Cygon or Orthene as a control. Do not use Cygon on **hollies.**‡

☞ Continue to watch **Red Tip Photinia** for signs of leaf spot. When seen, immediately spray affected and adjacent plants with Daconil.‡

☞ Lacebugs are terrible pests which attack the foliage of **azalea** and **Pyracantha.** The damaged leaves have a silver appearance. Turn the leaf over and inspect for brown dots of residue which indicate the presence of this pest. This time of the year, you may even see this terrible pest feeding on the undersides of the leaves. Spray with Orthene.‡

Water

☞ Slowly soak shrubs and vines if there has been no significant rain in a week. This is especially important for this year's plantings. I prefer watering with a water-breaker nozzle attached to the hose. Place the nozzle next to the trunk and slowly soak until water puddles around the plant.**

Other

☞ Mulch all shrubs and vines to conserve moisture during the summer. Do not allow the mulch to crowd or pack against the lower stems and trunks.††

☞ Begin making semi-hardwood cuttings of shrubs like **azalea, Camellia,** and **Hydrangea.** Root them in a peat-light mixture or perlite rooting bed in a shaded location. Mist them frequently to keep them from drying out.‡‡

---

† See "How to Fertilize Shrubs and Vines," p. 30

‡ See "Controlling Insects and Diseases," p. 80

‡ See "Controlling Insects and Diseases," p. 80

** See "Proper Watering," p. 130

†† See "Mulching: A Lesson from Nature," p. 243

‡‡ See "Semi-Hardwood Cuttings," p. 174

Fresh grapes are a delight in mid-summer.

III. *Fruits*

Fruits are amazing! Of all the produce in the Southern garden, there is nothing as awe-inspiring as the fruit harvest. While we are busily hoeing, cultivating, fertilizing, and watering our vegetables, it seems like there is nothing to do but sit back and watch our fruit ripen. Of course, the pruning, fertilizing, and mulching we did back in January is too distant a memory to be weighed into the equation. For now, it is fine with me to consider these fruits a delightful surprise gift from nature.

While late peaches are ripening, blueberries are just beginning. Grapes, strawberries, and the first summer apples are also ready. It seems as if the biggest chore of the summer fruit harvest is finding enough new dessert recipes to handle what we've grown.

SECRETS OF THE BERRY PATCH
(Pruning Semi-Bush Fruits)

One of nature's finest gifts to Southerners is the blackberry bush, which grows wild through much of the South, offering delicious free fruit to anyone who dares to enter the briar patch. Most of us never stop to think why the briar patch is the way it is—a twist-ed tangle of more dead canes than live ones. A briar patch gives us wonderful insight into the growing pattern of **blackberries** and most other cane-producing fruits like **raspberries**, **dewberries**, and **boysenberries** (which I call semi-bush fruits).

We learn from the briar patch that there are three kinds of stems: fresh new shoots, healthy shoots which produce fruit, and older canes which are either

After fruiting, blackberry canes die, leaving a thorny thicket.

New summer shoots of blackberry will fruit next summer.

dead or dying. With semi-bush fruits, canes grow one year in order to produce fruit the second year, and then never produce again and die. After fruiting, these canes are useless and die quickly, which is the reason the briar patch becomes such a tangled mess. If you look at the bottom of a briar patch, you will see many new shoots starting to sprout, even as early as **blackberry** picking time.

Experienced fruit growers never have to struggle in a briar patch when they harvest their berries because of the way they train their plants. Each year after harvest, they remove the canes which bore fruit to let the new shoots grow which will produce next year, without competition from the useless ones.

If you train semi-bush fruits properly, you allow them to grow and be pruned more easily. This type of berry should be planted in rows at least eight feet apart. Place eight-foot-long permanent, treated posts 12 feet apart in the row and two feet into the ground. Run two or three wires horizontally between the posts, securing them tightly. Put the first wire two feet above the ground and run the rest like a ladder,

each two feet above the last. Plant two to four plants between each set of posts, depending on the type of berry and whether it is a bush cultivar or a trailing cultivar. Tie the first year's growth to the wires. These will not bear the first season.

New shoots will sprout from the base of each plant during the second season. Keep them separate from last year's canes, the ones which produce berries this summer. After harvesting fruits this summer from the second year canes, remove them as soon as possible, then tie this year's shoots to the wires. New shoots will continue to sprout through the summer and should be tied as soon as they reach the wires. These will produce delicious fruit next summer.

FRUIT ACTIVITIES FOR JULY:

Plant

☛ July is *not* the best time to plant B&B and container-grown fruits. Wait until the late fall/winter when you won't shock the plant as much.

Prune

☛ This season's new growth is emerging on fruit trees. Next year's fruit will be set on this new growth, so if you do anything to disturb it, you will disturb next year's crop.

☛ Remove all canes of semi-bush fruits like **blackberries** and **raspberries** which have finished fruiting. This will encourage new shoots on which next year's berries will be set. After removing the old canes, train this year's growth onto the fence or trellis.*

☛ Remove any Black Knot Galls on plum stems.

Fertilize

☛ Fertilize **figs** with a 15-15-15 fertilizer. Use about 1/2 pound per three feet of height. This is the second application of the year. If you missed the first application in early spring, apply this same amount.

* See "Secrets of the Berry Patch," p. 155

☞ Fertilize **apples** and **pears** if they are growing poorly. Use 15-15-15 fertilizer according to the amount of growth desired.†

Spray

☞ **Grapes**, late **peaches**, and **summer apples** ripen in July, but other fruits which ripen in August and September need help to have good fruit. Continue a regular control program for fruit insects and diseases. The most practical method of control is a complete home orchard spray. Continue applications at recommended intervals until the fruit ripens. Read the directions and do not spray fruits too close to harvest.

☞ Watch for spider mites on **raspberries** and other semi-bush berries. Their presence is evident when the foliage has a silvery gray appearance. Spray with Kelthane to control this serious pest.‡

☞ Japanese Beetles continue to be a serious problem this month. They attack **grapes**, **plums**, and other fruits. Those which have finished fruiting should be sprayed or dusted with Sevin to prevent severe leaf damage and defoliation. Beetle traps work as well, but remember to place them downwind from your fruit. You don't want to attract the beetles to your fruiting plants.‡

☞ Spray **bunch grapes** until the fruit is harvested with a complete home orchard spray to prevent brown rot and control leaf worms and Japanese Beetles.‡

☞ Brown rot continues to be a serious disease problem for late-ripening **peach** cultivars. If you are to harvest good fruit, you must remain diligent with your complete home orchard spray program to control this disease.‡

Water

☞ Keep **fig** bushes well watered and mulched. **Figs** are growing larger now and need water to develop well.

☞ It is important to slowly soak fruit trees and bushes if there has been no significant rain in a week, especially if you planted them this year.**

Other

☞ Keep fruit harvested as it ripens. If you leave fruit hanging on the tree after your spray program is completed, you are issuing an invitation for insects and diseases.

☞ Remove all undeveloped fruit which failed to ripen for whatever reason. Never leave it on the tree.

☞ When mowing in orchard areas, be careful not to hit the bark of fruit trees with the mower. Any damage to the bark will provide an entrance place for borers.

☞ Keep fruits mulched with pine straw to prevent weeds and grasses from competing for water and fertilizer, but do not pile the mulch against the trunks of fruit trees.††

☞ Allow **strawberry** runners to develop into new daughter plants. This will increase your next year's harvest.

☞ Cover **fig** bushes with a net to keep birds from ruining the fruit.

† See "How to Fertilize Fruit Trees," p. 37
‡ See "Controlling Insects and Diseases," p. 80

** See "Proper Watering," p. 130
†† See "Mulching: A Lesson from Nature," p. 243

Mass rose plantings are beautiful all summer.

IV. *Roses*

July is a the time to decide which new roses to add to your collection next year. While most roses look good in May and even June, July is the month to see if they can stand the test of a Southern summer. Roses which are growing and flowering well in the heat are those which you should consider for your future plantings. Also observe the quality of the flowers. Many Northern and Western varieties bloom poorly in our summer heat. Cool weather varieties may have brown edges to the petals and may shatter quickly, whereas hot weather varieties flower and hold well during hot summer weather here in the South.

Some great places to view roses are the various public gardens around the South. Most have numerous rose beds which are likely to contain some interesting newer cultivars. Watch out, though. When you finally head out to the parking lot, you will probably have a pad with the scribbled names of 15 new roses you want to add to your own garden. When admiring a beautiful rose bed, it is hard to remember that 15 scribbled names also means 15 holes to dig next winter.

ROSE ACTIVITIES FOR JULY:

Plant

☞ July is *not* a good time to plant bare-root and container-grown roses. Wait until the late fall/winter when you won't shock the plant as much.

Prune

☞ Groom roses constantly. Never leave a dead or dying stem on the plant because the disease will spread to healthy canes. Also remove any weak, broken, or spindly shoots.*

* See "Grooming Roses," p. 110

☛ Remove all dead flowers by clipping above a five-leaflet set, as if you were cutting the flower to take inside.*

Fertilize

☛ In hot, dry conditions, keep plants growing with light applications of a complete rose fertilizer on your regular six-to-eight-week program. Supplement this program by spraying the foliage and new shoots with a water-soluble fertilizer solution like Peters.

Spray

☛ Keep going with your complete rose spray program every 10 to 14 days according to the directions. Use a combination insecticide and fungicide spray and continue applications through September.

☛ Watch out for Japanese Beetles. Your normal spray program will not control these pests. Use Japanese Beetle traps or supplement your spray program with Sevin.†

☛ Blackspot continues to be a major summer problem for roses. Watch out! Consistent applications of your regular spray should prevent heavy damage.†

☛ During hot, dry weather, thrips may also become a problem. Infected rose blossoms will turn brown on the petal edges. Check for these pests by pulling one of the discolored flowers apart. There will be rod-shaped thrips feeding at the base of the petal. Control thrips with Orthene.†

☛ Bud worms eat holes in maturing rose buds. They are usually controlled by your regular complete spray program, but applying Bacillus thuringiensis (BT) is a good supplemental control method.†

Water

☛ Water when there has been no significant rain for a week. A soaker hose is a good way to prevent wetting the foliage and thereby encouraging diseases.

Soak the bed thoroughly. Shallow watering does more harm than good by drawing the roots to the surface where they will dry out more quickly.‡

Other

☛ Observe various rose cultivars in public gardens and in the gardens of friends. Consider any roses which are growing and flowering well in the heat for your future plantings.

☛ Remember to cut flowers correctly. Always make the cut above a joint where a five-leaflet originates. Cutting at this point encourages a strong new shoot and blossom to form.*

☛ Many **Hybrid Tea** and **Grandiflora** roses have several flowers in a cluster (called a candelabra) which may not all bloom at the same time. Remove each spent flower in the cluster as it finishes blooming. When all the flowers are done, cut the whole cluster stalk back to a five-leaflet set.*

☛ Keep roses well mulched with pine straw during the summer. Add fresh mulch when you can see bare ground around the plants, but do not pile mulch against the crown or lower stems. Many problems like cankers and botrytis occur when mulch covers the lower stems.**

☛ Cut roses will last longer in an arrangement when the stems are recut underwater before placing in the vase. This allows water, not air, to travel up the stem.

‡ See "Proper Watering," p. 130

* See "Grooming Roses," p. 110

** See "Mulching: A Lesson from Nature," p. 243

* See "Grooming Roses," p. 110

† See "Controlling Insects and Diseases," p.80

V. *Flowers and Colorful Garden Plants*

By July, our ice tea can't keep the mint bed under control. It has grown tall and spread everywhere. Mint jelly, mint tea, mint garnishments, mint lemonade—enough! The only answer to keeping mint out of our ice cream is the weed-eater. Cutting them back to the young basal shoots will force fresh growth for tender new leaves the rest of the summer, but also cut down on the abundance of unused foliage.

Mint is a wonderful herb but can crowd out other plants unless kept restricted.

Besides chopping back my mint, July is my time to stand back and admire the flower bed. Annuals and perennials have all grown to fill their designated spaces and are looking strong and healthy. Every July I take a picture of my garden so that next winter I have something to remind me of these sunny warm colorful days. The picture also inspires me to order mail-order seeds in time for planting.

Admiring the garden in July is a good way to slow down after the frantic planting of April, May, and June and enjoy our gardens as they grow.

STOP THOSE MOSQUITOES!

By July in the Southern garden, most of us are cautious about working outside in the evenings. A couple of months of mosquito bites have taught us that gardening is not always pain free. To my dismay, I have found that over the past couple of years mosquitoes have been attacking me in the afternoons. I have been unable personally to substantiate reports of a new breed of daytime mosquito moving into the South. These mosquitoes supposedly have a distinct color pattern, but I have decided not to participate in any field research to identify them.

There are several ways to cut down on mosquito populations and make our gardens more habitable in the evenings. Some of these methods coincide perfectly with our regular gardening activities. For instance, we can grow **Birdhouse** or **Martin Gourds** (Lagenaria siceraria) to hang for the purple martins. Purple martins are a type of swallow which nest in colonies and are renowned for their consumption of deleterious insects like gnats and mosquitoes. Each year people who are lucky enough to have a colony of purple martins rejoice at the sight of their return from wintering in Central and South America. Purple martins come back to the same spot year after year to nest and eat insects over the summer months.

Setting up a nesting area for purple martins is not difficult at all, but remember to grow enough gourds for a colony (two or three plants will supply about eight gourds). Once the gourds have grown and hardened on the vine, bore a 2 1/2-inch-wide hole on the side of the bottom portion of the gourd. Empty out the seeds and bore a smaller hole at the top to insert a rope to hang it from. **Martin Gourds** are usually hung on several cross beams nailed to an upright pole which is situated in an open area. Start with two rows, each holding four or five gourds, with the lower row no lower than 15 feet off the ground. As your purple martin colony expands, you can grow more gourds to house them.

Purple martins will also nest in man-made bird-

Insect-eating purple martins can be attracted by hanging groups of Martin Gourds for them to nest in.

Martin Gourds or houses should be in the open.

houses. These are unique in that they are multi-room dwellings. Some designs are for a single-story birdhouse with eight rooms while others are two-story birdhouses with up to 16 rooms. The main consideration in designing your own purple martin house is that each individual room should be six inches by six inches and the entry hole should be 2 1/2 inches in diameter. The hole should be one inch above the floor. The birdhouse should be fastened on top of a 15-to-20-foot pole and situated in an open area.

Purple martins are somewhat picky. They like open areas, especially near a pond or lake. In fact, there are probably a lot of purple martin houses around the South that have never been the home of a purple martin. Don't be deterred. Even if the purple martins don't arrive, there are lots of other fun and interesting birds who will gladly make a home out of your gourds.

Bats are another insect-eating friend around the garden. I often see them at twilight high above my garden. Their amazingly quick jerks and turns seem out of place on a lazy summer evening, but when you realize that some bats eat as many as 500 insects an hour, it is understandable why they have to move so fast.

It is unfortunate that as we build new houses and develop the surrounding areas, we are destroying many of the trees and natural habitats that bats like to live in. Building a bat house is a good way to attract bats as well as to help out the ones already living near your house. And with the added bonus of losing 500 insects an hour, it seems like an investment well worth making.

While detailed plans of various bat houses are available from your local Cooperative Extension Service, the main idea behind them is pretty simple. A bat house is basically a box made of rough wood with several wooden panels dividing the inside. Bats enter the bottom of the box and crawl up between the panels in order to nest overnight. The panels are spaced at different intervals so that young bats can feel cozy in one slot, while the fatter, more mosquito-laden bats can still squeeze in some of the larger slots. Your box should contain at least four slots with the smallest slot 3/4 of an inch wide, and each additional slot 3/16 of an inch wider.

The outer dimensions will change depending on the number of panels and slots you allow. Panels, however, should be about two feet wide and about 20 inches high. The back of the box should be 30 inches high so that there is a 10-inch landing area below the back panel.

Bat houses should be hung 12 to 15 feet above the ground on the side of a tree, barn, or outbuilding. The spot should get enough sun to warm it during the day, but not so much as to make it unbearably hot. Try to find a spot which faces east to southeast and gets plenty of morning sun. Bats may move into your bat house in as little as several weeks, but sometimes they don't find it for a year or two. Don't give up hope, though, because just like purple martins, once they move in, you have probably made a friend for life.

Summer evenings in July and August always seem a little better when you look up and spot a bat busy at work or a purple martin swooping here and there. While no garden is completely mosquito-free, having these flying friends around at least makes me feel that mosquitoes were created for a reason other than to eat me.

FLOWER ACTIVITIES FOR JULY:

Plant

☛ Last call for planting annual, perennial, and biennial herbaceous garden plants like **Ageratum**, **Begonia**, **Coleus**, **Geranium**, **Impatiens**, **Salvia**, **Astilbe**, **Shasta Daisy**, **Purple Cone-Flower**, and **Rudbeckia**. Work the ground well, add humus, and plant as if it were spring. Keep new plantings well watered so they will grow quickly and start performing.*

☛ Cut **Bearded Iris** leaves back in a fan after the tips begin to brown. If you want to move them to a new spot or divide the clumps, reset them as soon as the leaves turn brown and die back. First, lift and separate

See "How to Plant a Flower Bed," p. 62

the clumps. Then dust them with sulfur to prevent rot and reset them shallowly in a well-drained, sunny spot.*

Prune

☞ Groom herbaceous flowering plants like **Impatiens**, **Begonia**, and **Salvia** by removing spent flowers, seed pods, yellow leaves, and improper growth. Plants which have grown tall and spindly may be topped to force side growth.†

☞ Do not pinch **chrysanthemums** and **dahlias** after July 1 or you might disrupt the bloom.

Fertilize

☞ Continue fertilizing plants with 5-10-15 on a six-to-eight-week schedule through the end of the season.

☞ Fertilize **chrysanthemums** and **dahlias** with a 5-10-15 formula every four to six weeks until they bloom.

☞ During dry weather, spray a water-soluble fertilizer solution like Peters on foliage as a supplement to keep plants growing well when their roots are not as active and they are not taking up fertilizer from the soil.

Spray

☞ Watch carefully for insects and diseases on flowers. Insects are the greatest problem. Fast succulent growth is highly susceptible to aphid, spider mite, leaf hopper, thrip, and worm damage. Orthene is an excellent all-around control.‡

☞ Large attacks of worms on a particular plant, like **Geranium**, can be controlled by Dipel dust or Thuricide spray containing Bacillus thuringiensis (BT), an excellent biological control.‡

☞ Slugs and snails may still be bad on **Hosta**, **Caladium**, **Elephant Ear**, **Coleus,** and other succulent summer flowers. Use a snail bait or shallow pans of stale beer to kill them.‡

☞ As in other areas of the garden, Japanese Beetles are often a serious problem this month. Plants can be sprayed or dusted with Sevin to prevent damage. Beetle traps work as well, but remember to place the traps downwind from your garden.‡

Water

☞ Water plants thoroughly with one inch of water per week if there has been no significant rainfall.**

☞ Hanging baskets will need more water during the hot summer months, but do not overwater them. Soak them thoroughly, then soak them again only when the surface is dry. I take mine out in the yard to wash them down (or put them out when it rains) to remove dust and to keep them more attractive.

Other

☞ Remove spent flowers as soon as they become unattractive unless the seeds are to be harvested. Allowing seeds to develop reduces the vigor of plants and produces fewer flowers.†

☞ Keep beds and borders free from weeds, which compete with good plants for water and fertilizer.

☞ Mulch beds with dry grass clippings or pine straw to reduce weed problems and to conserve moisture. Mulch eliminates the need to cultivate the soil because it keeps the soil moist and prevents the sun from baking it hard.††

☞ If no mulch is used, cultivate beds and borders frequently to keep the surface loose, allowing air and moisture to enter the ground while controlling weeds.

☞ Some flowering plants may become top-heavy and fall over. Stake them with small green bamboo stakes which do not show.

---

* See "How to Plant a Flower Bed," p. 62
† See "Grooming and Pinching Flowers," p. 137
‡ See "Controlling Insects and Diseases," p. 80

‡ See "Controlling Insects and Diseases," p. 80
** See "Proper Watering," p. 130
† See "Grooming and Pinching Flowers," p. 137
†† See "Mulching: A Lesson from Nature," p. 243

Harvest sweet corn when the silks are brown to the tip and the ear feels firm.

VI. *Vegetables*

While the official beginning of summer was back in June, my definition of the start of summer is when my cool-weather crops have finished and squash, beans, tomatoes, peppers, sweet corn, and pole beans begin to grace my table. What is more like summer? There is something about the sight of sweet corn tassling in the garden that slows life down and makes it a little bit more meaningful. It even sounds like fun to say, "I'll be out on the porch shucking the corn."

For most of us, vegetable gardening has been a fairly continuous activity since April. Don't let the drudgery of hoeing summer weeds get you down. Take a moment to scout for bugs, notice the two different flowers on your squash, or dream up a new way to train your pole beans. Investigation and innovation are what keep vegetable gardening new and exciting every year.

VEGETABLE ACTIVITIES FOR JULY:

Plant

☛ Plant cowpeas like **Lady Peas**, **Black-Eyed Peas**, and **Crowder Peas** in bare garden areas. All cowpeas are a good green-manure cover crop (plow them under while the stems are still succulent). They can also be left to maturity for their excellent edible peas. Both methods help to build the soil and prevent bare ground from washing.*

Prune

☛ Train and support **tomatoes**, **cucumbers**, **pole beans**, and **peppers** on a regular basis.†

Fertilize

☛ If **sweet corn** is not dark green when it tassles, apply 15-15-15 fertilizer at the rate of 1/2 pound per 10 feet of row.‡

☛ **Tomatoes**, **peppers**, **eggplant**, **cucumber**, and **okra** should be fertilized with 5-10-15 every six weeks throughout their growing season. Application is at a rate of approximately one pound per 10 feet of row.‡

☛ Continue to fertilize other growing vegetables with 5-10-15 about every six weeks until harvest is over. Application is at a rate of approximately one pound per 10 feet of row. ‡

Spray

☛ There are numerous insects and diseases which feed on vegetables in our gardens throughout the season. The first step to effective control is detecting the pest before it has damaged your crop extensively. Once you spot a problem, take an infected leaf, flower, or fruit to your local nurseryman or Cooperative Extension Service agent for identification. There are a wide variety of organic and inorganic materials which control most garden pests.

☛ Spray or dust frequently to control fruit worms, blights, and other diseases, especially on **tomatoes**. I like to use BT for worms and a home vegetable spray or dust for the diseases.‡

☛ Watch for Asparagus beetles which will quickly eat **Asparagus** foliage and damage plants. Sevin should give you good control.‡

☛ Blossom End Rot, which results in black corking of the bottom (blossom end) of **tomatoes, peppers,** and **eggplants**, is caused by a calcium deficiency aggravated by improper watering (too much or too little). Apply a calcium solution to the foliage and correct the watering problem. Liming during the winter will also help correct this problem for the next season.‡

☛ Japanese Beetles continue to be a serious problem this month. Spray or dust vegetables with Sevin. Beetle traps work as well, but remember to place the traps downwind from your garden.‡

☛ Dust **sweet corn** silks with Sevin or BT to prevent earworms from ruining your **corn** crop. Read the label to find how many days before harvest you can still dust.‡

Water

☛ Water vegetables thoroughly with about one inch of water if there has been no significant rainfall for a week.‡

☛ Cracking of **tomato** fruit is generally caused by uneven watering, whether from rain or irrigation. If cracking occurs, use a soaker hose and let water run for several hours. Do not use again for three or four days. If you keep **tomatoes** properly watered, they will not crack after a heavy rain.‡

---

* See "Planting Cover Crops," p. 205

† See "Training Vegetables off the Ground," p. 118

‡ See "Fertilizing, Spraying, and Watering Vegetables," p. 115

‡ See "Fertilizing, Spraying, and Watering Vegetables," p. 115

Other

☛ Suckering **tomatoes** (removing the fast growing shoots between the leaf and the stem) will reduce the number of fruit, even though what is left will be larger. It's your choice as to whether to sucker, partially sucker, or sucker not at all.

☛ Harvested **sweet corn, lettuce, melons**, and **green onions** will hold their quality if you plunge them into an ice-water bath for 20 minutes before storing.**

☛ Keep vegetables free of weeds by hoeing or mulching (mulching also conserves moisture in the ground). Weeds can devastate crops during July by competing with them for essential nutrients and also by harboring damaging insects.

☛ Remove all finished crops as soon as possible and plant the bare areas with a cover crop like **cowpeas**. Old dying plants are perfect breeding grounds for insects and diseases.*

☛ Harvest frequently and correctly. Vegetables left too long on the plant lose taste and quality.**

** See "Harvesting Vegetables and Keeping Them Tasty," p. 140
* See "Planting Cover Crops," p. 205

VEGETABLE:	HARVEST:
Onions and Shallots	When the tops break over and yellow
Cucumbers, Squash, Zucchini	While still small and tender
Cantaloupe	When the vine pulls easily and cleanly from the melon
Pole Beans	Before you see the seeds bulging
Okra	Before it is five inches long
Watermelons	When the pigtail dies
Tomatoes, Peppers, Eggplants	Harvest frequently and remove unusable fruit
Sweet Corn	When the silks are brown

NOTES

Leaves of Begonia deliciosa are beautiful all year.

VII. *Houseplants*

Most summers I end up buying several new houseplants. Gardening fever takes hold, and since I have usually finished filling every remaining spot of my annual bed by mid-summer, I turn my attention to the porch and patio. Bare corners, beware!

There are a couple of things to remember when buying summer houseplants. First, watch out for insects and diseases. Observe new plants a few days before you place them in the vicinity of your other plants. Aphids can travel! Another thing to remember is that houseplants are not always grown in the best potting mixture. Plant growers often use an "economy mix" made up mostly of ground bark and other cheap components. They complement the poor soil by adding plenty of fertilizer so the plant will continue to grow. This is fine for the short-term, but is not conducive to a plant's long-term health. I like to repot my newly purchased houseplants in a peat-light potting mixture which will help them to grow healthily all year.

HOUSEPLANT ACTIVITIES FOR JULY:

Plant

☛ Houseplants, especially newly purchased ones, can be repotted at any time during the year. Use a pot at least two sizes larger so the plant will have plenty of room to grow. I prefer to grow most of my houseplants in a peat-light potting mixture.*

Prune

☛ Groom indoor plants whenever they need it. Remove weak branches or stems as well as off-color leaves.

Fertilize

☛ Fertilize with a full-strength, water-soluble fertilizer solution every time you water. As an alternative,

* See "Repotting Houseplants," p. 67

I also like to use fertilizer spikes or Osmocote slow-release fertilizer, which lasts several months.†

Spray

☛ Check all indoor plants for insects such as spider mites, scale, and mealybug. I like to use a houseplant systemic insecticide to control them, because it is easier and safer than spraying inside. If you do spray, remember to apply the insecticide to the undersides of the leaves. I prefer to take my houseplants outside to spray since most insecticides smell bad.‡

☛ Be careful when spraying **ferns**. Some insecticides are harmful to them. *Always read the label for warnings about **ferns** and other plants.*

Water

☛ Keep an eye on houseplants during the summer. When they look limp, check for dry soil. If it is dry, water thoroughly in a sink or bathtub, letting the water drain completely, and don't water again until the surface is dry once more. Between waterings, mist with plain water on a regular basis. If the limp plants are in moist soil, do not water, but allow the soil to dry a bit and mist frequently.†

☛ Tip-burn or edge-burn on leaves indicates that more water is being lost than is being absorbed by the roots. Check for dry soil, too much sunlight, or drafts from air-conditioning vents. Overwatering can also cause this condition.†

Other

☛ With proper care, houseplants can be propagated at any time during the year. Since July is a hot month, keep cuttings out of direct sunlight and mist them frequently so they don't dry out.**

☛ Remember that the position of the sun continues to change in the sky. Windows which received plenty of light last month might be losing some exposure.

---

† See "Houseplant Care and Maintenance," p. 232

‡ See "Common Houseplant Ailments," p. 280

† See "Houseplant Care and Maintenance," p. 232

** See "Propagating Herbaceous Houseplants and Garden Plants," p. 225

NOTES

VIII. *Lawns*

During the summer months, caring for summer grasses like Bermuda Grass is rather straightforward. When they are not dark green, fertilize them. When it doesn't rain, water them. Nothing could be simpler (as long as you don't mind opening up your wallet).

Things are a little different with evergreen grasses like the fescues. Since they are not squarely in the growth phase of their life cycle, we have to be more aware of what they are up to so that we can effectively care for them.

In late May and June, evergreen grasses were in the reproductive phase of their life cycle and would have produced seeds if left uncut. This month, they are recuperating and although they are still growing (and still need to be cut), they are not in a heavy growth phase like they were in cool weather. This means that if we decide to fertilize, most of the nutrients will dissipate before being absorbed by the grass and overfertilizing can harm them.

The best way to care for evergreen lawns in July is to keep them watered when it is dry and not cut them too close to the ground. Also, control weeds which might choke them out as well as insects and diseases which can overcome them in their weakened state. Fertilize only when they are light green and do it carefully. Since they are not rapidly growing, fertilizing evergreen lawns may encourage more weeds than grass.

LAWN ACTIVITIES FOR JULY:

Plant

☛ Continue planting or reseeding summer grasses like **Bermuda Grass**, **Zoysia**, **Centipede**, and **St. Augustine** until early August.*

☛ Do not plant evergreen grasses like **fescue** until September.

Fertilize

☛ Keep summer grasses like **Bermuda Grass**, **St. Augustine**, and **Zoysia** well fertilized with a high-nitrogen lawn fertilizer. (**Centipede** usually does not need fertilizing unless it is a light green or yellow, at which time it should be fertilized with a Centipede-specific fertilizer.) This application will be good for another 90 days.

☛ Do not fertilize evergreen grasses unless the color is light green or yellow. Then fertilize with a high-nitrogen lawn fertilizer at one-half the recommended rate.

Spray

☛ Watch for chinch bugs. They cause brown patches in **Centipede** and **St. Augustine** lawns. Remove a plug of sod with a bulb planter. Slowly immerse the plug in a bucket of water. Look for small insects to rise. Apply a soil insecticide like Diazinon to the whole area where you find chinch bugs.†

☛ Spray weeds to keep them from crowding out your grass.

☛ Watch for insect and disease problems. Insects cause irregular dead areas while diseases cause well-defined dead areas. Take a plug of grass which has both dying and healthy grass to your local nurseryman or Cooperative Extension Service agent for identification.†

Cut

☛ **Hybrid Bermuda Grass** may need cutting twice a week.

* See "Planting and Reseeding Summer Lawns," p. 98

† See "Controlling Insects and Diseases," p. 80

☛ Cut summer grasses often to prevent browning. If you wait until the grass is tall before cutting, you will remove the green part, leaving brown stems. This condition will remain until new green leaves grow.

☛ In the summer months, cut evergreen grasses at the highest level for the type. See chart below.

☛ Cut grasses at the proper height:

SUMMER GRASSES	HEIGHT
Common Bermuda Grass	2 inches
Hybrid Bermuda Grass	1 to 1 $^1/_2$ inches
Centipede	1 $^1/_2$ to 2 inches
St. Augustine	2 to 2 $^1/_2$ inches
Zoysia	1 to 2 inches

EVERGREEN GRASSES	HEIGHT
Kentucky 31 Tall Fescue	3 to 3 $^1/_2$ inches
Turf-type Tall Fescues	3 inches
Fine Fescues	1 $^1/_2$ to 2 inches
Kentucky Bluegrass	2 to 2 $^1/_2$ inches

Water

☛ Keep lawns watered during dry spells. Place a one-pound coffee or straight-sided can halfway between the sprinkler and the end of the fall of water. Allow the sprinkler to run until there is one inch of water in the can. If water starts puddling on the surface of the lawn, turn off the water and check the amount in the can. If there is one-half inch, do not water again for three or four days. If there is an inch, do not water for a week. If it puddles when there is less than one-half inch, let it soak in and then continue watering until there is one-half inch in the can.‡

‡ See "Proper Watering," p. 130

NOTES

August

IN THE SOUTHERN GARDEN

August separates the sheep from the goats when it comes to gardening. There are those who take every opportunity to be in the garden doing something, even if conditions aren't perfect, and there are those who feel that gardening is mainly a spring activity when *everybody* is outside planting something and who now grumble at cutting the lawn regularly while it's hot and muggy. During Dog Days, there are times when neither the sheep nor the goats have much enthusiasm for doing jobs like hoeing weeds. Frankly, many really useful gardening projects are set aside to be done after vacation or after Labor Day, which coincidentally is when Dog Days are over and the weather is more pleasant. That's too bad, because there are some very time-specific activities in August like starting seeds of fall vegetables, making semi-hardwood cuttings of broadleaf evergreens, and planting cover crops on bare garden areas.

Many of us tend to make a garden just a place for activity. But a garden is meant to be more than just activity. It does take activity to make it beautiful and productive, but the real definition of a garden is a place to be refreshed and inspired. August is a good time to think about what could make your garden a more inviting and enjoyable place to be. Perhaps a bench placed in a nice shady spot is all that is needed, but let your creative mind go to work. A fountain, pool, or waterfall can create a cool feeling. A simple, easily made arbor covered by a beautiful vine can be an excellent focal point as well as a wonderful place to sit on a hot day.

Don't restrict your yearly changes to types and cultivars of flowers and vegetables. Also try to create new ways to make your garden a more enjoyable place to spend your time.

AT LEFT: *Summer Hydrangea (Hydrangea paniculata)*

I. *Shade and Flowering Trees*

In August all is green. Walking around the South sometimes makes you feel like you are in a jungle. The humidity is heavy in the air around you, and leafy branches hang down, offering brief respites from the sun.

Suddenly in mid-August among all the green, the Sourwood stands out as a glorious reminder that we are in the South and not the tropics. Its tiny flowers cascade in a soft flow of white among branches high and low. By the end of the month, the Sourwood's leaves have already turned their fall color — scarlet red. With its white touch of spring, and a colorful glimpse of autumn to come, the Sourwood is a reminder that the South is a place of seasonal rejuvenation rather than constant tropical heat.

Why the Sourwood has chosen August to bloom, I do not know. Perhaps it is a hidden pact with the bees, which in turn make Sourwood honey. Whatever the reason, I am thankful for the diversity it lends to our Southern landscape.

TREE ACTIVITIES FOR AUGUST:

Plant

☞ August is really too hot to plant B&B and container-grown trees. Wait for the cool weather of late fall/winter.

Prune

☞ Summer is not the time to prune tree limbs. If there is a broken branch, however, remove the limb (including the jagged break or split) with a clean cut.*

Spray

☞ Look for damaging insects on evergreen trees like **magnolias** and **hollies**. Scale, spider mites, lacebug, leaf miner, spittlebug, and leaf hopper are still around in August. Use Cygon or Orthene to control them. Do not use Cygon on **hollies**.†

☞ Protect flowering trees like **flowering peaches** and **flowering plums** from Japanese Beetle damage by spraying with Sevin or putting traps downwind from the tree.†

☞ If insects or diseases you're not familiar with show up on trees, take a branch containing some of the infected area to your local nurseryman or Cooperative Extension Service agent for identification and suggested controls.†

☞ Flowering trees are susceptible to Southern borers just like fruit trees. Borer control takes place in August. Two sprayings are needed. In the lower South, spray immediately after the fruit harvest and again in early September. In the middle and upper South, spray on the first of August and the first of September. Thiodan is the recommended material to use.

Water

☞ Newly planted trees should be soaked once a week throughout the month if there is no significant rain.‡

☞ During periods of extreme drought, large trees may need watering. Watch for discoloration, drying, die-back, and premature leaf-fall as signs that the tree is being affected. Use a watering spike placed intermittently around the perimeter of the tree's roots, approximately under the edge of the farthest reaching limbs. Water thoroughly.‡

* See "Pruning Shade and Flowering Trees," p 4

† See "Controlling Insects and Diseases," p. 80

‡ See "Does Your Tree Have Enough Water?" p. 150

Other

☛ Keep spring-planted trees well mulched to conserve moisture when it is hot and dry. Do not let mulch pack around the trunk.**

☛ Be extremely careful when mowing or using a power

** See "Mulching: A Lesson from Nature," p. 243

trimmer around old and new trees. *Do not hit or damage the bark.* Even the slightest damage may make an entrance for borers (which are a serious problem in August) or other damaging insects. This is true for all trees in the landscape or natural area, including planted and native trees. **Dogwood, flowering peach, flowering cherry,** and **flowering plum** are highly susceptible to borer attacks. Shade trees like **pines** are also attacked by various borers and bark beetles.

NOTES

"Hearts A' Bustin' With Love" (Euonymus americana)

II. *Shrubs and Vines*

August is not the best month of the year for showy colors on shrubs around the garden. All of the spring-flowering shrubs have long since finished blooming, and they are spending their summer afternoons preparing buds for *next* year's bloom. Most summer-flowering shrubs have finished as well, but a few, like my Hydrangea paniculata, are a welcome sight with its puffs of fluffy white blossoms flourishing despite the heat.

Another August wonder is the "Hearts A' Bustin' With Love" (Euonymous americana), a delightful shrub which grows wild among pine trees. While it can be planted, I prefer to stumble upon this plant when walking in the woods. Their pretty seed pods *do* look like they are busting with love as they break open to offer their bright red seeds. I can't help but stop and admire them and wonder about the poetic person who gave them their name.

SEMI-HARDWOOD CUTTINGS

Many of us are now growing plants which came from the dormant cuttings we made back in January and February. We took cuttings when our shrubs were dormant so as not to shock the plant too much. As warm weather arrived, the cuttings began to emerge from dormancy just like their parent shrub, and the cuttings developed roots.

In July and August we can make cuttings again. Some of my favorite shrubs to make cuttings of are **Camellia**, **azalea**, **Rhododendron**, and **Hydrangea**. Unlike dormant cuttings, semi-hardwood cuttings are active and growing when we cut them from the mother plant. For this reason, they require a little more attention, but not too much more. Also, they will root faster than dormant cuttings, so we don't have to wait as long to see our results. Cuttings are especially useful if you are doing any summer pruning because you are making use of a part of the plant you would otherwise throw away.

Semi-hardwood cuttings are made from this year's new growth and are so named because the wood has toughened up since emerging but is not old and hard like last year's wood. This wood will root more vigorously than older wood because it contains more of the plant's growth hormones. Cuttings will usually root in six to eight weeks, compared to the eight to 12 weeks for dormant cuttings.

Semi-hardwood cuttings can be set in many different ways. Those of you who prepared a rooting bed or cold frame for dormant cuttings can use the same bed

Semi-hardwood is identified by the lighter colored new growth, on the right. Make cuttings in August from this new growth.

Semi-hardwood cuttings will develop healthy roots in 6-8 weeks.

(see January, "Making Dormant Cuttings of Shrubs and Roses"). Cuttings can also be rooted directly in a pot of peat-light potting mixture or pure perlite. Seedling flats or trays will work as well. The main factor is to root your cuttings in airy, well-drained soil or rooting medium. Placement of the rooting bed, pot, or flat is also very important. Since your cuttings are alive and growing, yet have no root system, they need a moist, humid environment to be successful. Professional operations use timed spray systems which briefly mist the cuttings every minute or so to prevent them from drying out. The amateur gardener can manage by keeping them out of direct sunlight and hand misting them every day.

Cuttings are made in the same way as dormant cuttings. Semi-hardwood is found at the extremities of the shrub and is identified by the lighter colored wood. Make cuttings four to six inches long, with the basal cut 1/4 inch below a bud (see January, "Making Dormant Cuttings of Shrubs and Roses"). It is more important to cut below a bud than to stay in the four-to-six-inch range. Do not cut back into last year's growth. Also, tip growth is more vigorous than side shoots and will root the fastest.

Before you set your cuttings, you might want to recut the basal cut on an angle (don't cut closer to the bud than 1/4 of an inch) and treat it with a rooting compound like Hormodin or Rootone. Some people prefer to shave off a portion of bark instead of cutting on an angle. Semi-hardwood cuttings require one more step of preparation than dormant cuttings. Since your cutting is active and growing, water will be evaporating from its leaves (the process of transpiration). Without roots, the cutting cannot absorb enough water through the basal cut to compensate for the amount of evapo-

ration. The ensuing dehydration is the most common killer of semi-hardwood cuttings. In order to cut back the amount of water loss, it helps to remove all but two or three leaves. Don't remove too many leaves, however, since the cutting is alive and needs some leaf area to feed itself. Also, remove any flower buds from the cutting so it will concentrate its effort on growing roots. Once your cuttings are prepared, set them no closer than two inches apart in the pot, tray, or rooting bed, and remember to mist them frequently.

As you wait for your cuttings to root, care for them just like any other indoor plant. Watch for signs they are too dry, too wet, light-deprived, or infested with insects. A well-cared-for cutting will root quickly, while a deprived one may linger in the bed for months without ever growing roots.

After six to eight weeks, most semi-hardwood cuttings will have rooted. Those you have set directly in a peat-light mixture can be allowed to continue growing in the same pot. Others will need to be transplanted into a pot filled with a peat-light mixture for at least one season before they are planted outside. Potted cuttings will need little tending except for water and fertilizer. The first winter, however, keep them in a sheltered area or a cold frame to protect them from the most bitter winds and temperature drops.

"SNAKES, SKEETERS, AND KUDZU"

I hear there are gardeners far to the north of us who recommend that we Southerners plant a wonderful vine named kudzu. This vine is said to grow rapidly, cover arbors with dense foliage, and stop erosion on troublesome banks. In short, they claim Kudzu will help us beautify our otherwise boring landscape. Whoever these people are, I hope they will stop on their way back from Disney World and collect some of our most vigorous specimens to take back to plant in their own yards.

I once heard an older Southern farmer proclaim the three things he hated most were "snakes, skeeters, and Kudzu." I think that those of us who have personally encountered Kudzu would probably put it on our own lists as well.

Kudzu is an abomination. It is a mean vine that doesn't cooperate in any way with the rest of nature. Its sole purpose in life is to cover anything and everything in its path until it dominates an entire area. If left untended, Kudzu will climb trees, strangling them until they die. Kudzu will also completely cover an old farm building until all that is left is a mound in a field of green. There is a patch near my house that is trying to cover a road. Every day tendrils grow out and are smashed by the passing cars. It is our duty as Southerners to try to remove as much Kudzu as possible from the landscape in our lifetime.

Kudzu (Pueraria lobata) is a woody vine native to China and Japan. Its leaves grow up to six inches and an established vine can grow up to 60 feet in a season. It is deciduous and hardy in the South. As spring arrives, Kudzu begins an enormous growth spurt which peaks in mid-summer. In August it begins to slow down and does not grow considerably for the rest of the season. Its reddish-purple flowers bloom in late summer.

Now that you know the enemy, you can plan your attack. Kudzu is best confronted when it is at its weakest point. Though some people think winter is the best time, that is not the case. In winter, Kudzu is dormant and hiding safely beneath the surface of the ground. The time to attack is when it is active and more vulnerable.

By the last two weeks of August, Kudzu plants have expended most of their stored energy. The growing season has exhausted them, and they sit back and proudly admire their 60-foot-long vines. The time is now! The key to success is to attack the entire area at one time. Kudzu has the unfortunate ability to "segment" itself from dead parts of the vine. This means that killing one end of the vine won't necessarily affect the other 60 feet. Kudzu vines root along many parts of the vine, and any given section is capable of sustaining itself.

There are two different methods of attack: spraying with a potent weed killer like Roundup, or mowing/weed-eating all the foliage. Spraying is more effective, but mowing is effective if you keep it up for a season or two. The idea is to kill as many leaves as possible. When the foliage is removed, the vines can no longer feed themselves. Since they have not yet stored any food in August, many vines will not have the strength to sprout new leaves to feed themselves and they will die. Keep watch, though. Some particularly tough plants may sprout some more leaves before frost. When they appear, try to wipe them out with a second attack.

The battle may have been won, but the war is not yet over. Our foe will be regrouping over the winter months. There may also be some latent seeds in the soil. The following spring, you must watch carefully for the remaining Kudzu to emerge. Early in the spring season, spray or mow these new leaves before they have a chance to establish themselves. With luck, this will be the final blow. Those of us who mowed or weed-eated may have to fight the battle over one more season.

Having fulfilled your Southern duty, the best thing to do now is to plant a beautiful **Carolina Jessamine** on the nearest arbor to show any Northerner who might be passing through what a true Southern vine looks like.

Kudzu threatens plants and structures all over the South.

Kudzu can grow 60 feet in a season and covers everything in its way.

SHRUB AND VINE ACTIVITIES FOR AUGUST:

Plant

☞ August is *not* a good time to plant B&B and container-grown shrubs or vines. Wait until the late fall/winter when you won't shock the plant as much.

Prune

☞ Do not prune spring-flowering evergreens like **azalea**, **Camellia**, and early-flowering cultivars of **Rhododendron** (those which bloomed in April and May). They have started setting flower buds for next spring's blossoms. Pruning will reduce or remove the flowering potential.

☞ Late-flowering cultivars of **Rhododendron** and **Mountain Laurel** (both of which bloom in June and early July) can still be pruned in early August, but do so as soon as possible before the new growth darkens.*

☞ Do not prune summer-flowering shrubs like **summer hydrangeas** or you might disturb the bloom.

Fertilize

☞ Do *not* fertilize spring-flowering shrubs like **azalea**, **Camellia**, and **Viburnum** (you will disturb bud formation) or broadleaf evergreens like **Burford Holly** and **Box Leaf Holly** in August.

☞ Do not fertilize summer-flowering shrubs like **Althaea**, **Butterfly Bush**, or **Hydrangea** because you might disturb the bloom. Summer-flowering shrubs are fertilized in the early spring before their growth spurt begins. However, you may fertilize any which are off-color and showing signs of fertilizer deficiency.†

Spray

☞ Watch out for damaging insects on evergreens, especially **Euonymus**, **azalea**, **Camellia**, **Pyracantha**, **Gardenia**, and **Photinia**. Scale, spider mites, lacebug,

leaf miner, spittlebug, and leaf hopper are still active in August. Use Cygon or Orthene as a control. Do not use Cygon on **hollies.**‡

☞ Continue to watch **Red Tip Photinia** for signs of leaf spot. If detected, immediately spray affected and adjacent plants with Daconil.‡

☞ Lacebugs are terrible pests which attack the foliage of **azalea** and **Pyracantha**. The damaged leaves have a silver appearance. Turn the leaf over and inspect for brown dots of residue which indicate the presence of this pest. This time of the year, you may even see this insect feeding on the undersides of the leaves. Spray with Orthene.‡

☞ Apply Giberellic Acid to fall and winter-flowering **Camellia** buds for larger and earlier flowers.

☞ Spray **Kudzu** with Roundup or mow all visible foliage in the last two weeks of August. **Kudzu** is at its weakest at this time of the year.**

Water

☞ Slowly soak shrubs and vines if there has been no significant rain in a week. This is especially important for the current year's plantings.††

Other

☞ Mulch all shrubs and vines to conserve moisture during the hot month of August. Do not allow the mulch to crowd or pack against the lower stems and trunks.‡‡

☞ Continue making semi-hardwood cuttings of shrubs like **azalea**, **Camellia**, and **Hydrangea**. Root them in a peat-light mixture or perlite rooting bed in a shaded location. Mist them frequently to keep them from drying out. Cuttings made last month may be ready to transplant.***

---

* See "Pruning Flowering Shrubs and Vines," p. 31

† See "How to Fertilize Shrubs and Vines," p. 30

‡ See "Controlling Insects and Diseases," p. 80

** See "Snakes, Skeeters, and Kudzu," p. 175

†† See "Proper Watering," p. 130

‡‡ See "Mulching: A Lesson from Nature," p. 243

*** See "Semi-Hardwood Cuttings," p. 174

Blight-resistant Orient Pear is best for the South.

III. *Fruits*

Last month, my tomatoes really made it feel like summer. Now with hot days and hot nights, I wonder if it is about time for all this foolishness to be done with. If I were to consult my tomatoes, they would inform me that their harvest is far from finished. Is there no reprieve?

Luckily, there are two sides to every story. All it takes is a walk down to visit the fruit trees to know that summer won't last forever. The apples are on their way! More than any other fruit, I admire my apples and check their progress with diligence. Maybe it is because they take longer to ripen that I consider them special. They seem to be holding out on me as I fill my pail with blueberries and pluck a few figs.

The Orient pears are also getting ready for the end of summer. Remember to harvest them when they first show color so they won't fall and bruise. Take them inside, wrap them with newspaper, and store them in a cool place. They will ripen nicely off the tree and add a new menu item to your meals — pear salad!

FRUIT ACTIVITIES FOR AUGUST:

Plant

☛ August is *not* a good time to plant B&B and container-grown fruits. Wait until cool weather returns in the late fall.

Prune

☛ This season's new growth is emerging on fruit trees. Next year's fruit will be set on this new growth, so if you do anything to disturb it, you will disturb next year's crop.

☛ Remove all canes of semi-bush fruits like **blackberries** and **raspberries** which fruited this summer. This will encourage new shoots from the crown on which next year's berries will be set. After removing the old canes, train this year's growth onto the fence or trellis.*

Fertilize

☛ Fertilize **peaches**, **nectarines**, and **plums** with 15-15-15 in the early part of the month. Use one-half pound per year of age of the tree up to a maximum of five pounds. This is the second application of the year.†

☛ Fertilize **apples** and **pears** if they are growing poorly. Use 15-15-15 fertilizer according to the amount of growth desired.†

Spray

☛ Continue a regular control program for fruit insects and diseases using a complete home orchard spray. Continue applications at recommended intervals until the fruit ripens. Read the directions and do not spray too close to harvest.

☛ Watch for spider mites on **raspberries** and other semi-bush berries. Their presence is evident when the foliage has a silvery gray appearance. Spray with Kelthane to control this serious pest.‡

☛ Japanese Beetles continue to be a serious problem this month. They attack **grapes**, **plums**, and other fruits. Those which have finished fruiting should be sprayed or dusted with Sevin to prevent defoliation. Beetle traps work as well, but remember to place the traps downwind from your fruits.‡

☛ Spray **bunch grapes** until the fruit is harvested with a complete home orchard spray to prevent brown rot and control leaf worms and Japanese Beetles.‡

☛ Southern borer control on **peaches**, **nectarines**, **plums**, and **cherries** takes place in August. Two sprayings are needed. In the lower South, spray immediately after harvest and again in early September. In the middle and upper South, spray on the first of August and the first of September. Thiodan is the recommended material to use.

Water

☛ Keep **figs** well watered and heavily mulched for good, tasty fruits.

☛ Slowly soak fruit trees and bushes if there has been no significant rain in a week. This is especially important for this year's plantings.**

Other

☛ Keep fruit harvested as it ripens. Fruit left hanging on the tree after your spray program is completed is an invitation to insects and diseases.

☛ Remove all undeveloped fruit which failed to ripen for whatever reason. Never leave it on the tree.

☛ Harvest **pears** as they begin to turn color and before they fall. Do not leave them to ripen on the tree or they will be damaged as they fall and hit the ground. Pears may be harvested slightly green and wrapped in newspaper to ripen fully.

☛ Cover **fig** bushes with a net to prevent birds from ruining the fruits.

☛ Keep **strawberries** — as well as other fruits — mulched to discourage weeds. Grass clippings are an excellent mulch for **strawberries**.††

☛ Allow **strawberry** runners to develop into new daughter plants. This will increase your next year's harvest.

☛ Be careful when mowing in orchard areas not to hit the bark of fruit trees with the mower. Any damage to the bark will provide an entrance place for borers. This is especially important in August when the adult borer moths are flying.

---

* See "Secrets of the Berry Patch," p. 155

† See "How to Fertilize Fruit Trees," p. 37

‡ See "Controlling Insects and Diseases," p. 80

** See "Proper Watering," p. 130

†† See "Mulching: A Lesson from Nature," p. 243

Pink Hybrid Tea Rose

IV. *Roses*

In August, the secret of the rose is laid out for all to see. Most of our roses are looking pretty poor. Rose hybridizers around the country have worked so hard trying to make bigger, more beautiful roses that they have largely neglected to develop disease- and heat-resistant cultivars. Unfortunately, roses sell because they have a pretty picture on the tag, and that picture certainly wasn't taken in August.

There are some ways that we can help our roses during August. One of my favorites is to spray them with a water-soluble fertilizer solution like Peters. This is a good way to give them a little lift. Unfortunately, many have lost leaves, have Blackspot, and are not producing many new buds. These roses can be cut back one-third to force new healthy growth. The new canes should produce some fine roses in the cooler months before frost arrives.

ROSE ACTIVITIES FOR AUGUST:

Plant

☛ August is *not* a good time to plant bare-root and container-grown roses. Wait until the late fall/winter when you won't shock the plant as much.

Prune

☛ At the end of August, large rose bushes may be pruned back one-third to force strong growth for fall blossoms.

☛ Groom roses constantly. Never leave a dead or dying stem on the plant because the disease will spread to healthy canes. Also remove weak, broken, or spindly shoots.*

☛ Remove all dead flowers by clipping above a five-leaflet set, as if you were cutting the flower to take inside.*

Fertilize

☛ In hot, dry conditions, keep plants growing with light applications of a complete rose fertilizer on your regular six-to-eight-week program. Supplement this program by spraying the foliage and new shoots with a water-soluble fertilizer solution like Peters.

Spray

☛ Continue with your complete rose spray program every 10 to 14 days according to the directions. Use a combination insecticide and fungicide spray and continue applications through September.

☛ Watch out for Japanese Beetles. Your normal spray program will not control these pests. Use Japanese Beetle traps or supplement your spray program with Sevin.†

☛ Blackspot continues to be a major problem during August. Don't let up! Consistent applications of your regular spray should prevent heavy damage.†

☛ Thrips may become a problem during hot, dry weather. Infected rose blossoms will turn brown on the petal edges. Check for these pests by pulling one of the discolored flowers apart. You will see rod-shaped thrips at the base of the petal. Thrips are controlled with Orthene.†

☛ Bud worms eat holes in maturing rose buds. They are usually controlled by your regular complete spray program, but applying Bacillus thuringiensis (BT) is a good supplemental control method.†

Water

☛ Water when there has been no significant rain for a week. A soaker hose is a good way to prevent wetting the foliage and thereby encouraging diseases. Soak the bed thoroughly. Shallow watering does more harm than good by drawing the roots to the surface where they will dry out more quickly.‡

Other

☛ Continue to observe various rose cultivars in public gardens and in the gardens of friends. Roses which are growing and blooming well in the heat are those which you should consider for your future plantings.

☛ Remember to cut flowers correctly. Always make the cut above a joint where a five-leaflet originates. Cutting at this point encourages a strong new shoot and blossom to form.*

☛ Many **Hybrid Tea** and **Grandiflora** roses have several flowers in a cluster (called a candelabra) which may not all bloom at the same time. Remove each spent flower in the cluster as it finishes blooming. When all the flowers are done, cut the whole cluster stalk back to a five-leaflet set.*

☛ Keep roses well mulched with pine straw during the summer. Add fresh mulch when you can see bare ground around the plants, but do not pile mulch against the crown or lower stems. Many problems like cankers and botrytis occur when mulch covers the lower stems.**

☛ Cut roses will last longer in an arrangement when the stems are recut under water before placing in the vase. This allows water, not air, to travel up the stem.

---

* See "Grooming Roses," p. 110

† See "Controlling Insects and Diseases," p. 80

‡ See "Proper Watering," p. 130

* See "Grooming Roses," p. 110

** See "Mulching: A Lesson from Nature," p. 243

V. *Flowers and Colorful Garden Plants*

Variegated Hosta enjoys shady spots out of the August sun.

Arriving home in August is especially nice. Every trip out seems to be a test of our will against that of the sun. We race across blazing hot parking lots trying to find another air-conditioned haven. And when we return, we have to face the dreaded oven our car has become in the meantime. Sticking to the car seat, we can only plead with the air-conditioner to hurry.

Home is different. The grass absorbs sun happily, making use of the rays that the black parking lot across town bounced back in our face. Our shade trees gladly take the brunt of the sun and leave a cool reminder of their presence below. Off to the side of the garden, our hostas sit comfortably in the shade and seem to mock the annuals and perennials who claimed they could take full sun.

To give our flowering plants a little credit, the beating sun is not their problem. Despite their strained look in August, these plants were made for full sun. Weeds, insects, drought, and a lack of grooming affect flowering plants much more than the sun in August.

Weeds and drought can be attacked with one fell swoop. Pull what weeds you have and apply a thick mulch. Then soak the bed thoroughly. The mulch will cool the hot August ground, prevent water from evaporating as quickly, and block returning weeds.

Grooming is a different problem. By August, many of our flowers like Impatiens, Begonia, and Salvia have grown so well they have become top-heavy. Instead of staking these tall, spindly plants, top them to force new, more vigorous growth. Cutting back will also help them to bush out.

By early September, most flowering plants will have rebounded and will be ready to stand their ground against the quips of any nearby hostas.

FLOWER ACTIVITIES FOR AUGUST:

Plant

☛ Plant new or old potted **chrysanthemums** at the end of the month for fall flowers.*

☛ Start seeds of hardy annuals, perennials, and biennials like **pansy**, **English Daisy**, and **Purple Coneflower** around mid-August. Plant seeds in trays and then place them in a cool location. For best results, use a peat-light mixture and cover them shallowly. Place a piece of clear plastic or a clear plastic dome over the tray to prevent the soil from drying out.†

* See "How to Plant a Flower Bed," p. 62

† See "Starting Seeds Inside," p. 18

☛ Transplant **Bearded Iris** any time this month. Cut leaves in a fan below where they are dying back, and set them with the top of the root at the surface of the soil. Use bone meal when you plant. Remember, **Bearded Iris** need full sun to bloom well.*

Prune

☛ Groom herbaceous flowering plants like **Impatiens**, **Begonia**, and **Salvia** by removing spent flowers, seed pods, yellow leaves, and improper growth. Plants which have grown tall and spindly may be topped to force side growth. ‡

Fertilize

☛ Continue fertilizing herbaceous plants with 5-10-15 on a six-to-eight-week schedule through the end of the season. Poorly-growing annuals and perennials may need special attention.

☛ Continue to fertilize **chrysanthemums** and **dahlias** with a 5-10-15 formula every four to six weeks until they are in bloom.

☛ During dry weather, spray a water-soluble fertilizer solution like Peters on foliage to keep plants growing well.

Spray

☛ August is the worst month for insects. Keep ahead of the insect population by keeping a close eye on flowers and herbaceous plants. Fast succulent growth is especially susceptible to aphid, spider mite, leaf hopper, thrip, and worm damage. Orthene is an excellent all-around control.**

☛ Large attacks of worms on a particular plant, like **Geranium**, can be controlled by Dipel dust or Thuricide spray, which contain Bacillus thuringiensis (BT), an excellent biological control.**

☛ August can also be a terrible month for Japanese Beetles. Spray or dust plants with Sevin to prevent damage. Beetle traps work as well, but remember to place the traps downwind from your garden.**

Water

☛ Water plants thoroughly with about one inch of water per week if there has been no significant rainfall.††

☛ Hanging baskets will need more water during the hot summer months, but do not overwater them. Soak them thoroughly, then soak them again only when the surface is dry. They especially like to be washed down with the hose, or put out in the rain.

Other

☛ Keep flower borders and beds free from weeds. A heavy mulch of grass clippings makes it easy. Late summer and fall weeds are especially bad in August.‡‡

☛ Remove spent flowers as soon as they become unattractive unless the seeds are to be harvested. Allowing seeds to develop reduces the vigor of plants and produces fewer flowers.‡

☛ Cultivate unmulched bare areas to break the soil's crust. This allows moisture to penetrate the ground.

☛ Stake tall-growing annuals and perennials like **Salvia** and **Shasta Daisy** to prevent their falling over during heavy rains and wind. **Dahlias** will grow tall and must be staked. I like to use green bamboo stakes which do not show.

---

* See "How to Plant a Flower Bed," p. 62

‡ See "Grooming and Pinching Flowers," p. 137

** See "Controlling Insects and Diseases," p. 80

** See "Controlling Insects and Diseases," p. 80

†† See "Proper Watering," p. 130

‡‡ See "Mulching: A Lesson from Nature," p. 243

‡ See "Grooming and Pinching Flowers," p. 137

Zucchini squash

VI. *Vegetables*

August is a good month in the summer vegetable garden. By this time of the year, we have fallen into a nice routine in caring for our vegetables. Our tomatoes are going strong, peppers seem to be too prolific, and then there are the zucchini. What were we thinking? Seven zucchini plants seemed like such a manageable number back in May, but by August we have worn out the neighbors with our kind gifts. Deciding not to carry through with the idea of leaving anonymous zucchini donations in random mailboxes, I am likely to give extras the heave-ho into our compost pile after I have frozen all I can possibly eat this winter.

In August it is also the time to start thinking about the fall vegetable crop. Vegetables like broccoli and lettuce can be started from seed this month. With six weeks to grow, they will be ready to usher in cooler evenings, marking the South's next beautiful season.

VEGETABLE ACTIVITIES FOR AUGUST:

Plant

☞ **Bush beans** can be planted this month for a fall crop. Watch out, however, for the Mexican Bean Beetle and other insects.*

☞ Remove any plants which have finished producing. Work bare areas and plant a cover crop of **Crimson Clover** at the end of the month.†

☞ Start seed of cool weather vegetables like **broccoli, cabbage, cauliflower, collards,** and **lettuce** for transplanting to the garden in early September.‡

Prune

☞ Continue to train and support **tomatoes, cucumbers, pole beans,** and **peppers** on a regular basis.

Fertilize

☞ Fertilize as you plant in the garden with 15-15-15. This application should be good for about six weeks. Application is at a rate of approximately one pound per 10 feet of row.**

☞ **Tomatoes, peppers, eggplant, cucumber,** and **okra** should be fertilized with 5-10-15 every six weeks throughout their growing season. Application is at a rate of approximately one pound per 10 feet of row.**

☞ During periods of dry weather, spray the foliage of **eggplant, tomato,** and **pepper** plants with a water soluble fertilizer solution like Peters.

☞ Continue to fertilize other growing vegetables with 5-10-15 about every six weeks for the rest of the season. Application is at a rate of approximately one pound per 10 feet of row. **

* See "Planting a Vegetable Garden," p. 92
† See "Planting Cover Crops," p. 205
‡ See "Starting Seeds Inside," p. 18
** See "Fertilizing, Spraying, and Watering Vegetables," p. 115

Spray

☞ The first step to effective pest control is detecting the pest before it has damaged your crop extensively. Once you spot a problem you are not familiar with, take an infected leaf, flower, or fruit to your local nurseryman or Cooperative Extension Service agent for identification. There is a wide variety of organic and inorganic materials to control most garden pests.

☞ Spray or dust frequently to control fruit worms, blights, and other diseases, especially on **tomatoes.** I like to use BT for worms and a home vegetable spray or dust for the diseases.**

☞ White fly may be a serious problem this month on **tomatoes, peppers, eggplants,** and **squash.** There are no effective preventive measures, so it is important to control the population before they increase to damaging levels. Hang sticky yellow strips (available at garden centers) among your plants to trap these pests.**

☞ Tomato Hornworms and fruit worms are active this month. Keep fruiting plants sprayed or dusted with Bacillus thuringiensis (BT).**

☞ Keep an eye out for Japanese Beetles. Spray or dust vegetables with Sevin. Beetle traps work as well, but remember to place the traps downwind from your garden.**

☞ Keep **pole beans** sprayed or dusted with Sevin for worms and beetles.**

☞ Blossom End Rot, which results in black corking of the bottom (blossom end) of **tomatoes, peppers,** and **eggplants,** is caused by a calcium deficiency aggravated by improper watering (too much or too little). Apply a calcium solution to the foliage and correct the watering problem. Liming during the winter will also help correct this problem for the next season.**

☞ Watch for Asparagus beetles which will quickly eat **Asparagus** foliage and damage plants. Sevin should give you good control.**

** See "Fertilizing, Spraying, and Watering Vegetables," p. 115

☞ Dust late maturing **sweet corn** silks with Sevin to prevent earworms from ruining your **corn** crop. Read the label to find the number of days before harvest that you can still dust.**

Water

☞ August can be an especially dry month. Water vegetables thoroughly with about one inch of water if there has been no significant rainfall for a week.**

☞ Cracking of **tomato** fruit is generally caused by uneven watering, whether from rain or irrigation. If cracking occurs, use a soaker hose and let water run for several hours. Do not use again for three or four days. If you keep tomatoes properly watered, they will not crack after a heavy rain.**

Other

☞ Suckering **tomatoes** (removing the fast growing shoots between the leaf and the stem) will reduce the number of fruit, but what is left will be larger. Some gardeners partially sucker their plants to strike a happy medium. The choice is yours.††

☞ Keep vegetables free of weeds by hoeing or mulching. Weeds compete with vegetables for essential nutrients and harbor damaging insects.

☞ Harvested **sweet corn** and **melons** will hold their quality if you plunge them into an ice-water bath for 20 minutes before refrigerating.‡‡

** See "Fertilizing, Spraying, and Watering Vegetables," p. 115

†† See "Training Vegetables off the Ground," p. 118

‡‡ See "Harvesting Vegetables and Keeping Them Tasty," p. 140

☞ Remove all finished crops as soon as possible and plant the bare areas with a cover crop like **Crimson Clover** at the end of the month. Old dying plants are perfect breeding grounds for insects and diseases.†

☞ Harvest frequently and correctly. Vegetables left too long on the plant lose taste and quality.‡‡

VEGETABLE:	HARVEST:
Shallots	When the tops break over
Pole Beans	Before you see the seeds bulging
Cucumbers, Squash, Zucchini	While still small and tender
Cantaloupe	When the vine pulls easily and cleanly from the melon
Watermelons	When the pigtail dies
Tomatoes, Peppers, Eggplants	Harvest frequently and remove unusable fruit
Okra	Before it is five inches long
Sweet Corn	When the silks are brown

† See "Planting Cover Crops," p. 205

‡‡ See "Harvesting Vegetables and Keeping Them Tasty," p. 140

NOTES

Swedish Ivy (Plectranthus nummularius) is often called Creeping Charlie by Southerners.

VII. *Houseplants*

These days our lives are run by schedules. We make lists, carry daily planners, and sometimes schedule our lives on a computer. Tuesdays and Thursdays are choir practice. Wednesdays and Saturdays are softball games. And all too often, Saturday afternoons are scheduled as the time to plant, water, fertilizer, hoe, mulch, and enjoy gardening. Scheduling a time to garden is wonderful for us. It helps us set aside a time to enjoy ourselves. Unfortunately, it is not as wonderful for our plants.

Just like the weather, a plant's needs are unpredictable. Rain, sun, insects, diseases, weeds, moles, and many other conditions all contribute to the variable nature of gardening. Success is often achieved by keeping an eye on your plants rather than your daily planner.

We run into the most problems when dealing with houseplants. From our point of view, they thrive in the sterile atmosphere of our homes. Insects and diseases aren't nearly as bad as outside, weeds are not a problem, and we don't have to rely on the rain to water them. All too often we are lulled into a regimen of watering houseplants once a week on a particular afternoon.

This kind of scheduling can be tough on houseplants. Watering diligently once a week might keep a house-plant's roots soggy, slow down its growth, and cause it to shed leaves. Another common problem in August is that your houseplant has grown so well over the summer that watering once a week doesn't provide the plant with enough water.

But don't miss the point. Caring for houseplants isn't just a matter of readjusting your schedule every now and then. It is a matter of looking to them rather than to your daily planner for the best time to water. For those of you addicted to a life of schedules, I suggest the following entry for all 365 days of the calendar: "Go see how my houseplants are doing."

HOUSEPLANT ACTIVITIES FOR AUGUST:

Plant

☛ Houseplants, especially newly purchased ones, can be repotted at any time during the year. Use a pot at least two sizes larger so the plant will have plenty of room to grow. I prefer to grow most of my houseplants in a peat-light potting mixture.*

Prune

☛ Groom indoor plants whenever they need it. Remove weak branches or stems as well as off-color leaves.

Fertilize

☛ Fertilize with a full-strength, water-soluble fertilizer solution every time you water. Or, as an alternative, use fertilizer spikes or Osmocote slow-release fertilizer, which lasts several months.†

Spray

☛ Check all indoor plants for insects such as spider mites, scale, and mealybug. I like to use a houseplant systemic insecticide to control them. It is easier and safer than spraying inside. If you do spray, remember to apply the insecticide to the undersides of the leaves. I prefer to take my houseplants outside to spray since most insecticides smell bad.‡

---

* See "Repotting Houseplants," p. 67

† See "Houseplant Care and Maintenance," p. 232

‡ See "Common Houseplant Ailments," p. 280

☛ Be careful when spraying **ferns**. Some insecticides are harmful to them. *Always read the label for warnings about **ferns** and other plants.*

Water

☛ Keep an eye on houseplants during the summer. When they look limp, check for dry soil. If it is dry, water thoroughly in a sink or bathtub, letting the water drain completely, and don't water again until the surface is dry once more. Between waterings, mist with plain water on a regular basis. If the limp plants are in moist soil, do not water but allow the soil to dry a bit and mist frequently.†

☛ Tip-burn or edge-burn on leaves indicates that more water is being lost than is being absorbed by the roots. Check for dry soil, too much sunlight, or drafts from air-conditioning vents.†

Other

☛ With proper care, houseplants can be propagated at any time during the year. Since August is a hot month, keep cuttings out of direct sunlight and mist them frequently so they don't dry out.**

☛ Remember that the position of the sun continues to change in the sky. Windows which received plenty of light last month might be losing some exposure.

---

† See "Houseplant Care and Maintenance," p. 232

** See "Propagating Herbaceous Houseplants and Garden Plants," p. 225

NOTES

Keep summer weeds cut before they go to seed in August.

VIII. *Lawns*

By August, our lawns (especially evergreen grasses) are looking pretty poor. It's hot and dry, and our pre-emergence weed killer has given out. Weeds seem to be sprouting up everywhere. I don't know how these rascals are able to thrive when our carefully tended lawns cannot. Maybe we should switch to a carefree, all Pigweed lawn.

In August, many weeds begin to produce seeds. It is crucial to keep lawns cut so that weeds cannot form seed heads. If you are going on a week-long vacation in August, have someone come cut your yard. It is money better spent than on herbicides to control a thousand newly sprouted weeds.

There is also some good news. Before you panic at the sight of rampant crabgrass and goosegrass, remember that it will die in September. If you have an evergreen lawn, wait until the crabgrass dies, and then reseed your grass. Evergreen grasses like cool weather and will take over the crabgrass's territory.

LAWN ACTIVITIES FOR AUGUST:

Plant

☛ You can still plant summer grasses like **Bermuda Grass**, **Centipede**, **St. Augustine**, and **Zoysia** with care during the first half of the month.*

☛ Do not plant evergreen grasses like **fescue** until September.

Fertilize

☛ Keep summer grasses like **Bermuda Grass**, **St. Augustine**, and **Zoysia** well fertilized with a high-nitrogen lawn fertilizer. (**Centipede** usually does not need fertilizing unless it is a light green or yellow, at which time it should be fertilized with a Centipede-specific fertilizer. Never use lime on **Centipede**.) This application will be good for another 90 days.

☛ Do not fertilize evergreen grasses unless the color is light green or yellow. Then fertilize with a high-nitrogen lawn fertilizer at one-half the recommended rate. If at all possible, it is best to wait until September to fertilize evergreen grasses. Fertilizing now will help weeds and weedgrasses more than your evergreen grass.

Spray

☛ Weeds and weed grasses invade lawns this time of the year, especially in those evergreen grass lawns. Spray weeds early this month with a recommended herbicide and keep weed grass seed stalks cut off when you mow. It is important to prevent crabgrass, goosegrass, and crow's foot grass from producing and dropping huge numbers of seeds. Always use a herbicide recommended for southern summer grasses and on **Centipede** and **St. Augustine** use only those recommended and use them with extreme care. †

☛ Chinch bugs remain a problem, causing brown patches in **Centipede** and **St. Augustine** lawns. Remove a plug of sod with a bulb planter. Slowly immerse the plug in a bucket of water. Look for small insects to rise. Apply a soil insecticide like Diazinon to the whole area where you find chinch bugs.†

☛ Watch for insect and disease problems. Insects cause irregular dead areas while diseases cause well-defined dead areas. Take a plug of grass which has both dying and healthy grass to your local nurseryman or Cooperative Extension Service agent for identification.†

☛ Watch for Fall Armyworms. These come in droves and can ruin a lawn overnight. The first indication of this potential disaster is very heavy moth activity, especially around shrubs next to your lawn. Be ready to spray or apply granules of Diazinon as soon as you see the first worms in your lawn.†

Cut

☛ Keep all types of lawns mowed at the right height. Summer grasses are more tolerant than evergreen ones. The **fescue** grasses can be damaged severely when cut too short in August's heat.

☛ **Hybrid Bermuda Grass** may need cutting twice a week.

☛ Cut summer grasses often to prevent browning. If you cut grass after it is very tall, you remove the green part, leaving brown stems. This condition will remain until new green leaves grow.

☛ Thinning of **fescue** lawns may be due to cutting too short. Check your cutting height.

---

* See "Planting and Reseeding Summer Lawns," p. 98
† See "Controlling Insects and Diseases," p. 80
‡ See "Proper Watering," p. 130

☛ Cut grasses at the proper height:

SUMMER GRASSES	HEIGHT
Common Bermuda Grass	2 inches
Hybrid Bermuda Grass	1 to 1 $\frac{1}{2}$ inches
Centipede	1 $\frac{1}{2}$ to 2 inches
St. Augustine	2 to 2 $\frac{1}{2}$ inches
Zoysia	1 to 2 inches

EVERGREEN GRASSES	HEIGHT
Kentucky 31 Tall Fescue	3 to 3 $\frac{1}{2}$ inches
Turf-type Tall Fescues	3 inches
Fine Fescues	1 $\frac{1}{2}$ to 2 inches
Kentucky Bluegrass	2 to 2 $\frac{1}{2}$ inches

Water

☛ Keep lawns watered during dry spells. Place a one-pound coffee can halfway between the sprinkler and the end of the fall of water. Allow the sprinkler to run until there is one inch of water in the can. If water starts puddling on the surface of the lawn, turn off the water and check the amount in the can. If there is one-half inch, do not water again for three or four days. If there is an inch, do not water for a week. If the ground puddles when there is less than one-half inch, let it soak in and then continue watering until there is one-half inch in the can.‡

‡ See "Proper Watering," p. 130

NOTES

September

IN THE SOUTHERN GARDEN

September is a time of change. Nights are suddenly cooler and daytime temperatures more moderate, children are back in school, trees show the first hint of fall color, and flowers bloom furiously as if they realize their end is near. Fall starts officially with the Fall Equinox on either September 22 or 23, when daytime hours equal night hours.

September brings a new season for us. Every year, garden activities change as the days grow longer or shorter and weather grows warmer or cooler. Gardening follows the seasons more than it does the calendar, and despite the calendar, September is as much a beginning as an ending. I always consider it the start of a season when I can start planting without fear of intense heat and droughts.

My garden soil is always my primary concern because it brings forth life, fruit, and beauty. Now that most vegetables and many flowers have finished for the year, I think about what I need to do to improve my soil before next year rolls around and it is time to plant spring gardens. I depend on cover crops to add humus and nutrients and improve soil structure, since growing humus is far easier than spending time and effort to dig in compost; besides, it is cheaper. In addition to building the soil, cover/green-manure crops prevent soil erosion during the heavy rains of winter and spring. In the South, the best cover crop to plant in September is Crimson Clover, a deep-rooted legume which holds the soil and adds green manure and nitrogen.

Since most of us gardeners prefer planting to the more mundane garden jobs, the change in weather and the beginning of a new planting season is particularly welcome. From now until hot weather next May, we do our major plantings of the year.

In September we can start planting hardy plants like peonies, Iris, hardy perennials, hardy annuals, hardy biennials, and hardy vegetables, all of which can stand our cold winters. The reason to plant hardy perennials and biennials in the fall is to "trick" them into acting like they have been growing two years, which results in better flowers next spring and summer.

Fall is a great gardening time because there are still flowers in bloom and fruits to harvest. They provide far more inspiration to be outside in the garden in September than there will be in the cold winter months to come.

AT LEFT: *Attractive seed pod of Southern Magnolia (Magnolia grandiflora)*

Sugarberry or Hackberry (Celtis occidentalis)

I. *Shade and Flowering Trees*

Life is changing in September. The children are back in school, the nights begin to cool off, and once again we remember our trees. All summer their stolid presence in our landscape went unnoticed except when we gratefully accepted the cool of their shade. Now the scarlet red Sourwoods, and the rustle of leaves in the cool breezes of late September remind us once more that our trees are an active and changing part of our landscape.

While there may be some rain by the end of September, the beginning is often a dry reminder of August. If the summer has been particularly dry, drought problems may just now be showing up on your established shade and flowering trees. Water them! Just because it doesn't feel like August doesn't mean your tree isn't being affected. Fifteen feet below the surface of the ground, it may feel like we are in the middle of a full-fledged summer drought.

TREE ACTIVITIES FOR SEPTEMBER:

Plant

☛ Wait until later in the fall to plant B&B, bare-root, and container-grown flowering and shade trees. The trees being sold this time of year are not as desirable because they have just endured a hot summer in a pot or burlapped ball of earth. Trees sold later in the season will have been dug recently.

Prune

☛ *Do not prune* trees this month. Pruning could force tender growth which might be killed by the first hard freezes. Also, many flowering trees have set their blossom buds for next year. Pruning would remove many of next year's flowers.

Fertilize

☛ *Do not fertilize* trees this month. Just like pruning, fertilizing could force tender growth which might be killed by the first hard freezes.

Spray

☛ Watch for insects like scale. Spray with Orthene for general control and Cygon for scale on all except **hollies.***

☛ Finish last month's Southern borer control on **flowering peaches, flowering cherries,** and **flowering crabapples** by spraying for the second time in early September. Thiodan is the recommended material to use.

Water

☛ Slowly water trees if there has been no significant rain in a week. This is especially important for the current year's plantings.†

☛ The effects of a summer drought may just now be showing up on large trees. Watch for discoloration, drying, die-back, and premature leaf-fall as signs that the tree is being affected. Use a watering spike placed intermittently around the perimeter of the tree's roots, approximately under the edge of the farthest reaching limbs. Water thoroughly.†

Other

☛ Keep newly planted trees well mulched to conserve moisture when it is hot and dry, especially in early September. Do not pile mulch against the trunks.‡

☛ Be extremely careful when mowing or using a power trimmer around old and new trees, especially **dogwoods, flowering cherries, crabapples, flowering peaches,** and **flowering plums.** Do not hit or damage the bark. Even the slightest damage may make an entrance for borers or other damaging insects. This is true for all trees in the landscape or natural areas, including planted and native trees.

---

* See "Controlling Insects and Diseases," p. 80

† See "Does Your Tree Have Enough Water?" p. 150

† See "Does Your Tree Have Enough Water?" p. 150

‡ See "Mulching: A Lesson from Nature," p. 243

NOTES

Sweet Autumn Clematis is covered with white fragrant flowers as the weather cools.

II. *Shrubs and Vines*

September is a slow month for shrubs and vines. The summer-flowering shrubs have all but finished, and our annual vines are lacking the luster they dazzled us with in the summer months. Everywhere we look, there are buds forming on our shrubs. The spring-flowering shrubs like azalea, Rhododendron, and Spiraea have all set buds, but we are left to dream about their color all winter long.

There is an exception! The fall and winter-flowering Camellia sasanqua and Camellia japonica cultivars are getting ready to bloom. Although the Camellia sasanqua blossoms are not as striking as some of the Camellia japonica cultivars, their early bloom more than makes up for any shortcomings.

If you are looking for a new activity this month, try "gibbing" your Camellia japonica. Giberellic Acid applied to fall and winter-flowering Camellia japonica buds will cause them to flower earlier than normal and also increase their flower size. This is especially helpful in preventing cold damage. All you have to do is remove the closest vegetative bud to the flower bud and put a drop of the acid in the little pit where the vegetative bud was attached to the main stem. It is fun to experiment by gibbing some and leaving others to develop on their own.

SHRUB AND VINE ACTIVITIES FOR SEPTEMBER:

Plant

☞ Wait until November to plant new shrubs and vines like **azalea**, **Camellia**, **Hydrangea**, **Carolina Jessamine**, and **hollies**. Dormant plants won't be as shocked when you plant them.

Prune

☞ *Do not prune* shrubs and vines this month. Pruning may force tender growth which might be killed by the first hard freezes. Also, many flowering shrubs have set their blossom buds for next year. Pruning will remove many of your next year's flowers.

Fertilize

☞ *Do not fertilize* shrubs and vines this month. Just like pruning, fertilizing may also force tender growth which might be killed by the first hard freezes.

Spray

☞ While insects and diseases aren't as bad in September, it is still important to keep them under control. Remember the old saying, "One aphid killed in the fall is a thousand killed in the spring." If you find a problem you can't identify, take an infected branch or leaf to your local nurseryman or Cooperative Extension Service agent for identification. There's a wide variety of organic and inorganic materials to control most garden pests.*

☞ Watch for insects like lacebug and scale. Spray with Orthene for general control and Cygon for scale except on **hollies**.*

Water

☞ Slowly soak shrubs and vines if there has been no significant rain in a week. This is especially important for the current year's plantings.†

Other

☞ Keep an eye on your summer semi-hardwood cuttings. Many will have rooted by now and can be transplanted. Remove them carefully from the rooting bed using an old spoon or small trowel. Leave any rooting material which is "attached" to the roots. Pulling it off could harm the tender roots.‡

☞ Use Giberellic Acid on fall and winter-flowering **Camellia japonica** buds which you want to flower earlier and be larger. Remove the closest vegetative bud to the flower bud and put a drop of the acid in the little pit where the vegetative bud was attached to the main stem.

☞ Mulch shrubs and vines to conserve moisture, especially during the first half of the month. Do not allow the mulch to crowd or pack against the lower stems and trunks.**

---

* See "Controlling Insects and Diseases," p. 80

† See "Proper Watering," p. 130

‡ See "Semi-Hardwood Cuttings," p. 174

** See "Mulching: A Lesson from Nature," p. 243

September brings the first fall apples, especially in the Southern mountains.

III. *Fruits*

It's apple time in the South and you don't have to look far to find a small-town apple festival. Although I prefer picking homegrown apples, it is always fun to visit some of these festivals to experience the community activities which accompany harvest time — country music, funnel cakes, and folk art, to name a few.

Besides apples, pears continue to ripen in September. It is still important this month to harvest them before they fall from the tree. Inevitably some will slip by and end up rotting on the ground. Watch out because the yellow jackets love to light on these fallen pears and it's easy to step on one and get stung.

There is another autumn delight in September — wild muscadines! It is so nice to stumble on a vine while walking in the woods. There is nothing like squeezing muscadines so the pulp pops into your mouth, leaving the bare skin behind. Even when you pop one that isn't quite ripe and your face wrinkles up like a raisin, it's hard not to try just one more.

FRUIT ACTIVITIES FOR SEPTEMBER:

Plant

☞ The best time to plant fruit trees (**peaches, pears, apples, etc.**) and semi-bush fruits (**blackberries, raspberries, etc.**) and bush fruits (**blueberries**) is from November to February. September is a good month to decide which cultivars to plant this winter. Talk to friends and neighbors to find out which fruit cultivars grew and produced well for them over the summer.

Prune

☞ Remove all canes of semi-bush fruits like **blackberries** which fruited this summer. This will encourage new shoots from the crown on which next year's berries will be set.*

☞ *Do not prune* fruits this month. Fruit trees, semi-bush fruits, and bush fruits are growing well and forming buds. Next year's fruit will be set on this new growth, so don't do anything to disturb it or you will disturb next year's crop.

Fertilize

☞ *Do not fertilize* fruits this month. Fertilizing them may disturb bud formation.

Spray

☞ Continue a regular control program for insects and diseases on fruits which haven't yet ripened. A complete home orchard spray is the most practical method of control. Continue applications at recommended intervals until the fruit ripens.

☞ Finish last month's Southern borer control program on **cherries, nectarines, peaches,** and **plums** by spraying for the second time in early September. Thiodan is the recommended material to use.

Water

☞ Slowly soak fruit trees and bushes if there has been no significant rain in a week. This is especially important in the first part of the month which is usually as dry as summer.†

Other

☞ **Flowering crabapple** fruit will be ripening this month. The larger fruited varieties are spectacular in the fall. You can also make delicious jelly from them.

☞ Continue to harvest **pears** before they fall from the tree. If they are not completely ripe, you can ripen them in the house by wrapping each in a piece of newspaper and placing in a cool spot.

☞ Harvest **muscadines** and **scuppernongs** as soon as they are ripe or the birds will get more than you do.

☞ Be careful when mowing in orchard areas not to hit the bark of fruit trees with the mower. Any damage to the bark can provide an entrance place for borers, especially in early September when the adult moth is laying her eggs.

☞ Keep fruits mulched with pine straw to prevent weeds and grasses from competing for water and fertilizer. However, do not pile the mulch against the trunks of fruit trees.‡

---

* See "Secrets of the Berry Patch," p. 155

† See "Proper Watering," p. 130
‡ See "Mulching: A Lesson from Nature," p. 243

Cooler nights cause roses to start growing and blooming.

IV. *Roses*

As the nights begin to cool in mid to late September, roses will begin to grow and bloom more productively. They really didn't like the hot, humid weather we offered them in July and August. September and October are more their speed.

Many of us cut back our larger rose plants by one-third in August. If you didn't, you can still do so in early September. This grooming will encourage the plant to send up some vigorous new canes to provide us with one final show before freezes take their toll. Also remember to keep your roses well fertilized so that they will be encouraged to sprout new growth.

As new rose canes sprout and develop, it is nice to know that Blackspot will not be as much of a problem as it was in August. Without as much threat from insects and diseases, I have added hope for these new canes in cooler weather. While the number of blooms won't compare to last May, they will be a welcome sight on the crisp mornings to come.

ROSE ACTIVITIES FOR SEPTEMBER:

Plant

☞ November will be the start of rose planting time again. Visit rose gardens of friends and institutions to find varieties which you think will go well in your garden. Fall rose catalogs will soon be in the mail, and they are also a good source of information about new and old varieties.

Prune

☞ Get ready for fall blossoms by cutting back your plants one-third if you haven't done so already. Fertilize after pruning (on your regular schedule) and keep them soaked if the weather becomes dry. Remove any leaves with Blackspot.

☞ Groom roses constantly. Never leave a dead or dying stem on the plant because the disease will spread to healthy canes. Also remove weak, broken, or spindly shoots.*

☞ Remove all dead flowers by clipping above a five-leaflet set, as if you were cutting the flower to take inside.*

Fertilize

☞ In hot, dry conditions, keep plants growing with light applications of a complete rose fertilizer on your regular six-to-eight-week program. Supplement this program by spraying the foliage and new shoots with a water-soluble fertilizer solution like Peters.

Spray

☞ Continue with your complete rose spray program every 10 to 14 days according to the directions. Use a combination insecticide and fungicide spray and continue applications through the end of the month.

☞ Bud worms eat holes in maturing rose buds. They are usually controlled by your regular complete spray program, but applying Bacillus thuringiensis (BT) is a good supplemental control method.†

Water

☞ Water roses when there has been no significant rain for a week. Use a soaker hose to prevent wetting the foliage and thereby encouraging diseases. Remember to soak the bed thoroughly.

Other

☞ Remember to cut flowers correctly. Always make the cut above a joint where a five-leaflet originates. Cutting at this point encourages a strong new shoot and blossom to form.*

☞ Many **Hybrid Tea** and **Grandiflora** roses have several flowers in a cluster (called a candelabra) which may not all bloom at the same time. Remove each spent flower in the cluster as it finishes blooming. When all the flowers are done, cut the whole cluster stalk back to a five-leaflet set.*

☞ Keep roses well mulched with pine straw during September. Weeds continue to grow! Add fresh mulch when you can see bare ground around the plants, but do not pile mulch against the crown or lower stems. Problems like cankers and botrytis may still occur this month if the mulch covers the lower stems.‡

☞ Cut roses will last longer in an arrangement when the stems are recut underwater before placing in the vase. This allows water, not air, to travel up the stem.

† See "Controlling Insects and Diseases," p. 80

* See "Grooming Roses," p. 110

‡ See "Mulching: A Lesson from Nature," p. 243

* See "Grooming Roses," p. 110

Rudbeckia produces enough seeds to plant some yourself and give some away.

V. *Flowers and Colorful Garden Plants*

With the children back in school, and family vacations behind us, planting time is here again. We can once again carefully plant seeds in trays or pots and check them daily to see if they are moist enough to germinate. We can also make cuttings of our summer annuals and tend them faithfully with mist bottle in hand. There is even time to plant a few more chrysanthemums to color the garden until hard freezes arrive.

Over the summer months you have probably collected seeds from your own plants and from those of your friends. It is fun to call up friends to see if they can use some extra Rudbeckia seeds. They in turn offer a handful of Marguerite Daisy seeds. Then it is time to spread out all your seed and decide which can be planted now and which should be left for spring.

Rudbeckia, pansies, Shasta Daisy, Impatiens, Salvia, Geranium, and Hosta: It is nice once again to be seeding, propagating, and growing these old friends. Summer was nice, but it is always a welcome change to have something to do besides mulching, watering, and grooming.

FLOWER ACTIVITIES FOR SEPTEMBER:

Plant

☛ Continue planting seeds of hardy annuals, perennials, and biennials like **pansy**, **English Daisy**, **Dianthus**, **Foxglove**, **Shasta Daisy**, **Rudbeckia**, **Purple Cone-Flower**, and **Larkspur** in seed trays or pots in order to have stocky plants for transplanting into the garden in late October or early November. Start seeds in a peat-light potting mixture. Cover trays with a tray dome or a piece of clear plastic to keep them from drying out.*

* See "Starting Seeds Inside," p. 18

☛ Plant new or old potted **chrysanthemums** for colorful fall flowers which will last until hard freezes occur.

☛ Plant **peonies** and **Bearded Iris** this month. Always plant them shallowly. **Peonies** do best in morning sun, planted in well-drained and limed beds, and mulched to keep the soil cool. Plant them with the pink buds just above the soil. **Bearded Iris** need normal, well-drained soil, and full sun.

Prune

☛ Groomed annuals and perennials like **snapdragons, Salvia, marigolds,** and **hollyhocks** now begin to show more signs of life. They can be fertilized with a 5-10-15 formula, and mulched well.†

☛ Remove spent flowers regularly and do not let them produce seed. Developing seed pods reduce the amount of bloom.†

Fertilize

☛ After you groom them, fertilize annuals and perennials. The plants will burst forth with more blossoms in late September and until frost in late October if you give them these incentives.†

☛ Continue fertilizing plants with 5-10-15 on a six-to-eight-week schedule through the end of the season.

☛ During dry weather, spray a water-soluble fertilizer solution like Peters on foliage to keep plants growing well.

Spray

☛ Watch carefully for insects and diseases on flowers. Insects are still active in September. Tender flowers are highly susceptible to aphid, spider mite, leaf hopper, thrip, and worm damage. Orthene is an excellent all-around control.‡

☛ Worms are particularly bad this time of year. Keep flowering plants sprayed or dusted with Bacillus thuringiensis (BT).‡

☛ Lift pots of porch and patio plants to check for sowbugs and pillbugs. If you see them, dust underneath with Diazinon. Dust the surface of the soil and water thoroughly. Clean these infestations up now to have good, clean, and healthy plants to bring inside just before frost.‡

Water

☛ Water plants thoroughly with about one inch of water per week if there has been no significant rainfall.**

Other

☛ Keep beds well mulched to prevent fall weeds from taking over. Besides being unsightly, these competitors for water and fertilizer will keep garden plants from performing as well as they should.††

☛ When plants fall over from too much weight, stake them up with green bamboo stakes. Don't wait too long to do this or the plants will be misshapen when they are finally propped up.

☛ Make your first cuttings of **Begonia, Coleus, Geranium,** and **Impatiens.** Root them in peat-light or perlite-filled pots or trays. Make cuttings several times until just before frost to be sure you have well-rooted plants to overwinter.‡‡

☛ Tropical flowering plants like **Hibiscus, Ixora,** and **Allamanda** which have been outside all summer may need repotting. Ease the ball of soil out of the pot and look at the roots. If they are matted against the outside of the ball, it is time to repot. Always use a peat-light potting mixture and a pot at least two sizes larger.***

‡ See "Controlling Insects and Diseases," p. 80

** See "Proper Watering," p. 130

†† See "Mulching: A Lesson from Nature," p. 243

‡‡ See "Propagating Herbaceous Houseplants and Garden Plants," p. 225

*** See "Repotting Houseplants," p. 67

† See "Grooming and Pinching Flowers," p. 137

‡ See "Controlling Insects and Diseases," p. 80

VI. *Vegetables*

These days we can buy almost any vegetable at any time of the year. Although they taste horrible, we can drop by the supermarket in December and buy some "fresh" tomatoes. Potatoes, squash, greens, lettuce, and even zucchini are also available almost year-round.

Thank goodness vegetable gardening is different. Just about the time one harvest is getting tiresome, here comes another season offering a new cast of players to liven things up. It is this kind of diversity that keeps us vegetable gardening from April to October, and even during the winter months.

September is the beginning of a new round in the garden. The cool-season crops we last saw in the June harvest are ready to be planted again. Some, like collards, spinach, beets, and carrots, should be planted as soon as possible so they will mature before the first freezes. Others, like broccoli, cabbage, and lettuce, which you started from seed last month, can now be transplanted.

Before you know it, there will be new vegetables on the table. I think avoiding the supermarket and doing without broccoli for the last several months has been a good thing. I know that the anticipation will make it taste that much better.

THE FALL VEGETABLE GARDEN

Fall vegetable gardens were once as important as spring ones, but now it usually takes a drive into the country to see **onions, cabbage, collards, turnips, lettuce, rapegreens, mustard greens,** and even **beets** and **carrots** growing in the fall. In the old days, people always grew a fall crop of **Irish potatoes** to store during the winter, and depended on fresh greens for healthy meals until severe freezes finally killed all but the toughest plants like winter **cabbage** and **onions.** Modern gardeners prefer to shop at the supermarket rather than enjoy this second fresh vegetable season. It is even hard in the fall to find vegetable plants in nurseries or garden centers. Those of us who want a fall garden may have to take a trip to a country store to find the seeds and plants we need.

By September, about all that is left in most vegetable gardens are **tomatoes, peppers, eggplant, okra,** and yet-to-be-harvested **sweet potatoes.** There is still plenty of potential for all of these if you groom and fertilize them, just as you do flowers. The other summer vegetables have finished producing and should be removed from the garden since they provide perfect harbors for insects and diseases.

Consider the advantages of growing fall vegetables. Homegrown fresh vegetables are even tastier in the fall when compared to supermarket vegetables from distant production areas, and they are easy to plant after you remove summer vegetables which have finished producing.

Develop a fall vegetable garden using the same basic techniques I suggested in "Planting a Vegetable Garden" last April. Prepare the soil and plant

Plant broccoli plants in early September for a fall crop.

Sow small seeds of crops like turnips and mustard carefully and not too deeply for quick germination and a good fall crop.

in the same way. Root crops like **onions, turnips, radishes, beets,** and **carrots** should be planted on beds, while **greens, lettuce, cabbage,** and **broccoli** can be planted either on beds or flat. You need to fertilize with a 15-15-15 formula when you plant (one pound per 10 feet of row), just as in the spring, but subsequent applications of 5-10-15 won't be necessary. September and October are usually dry months, unless hurricanes sweep through the South bringing deluges of rain. Keep your hose and sprinklers ready since fall vegetables need the same one inch of water a week as they did during the spring and summer.

Plant as early as possible in September to give your fall vegetables plenty of time to mature before hard freezes in November bring an end to the fall vegetable season. September is too late to start seeds of **onions, cabbage, broccoli,** and **lettuce** for plants to set in the garden this fall. Find a good nursery or country store and purchase plants. You can still seed **beets, carrots, radishes, turnips,** and various **greens** in *early* September; they will have plenty of time to mature before hard freezes.

The following chart indicates which fall vegetables are best planted by seeding and which by setting out plants:

FALL VEGETABLE PLANTING GUIDE

FALL VEGETABLE	HOW TO PLANT
Beets	Seeds
Broccoli	Plants
Cabbage	Plants
Carrots	Seeds
Collards	Seeds or Plants
Garlic	Cloves
Kale	Seeds
Lettuce	Plants
Mustard Greens	Seeds
Onions	Plants or Sets
Parsley	Seeds or Plants
Radish	Seeds
Rapegreens	Seeds
Spinach	Seeds
Turnips	Seeds

PLANTING COVER CROPS

Planting a cover crop is one of my favorite ways to build the soil. There is something naturally exhilarating about watching **Crimson Clover** grow on a garden plot and imagining the hidden processes going on underground to help build the soil. It is much like finding a ladybug in the garden and carefully helping her on her way. It is an exhilaration born of cooperating with something as small as a bug or the nitrogen-producing bacteria on the roots of a leguminous cover crop.

A cover crop is any crop grown to build the soil or prevent soil erosion. Growing a cover crop is often called "green manuring" since we are growing the crop to plow under and add organic matter (humus) to the soil. There are two types of cover crops: leguminous and non-leguminous crops. A legume is a plant which has nitrogen-fixing bacteria on its roots. **Crimson Clover, Austrian Winter Peas,** and the various **cowpeas** are the leguminous cover crops most often grown in the South. In the North, cold weather prevents growing legumes all year round. They must resort to growing non-leguminous cover crops like **Ryegrass, rye,** and **buckwheat.** Since legumes have the added benefit of nitrogen-fixing bacteria, we should stick to growing legumes and leave the **Buckwheat** to those in northerly climates.

Cover crops benefit the soil in many ways. First, a legume, with its nitrogen-fixing bacteria, absorbs nitrogen from the air, processes it into a form plants can use, and stores it in nodules on the roots of the plant, later to be released into the soil when the crop is plowed under. Second, the root action of a cover crop loosens and prevents the soil from compacting.

Leguminous crops like Crimson Clover produce nitrogen-fixing bacteria nodules on the roots which add much needed nitrogen to the soil.

Green-manure/cover crops like Crimson Clover produce large amounts of humus to be worked in gardens next spring.

Crimson Clover seeds are tiny and can be mixed with dry sand to aid in sowing.

Third, when turned under, a cover crop is a major source of humus as it decomposes. And finally, a cover crop prevents soil erosion. When combined, these benefits make a compelling reason to plant a cover crop, especially since it is such an easy task.

Leguminous cover crops can be planted to improve the soil in any garden area. Lawns, flower beds, vegetable gardens, and steep banks are all candidates. However, vegetable and flower gardens are the most usual spots since yearly crops tend to deplete the soil. We also spend most of our allotted garden funds on flowers and vegetables, so we expect them to perform well. Growing a legume in the off-season is a great way to help our plants do their best.

In the South, we usually plant cover crops at two times of the year: immediately after our summer vegetable harvest is finished, or in the fall. Summer legumes like **cowpeas** (**Lady Peas**, **Black-Eyed Peas**, and **Crowder Peas**) are planted after our short harvest crops like **sweet corn**, **bush beans**, and **cantaloupe** are finished. They are grown through the end of summer and plowed under in the early fall since they will die with the first hard freeze.

Fall cover crops like **Crimson Clover** and **Austrian Winter Peas** are planted in the fall to build the soil and prevent erosion over the winter months. Both **Crimson Clover** and **Austrian Winter Peas** are hardy, but **Crimson Clover** should be planted before mid-October because it needs warmer weather to establish itself. **Austrian Winter Peas** can still be planted after mid-October since they grow better in cool weather. All cover crops should be turned under before they go to seed so they won't proliferate as weeds in your later plantings.

While it is best to sow your cover crop on well-turned soil, I have had good germination even on untilled areas which I worked with a stiff garden rake. Since cover crops are normally planted on areas where we plan to garden, it is a good idea to go ahead and prepare the soil just as if you were planting your regular garden.

The trickiest part of planting a cover crop is sowing the seed. It is not worth it to use a push- or pull-type broadcast spreader. It is hard to roll a spreader over worked ground, and it will probably not broadcast evenly. The best method is to use a hand-crank broadcast spreader or broadcast the seeds yourself by hand. It takes a little practice to become adept at hand-broadcasting seed. It is an old method but not necessarily simple (remember the famous painting "The Sower" by Van Gogh).

Crimson Clover is the hardest to work with since the seeds are tiny. A common method of easing the burden is to evenly mix the seeds in a neutral medium like dry sand. You will still apply the same amount of seeds per given area, but the overall bulk material applied will be larger and easier to handle.

Hand-broadcasting seed is much like side-arming a baseball pitch. Grab a handful of seed, reel back, and throw your pitch. The seeds should scatter as they leave your hand and cover about three square feet of ground. The best advice is to hand-broadcast boldly and confidently. Without confidence, your throw will probably peter out at the end, the seeds will leave your hand in one clump, and you will have a garden pockmarked with thick, scattered patches of your crop.

There is one additional step for leguminous cover

Scatter Crimson Clover seeds and gently rake in so they will germinate evenly and quickly.

crops. Some seed is sold with a separate pack of nitrogen-fixing bacteria. The bacteria is specific to your cover crop and needs to be mixed with the seeds before sowing so that it can later attach itself to the roots of the young legumes. Read the directions for the recommended method of application.

After sowing the seeds, gently rake them in with the back side of a garden rake. They should not be covered too deeply. It is also a good idea to water the plot thoroughly to get them going. Germination usually ranges from one to two weeks.

Sometimes leguminous cover crops like **Crimson Clover** will be a light green color in their first few weeks of growth. The nitrogen-fixing bacteria is not producing enough nitrogen to supply the growing plant. Broadcast a light application of 15-15-15 fertilizer to green them up. Don't worry, though; soon the bacteria will be producing an excess of nitrogen and storing it in nodules on the **clover's** roots. When you plow under the mature **clover**, the nitrogen nodules will be left in the soil to supply your flowers or vegetables with this essential nutrient.

Finally, remember that it takes about a month for a cover crop to decompose in the ground. Turn under your crop at least a month in advance of your fall or spring plantings.

TYPE OF COVER CROP	WHEN TO SOW	BROADCAST RATE PER 1000 SQ.FT.
Cowpeas (**Lady Peas**, **Black-Eyed Peas**, and **Crowder Peas**)	Summer	5-10 lbs.
Crimson Clover	Fall, before mid-October	2-3 lbs.
Austrian Winter Peas	Fall, Winter	5-10 lbs.

VEGETABLE ACTIVITIES FOR SEPTEMBER:

Plant

☛ **Beets, carrots, collards, mustard greens, onions** (plants and sets), **parsley, radishes, rapegreens, spinach,** and **turnips** can be planted from seed all month. The earlier you can plant, the better.*

☛ **Broccoli, cabbage, cauliflower, onion, collards,** and **lettuce** seedlings started last month or purchased at the nursery can now be set in the garden.*

☛ Prepare the ground for fall plantings just as well as you did last spring. Add organic material, then till deeply. Broadcast limestone over the surface at a rate of 50 pounds per 1000 square feet. Make rows, work in a 15-15-15 fertilizer at a rate of one pound per 10 feet of row, and then plant the seed or plants. Remember to plant **onions, turnips** (for bottoms), **beets, radishes,** and **carrots** on beds rather than flat in a furrow.*

☛ Plant **Crimson Clover** rather than **cowpeas** in bare garden areas as an excellent green-manure cover crop. **Crimson Clover** is hardy and will last through the winter.†

Prune

☛ Groom **tomato** plants if they are looking bad and not producing well. Remove weak growth and spray for diseases with a complete tomato spray to which you have added a water-soluble fertilizer solution like Peters. Fertilize around the plants with a 15-15-15 formula and soak the bed well. Be sure that the mulch is thick enough to prevent fall weeds. Soon plants will produce new growth and flowers for an October harvest.

Fertilize

☛ Fertilize vegetables as you plant with a 15-15-15 fertilizer. Application is at a rate of approximately one pound per 10 feet of row. This application should be good for about six weeks.‡

☛ **Tomatoes, peppers, eggplant, cucumber,** and **okra** should be fertilized with 5-10-15 every six weeks throughout their growing season until they are groomed in the fall (if they need grooming); then it is best to use 15-15-15. Application is at a rate of approximately one pound per 10 feet of row.‡

☛ Continue to fertilize other growing vegetables with 5-10-15 about every six weeks for the rest of the season. Application is at a rate of approximately one pound per 10 feet of row.‡

Spray

☛ The first step to effective pest control is detecting the pest before it has damaged your crop extensively. Once you spot a problem you are not familiar with, take an infected leaf, flower, or fruit to your local nurseryman or Cooperative Extension Service agent for identification. There's a wide variety of organic and inorganic materials to control most garden pests.‡

☛ Spray or dust frequently to control fruit worms, blights, and other diseases, especially on **tomatoes.** I like to use Bacillus thuringiensis (BT) for worms and a home vegetable spray or dust for the diseases.‡

☛ Whitefly may be a serious problem this month on **tomatoes, peppers, eggplants,** and **squash.** There are no effective preventive measures, so it is important to control the population before they increase to damaging levels. Hang sticky yellow strips (available at garden centers) among your plants to trap these pests. A spray of an insecticidal soap may also help.‡

☛ Tomato Hornworms and fruit worms are active this month. Keep fruiting plants sprayed or dusted with Bacillus thuringiensis (BT). If you are not getting good control, spray or dust with Sevin.‡

☛ Keep **pole beans** sprayed or dusted with Sevin for worms and bean beetles.‡

* See "Planting a Vegetable Garden," p. 92
† See "Planting Cover Crops," p. 205
‡ See "Fertilizing, Spraying, and Watering Vegetables," p. 115

‡ See "Fertilizing, Spraying, and Watering Vegetables," p. 115

☛ Blossom End Rot, which results in black corking of the bottom or blossom end of **tomatoes, peppers,** and **eggplants**, is caused by a calcium deficiency aggravated by improper watering (either too much or too little). Apply a calcium solution to the foliage and then correct the watering problem. Your next fruits should be free from the problem. Liming during the winter will also help correct this problem for the next season.‡

☛ Watch for Asparagus beetles which will quickly eat **Asparagus** foliage and damage plants. Sevin should give you good control.‡

Water

☛ Water vegetables thoroughly with about one inch of water if there has been no significant rainfall for a week.‡

Other

☛ Remove all finished crops as soon as possible and plant the bare areas with a cover crop like **Crimson Clover**. Old dying plants are perfect breeding grounds for insects and diseases.†

☛ Remove and dispose of over-ripe vegetables from your plants every day. Left on the plants, they attract insects and diseases.

☛ Keep vegetables free of weeds by hoeing or mulching. Weeds compete with vegetables for essential nutrients and harbor damaging insects.

☛ Harvest frequently and correctly. Vegetables left too long on the plant will lose their best taste and quality.**

VEGETABLE	HARVEST
Cucumbers, Squash, Zucchini	While still small and tender
Pole Beans	Before you see the seeds bulging
Tomatoes, Peppers, Eggplants	Harvest frequently and remove unusable fruit
Various Greens	When the leaves are large but still tender
Okra	Before they are five inches long

‡ See "Fertilizing, Spraying, and Watering Vegetables," p. 115
† See "Planting Cover Crops," p. 205

** See "Harvesting Vegetables and Keeping Them Tasty," p. 140

NOTES

VII. *Houseplants*

Most of the houseplants we grow are native to the equatorial regions of the world. We use them as houseplants because they grow naturally on the shaded jungle floor and don't mind the lack of light available in our homes.

In the equatorial regions, plants get about 12 hours of daylight and 12 hours of night all year round. In the South, March 20/21(the Spring Equinox) and September 22/23 (the Fall Equinox) mark the days on which day and night are equal. In other words, this month is one of the times each year when our houseplants feel most at home.

I like to propagate my houseplants in September. They have grown well over the summer months and filled out their pots. Many need to be divided, some have grown "leggy" and need to be cut back, and others are getting too tall for their designated spot. Propagation is a good way to reduce the size of my present stock and create new plants to fill my home or to give as Christmas presents. It is also a fun hobby. There are lots of different methods, procedures, and equipment to try out.

While the main reason I propagate in September is that plants have plenty of summer growth, I also like to think that it will be less of a shock to them if the light conditions are close to their native habitat and they feel at home.

HOUSEPLANT ACTIVITIES FOR SEPTEMBER:

Plant

☞ Check for plants which are pot-bound and need repotting, including those you purchased last spring. Repot in early September to give plants plenty of time to become re-established before being moved inside. Use a peat-light potting mixture. Check for insects while the plant is out of its pot.*

☞ **Hibiscus**, **Allamanda**, **Ixora**, and many other tropical flowering plants can be rooted this month for additional plants next year. Take cuttings from young shoots with developed leaves. Root in a peat-light mixture or in perlite. Pot them when the roots are one inch long, and overwinter in a bright, warm spot.†

☞ Fall is a good time to propagate houseplants. One of my favorite things to do is propagate pot-bound plants through division. In this way, one established plant becomes many. These will make great Christmas gifts for family and friends.†

Prune

☞ Groom indoor plants whenever they need it. Remove weak branches or stems as well as off-color leaves.

Fertilize

☞ Fertilize with full-strength, liquid fertilizer every time you water. Or, use fertilizer spikes or Osmocote fertilizer, both of which last several months.‡‡

Spray

☞ Check all indoor plants for insects like spider mites, scale, and mealybug. Using a dry houseplant systemic insecticide to control them is easier and safer than spraying inside. If you do spray, remember to apply the insecticide to the undersides of the leaves. I prefer to take plants outside on a warm day to spray.**

☞ If sowbugs or pillbugs were found when repotting, treat the soil with Diazinon.*

---

‡ See "Houseplant Care and Maintenance," p. 232

** See "Common Houseplant Ailments," p. 280

* See "Repotting Houseplants," p. 67

---

* See "Repotting Houseplants," p. 67

† See "Propagating Herbaceous Houseplants and Garden Plants," p. 225

☞ Be careful when spraying **ferns**. Some insecticides are harmful to them. *Always read the label for warnings about **ferns** and other plants.*

Water

☞ Continue to watch houseplants. When they look limp, check for dry soil. If it is dry, water thoroughly in a sink or bathtub, letting the water drain completely, and don't water again until the surface is dry once more. Between waterings, mist with plain water on a regular basis. If the limp plants are in moist soil, do not water. Allow the soil to dry a bit and mist it frequently instead.‡

☞ Tip-burn or edge-burn on leaves indicates that more water is being lost than is being absorbed by the roots. Check for dry soil, too much sunlight, or

drafts from heating vents. Overwatering can also cause poor root development which results in the same symptoms.‡

Other

☞ September 22/23 marks the Fall Equinox, the official end of summer. On this day, the number of light and dark hours are equal. After September 22/23, the daylight hours will continue to decrease until the Winter Solstice around December 21. This decrease of natural light marks the beginning of a slow-growth period for houseplants. Also, remember to check your houseplants periodically as the sun's position in the sky changes. Windows which currently receive enough light may lose some as the sun's position lowers in the sky.

‡ See "Houseplant Care and Maintenance," p. 232

‡ See "Houseplant Care and Maintenance," p. 232

NOTES

VIII. *Lawns*

The story of our grass continues. All summer we have been cutting — week after week, month after month. When there was a patch of weeds and we found the need to do something to our lawns besides cutting, there always seemed to be some reason to wait. "Leave them until next year; we'll certainly get the pre-emergence down in time *next year*."

September is a month of action in the world of grasses. It is another turning point in their life cycle and a time for us to work on them *this year*. The evergreen grasses, also known as cool-season grasses, are ready to grow again after the hot summer. The cooler nights in late September inspire them. Planting, reseeding, fertilizing, and liming are all ways to turn your lawn into the prize-winner it wants to be.

The summer grasses are different. I like to think of them in the same category as my annual flowering plants. They revved up last April and performed wonderfully all summer. By September, they are not in their prime, just like our annuals which have grown spindly and aren't producing as many flowers. Don't fertilize summer grasses this time of year because it will force new growth which won't have time to harden-up before freezing weather arrives. Fall and winter are the time for summer grasses to rest and "lie low."

Try not to put off your lawn work until next year. Evergreen grasses started now will be in much better shape next year than if you wait and plant in March. Summer grasses will also emerge quickly and strongly next spring if they "retire" for the season in good health.

Evergreen lawns start growing well in September.

September is the best time of the year to plant evergreen lawns.

LAWNS IN THE FALL

The nights are cooler now and the days more comfortable than just a few weeks ago. Not only are gardeners happy with these changes; evergreen lawns are too. Summer has not been the best time for these grasses, which have been existing only with a great deal of help from us; **fescues** and **bluegrasses** needed pampering to keep them free from weeds and growing well. On the other hand, summer <u>is</u> the best time of the year for the other group of lawn grasses which we grow in the South — southern summer grasses like **Bermuda Grass, Zoysia, Centipede,** and **St. Augustine**. In September, with the change in weather, they start their slower growth cycle which ends with frost. Then they go dormant and remain brown until after danger of frost next spring, when they begin to grow again.

September is the best time of the year to start a new evergreen lawn but not a good time to plant Southern summer grass lawns. Summer lawns should be planted when the weather is warmer during the late spring and summer. I have described how to plant and reseed evergreen grasses in March ("Planting and Reseeding Evergreen Lawns") and how to plant and reseed summer grasses in April ("Planting and Reseeding Summer Lawns"). The principals are the same for starting or reseeding an evergreen lawn this month, though there are a few other things to consider when starting a new lawn in the early fall.

The fall is drier than the spring, and gardeners need to water frequently and correctly. This "how to" is explained in detail in the lawn articles mentioned above as well as "Proper Watering" in June.

Since this is the best time of the year to start a new evergreen lawn, garden centers and nurseries are filled with the standard types like **Kentucky 31 Fescue,** the new **turf-type tall fescues,** the shade-tolerant fescues like **Creeping Red** and **Chewing,** and **Kentucky Bluegrass**. In addition, there are lawn mixtures containing sun and shade-tolerant evergreen grasses. These can be a blessing to the lawn grower who has a combination of exposures. However, be careful when purchasing a lawn mixture. Many of those found on the market, especially at low prices, contain high percentages of annual grasses like **Ryegrass** which will grow well through the winter and die next May or June at the end of their life cycle. *Always* read the label affixed to the bag. This label is a government requirement and states the germination rate (%) and the amounts of all grasses in the bag. The key to a good mixture is that it has *no* **Ryegrass** or other annual grasses. A good mixture for the South should have more **turf-type fescues** than **Kentucky 31** and more shade tolerant fescues like **Creeping Red** and **Chewing** than **Kentucky Bluegrass.**

Estimate the amount of direct sun and filtered sun which your lawn area will get. If you have 50% of each, your mixture should have 50% **Kentucky 31 Fescue** and the **turf-type fescues**, and 50% **Chewing fescue, Creeping Red fescue,** and **Kentucky Bluegrass.** As the percentages of sun and filtered shade change, the mixture should also change.

Mixtures are easier to plant since you do not have to worry whether you are planting the best grass in each type of exposure. But because the quality of many mixtures is poor, I prefer to sow individual grasses in each area with some of each in the transitional parts of my lawn.

LAWN ACTIVITIES FOR SEPTEMBER:

Plant

☛ It is time to plant evergreen lawns like **Kentucky 31 Fescue, Creeping Red Fescue, Chewing Fescue, Kentucky Bluegrass,** and **Bentgrass** (with caution). *

☛ Reseed bare areas of evergreen lawns as soon as the weeds are dead. Do not just sow seed over the lawn to thicken it up. Work the bare or thin areas with a potato hook, apply lime, fertilize, and then reseed.*

Fertilize

☛ Fertilize established evergreen lawns with a high-nitrogen, slow-release lawn fertilizer.†

☛ There is no need to fertilize summer grass lawns this month.

☛ Apply lime to evergreen lawns at the rate of at least 50 pounds per 1000 square feet. This is helpful every fall. Dolomitic limestone in pellet form is the easiest form to use.†

☛ Remember that summer grasses like **Bermuda Grass** and **Zoysia** should not normally be limed every year. **Zoysia** should be limed only if a pH level has been taken and it is less than 6 pH. **St. Augustine** and **Centipede** should never be limed.

Spray

☛ Control broadleaf weeds with a good lawn weed killer. Be sure and spray with the type which is recommended for your grass.†

☛ Watch for Fall Armyworms. They come in droves and can ruin a lawn overnight. The first indication that you will have of this potential disaster is very heavy moth activity, especially around shrubs next to your lawn. Be ready to spray or apply granules of Diazinon as soon as you see the first worms in your lawn.

Cut

☛ Mow at the recommended heights through September.

☛ **Hybrid Bermuda Grass** may need cutting twice a week.

☛ Cut summer grasses often to prevent browning. Cutting grass after it is very tall removes the green part, leaving brown stems. This condition will remain until new green leaves grow.

* See "Lawns in the Fall," p. 213
† See "Fertilizing and Controlling Weeds in Lawns," p. 80

† See "Fertilizing and Controlling Weeds in Lawns," p. 80

☞ Cut grasses at the proper height:

SUMMER GRASSES	HEIGHT
Common Bermuda Grass	2 inches
Hybrid Bermuda Grass	1 to 1 $\frac{1}{2}$ inches
Centipede	1 $\frac{1}{2}$ to 2 inches
St. Augustine	2 to 2 $\frac{1}{2}$ inches
Zoysia	1 to 2 inches

EVERGREEN GRASSES	HEIGHT
Kentucky 31 Tall Fescue	3 to 3 $\frac{1}{2}$ inches
Turf-type Tall Fescues	3 inches
Fine Leaf Fescues	1 $\frac{1}{2}$ to 2 inches
Kentucky Bluegrass	2 to 2 $\frac{1}{2}$ inches

Water

☞ Keep evergreen lawns well watered in dry periods to encourage heavy growth before cold weather.‡

Other

☞ Do not worry about **crabgrass** which is an annual and should be turning reddish purple before dying. Pull out dead or dying clumps to allow lawn grasses to quickly fill in the bare areas.

‡ See "Proper Watering," p. 130

NOTES

October

IN THE SOUTHERN GARDEN

Nature reserves some of her greatest beauty for October, the last month before cold brings an end to the growing season. Frosty weather starts in the Southern mountains in October and creeps southward until it reaches the deep South in November. Before the freezes, the chilly nights of October paint the forests a beautiful blend of yellow, gold, red, orange, and purple. Mountains seem to be on fire in the early-morning and late-afternoon sun as maple, hickory, and oak leaves compete for first prize in nature's beauty contest.

Home landscapes join in the contest for best color of the year, not only with maples, oaks, and Gingko trees but also with brightly colored leaves on shrubs like Oakleaf Hydrangea, Pyracantha, and Nandina. Crabapple trees try to outdo their beautiful spring flowers with their red fall fruits. Hollies sport dark red berries. Annuals which colored our flower beds all summer become brilliantly colored with October's chilly nights.

Some of my most vivid memories as a boy growing up in the country are of cool October days and chilly nights. Sweet potatoes came from the ground like nuggets of gold; the garden yielded fresh greens and the last of the tomatoes and peppers. My friends and I could always find a few wild muscadines (bullaces to us back then) to relish as we rode our ponies through the forests. It was a happy time for all of us in the country because the results of summer's work meant a gracious plenty for the winter. On chilly nights, we celebrated the harvest with 'possum and 'coon hunts, and I can still hear the howls of Red Bone hounds as they picked up a scent. We called the full moon at the end of October the Harvest Moon, a special time when hogs were killed and there was fresh sausage on the breakfast table.

Though times have changed, October's chilly nights still herald the end of the growing season and the final harvests of the year. Friday night high school football replaces 'possum hunts, and hay rides provide just as much fun for the young. Sweet potatoes and fresh pork meat are no longer required for eating well until gardens produce again in the spring. Nowadays, our frozen homegrown blueberries and sweet corn are what remind us on a cold winter night of the wonders produced by our summer garden.

AT LEFT: *Maples are brilliantly colored in October.*

Sugar Maple (Acer saccharum) is spectacular in the fall.

I. *Shade and Flowering Trees*

Autumn in the South provides a new perspective on the garden. While we normally choose a new tree for our landscape according to its size or flowering potential, there is also the option to choose trees by their fall color. While we usually don't consider fall color as the primary attribute of a tree, keeping it in mind does help to make the garden beautiful throughout the year.

Some of our most beautiful trees in the fall are Sugar Maple, Red Maple 'October Glory,' Gingko biloba, true Pin Oak (Quercus palustris), Sweet Gum, and Bradford Pear. 'October Glory' is a Red Maple cultivar which was specially selected for its color. If you're going to plant a Red Maple anyway, why not consider 'October Glory'? There are other cultivars of the major trees chosen for their spectacular color, which can spice up your autumn landscape and add a new diversity of color to your yard.

While autumn is normally noted for its leaves, don't forget the bright red fruit adorning the Callaway Crabapple. Its fruit is larger than most crabapples and makes quite a display. The various cultivars of American Holly also produce a multitude of red berries as a beautiful accent against their dark green foliage.

Although autumn color may provide the inspiration to plant a new tree, remember that autumn is not the best time to plant. You would be wise to wait until the trees are fully dormant so they won't be as shocked in handling. Professional growers also wait until trees are dormant to dig them in the fields. The trees you will find in nurseries this month are probably left over from last year and are not as desirable as the ones to come in the winter months.

TREE ACTIVITIES FOR OCTOBER:

Plant

☞ Begin planting B&B and container-grown trees whenever the ground is not moist. It might be wise, however, to wait until next month when trees are fully dormant and nurseries have their new stock. If you do plant, make sure to plant trees at the correct depth in a well-prepared hole, and stake them to prevent swaying. Never plant trees deeper than they were growing in the nursery. When planting B&B and container-grown trees, it is a good idea to leave the top of the root ball showing after planting. Plant bare-root trees with the soil level one inch above the top root.*

☞ Choose planting stock carefully. New shade trees should be straight, should have a dominant central shoot or leader, should have tight, smooth bark, and should not be loose in the ball or container. Carefully choose flowering trees which are free from scars, indicating that they have been grown well.

☞ When handling B&B and container-grown trees, never pick them up by the stem. The roots in the pot or ball of earth are liable to break.

Prune

☞ *Do not prune* trees this month. Many flowering trees have set their blossom buds for next year. Pruning would remove many of next year's flowers. The best time to prune shade and flowering trees is later in the winter when they are dormant.

Fertilize

☞ *Do not fertilize* trees this month. The best time to fertilize shade and summer-flowering trees is in early spring when they are emerging from dormancy. Spring-flowering trees are fertilized in the spring as their flower petals fall.

Spray

☞ Clean up infestations of scale on evergreen trees while the insects are still active. Spray with Cygon or Orthene except on **hollies**. Use Orthene on **hollies**.†

Water

☞ Water newly planted trees thoroughly, even if the ground is wet, in order to settle the soil around the roots. Don't worry if it should freeze before the ground dries out. When it freezes, wet soil insulates the tree's roots more than dry soil.‡

Other

☞ Mulch newly planted trees with pine straw or pine bark. Do not allow the mulch to pack against the tree's trunk. Pests like the vole (pine mouse) will crawl up through the mulch and chew off the tree's bark near the ground. If you do see vole damage, you might want to get a vole trap or a mean cat.**

☞ Check mulch around older trees and replenish with fresh mulch if needed. The mulch that has been around trees all summer probably contains overwintering insects which are settling in for the winter.**

☞ Stake newly planted shade and flowering trees, especially if they were purchased bare-root. Attach three wires to the trunk about four or five feet off the ground which run to wooden stakes driven at intervals around the tree. Make a collar of old watering hose to prevent the wire from cutting into the trunks.

☞ Keep falling leaves from piling up against the trunks of your trees. Leaves will trap too much water against the trunk and cause various problems.

† See "Controlling Insects and Diseases," p. 80

‡ See "Helping Plants Survive the Cold," p. 269

** See "Mulching: A Lesson from Nature," p. 243

* See "Planting Trees and Shrubs," p. 264

Oakleaf Hydrangea (Hydrangea quercifolia) turns a rusty red in fall.

II. *Shrubs and Vines*

October is normally a time to admire the fall leaf color of our trees. When a Sugar Maple turns a whole corner of your garden orange, it is hard to notice anything else.

The fact is, shrubs are also a major source of fall color in the garden. The Oakleaf Hydrangea turns a rusty red and is stunning when planted in a long line. The deciduous Euonymous alatus turns a bright red as does the Red Tip Photinia. Nandina can range from a dark red to the bright, orange-red of some cultivars. These colorful shrubs add a layered dimension to the landscape as they sit nestled back behind a large shade tree and draw your eye with a contrasting color.

An added colorful autumn sight are the red berries on Nandina and many hollies. After you have finished enjoying their colorful clusters nestled in among the leaves, you can harvest the seeds to grow some more shrubs next spring. Don't wait too long, however, because the birds might beat you to them.

SHRUB AND VINE ACTIVITIES FOR OCTOBER:

Plant

☞ Begin planting container-grown and B&B shrubs this month. (Don't plant bare-root shrubs and vines until later in the winter.) It might be wise, however, to wait until next month when shrubs and vines are fully dormant and nurseries have their new stock. If you do plant, prepare the holes as carefully as you do for shade trees.*

Prune

☞ *Do not prune* shrubs and vines this month. Pruning could force tender growth which might be killed by the first hard freezes. Also, spring-flowering shrubs and vines like **azalea, Forsythia, Spiraea, Flowering Quince, Camellia, Rhododendron, Carolina Jessamine,** and **Wisteria** have set their blossom buds for next year. Pruning would remove many of your spring flowers.

Fertilize

☞ *Do not fertilize* shrubs and vines this month. Just like pruning, fertilizing could force tender growth which might be killed by the first hard freezes. It also makes plants more susceptible to early cold damage. Non-flowering shrubs and vines like **boxwoods, Box Leaf Holly, Burford Holly** and **English Ivy** are fertilized in the early spring. Spring-flowering shrubs and vines like **azalea, Forsythia, Spiraea, Flowering Quince, Camellia, Rhododendron, Carolina Jessamine,** and **Wisteria** are fertilized in the spring after they flower. Summer-flowering shrubs like Butterfly Bush are fertilized in the early spring.

Spray

☞ Watch for lacebugs on **azalea** and **Pyracantha.** The leaves will turn a silvery color, and the undersides will have brown residue. Spray them with Orthene. It is important to kill the adults before they lay eggs which would overwinter and emerge next spring to attack your plants again.†

☞ Watch for scale on evergreens like **boxwoods, Euonymus,** and **Burford Holly.** Spray with Cygon or Orthene to control it, except do not use Cygon on **hollies.** It is important to clean up the scale while they are still active.†

Water

☞ Water newly planted shrubs and vines thoroughly, even if the ground is wet, to settle the soil around the roots. Don't worry if it is going to freeze before the ground dries out. When it freezes, wet soil insulates the roots more than dry soil.‡

Other

☞ Mulch shrubs and vines, especially newly planted ones, with pine straw, but leave the space around the trunks or lower stems free of mulch.**

☞ Keep falling leaves from piling up against the trunks and stems of plants, especially **boxwoods** and **azaleas.** They can cause crown rooting (shifting the root structure upward) and make the shrub more susceptible to drying out in cold or dry weather.

* See "Planting Trees and Shrubs," p. 264
† See "Controlling Insects and Diseases," p. 80
† See "Controlling Insects and Diseases," p. 80
‡ See "Helping Plants Survive the Cold," p. 269
** See "Mulching: A Lesson from Nature," p. 243

III. *Fruits*

After a long season of fruit harvests, the season is finally over. While there still may be some apples and pears in the refrigerator, most of our fruits are either canned, preserved, or a memory of warmer days.

While it may seem like an age until next summer's harvest, our fruit trees, bush fruits, and semi-bush fruits have already set buds for next year. If you need a little lift as cold weather approaches, walk out to check on these fruit buds. There are always too many to count and it is inspiring to know they are there, waiting for warm weather in the spring to flower and begin producing fruit.

There is still plenty of time before the fruit season begins in January and February with the first applications of dormant spray. Don't rush things and buy new fruit plantings this month. If you wait until November and December to plant a new tree or bush, your new fruit will start off on a better foot since it will be fully dormant.

FRUIT ACTIVITIES FOR OCTOBER:

Plant

☛ The best time to plant fruit trees is from November to February when they are dormant.

☛ Begin planting container-grown and B&B bush fruits (**blueberries**), semi-bush fruits (**blackberries, raspberries etc.**), and fruiting vines (**muscadines, scuppernongs, and grapes**). It might be wise, however, to wait until next month when they are fully dormant, and nurseries have new stock. If you do plant, prepare the holes as carefully as you do for shade trees.*

Prune

☛ *Do not prune* fruit trees, bush fruits, or fruiting vines this month. Remember, fruits have set their buds by October. Any pruning would probably remove some buds and reduce next season's harvest. Wait until January/February to prune fruit trees.

☛ If you have not done so already, remove the older canes on semi-bush berries like **raspberries** and **blackberries** which bore this past summer. Leave the new growth to produce next summer's fruit. Train this new growth onto a fence or trellis. †

Fertilize

☛ *Do not fertilize* fruits like **apples**, **peaches**, and **pears** until early spring when their buds begin to swell.

Spray

☛ There is no need to spray fruits until later in the winter. Application of dormant spray begins in Janaury.

Water

☛ Thoroughly water any newly planted bush or semi-bush fruits even if the ground is wet. This is done to settle the soil around the roots. Don't worry if it is going to freeze before the ground dries out. When it freezes, wet soil insulates the roots more than dry soil.‡

Other

☛ Be careful when mowing in orchard areas not to hit the bark of fruit trees with the mower. Any damage to the bark will provide an entrance place for borers.

☛ Keep fruits mulched with pine straw to prevent weeds and grasses from competing for water and fertilizer. However, do not pile the mulch against the trunks of fruit trees.**

---

* See "Planting Trees and Shrubs," p. 264
† See "Secrets of the Berry Patch," p. 155

‡ See "Helping Plants Survive the Cold," p. 269
** See "Mulching: A Lesson from Nature," p. 243

Roses are our best plants for color all season.

IV. *Roses*

It is amazing to think back on the rose season and realize that our roses have been blooming since late April. What an incredible plant! Some years, depending on the weather, we might have a few rose blossoms up until Thanksgiving. Even if we see the last blooms in October, our roses have once again proven themselves over a long growing season.

Next month, new rose stock will begin showing up in local nurseries. We will finally get the chance to fill out our beds and make the additions we've been dreaming about all summer. You can never have too many roses!

As you finish up the season, don't groom your roses too heavily — just cut off flowers to take inside, or remove spent flowers. Next month we will cut back tall roses by one-third for the winter months.

ROSE ACTIVITIES FOR OCTOBER:

Plant

☞ Wait until next month to begin planting new container-grown and bare-root roses when they are dormant and fresh new stocks are in nurseries.

Prune

☞ Remove all dead flowers by clipping above a five-leaflet set, as if you were cutting the flower to take inside.*

Fertilize

☞ Fertilize for the last time this season with a complete rose fertilizer. If you fertilized at the end of September, you can skip this application.

Spray

☞ Begin winding up your regular spray program. It is a good idea to spray one last time before the weather turns cold to control insects and diseases before they overwinter.

Water

☞ Water rose beds during any periods of dry weather. October is generally one of our driest months. Use a soaker hose to prevent wetting the foliage and thereby encouraging diseases. Remember to soak the bed thoroughly.†

Other

☞ Remember to cut flowers correctly. Always make the cut above a joint where a five-leaflet originates. Cutting at this point encourages a strong new shoot and blossom to form.*

☞ Many **Hybrid Tea** and **Grandiflora** roses have several flowers in a cluster (called a candelabra) which may not all bloom at the same time. Remove each spent flower in the cluster as it finishes blooming. When all the flowers have finished, cut the whole cluster stalk back to a five-leaflet set.*

☞ Keep roses well mulched, but do not pile mulch against the crown or lower stems. Many problems like cankers and botrytis occur when mulch covers the lower stems. Also, it is a good idea to replace summer mulch in the fall to dispose of any overwintering insects and diseases.‡

☞ Cut roses will last longer in an arrangement when the stems are recut underwater before placing in the vase. This allows water, not air, to travel up the stem.

* See "Grooming Roses," p. 110

† See "Proper Watering," p. 130

* See "Grooming Roses," p. 110

‡ See "Mulching: A Lesson from Nature," p. 243

NOTES

V. *Flowers and Colorful Garden Plants*

Here come the first frosts and our annuals know it. Although they are still brightly colored, the cooler weather has slowed their growth down to a crawl, and their season is almost over. Before they die, take a final look around your flower bed with an eye for fungus and disease. Now is the time to recognize problems which need to be fixed before your new plantings next April.

As soon as frost has killed my annuals, I like to jump right in and dig the geraniums. Before hard freezes arrive and brown their tops completely, there is plenty of life left in them. These tough plants can be stored dry in plastic bags in the garage or a dry part of a greenhouse (see picture p. 43). Next spring they can be potted and will spring back to life soon in a sunny window inside the house. Once the frost danger has passed, they will be ready to grace our gardens for another growing season.

While most of the garden is preparing for the winter months, thank goodness for the hardy annuals and perennials like pansies, Purple Cone-Flower, and Dianthus. Setting out new plants and seedlings is a wonderful way to beat the cold and keep us in the gardening mood through the end of the year.

Propagating Herbaceous House-plants and Garden Plants

If we're not careful, gardening can become an expensive hobby. Our excitement often translates into purchasing more and more plants. Then we have to buy more fertilizer to keep our new plants growing, maybe a new pair of shears to keep them pruned, and bigger and better pots to showcase them. While gardens do respond favorably to such high-priced treatment, there is an alternative.

Propagating is when we purposely cause a plant to reproduce naturally. It is the simplest way to avoid buying plants while increasing the number of plants in your house and garden. The greatest part of plant propagation is that it is a hobby in and of itself. There is always a new method to try, technique to perfect, or new plant to propagate. Since there is little or no cost to making more cuttings, our attempts can be limitless. I have found it one of the best ways to stay busy in the garden without ending up at a nursery buying five new plants.

During the gardening year, there are several distinct propagation seasons. In January and February, we take dormant cuttings of woody shrubs and vines (see January, "Dormant Cuttings of Shrubs and Roses"). In July and August, we take semi-hardwood cuttings of woody shrubs and vines, especially broadleaf evergreens (see August, "Semi-Hardwood Cuttings"). While herbaceous (non-woody) houseplants and garden plants can be propagated successfully throughout the year, there is usually a concentrated effort in September and October. This is when we take cuttings of our annuals to overwinter before they are killed by frost, propagate houseplants which have grown too large over the summer, and get new plants started to use as Christmas presents.

Since propagation is causing a plant to reproduce naturally, the propagation technique we use depends on whether a particular plant reproduces sexually or asexually. Sexual reproduction occurs when a flower is pollinated and a seed is produced. The pollen might come from the same plant or from a different plant of the same species. Plants spread their seeds in many ways. With some, like the **Witch Hazel**, **Cleome**, **Impatiens**, and **Sweet Shrub**, seed pods burst open, flinging the seed out from the plant. Others, like **maples**, have "winged" seeds which are carried some

Swedish Ivy and other houseplants which have grown large over the summer can be propagated by stem cuttings in October.

distance from the tree by the wind. **Magnolia gran-diflora** seeds are spread by woodpeckers, which eat them and spread them throughout the neighboring woods. Other plants like the **Moonflower** merely drop their seeds to the ground below.

Sexually propagating a plant is a technical way of saying "planting a seed." There are many herbaceous houseplants and garden plants like **Hosta**, **Leopard Flower**, **Rudbeckia**, and **Marguerite Daisy** which are easily propagated by seeds. Planting seeds is covered in January's "Starting Seeds Inside".

Asexual reproduction occurs when a piece of a plant grows roots and is able to sustain itself apart from the mother plant. The new plant has the same genetic material as the mother plant and will bear a resemblance to it (some people propagate to retain a particular plant's unique characteristics). Plants naturally reproduce asexually when a piece of the plant breaks off and roots nearby (**Spider Plant**), when a limb is trapped against the ground and grows its own roots (**Rhododendron**), when a vine's runner grows its own roots (**Pothos**), and in many other situations.

Fall is a great time to asexually propagate houseplants like **Peace Lily** and **Piggyback**, and herbaceous garden plants like **Hosta**, **Liriope**, **Impatiens**, and **Salvia**. Some of the most common methods of propagating these plants are by divisions, stem cuttings, and leaf cuttings. So how do you know which method to use? Gardeners and garden books are a great source of information about propagation, but the bottom line is that propagation is based on experience. Make your best guess as to what method should be used and try it out. If you don't succeed, try a different method next time. You may even want to try several methods at the same time. Here are the basics of the most commonly used methods.

Divisions

Dividing a plant is one of the most basic methods of propagation. Many plants grow in clumps which break apart when they become mature. **Hosta** is a good example. Dig up a **Hosta** clump in your garden. The clump is segmented with thinner, weaker connections between the different sections. You will notice that there are roots which seem to belong to a certain side of the plant. Divide the plant by breaking these connections so that the segments are free from one another. Each

Dig and divide semi-hardy clump plants like Dahlia before a killing frost. Store over the winter and plant next spring.

segment of the clump should have a fair amount of roots and leaf material. Repot or replant each segment as if it were a newly purchased plant. Soon it will begin expanding and grow into a mature plant.

Stem Cuttings

Cuttings of herbaceous (nonwoody) houseplants and garden plants are different from the dormant cuttings and semi-hardwood cuttings you made from shrubs and vines. Herbaceous plants tend to root quickly, but are also susceptible to wilting, fungus, disease, and insects because of their succulent growth. Perennials and houseplants tend to be a little easier to propagate. Houseplants native to the jungle floor, like **Pothos**, are very easy to root. **Creeping Charlie (Swedish Ivy)** roots in as little as one week in the right conditions.

Take your cuttings from the vigorous extremities of the mother plant. While tip-growth will root the fastest, any young wood is likely to root. Make your cuttings four to five inches with the basal cut 1/4 inch below a node or bud. It is more important to make the basal cut below a bud than to stay within the four-to-five-inch range. Remove all but three or four top leaves from the cutting to reduce the amount of water evaporating from the leaves. Root cuttings in a peat-light or perlite-filled pot, tray, or rooting bed. These rooting mediums are sterile and you will be less likely to have fungus problems.

I prefer to use a rooting compound with a fungicide, like "Rootone F," on herbaceous plants. Dip the basal cut in the compound before setting it. Stick the cutting one to two inches into the mixture so that at least

1 – Make the basal cut below a bud or node.

2 – Remove all but three or four leaves to reduce water evaporation from the leaves.

3 – Cutting ready to place in rooting medium.

one bud is below the surface. If there are several buds on the stem, you are likely to get roots from each bud!

It is especially important to mist your cuttings frequently. Herbaceous plants wilt easily and won't survive to root if they are not cared for properly. Herbaceous plants are also more sensitive to temperature. Keep your cuttings in a warm spot so that you trick them into thinking it is spring, and time to grow.

Propagated Piggyback plants will sprout roots from the base of the leaf and petiole.

Leaf Cuttings

Some plants like **Piggyback (Tolmiea menziesii)** and **African Violet** don't have much of a stem to use when making a cutting. These plants can be propagated by leaf cuttings. A leaf cutting is made by sticking the petiole, the stalk which supports the leaf, into the rooting mixture rather than the stem itself.

First, cut off a healthy leaf from the extremity of the plant. Don't worry about locating a bud; just cut the leaf with at least an inch of petiole. When you set the leaf cutting, the leaf will sit on top of the rooting medium with the petiole sticking down into the soil. You might need to trim the one inch petiole into a stub which will stay underground if it is abnormally curled.

If you keep the leaves well misted so they don't dry out, they should root within several weeks. A hint with **Piggyback** plants: choose a leaf that has a daughter leaf riding piggyback, it will root faster.

Layering

There are several different methods of layering a plant, but not all are feasible for herbaceous plants, which are more fragile than woody shrubs and vines. One of the simplest methods is actually a very old technique. The ancient Chinese are known to have layered plants.

The modern way is to "plant" a piece of a plant in a different pot while it is still attached to the mother plant. This type of layering is easiest with viny plants or plants with a limber stem because you don't have to worry about breaking the stem when you bend it over.

First, fill the new pot three-fourths full with a peat-light potting mixture. Then lay the vine or branch across the top of the new pot, still attached to the mother plant, and cover the stem with about one inch of soil. If it won't stay down, you can put a stone on top of the branch or fashion your own device with stakes. Continue to grow the plants side by side until the bent-over stem has rooted in the new pot. Then cut the connecting stem where it enters the new pot. Both plants will continue to grow, relying on their own root systems.

One way the ancient Chinese layered was to knock a hole in the bottom of the new pot and feed the branch or vine up into the pot through the hole. Then they would fill the pot with soil so that the branch or vine "grew" out of the soil like a normal plant. Once it had rooted, they would cut the branch or vine where it entered the bottom hole of the new pot. The problem is that the new pot has to be placed on boards or bricks so that it won't crush the stem entering the bottom. I have found this method difficult because the new pot is constantly falling off the bricks.

Alternatives

There are several other propagation techniques which are not as common as those mentioned above. Modern air-layering (which is often used with woody plants) is sometimes used on houseplants like **Rubber Plant** which have a woodier stem. The method is to remove a section of bark from around the stem, treat the exposed area with rooting compound, place damp sphagnum peat moss over the "wound," and wrap the branch and peat moss with plastic. After tying the plastic shut, you have situated a rooting medium on the branch for the plant to root into. Once it has rooted, you can cut off the branch and pot it like a new plant. Another variation is to root stem or leaf cuttings of plants like **Wandering Jew (Zebrina pendula)** in a glass of water instead of sticking them in a rooting mixture. There is also a technique known as cane cuttings which is limited to use on plants like **Dracaena**.

Whichever method you choose to propagate your plant, the end result is the same: a free plant! It is a great feeling to master even the basic forms of propa-gating because the number of plants in your garden will increase without the worry that you are draining your bank account too quickly. Before you know it, your house will be jammed with plants, and you'll have to build a greenhouse to handle all your over-wintering tropicals.

FLOWER ACTIVITIES FOR OCTOBER:

Plant

☞ Plant hardy annual, perennial, and biennial plants like **pansy**, **English Daisy**, **Dianthus**, **Foxglove**, **Shasta Daisy**, **Rudbeckia**, **Purple Cone-Flower**, and **Larkspur** outside all month.*

☞ Begin transplanting seedlings of the hardy annuals, perennials, and biennials which you started from seeds in August and September.†

☞ Plant potted, blooming **chrysanthemums** the first part of the month to have flowers until hard freezes.

☞ If you have already purchased spring-flowering bulbs, wait until November to plant unless you are in the mountains of the South. If you are not going to plant, keep the bulbs cool until planting time.‡

Prune

☞ As annual and perennial tops die, cut the plants to the ground and remove all dead material. Dead plants are an invitation to fungus and disease.

Fertilize

☞ Fertilize as you plant with 15-15-15. This is the only application needed until spring.

☞ There is no need to fertilize established flowers and colorful garden plants this late in the season.

---

* See "How to Plant a Flower Bed," p. 62

† See "Starting Seeds Inside," p. 18

‡ See "Southern Flowering Bulbs, Corms, Tubers, and Roots," p. 252

Spray

☞ Control any remaining insects and diseases on perennials with Orthene to prevent them from over-wintering on the clumps or in the mulch.

Water

☞ Water newly planted flowers and garden plants thoroughly with about one inch of water per week if there has been no significant rainfall. October is one of the driest months of the year.**

Other

☞ Continue to take cuttings of **Begonia**, **Coleus**, **Geranium**, and **Impatiens**. Root these in peat-light or perlite-filled pots or trays. Make cuttings several times until just before frost to be sure you have healthy plants to overwinter. Remember to keep them misted so they will root quickly.††

** See "Proper Watering," p. 130

†† See "Propagating Herbaceous Houseplants and Garden Plants," p. 225

☞ Dig **geraniums** and store them before they are killed by hard freezes. Shake the soil off the roots and place the roots in a plastic bag for storing in a cool place over the winter.

☞ Mulch semi-hardy plants like **Canna, Tuberose,** and **Ginger Lily** to keep the roots or bulbs alive over the winter. In colder parts of the South where the temperature may drop below 15 degrees, dig the bulbs and store them in a cool, dry place.

☞ Dig tender tubers and roots like **Canna, Dahlia, Caladium,** and **Elephant Ears** as soon as frost burns the foliage. Keep **Canna** and **Dahlia** roots stored in a cool place. Do not set them in the garden until next spring when the ground is warm and the danger of frost has passed. Store **Caladium** and **Elephant Ear** tubers in a warmer spot than **Canna** and **Dahlia** roots.

NOTES

VI. *Vegetables*

October is the final month of the vegetable garden season for most of us. We will finally say goodbye to the tomato, eggplant, and pepper plants we have been tending since setting out last April. They will not make it past the first heavy frost. Try to get all the fruit harvested before frost strikes, and ripen the last tomatoes inside.

Our fall vegetables are also about ready to harvest. Broccoli, cauliflower, collards, beets, carrots, radish, greens, and sweet potatoes will all be ripening. They are a welcome sight in the garden this late in the season.

While most of us will sow a cover crop and put our vegetable gardens to bed for the winter, why not plant a

Plant onion sets closely to have plenty of green onions all winter.

row or two of onions, cabbages, and collard plants? These hardy plants will slowly grow and mature over the winter months and be ready to harvest in the early spring. Maybe this is the year to extend your vegetable garden season to include the entire year. Since we are blessed with mild weather in the South, we should take advantage of it.

HARVESTING AND STORING VEGETABLES IN THE FALL

Fall's frosty and freezing nights herald the end of the growing season for most garden vegetables. Frost ends summer vegetables like **tomatoes, okra** and **sweet potatoes,** while hard freezes finish hardy vegetables like **broccoli** and **cabbage.** A few, like **winter cabbage, kale**, and **collards**, survive all but extreme cold, while **onions** grow throughout the winter.

I discussed good harvesting and handling practices in "Harvesting Vegetables and Keeping Them Tasty" in June. Some of the principles must be modified in the fall since cold is the main problem, not heat.

Pick both green and red tomatoes right before the first killing frost. Green tomatoes with a radiating star on the bottom will ripen in a sunny window. Use other green tomatoes for frying.

Weather is fickle and the arrival of the first frost cannot be predicted in advance with much accuracy. Remember, once summer vegetables have been damaged by frost, they are ruined; therefore, harvest all tender vegetables *before* the general time for the first frost in your area (late October in the mid-South, often about the time of the full moon; earlier in the mountains; later in the coastal plains).

Harvest all mature fruits of **eggplants** and keep them in the refrigerator or some cool storage spot. Remove all **peppers** and **okra**, since small and immature fruits are usable as is. Pick all except the smallest **tomatoes**, both green and showing color. Look on the bottom for a radiating star which tells you that they will still ripen and place them on a sunny window ledge to ripen. Save those without the star for fried green tomatoes, a Southern delicacy.

Harvest **sweet potatoes** in October before any possible danger of frost and when the ground is cracking around the mother plant. Dig them very carefully because bruising makes them susceptible to rotting. I dig mine with a spading fork because it is less likely to damage the tender potatoes. Separate them into two groups: those which have no cuts and apparent bruises, and those which do. Wash the bruised or cut ones and cook them as soon as possible. Spread the whole, unbruised potatoes on newspapers in a warm place for a week to cure (toughen up). After they are cured, carefully wash off most of the dirt but do not try to scrub them until they are squeaky clean because you'll probably bruise them, like we once did. Store **sweet potatoes** in a cool place (about 55 degrees) where they cannot freeze. If they are stored in too warm a place, they will sprout, and if stored too cold, they will rot. Under proper storage conditions, they will last for many months.

Beets, carrots, and **turnips** can stand light frost but not hard freezes. Dig them for immediate use any time after the ground cracks around the mother plants. When a hard freeze is predicted, dig those still left in the garden. Remove their tops, wash them carefully, and store them in a cool place like your sweet potatoes. **Beets** and **carrots** also store well in the refrigerator's vegetable crisper. **Turnips** store better in a cool place.

Broccoli, fall cabbage, cauliflower, and **lettuce** must be harvested before the first hard freeze and stored in the refrigerator.

VEGETABLE ACTIVITIES FOR OCTOBER:

Plant

☛ Plant hardy **onions** (plants and sets), **winter cabbage** plants, and **collard** plants for an early spring harvest. **Cabbage** and **collards** will survive winters when temperatures remain above 15 to 20 degrees.*

☛ It is too late to plant September crops like **beets, carrots, radishes, turnips,** and **rapegreens.**

☛ Remove vegetable plants which have finished producing. Work these bare areas and sow them with a green-manure cover crop. **Crimson Clover** can be planted in the earlier part of the month (it needs warmer weather to become established), but after the 15th, plant **Austrian Winter Peas** instead. These leguminous green-manure crops will prevent washing, keep the soil loose through the winter, build nitrogen in the soil, and provide humus when you turn them under next spring. Do not use cover crops, however, in areas you are planning to plant in January.†

Fertilize

☛ There is no need to fertilize hardy **onions, cabbages,** and **collards** which are being grown for an early spring harvest.

Spray

☛ Watch for insects on **broccoli, cabbage, cauliflower,** and **collards.** Green worms may attack up until frost and can be treated with Bacillus thuringiensis (BT). Dipel dust and Thuricide spray are two forms of BT.‡

Water

☛ Water vegetables thoroughly with about one inch of water if there has been no significant rainfall for a week. October is one of the driest months of the year.‡

Other

☛ Dig **sweet potatoes** before the first hard frost. Start digging in October as soon as the ground begins to crack around the base of the plants, indicating large potatoes in the ground. Dig carefully, to prevent bruising or cutting the tender skin. Shake off excess soil, let potatoes cure in a warm place for several days, then wash off the remaining soil. A warning: Don't scrub off the soil — you'll damage the potato skin and cause it to start rotting.**

☛ Harvest all **tomatoes** before the first frost warning, even if they are green. **Tomatoes** with a radiating star on the bottom will ripen if placed in a sunny window. The rest can become fried green tomatoes!**

☛ Harvest any mature **eggplant** and **pepper** (hot and green) before the first frost.**

☛ Remember to harvest **broccoli** and **cauliflower** before the yellow flowers appear.**

☛ Dig **carrots, beets,** and **radishes** when the ground begins to crack at the stem of the plant.**

---

* See "Planting a Vegetable Garden," p. 92
† See "Planting Cover Crops," p. 205

‡ See "Fertilizing, Spraying, and Watering Vegetables," p. 115
** See "The Fall Vegetable Garden," p. 204

VII. *Houseplants*

October is a big month for houseplants. It is certainly a wake-up call to hear the first forecast of frost on the news and realize that your hanging baskets are still out on the porch and patio. Where will they all go? The rush is on as furniture is moved, pots are hauled inside, and patio plants are introduced to their new indoor environment.

Houseplants which have been inside all year are just as affected by the change of weather in October. Although the temperature doesn't change much for them, the furnace dries the air almost as much as the air conditioner did in July. Keep an eye out for signs of drying, like tip-burn on leaves, wilting, and leaf-drop. Ferns are usually affected the most and will lose at least a few fronds as they get used to the dry air. Keep them well groomed and mist them frequently to ease the transition.

The number of daylight hours continues to decrease in October, and houseplants will be growing more slowly. If you haven't cut back on the strength of your fertilizer application, now is the time. Once plants become adjusted to the dry winter environment, many will not require as much water. Remember to water only when the surface of the soil is dry to the touch. Overwatering is a major houseplant problem during the winter months.

HOUSEPLANT CARE AND MAINTENANCE

Growing plants indoors is as much a part of gardening as growing trees, shrubs, flowers, and vegetables outdoors. Houseplants bring life into homes just as ornamental plants bring life to landscapes. As a lover of green growing things, I need plants on a table inside as much as I need a green lawn covering my red clay yard or beautiful green shrubs hiding the concrete block foundation of the house.

However, homes are not ideal environments for growing plants. There is too little light for most plants, too little humidity for many because of heating and air conditioning, no seasonal changes allowing plants to go dormant, and no large areas of garden soil in which plants can expand their root system. Before the conveniences of electric lights and warm furnaces became common, it was not even possible to grow plants inside. In the days before artificial heat and light, bleak winter days were brightened with garden paintings or plants brought in from hothouses for a short stay. Now, by adapting outdoor plants to inside conditions, we are able to enjoy plants inside as well as in the garden.

Horticulturists have introduced a whole new class of plants to grow indoors. They come from the tropics, where they receive the same low light on dark tropical forest floors as they would inside a home. They are better suited to indoor growth conditions because their natural tropical habitats do not have the wide swings of daytime light and nighttime dark which are found in our part of the world. **Philodendron, Pothos, Corn Plant, Spider Plant**, and **Rubber Plant** are a few examples of tropical plants which do well under the adverse conditions of a home.

Though tropical plants survive quite well in the lower light levels found inside even the brightest homes, the low humidity caused by home heating and air conditioning is a far cry from the hot, muggy conditions of a tropical forest. Though desert plants like cacti grow well in low humidity like you find inside a house, their natural habitats are also extremely bright, making them poor candidates for doing well indoors. Since neither group is well-adapted to house conditions, gardening inside becomes the art of "making do." I have found tropicals easier to grow under normal conditions inside than all but one or

Pothos grows well even in the adverse conditions of our homes.

two desert plants. One of these is **Aloe vera,** which seems happy under a fluorescent light next to our kitchen sink, where it is ready if we should need it for a burn or scald.

You can decorate rooms with plants in two ways: (1) choose a plant for the conditions in a room, or (2) choose a plant for decorating purposes and adjust the conditions to fit its needs. Of the two, the easiest and most successful way is to choose the plant for a room's conditions.

Growing houseplants is like growing any plant: you need to understand their needs and give them all the help you can.

General Conditions for Houseplants

Light: Rooms usually have variable light conditions, being brightest near a window and darkest where artificial light is required to read. Direct sun through a window can damage plants by heating the leaf area above room temperature and causing high water loss. Keep plants back from any window where the sun would shine directly on their leaves.

You can soon tell if your plant is in a spot with good exposure. Plants become light in color and often grow spindly in too little light. Some plants like **Swedish Ivy (Plectranthus nummularias)** produce smaller, more dense leaves in low light than when grown in a better exposure, though they grow quite well under both conditions. Variegated plants like **Spider Plant (Chlorophytum comosum 'Vittatum')** and **Nephthytis (Syngonium podophyllum 'Albovirens')** often need less light than their green counterparts. In too much light, they may look washed out and "burned" rather than having the normal rich coloration.

Don't mistake naturally variegated plants, like this Nephthytis, for those suffering from lack of light or fertilizer.

Heat: Normal daytime winter thermostat settings from 68 to 72 degrees offer ample heat for most houseplants, but night time temperatures in a room should never fall below 58 to 61 degrees. Never place a plant near a hot-air vent, for it will rapidly dry the leaves, causing excessive water loss and a "burned" appearance. Never place plants next to a window because heat is quickly lost through the glass and the temperature of the leaves can drop below the air temperature in the room.

Humidity: Most plants grow better in higher humidity than is comfortable for humans. Heated houses are dry unless they have a humidifier connected with the heating system. Air conditioning dries the air even more than furnaces do, since a low humidity prevents the house from being muggy, sticky, and uncomfortable. Many plants which are native to tropical rainforests suffer inside from dry conditions in both summer and winter. Over time, however, many will develop a more active root system to supply ample moisture to the leaf area when excess water is being lost because of low humidity. Newly purchased plants suffer the most since they have been grown under high humidity in the nursery. You must give them extra care until they are adjusted to their new conditions.

Houseplant growers overcome dry conditions in a number of ways. Misting leaves with tepid water increases the humidity around a plant and reduces water loss. To be effective, mist several times a day (this may be a problem for some homeowners). I find a simple cold air vaporizer, like you use when you have a cold, makes an excellent humidifier when set among plants. There are also commercial humidifiers on the market which work well.

Soil: Few of us have indoor planting areas with large amounts of soil like outside gardens. More often, pots, tubs, and planter boxes have to take the place of well-prepared flower beds. Remember how important good soil preparation is for a flower bed? We till thoroughly, add humus to loosen the soil, and add perlite to improve drainage. Few commercial houseplant growers mix the soil for their pots, so I prefer to repot bought plants, using a more suitable soil mixture.

Choosing the right potting mixture is necessary. The mixture should be light, high in humus, and contain perlite for good drainage. Many houseplant

Peat-light potting mixes are light, high in humus, and contain perlite for good drainage. They make growing houseplants much easier.

potting soils found in garden centers and nurseries are the opposite. They are much too heavy, containing large amounts of peat-muck which holds too much water for too long. The "jungle mixes" I have tried to use are not like any natural jungle soil I have ever worked with in the tropics. True jungle soil is loose and friable, not heavy and wet. I always use a peat-light potting mixture which contains more peat moss than ground bark. A simple method of choosing a good potting mixture is to pick up a bag in a nursery. If it feels light, it is fine; if it feels heavy, put it back. Then read the ingredients listed on the label to get the one with the highest percentage of peat moss. If there is only one peat-light mixture available and it is high in bark, it is better to use than a heavy peat-muck mixture. A loose, porous potting mixture is always best. Another method is to buy perlite and peat moss separately and mix your own potting mixture at a ratio of about one to one. Watch out, though, this can be a messy endeavor.

Choosing the Best Container: Over the years I have seen almost every kind of container used for growing plants both inside and outside. When we moved into our home at Sweet Apple, we found an old iron wash pot used as a planter. Since then, we have used cedar, cypress, ceramic, treated wood, clay, and plastic planters, which better fit our lifestyle than the old wash pot.

Any type of container which has good bottom drainage is a candidate for growing plants. Water must never sit in the bottom of the container because anaerobic bacteria will build up and damage the plant's roots. I have found a clay pot with good drainage is the best all-around pot to use. Clay pots have the distinct advantage of allowing air to enter through the walls. Cedar tubs and planters are excellent for larger plantings, and cypress is also good but not as long-lasting. There can be some problems with chemical damage when using pressure-treated wood in small planters.

Using the right size container is also important. There should be at least two inches of fresh soil between the root ball and the edge of the pot. Use a saucer under the pot to prevent water damage to your furniture. Plastic saucers which look like clay serve this purpose well since they are waterproof.

Water: More houseplants are lost due to improper watering than for any other reason. Overwatering rather than underwatering a plant in a pot or tub can be much more damaging because roots must grow to take up moisture and nutrients. The white roots you see when you lift a plant out of its pot are the ones which absorb water and nutrients. Low oxygen in waterlogged soil allows undesirable anaerobic bacteria to develop instead of beneficial aerobic bacteria. Anaerobic bacteria give off toxic gasses which can damage or kill roots. The sour, gassy smell you notice in some soil is caused by these anaerobic bacteria. Watering properly is much easier when using a peat-light mixture described above. These mixtures are loose and porous, allowing excess water to drain away rather than staying in the pot. They also hold moisture in such a way that plenty of air remains in the pot for good root growth.

The best way to keep houseplants growing well is to follow the Primary Rule: *Water only when the plant needs it.* Water loss from the plant and from the soil's surface depends on the humidity in the house and the growth rate of the plant. Therefore, strict time schedules do not always work because you can water too little or too much without regard to the condition of the soil in the pot.

I prefer the finger test to see when a pot needs watering. Touch the surface of the soil and if it feels dry, water thoroughly, then don't water again until it feels dry once again. I like to place my houseplants in a sink or bath tub, then flood the peat-light mixture several times to force out unwanted gasses, bring in fresh air, and thoroughly wet the soil. Then I leave the pot where it will drain out any excess moisture before I put it back in its place.

Fertilizing: After I have watered and the pot has finished draining, I fertilize new plants with a solution of Peters or RaPidGro. I fertilize well-established plants with either fertilizer spikes or Osmocote slow-release pellets. Both work well. The amount of fertilizer depends on the plant's growth rate. During the winter when the days are short and houseplants grow minimally, I use a half-strength application of the fertilizer solution. During the spring and summer when plants are growing well, I use a full-strength solution, fertilizer spikes, or Osmocote.

You will find further information on growing houseplants in "Common Houseplants Ailments," in the December chapter, as well as in "Repotting Houseplants" in the March Chapter.

OWNING A GREENHOUSE

As October arrives in the Southern garden, the danger of frost begins to limit our gardening activity. Annuals die with the first freeze, perennials retreat to below ground, summer grasses turn brown, porch and patio plants must be brought inside, and most of our vegetables are finished for the season. Cold weather also limits the amount of time we can comfortably enjoy gardening outside.

October often inspires gardeners to want to own a greenhouse. As you pack a summer's worth of plants into every window spot in the house, it's hard not to think how wonderful it would be to have an area designated for growing plants through the winter months. You could mist to your heart's content without worry of soaking nearby furniture. Plants could be watered thoroughly without danger of the saucer overfilling. And more than anything, it would be a green haven to escape to during the lifeless winter.

Having a greenhouse is great. You can overwinter enough rooted annuals to fill your annual beds in the spring without a trip to the nursery. You can grow large patio plants over the winter which are too big to fit in the house. You can start vegetable and flower seeds early for setting out after the danger of frost. You can propagate numerous cuttings for Christmas presents or to expand your plant stock. In short, a greenhouse allows you to grow a lot more plants.

There are some drawbacks to owning a greenhouse, however. The initial start-up cost is relatively high. Besides the advertised price-tag of a pre-fabricated greenhouse or the cost of materials of a home-built one, there are many essential additions. A heating unit, propagation bench, shelving, irrigation equipment, ventilation fan, and plenty of pots are all necessities. While this expense may still be acceptable, remember that there is also a yearly heating bill to contend with. That can be the long-range heart-stopper.

Heating a greenhouse properly is the most important consideration in deciding whether or not to own one. Don't be fooled by talk of a "cool-weather greenhouse" which somehow manages without heat. The plants which would survive in such a greenhouse would most likely survive outdoors in the South. All you would be doing is creating a walk-in cold frame, and that is not the kind of place to escape to on a cold January afternoon.

A greenhouse should have a minimum temperature of 60 to 65 degrees for most tropical and herbaceous plants. Even in the South, this means buying a heater. Electric heaters are okay, but every winter there is the danger of losing power. Ice storms are common in the South, and brittle pine trees are prone to break onto power lines. Then it's panic time. Unless you have a back-up gas heater, you are likely to lose your entire stock in one night. Gas heaters are the most practical all-around method of heat. Propane and natural gas are both economical and reliable alternatives to electricity.

All of us have experienced the greenhouse effect in mid-July when we enter our baking-hot cars. Sunlight travels through the windows, warms the inside, and the heat cannot escape. It is very convenient to imagine this same effect eliminating our greenhouse heating bill in the winter. Unfortunately, this is not the case. The winter sun is much lower in the sky, cutting down on the most direct rays. Also, since the sun is so low in the sky, a tree or neighbor's house usually shades the greenhouse for some length of time during the day. And finally, greenhouses tend to leak a lot more than our cars. In order for the greenhouse effect to work, the heated air cannot escape all day so that it can warm our plants over the cold night. While the perfect location and the most airtight greenhouse will utilize the greenhouse effect to some degree, realistically we would still have to rely on artificial heat.

There is one final note on heating a greenhouse. Someone has posited the idea that if you paint 55-gallon drums black and place them in the greenhouse, they will absorb the sun's rays, hold the warmth, and slowly heat the greenhouse overnight. Without dissuading you from experimenting with *any* method of reducing the heating bill, I will say that you would have to have a very large greenhouse to be able to accommodate any number of 55-gallons drums, especially if they must be placed in the prime sunny areas reserved for our plants.

Besides heat, the other major continuing concern with a greenhouse is water. Creating a humid, tropically warm environment requires a fair amount of water, more than can be supplied by a watering can. The ideal situation is to have an underground pipe several feet below ground, which therefore won't freeze, leading to a faucet in the greenhouse. This continuous water supply will enable you to mist frequently and thereby propagate plants with much greater ease. I, personally, have raised plants in our greenhouse for 25 years using just an outside faucet and a garden hose. The South is graced with warm enough days in the winter to thaw the hose so that I can water. This is not to say that I haven't been caught by a long week of freezes and had to carry can after can of water up to the greenhouse. In these rough times I have had to look on with despair as my new cuttings wilt without proper misting. There is a trade-off.

All in all, though, owning a greenhouse is a delight. Stepping inside that humid, green environment on a bleak winter day raises your spirits immeasurably. It can become your own personal jungle, a place to delicately raise orchids, or merely a home for all the plants you have grown to love over the summer months. Whatever your motive, a greenhouse adds a whole new dimension to the gardening experience.

HOUSEPLANT ACTIVITIES FOR OCTOBER:

Plant

☛ Check houseplants and porch/patio plants for the need to repot. Repot if the roots have massed against the edge of the ball of soil and are dark in color. Always use a container which is at least two sizes larger. Also, check for sowbugs and pillbugs while the plants are out of the pot.*

☛ Pot cuttings of houseplants and tropicals as soon as they develop a root system. Use a peat-light potting mixture and begin applying a water-soluble fertilizer solution at one-half the recommended strength.†

Prune

☛ Groom indoor plants whenever they need it. Remove weak branches or stems as well as off-color leaves.

Fertilize

☛ As the days get shorter, plants will grow more slowly and need less fertilizer. Begin fertilizing with half-strength applications of a water-soluble fertilizer solution like Peters. Continue fertilizing every time you water.‡

Spray

☛ Check all indoor plants for insects such as spider mites, scale, and mealybug. Using a houseplant systemic insecticide to control them is easier and safer than spraying inside. If you do spray, remember to apply the insecticide to the undersides of the leaves.**

☛ Be careful when spraying **ferns**. Some insecticides are harmful to them. *Always read the label for warnings about **ferns** and other plants.*

* See "Repotting Houseplants," p. 67

† See "Propagating Herbaceous Houseplants and Garden Plants," p. 225

‡ See "Houseplant Care and Maintenance," p. 232

** See "Common Houseplant Ailments," p. 280

Water

☞ Watch houseplants carefully as cold weather approaches. When they look limp, check for dry soil. If it is dry, water thoroughly in a sink or bathtub, letting the water drain completely, and don't water again until the surface is dry once more. Between waterings, mist with plain water on a regular basis. If the limp plants are in moist soil, do not water but allow the soil to dry a bit and mist frequently.‡

☞ Tip-burn or edge-burn on leaves indicates that more water is being lost than is being absorbed by the roots. Check for dry soil, too much sunlight, or drafts from heating vents. *Overwatering* can cause roots to die, resulting in the same symptoms as underwatering.‡

☞ Adjust watering practices when the furnace begins to run. The air will be dry and plants will suffer. Be careful not to overwater. Regular misting with plain water will raise the humidity and help plants adjust to the drier environment.‡

☞ Keep **Christmas Cactus** barely moist and in dim light during October and early November to help them set buds.††

☞ **Ferns** which have been brought inside are particularly troubled by low humidity. Mist them frequently and remove any dead fronds as you see them.

Other

☞ Bring tender potted plants like **Hibiscus**, **Ixora**, and **Allamanda** inside before you turn on the furnace. They will adjust more quickly that way. It is also important to mist plants regularly as they get accustomed to the drier environment inside.

☞ Continue to propagate houseplants which have become large or pot-bound over the growing season.†

☞ Do not give *any* artificial light to **Poinsettias** which are being forced to bloom at Christmas until you see flower buds in November.††

☞ Houseplants which become lighter in color or have very long intervals between branches or stems (internodes) usually need more light.‡

☞ Newly purchased houseplants have been growing under ideal conditions at the nursery. When you bring them home, they may take a while to adjust to the drier conditions in your home. Water your new plants as prescribed above, but *do not overwater*! Mist them frequently and if they continue to do poorly, try placing a cool-air vaporizer near the plant for several days.‡

☞ Plants are very sensitive to the amount of light they receive. When moving plants inside for the winter, try to place them in the same light conditions they had while outside. One way to test light conditions is to use the light meter on your camera. Before moving the plant, test the spot outside. Then try to find a suitable place inside with approximately the same light meter reading.‡

---

‡ See "Houseplant Care and Maintenance," p. 232
†† See "Indoor Flowering Plants for the Holidays," p. 256
† See "Propagating Herbaceous Houseplants and Garden Plants," p. 225

†† See "Indoor Flowering Plants for the Holidays," p. 256
‡ See "Houseplant Care and Maintenance," p. 232

Even though it looks tender, cut new fescue when it reaches the proper cutting height to make it tough and cause it to spread.

VIII. *Lawns*

As Bermuda Grass and other summer grasses slow down, it is hard to believe that the grass cutting season is almost over. Even though it seemed like garden drudgery throughout the summer months, it is a little sad to say goodbye to that weekly get-away on the riding lawnmower. Don't get too nostalgic, however, and cut your summer grasses when they don't need it. This time of year it's a good idea to let them grow out to about three inches so they will harden up before the first killing frosts.

Evergreen grasses are a different story. Newly planted lawns and reseeded ones will be growing quickly in the cool weather they enjoy. Keep them well fertilized and cut when they reach the proper height in order to take full advantage of this growth period. Summer weeds are dying out, and evergreen grasses will quickly take over their area. Having a thick, healthy evergreen lawn is the best way to control the weeds which will emerge again next spring.

LAWN ACTIVITIES FOR OCTOBER:

Plant

☞ Summer grasses like **Bermuda Grass, Centipede, St. Augustine,** and **Zoysia** will be brown after the first hard frost. Many homeowners overseed these lawns with annual **Ryegrass** to have a green lawn all winter. Overseed in early October. This is not advisable on **Centipede** or **Hybrid Zoysia** because their thick turf prevents good germination of overseeded grasses.

☞ Continue planting **Kentucky 31 Tall Fescue, Turf-type Tall Fescues, Chewing Fescue, Creeping Red Fescues,** and **Bluegrass.***

Fertilize

☞ Fertilize evergreen lawns with a high-nitrogen, slow-release formula if you didn't in September.†

☞ There is no need to fertilize summer grass lawns this month.

☞ Lime evergreen lawns if you haven't done it in the last several months. Use 50 pounds of dolomitic limestone per 1000 square feet of lawn area.†

☞ Fertilize overseeded lawns with a 15-15-15 formula to start **Ryegrass** growing well.†

Spray

☞ Control broadleaf weeds with a lawn weedkiller recommended for your specific type of grass. Wait two weeks or the recommended time before reseeding.†

☞ Apply pre-emergence weed controls on lawns that had bad infestations of winter weeds (**Chickweed, Annual Bluegrass**) last year. This material will prevent winter weed seeds from germinating. Do not use on lawns which you plan to reseed this fall with evergreen grasses or annual **Ryegrass.**†

Cut

☞ It is wise to let summer grasses like **Centipede, St. Augustine,** and **Zoysia** grow to about three inches before the first frost. This way they will harden up and will be protected during winter cold. You won't have to cut them until they start growing again next spring.

☞ Keep new lawns cut at the proper height. Don't let them get too tall before you mow. Set the mower at the height listed below for your type of grass and begin cutting when grass reaches that height.

☞ Cut evergreen lawns at the proper height:

EVERGREEN GRASSES	HEIGHT
Kentucky 31 Tall Fescue	3 to 3 $\frac{1}{2}$ inches
Turf-type Tall Fescues	3 inches
Fine Leaf Fescues	1 $\frac{1}{2}$ to 2 inches
Kentucky Bluegrass	2 to 2 $\frac{1}{2}$ inches

☞ If you have seeded **Ryegrass** over **Bermuda Grass,** keep the **Ryegrass** cut about an inch above the base lawn. If you let it grow tall in clumps, it will damage your permanent grass.

Water

☞ Keep evergreen lawns well watered in dry periods to encourage heavy growth before cold weather.‡

---

* See "Planting or Reseeding Evergreen Lawns," p. 71
† See "Fertilizing and Controlling Weeds in Lawns," p. 73

‡ "See "Proper Watering," p. 130

November

IN THE SOUTHERN GARDEN

The first hard freezes slowly slide down out of the Southern mountains, and by the end of November the growing season is finished throughout most of the South. Our native persimmons are the last fruits of the season, hanging on leafless trees while waiting for a good freeze to make them tasty, even though 'possums seem to enjoy them any time they are a bright orange. Gingko is green one day and bright yellow a few days later, then loses all its leaves like a lady dropping a yellow skirt. If you don't like raking leaves week after week under oak trees, plant a Gingko and do the job just once.

I feel sad when my bright-colored annuals stand lifeless in the flower bed which has been so beautiful since last May when we planted it as our Mother's Day present for Betsy. Then sadness disappears and reality sets in, since November is a beginning as well as an ending. Now that plants are dormant once again, it is tree, shrub, vine, rose, bulb, and fruit planting time. The South is a great place to garden since each month there is something new to look forward to. As we pull up the last flowers of this season, we start planting bulbs for early color next spring.

Gardeners need to start preparations at the beginning of November for the holiday season which starts at the end of the month. How about a pot or two of Paperwhite Narcissus or a huge South African Amaryllis for yourself or a friend, to add to the holiday spirit? Half the fun is forcing your own, so start them in November for blooms in December.

Since everyone wants their homes and landscapes in order for holiday visitors, it's time to clean up dead annuals and perennial tops, take fallen leaves to the compost pile, and replace old mulch with fresh new material. Visitors provide a good excuse to clean up gardens, but a more important reason is to get rid of overwintering insects and diseases which can come back to plague plants next year.

America's great harvest feast, Thanksgiving, comes during the third week of November as a reminder of all the blessings our land produces. The harvests are over, and Thanksgiving gives Southerners a pause before we start winter and a whole new planting season.

AT LEFT: *Camellia sasanqua 'Sparkling Burgundy'*

Winter is a perfect time to see the framework of trees in our yard. This Sugar Maple is crowding the Norway Spruce.

I. *Shade and Flowering Trees*

It is finally time to plant shade and flowering trees in the South. All through the growing season we have been dreaming of a new flower color or beautiful new shade tree to transform the face of our landscape. We can at last realize our dream and carefully bring our plans to fruition.

While it might seem unfortunate that we don't plant at a time when the trees are in full form with leaves and flowers on display, the bare winter landscape is the perfect time to design a garden. In the winter, we can see the framework of the trees in our yard, and it is easier to choose a new tree that will fit a specific area. It's also easier to focus on this practical concern when we are not distracted by the fluff of leaves and flowers.

Even though newly purchased trees are dormant, treat them with care. Most of them have recently been dug in the fields, balled up in burlap, thrown on a truck, unloaded and hauled to their display bed at the nursery. And that's before you squeezed them in the trunk of your car! Remember when handling not to pick up young trees by the trunk or shake the trunk excessively. This is a sure way to break some of its vital roots.

MULCHING: A LESSON FROM NATURE

Mulching is a good idea taught us by nature itself. In a natural forest, leaves and pine straw cover the ground in a thick mat. This natural "mulch" prevents weeds from competing with the trees for nutrients, regulates the soil temperature, conserves water by cutting down on evaporation, and prevents the surface soil from washing. Natural mulch also returns nutrients to the soil as it decomposes.

When we gardeners apply mulch to attain these same benefits, the results are conclusive. Tests have shown that mulched flowers can produce up to three times as many blooms as unmulched plants. Mulching can also prevent bulbs from heaving from the ground in the winter and plants from drying in the heat of the summer. In general, mulched plants perform better and require less care from us.

Mulch is usually applied in the fall and in the spring. Mulch applied in the fall is termed "winter mulch" and is used mainly to regulate the soil temperature during cold periods, especially on shallow rooted evergreens. Mulch not only keeps the ground warmer than normal, but also causes the soil to both freeze and thaw more slowly than normal. Without mulch, the ground is likely to freeze and thaw very quickly, which tends to heave plants out of the ground. This is especially common with newly planted perennial bulbs and fall strawberries, both of which have not yet grown roots to anchor themselves. Heaving of established plants is just as damaging because it can break off many vital feeder roots.

Besides insulating the soil, winter mulch tends to trap more moisture in the ground. This is beneficial when it freezes, because wet soil insulates a plant's roots better than dry soil.

Summer mulch is applied in the spring and keeps the ground cool around shallow rooted plants, prevents the soil from drying out, and helps to control weeds. A plant's roots will generally grow much more quickly and vigorously in moist, mulched soil.

There are countless mulches available for use in the garden. In fact, "mulch" does not refer to any specific type of material; it refers to the use of the material. Some of the most common mulches are bark, cotton seed hulls, coffee grounds, pine straw, grass clippings, stones, leaves, peat moss, porous plastic, sawdust, and bark chips. All of these materials should be spread thickly enough to insulate and prevent weeds from sprouting. Generally, a two-to-four inch thick mulch is sufficient.

Watch out when using organic materials like bark chips or sawdust. If these materials are left too long, or are incorporated into the soil, they will rob the soil of nitrogen as they decompose. Although the nitrogen is eventually returned to the soil when decomposition is complete, this can take quite a while with materials high in cellulose. Nitrogen-deficient plants will turn yellow and will need to be fertilized with a complete fertilizer or with ammonium nitrate. Sawdust is especially troublesome in this respect since it is light and airy and roots tend to grow up into the mulch. It is also high in cellulose which is very slow in decomposing.

Whichever mulch you use, replace it every spring and fall, especially around roses, fruit trees, and bushes. Since insects and diseases tend to shelter and breed in mulch, replacing the material twice a year helps to keep their population in check. When changing

Mulching trees keeps the landscape tidy and attractive.

Do not pile mulch too high against the trunk.

mulch, watch out for chiggers, which especially love pine straw.

All year we have been warning against allowing mulch to crowd or touch the trunk or lower stems of plants, shrubs, and trees. Crowded trunks will stay moist, becoming more susceptible to insects, diseases, and rot. It also causes shallow-rooted plants to "crown root," shifting the root system upward. When it is dry, these roots will die and the plant will suffer.

The vole (pine mouse) is a pest that takes advantage of crowded trunks. The vole gets thirsty in the summer and hungry in the winter and will crawl up through the mulch and chew on your shrub or tree. The resulting damage looks a lot like when a beaver gnaws on a tree. The best prevention is to keep your mulch an inch or two from the trunk.

By taking a lesson from nature and mulching your trees, shrubs, and plants, you can help them to perform up to their natural potential. And besides, any idea that cuts down on the need to hoe weeds is certainly worth checking out.

TREE ACTIVITIES FOR NOVEMBER:

Plant

☞ Plant B&B, bare-root, and container-grown trees throughout the month when the ground is not frozen or likely to freeze soon. Make sure to plant trees at the correct depth in a well-prepared hole and stake them to prevent swaying (especially bare-root trees). Never plant trees deeper than they were growing in the nursery. When planting B&B and container-grown trees, it is a good idea to leave the top of the root ball showing after planting. Plant bare-root trees with the soil level one inch above the top root.*

☞ Choose planting stock carefully. New shade trees should be straight with tight, smooth bark, have a dominant central shoot or leader, and should not be loose in the ball or container. Choose flowering trees carefully as well. If they are free from scars, you can assume they have been grown well.

☞ Plant trees like **dogwoods** and **maples** dug from the wild only as a last resort and only if they are small. You are likely to cut their wide, sprangly roots drastically during digging, and then they will take forever to start growing vigorously again.

☞ Do not plant **Southern Magnolia** and **Cherry Laurel** until March.

☞ When handling container-grown or B&B trees, never pick them up by the trunk because roots in the ball of earth will break.

☞ It is best to plant trees when the soil is not too wet. However, if planting is necessary before the soil dries out, use dry peat moss as the soil amendment. It will absorb excess moisture and make it easier to prepare a good mixture to use in planting.

Prune

☞ Prune newly planted shade trees if necessary, removing any broken or damaged limbs with a clean cut. Never top a shade tree, however, or you will ruin its shape. †

☞ Wait until next month to begin major pruning of shade and flowering trees when you are sure the tree is thoroughly dormant.†

Fertilize

☞ Wait until early spring to begin fertilizing shade and flowering trees.

Spray

☞ Watch for scale on evergreen trees. Spray with Orthene or Cygon, except on **hollies**. Use Orthene on **hollies**.‡

* See "Planting Trees and Shrubs," p. 264

† See "Pruning Shade and Flowering Trees," p. 4

‡ See "Controlling Insects and Diseases," p. 80

Water

☞ Water newly planted trees thoroughly, even if the ground is wet, to settle the soil around the roots and drive out air pockets.**

Other

☞ Fallen leaves make a good addition to your compost pile. Before you take them out to the street for garbage collection, think about all the humus you are giving away.

☞ Mulch newly planted trees with pine straw or pine bark. Do not allow the mulch to pack against the tree's trunk.††

** See "Does Your Tree Have Enough Water?" p. 150

†† See "Mulching: A Lesson from Nature," p. 243

☞ Check mulch around older trees and replenish with fresh mulch if needed. If you haven't already, replace any mulch which has been around trees all summer. This mulch probably contains overwintering insects. ††

☞ Stake newly planted shade and flowering trees, especially if they were purchased bare-root. Attach three wires to the trunk at about four to five feet off the ground and run them to wooden stakes driven at intervals around the tree. Make a collar of an old watering hose to prevent the wire from cutting into the trunks.

☞ Rake fallen leaves away from trees. They do not make a good mulch and should not be allowed to pack on top of existing bark or pine straw mulches.

†† See "Mulching: A Lesson from Nature," p. 243

NOTES

Gardens around the South are blessed in November with the beautiful fall-blooming Camellia sasanqua, like Camellia sasanqua 'Snow-on-the-Mountain.'

II. *Shrubs and Vines*

November is the beginning of the shrub- and vine-planting season. While it isn't the most inspirational time to visit nearby nurseries, it is the best time to plant. It takes some degree of faith, though, to buy a new Forsythia and believe that its buds will break and leaves will adorn its bare limbs. It takes a lot of faith to buy a heavily pruned summer-flowering Hydrangea because not only do you have to trust that the leaves will emerge, you have to trust that the branches will sprout as well.

All around the South, gardens and yards will be colorful in November thanks to the fall-blooming Camellia japonica and Camellia sasanqua cultivars. These Camellia cultivars are truly a blessing and are sure to brighten your day as the first cold weather arrives. Keep them in mind as you plan out your garden and strive for year-round bloom.

Just because a shrub is growing in a one-gallon pot doesn't mean it requires less care in planting than an expensive tree in a five-gallon pot. Both plants are shocked by rough treatment and will grow much better in their first year if treated delicately.

SHRUB AND VINE ACTIVITIES FOR NOVEMBER:

Plant

☞ Plant all dormant container-grown, B&B, and bare-root shrubs like **Box Leaf Holly, Burford Holly, Forsythia, Hydrangea,** and **Spiraea** whenever the ground is not frozen or likely to freeze soon. Prepare the holes as carefully as you do for shade trees.*

☞ Plant hardy woody vines like **Carolina Jessamine** and **Chinese Wisteria** during periods of mild weather and when the ground is not frozen.*

* See "Planting Trees and Shrubs," p. 264

☛ Plant hardy ground covers like **English Ivy**, **Liriope**, **Vinca minor**, and **Spreading Juniper** whenever the ground is not frozen. Use well-rooted plants, not runners.*

☛ It is best to plant shrubs when the soil is not too wet. However, if planting is necessary before the soil dries out, use dry peat moss as the soil amendment. It will absorb excess moisture and make it easier to prepare a good mixture to use in planting.

Prune

☛ Heavy structural pruning of evergreen shrubs may be done this month, but if most of the leaf area is to be removed, I prefer to wait until mid-February to mid-March so I don't have to look at stubby plants so long.

☛ Prune broadleaf evergreens like **hollies, boxwood,** and **Euonymus**, and narrowleaf evergreens like **Juniper** and **arborvitae** to shape any time this month. Always prune so the top is narrower than the bottom, which keeps plants from becoming top heavy and unsightly.

☛ Do not prune spring-flowering shrubs and vines like **azalea, Rhododendron, Camellia, Forsythia, Flowering Quince, Spiraea, Viburnum,** and **Carolina Jessamine** until after they bloom next spring. They have already set their blossom buds and pruning would remove many of your spring flowers.

☛ Fall and winter-flowering **Camellia japonica** and **Camellia sasanqua** cultivars can be trimmed for shape after they bloom. Leave heavy pruning until February or March.†

☛ Wait until late winter to begin pruning summer-flowering shrubs like **Butterfly Bush, Barberry, summer hydrangeas,** and **Crape Myrtle.**

Fertilize

☛ *Do not fertilize* shrubs and vines this month. Plants are dormant and are not actively absorbing nutrients. Summer-flowering and evergreen shrubs and vines like **Butterfly Bush, Burford Holly** and **English Ivy** are fertilized in the early spring, and spring-flowering shrubs and vines like **azaleas** and **Wisteria** are fertilized in the spring after they flower.

Spray

☛ Continue to watch for scale on evergreens. Spray with Orthene or Cygon except on **hollies**. Use Orthene on **hollies**. It is important to clean these up while the pests are still active.‡

Water

☛ Water newly planted shrubs, woody vines, and ground covers thoroughly, even if the ground is wet, in order to settle the soil around the roots.**

Other

☛ Mulch shrubs and vines with pine straw, but do not let the mulch pile against the stems or trunks. If you haven't already, replace any mulch which has been around shrubs and vines all summer. This mulch probably contains overwintering insects.††

☛ Rake fallen leaves away from shrubs. They do not make a good mulch and should not be allowed to pack on top of existing bark or pine straw mulches. Leaves left too long might cause crown rooting which causes plants to be prone to drought damage.††

☛ Visit gardens which have plantings of **Camellia sasanqua** and fall blooming **Camellia japonica**. Choose cultivars for your garden from those in bloom.

---

* See "Planting Trees and Shrubs," p. 264

† See "Pruning Flowering Shrubs and Vines," p. 31

‡ See "Controlling Insects and Diseases," p. 80

** See "Proper Watering," p. 130

†† See "Mulching: A Lesson from Nature," p. 243

III. *Fruits*

There is a conspiracy in the fruit tree world! As hard as I look, it is still difficult to find a young "whip." A whip is a one-year-old fruit tree that has few if any side shoots. It looks like a stick with roots on one end, and it is the perfect tree to plant. Unfortunately, fruit tree growers are desperately growing trees which look prettier than a whip in the hope that we will buy more trees if they look nice. They tip the leader and main branches, even on peaches and nectarines, so that the young tree has a fuller form and they can charge more for it.

Before you buy a new fruit tree, read January's "Pruning Fruit Trees" to get an idea about the kind of tree you want to buy. Each kind of fruit tree needs to be pruned in a very specific way. These pruning techniques are designed to encourage as many healthy fruit as the tree can sustain. Unfortunately, the way the commercial growers who sell to our local nurseries prune seems to have little to do with the proper technique, and everything to do with making a sale.

In despair, I gave up my search recently and purchased a new two-year-old peach tree which had been pruned as if it were an apple, using the Modified Leader technique. It had a dominant six-foot-tall leader with seven major branches coming off the trunk. There was nothing to do but cut off the six-foot-tall tree at 22 inches and force it to branch out with two or three scaffold branches according to the proper Open Head/Basket method of pruning peach trees. And yes, I did have to pay for the four feet of tree I ended up throwing away!

This six-foot tall peach was originally pruned incorrectly.

The only answer is to lop it off at 22 inches and force scaffold branches to grow out and up. (See pictures on pp. 13 and 133 for properly pruned peach trees)

FRUIT ACTIVITIES FOR NOVEMBER:

Plant

☛ Plant B&B, bare-root, and container-grown fruits all month. This includes fruit trees (**peaches, apples, cherries, pears,** etc.), bush fruits (**blueberries**), semi-bush fruits (**raspberries, blackberries,** etc.), and vine fruits (**grapes, muscadines**).*

* See "Planting Trees and Shrubs," p. 264

☛ Plant **Chinese Chestnut, pecan, walnut,** and other nut trees. (Always plant two or three **Chinese Chestnuts** so they can cross-pollinate. Otherwise, you will not have a good nut harvest.)

☛ Plant **strawberries** as early in the month as possible and with caution. They need as much time as possible to develop good roots before heavy freezes arrive.

☛ Do not plant **figs** until February and March.

Prune

☞ If you have not done so already, remove the older canes on semi-bush berries like **raspberries** and **blackberries** which bore this past summer. Leave the new growth to produce next summer's fruit. Train this new growth onto a fence or trellis.†

☞ Do not prune fruit trees like **apples, cherries, peaches, pears,** and **plums** until January or early February.

☞ Wait until January and February to prune **grapes,** which is the best time.

Fertilize

☞ Apply dolomitic limestone around **figs**. Then mulch them heavily to protect the roots against extreme cold. This is done once a year.

☞ Do not begin fertilizing fruit trees like **apples, cherries, peaches, pears,** and **plums** until early spring when their buds begin to swell.

☞ **Grapes, blueberries, raspberries,** and **blackberries** are also fertilized in the spring.

Spray

☞ There is no need to spray fruits this month. The first spraying of the season begins in January/February with the application of a dormant spray.

† See "Secrets of the Berry Patch," p. 155

Water

☞ Water newly planted fruits thoroughly, even if the ground is wet, in order to settle the soil around the roots.‡

Other

☞ November-planted **strawberries** should be mulched heavily to prevent them from heaving out of the ground when the weather freezes.**

☞ Remove all old fruit which is still hanging on the trees or vines. These are full of disease spores which will infect next year's crop.

☞ Gather **pecans** and **walnuts** as soon as they fall to the ground. If you let them lie on damp soil, they will be ruined and the squirrels will get more than you will.

☞ Be careful when mowing in orchard areas not to hit the bark of fruit trees with the mower. Any damage to the bark will provide an entrance place for borers.

☞ Keep fruits mulched with pine straw to prevent weeds and grasses from taking over during the winter. However, do not pile the mulch against the trunks of fruit trees.**

‡ See "Proper Watering," p. 130
** See "Mulching: A Lesson from Nature," p. 243

NOTES

IV. *Roses*

In a warm year, we might still have a few roses in November. Even though these final blossoms of the year are a delight, all eyes are on next season with the anticipation of having a bigger and better rose bloom. For many of us, this means adding a few new roses to our collection.

November is the first month of the rose planting season. While it is okay to plant up through February, I like to order my roses no later than December. Depending on the season and grower, shipments might take as long as three or four weeks, and you don't want to get caught too late in the season.

Remember to plant when the ground is not frozen, and when it is not too wet. There will be plenty of warm spells throughout our mild winter which will be perfect for planting, so pick a good day. There is no better way to take advantage of a warm winter day than to get out in the garden and plant a new rose.

PLANTING BARE-ROOT ROSES

Roses are potentially our greatest flowering shrub, with an array of flowers unsurpassed by any other plant. The types vary from huge individually flowering plants to shrubs covered with masses of smaller blossoms. Most of the new types and cultivars bloom throughout the season, which is a rarity among flowering shrubs. Roses really are a must for every Southern garden.

It is important to plant and grow roses correctly or they will perform poorly and be an eyesore. The first step is choosing the right location. They require six hours of full sun each day during the growing season. It is also important to find a location with rich, high-humus, well-drained soil. If you have found such a spot, make sure there is enough space for your different cultivars. **Floribunda** and **Grandiflora** will need to be set 36 inches apart. **Hybrid Tea** should be set 30 to 36 inches apart, depending on the cultivar.

Roses need to be planted in well-prepared beds. After you have found a well-drained location, begin tilling or working the soil with a spade. Try to work the bed at least 12 inches deep and at least two feet wider than the outermost rose. Some professionals work the soil 36 inches deep! If the soil is sticky, add perlite or finely ground bark and work it in thoroughly. Depending on the situation, you might want to add humus, like peat moss, to condition the soil (see March, "How to Plant a Flower Bed"). If you are working with a new garden area, add limestone. Continue working the soil until all of the amendments are evenly distributed. Dig the actual

planting hole about one foot deep and two feet wide to begin with, then alter it according to the roots of the particular rose.

Prepare bare-root roses before you place them in

1 – Remove weak or dead canes, leaving three or four well-spaced canes to form the plant's structure.

2 – Tip rose roots until even, then plant on cones of soil to accommodate their natural root structure and prevent air pockets.

3 – Planting depth is critical. In the South, place the rose so the graft union is just above the surface of the soil.

the hole. First, soak the roots in a bucket of water for several hours. This will start water absorption. Next, prune off any roots which broke in handling. Use a sharp pair of pruning shears and try not to tear as you cut. Each new rose should have three or four healthy canes the size of your index finger. These canes should be at least 12 inches long. Prune off any canes which are unhealthy and cut back stems to a healthy bud.

When planting, it is important to place the rose properly in the hole so as to allow the plant to sit naturally with its roots extended. Make sure the hole is large enough to accommodate the roots without bending them. Next, make a cone of soil in the bottom of the hole to set the plant on. A rose's roots naturally grow downward and outward and without the cone, they would be flattened and might break when you pour the soil in the hole. As you place the plant in the hole, spread the roots out so they sit comfortably on the cone. Before filling the hole, check to see that the graft union (the swollen area below the limbs) is above the level of the ground. If it is not, remove the plant and build up the cone. Now fill the hole by packing loose, well-prepared soil around the roots. Once it is filled, make a collar of soil at the outer edge of the original hole to hold water. Finally, soak the newly planted bed after all the roses are set.

ROSE ACTIVITIES FOR NOVEMBER:

Plant

☞ Begin to plant dormant bare-root roses whenever the ground is not frozen. Before planting, trim long or broken roots and cut stems back to a healthy bud. Try new cultivars but keep old favorites as your major plantings until new ones have proven themselves in your garden.*

Prune

☞ Top-heavy roses may be pruned back about one-third to prevent swaying in the winds. *Do not prune heavily until early March.*

Fertilize

☞ There is no need to fertilize your roses this month.

Spray

☞ There is no need to spray roses until you apply lime sulfur as a dormant spray in January.

Water

☞ Water newly planted roses thoroughly, even if the ground is wet, in order to settle the soil around the roots.†

Other

☞ Remove fallen rose leaves from the bed to prevent blackspot, other diseases, and various insects from overwintering on the ground.

☞ Keep roses well mulched but do not pile mulch against the crown or lower stems. Many problems like cankers and botrytis occur when mulch covers the lower stems.‡

---

* See "Planting Bare-Root Roses," p. 250

† See "Proper Watering," p. 130

‡ See "Mulching: A Lesson from Nature," p. 243

V. *Flowers and Colorful Garden Plants*

Before the sight of dead annual and perennial foliage gets you down, cut your plants off, rake them up, and throw them in the compost pile. There is no time to lament the end of one season in the Southern garden! Head out to the nearest garden center and buy your spring-flowering bulbs, perennial roots, and a tray of pansies for good measure. It's time to plant again.

November is a good time to buy packaged plants like bulbs and roots. Keep a close watch on your local garden center so that you can buy when they have a fresh shipment. Often bulbs and roots are not stored in a cool enough location at the nursery and will begin sprouting within a few weeks of arrival. You do not want to buy them once they have sprouted.

Besides boosting your morale, removing dead plants from the garden is an important way to control insects and diseases. Many pests try to overwinter in dead foliage. Disposing of it properly will prevent them from emerging in the spring to attack newly sprouted perennials and succulent annuals.

SOUTHERN FLOWERING BULBS, CORMS, TUBERS, AND ROOTS

Each year the huge field in front of my boyhood home came alive with thousands of beautiful flowers heralding the arrival of spring. These **Laurens Koster Narcissus** were remnants of the days when the family's 1500-acre nursery grew large numbers of **Narcissus** bulbs to sell in our stores. They stopped production long before I can remember, but the remaining bulbs were scattered when the large field was plowed to plant other crops. They planted fescue grass when it first became popular and both the fescue and **Laurens Koster** formed a year-round alliance of beauty.

The favorite bulbs of the South are those which bloom in the spring, but as a boy I watched with fascination when **Resurrection Lilies** (**Lycoris squamigera** and **Lycoris radiata**) shot up from the ground in the late summer to form their clusters of fragrant pink or red "lilies" without a hint of the leaves which had come up, grown, and died down months before. We also waited eagerly for the fall **Rain Lilies** (**Zephyranthes**) to bloom in my mother's shaded garden, which were a signal that the hot summer was drawing to a close.

Spring-flowering **Snow Drops** (**Galanthus**), daffodils, **Dutch Iris**, sweet-scented **Jonquils**, all the **hyacinths**, **Scilla**, **Star of Bethlehem** (**Ornithogalum umbellatum**), **Ranunculus**, and **tulips** show that true spring has come to the South. While we may love others for nostalgic reasons, spring-flowering bulbs which complement **Forsythia**, **Flowering Quince**,

Bradford Pears, **flowering cherries**, **dogwoods**, **azaleas**, **snowballs**, and **Spiraea** let us know that winter weather is almost over.

November is the best time during the fall to plant spring-flowering bulbs, even though they are in the nurseries much earlier. I like to wait and plant when the ground is cool, which prevents them from sprouting too soon and sustaining winter damage. You can purchase bulbs earlier while selections are better and get exactly what you want. But you should still wait until November to plant them. Refrigerate earlier purchases or keep them in a very cool place until November planting time.

Peonies and **Bearded Iris** are also thought of as spring-flowering bulbs, though they are more like perennials. Plant both shallowly in the early fall as soon as they are available.

Depending on the type, spring-flowering bulbs can

Plant daffodils and other spring-flowering bulbs in November for masses of colorful flowers next spring.

either be planted in beds or be naturalized in open areas and woodlands. **King Alfred Daffodils** naturalize easily, requiring little attention after they are established. Birds seem to have seeded **Star of Bethlehem** in places where I have never planted them, and there are **King Alfred Daffodils** still growing which the previous owner planted on our land more than 30 years ago. Not all bulbs are as long-lasting. Most **tulips** last for only a few years in the South where warm soil causes them to multiply too rapidly and eventually disappear.

How Spring-Flowering Bulbs Grow: Each bulb is an embryonic plant with leaves, stems, and flower buds contained inside a storage organ filled with food which is available for growth when needed. Unlike most plants which grow during the summer, spring-flowering bulbs are dormant from the end of their growth cycle in late spring (when their foliage dies) until fall when they start developing roots to begin a new cycle of growth, bloom, and regeneration of the bulb. Gardeners need to understand a bulb's cycle to keep it growing well, since a mistake like cutting off the foliage too soon will prevent the plant from storing the food it needs for next year.

What Bulbs Need to Do Well: Most bulbs are subject to poor root development and rotting when grown in wet, sticky locations, so be sure to provide them with rich, well drained soil. Many, like **Narcissus, Dutch Hyacinths**, and **tulips**, require moderate sun. Our major spring-flowering types do best in moderately sweet soil of 6.0-6.5 pH. Yearly liming or fertilizing with bone meal will help these bulbs retain their vigor.

Planting Spring-Flowering Bulbs: Work the ground deeply and thoroughly, being sure it is pulverized deeper than the desired planting depth. Work in limestone or bone meal at the rate of 10 pounds per 100 square feet of bed area. Add peat moss and perlite if the soil is tight and sticky, using enough to develop a loose and friable structure (see March, "How to Plant a Flower Bed").

Plant at a depth of about 2 1/2 times the greatest diameter of the bulb. Instructions on the package tell you how deep to plant so you don't usually have to measure. In the South, **tulips** are a major exception if you want them to last for several years. Despite the label's direction, plant **tulips** about seven or eight inches deep to keep the bulbs cooler during the spring when they are regenerating and multiplying.

Bulbs which naturalize easily are stronger and compete well in woods and open areas. They may be spot planted by digging a slightly deeper than the proper planting depth and wider than the bulb's diameter. Place a tablespoonful of bone meal in the bottom of the hole, add an inch or two of soil, then set the bulb at its proper depth. Add peat moss to the soil taken from the hole until you have a loose, easily worked mixture to refill the hole over the bulb.

Fertilizing Bulbs: Bulbs need fertilizing each spring after they finish blooming to keep them beautiful year after year. Use a 5-10-15 fertilizer or a special bulb formula for best results. These fertilizers provide the nutrients needed for current growth and replenishment of the bulb for next year.

Bright tulips blend well with pansies and other spring flowers.

Sweet scented jonquils naturalize easily.

Bulb Problems: The major bulb types which we grow in the South have few insects or diseases. However, bulbs may not always live up to your expectations because of other problems.

HERE ARE A FEW RULES TO HELP YOU HAVE GOOD RESULTS:

1. Prepare the soil well.
2. Lime beds once a year.
3. Do not plant too early.
4. If you purchase them in the early fall, keep them cool until planting.
5. Plant at the right depth.
6. If you forget to plant your bulbs at the right time, plant them when you remember, even though it is past the recommended time. Stored bulbs cannot last from one year to another.
7. Fertilize bulbs as soon as the flowers die.
8. *Never cut off the leaves until they turn yellow.*

FLOWER ACTIVITIES FOR NOVEMBER:

Plant

☞ Plant hardy perennials like **Astilbe**, **Hosta**, **Delphinium**, **Foxglove**, and **Rudbeckia** this month. Dormant perennial roots are inexpensive and easy to plant.

☞ Finish transplanting seedlings (started from seed in August and September) of hardy annuals, perennials, and biennials in the early part of the month.*

☞ Prepare perennial beds well with peat moss and perlite. Perennials need good drainage. Add bone meal and work the bed deeply and thoroughly. Be sure to space the plants according to directions on the package. Perennials will grow rapidly when the weather begins to warm next spring.†

☞ Plant **pansy** and **English Daisy** this month. Mulch beds with pine straw to prevent the young plants from heaving out of the ground when it freezes.‡

☞ Plant spring-flowering bulbs now. Since bulbs need good drainage, work the bed well, add bone meal to sweeten the soil, and add 5-10-15 to stimulate growth. Plant all bulbs except tulips at the recommended depths. **Tulips** should be planted eight inches deep so they will last more than one or two years.**

Prune

☞ Remove all dead annual and perennial tops to prevent insects and diseases from overwintering and causing damage next spring.

☞ Cut back the dead foliage of established **Bearded Iris** and **Leopard Flower** (**Blackberry Lily**).

☞ Remove the dead tops of established **peonies** and replace mulch.

Fertilize

☞ There is no need to fertilize newly planted hardy perennials.

Water

☞ Water plants thoroughly after planting, even if the ground is wet, to settle the soil.

Other

☞ Mulch bare beds with pine straw to prevent winter weeds from getting out of control.‡

☞ Keep **Canna** and **Dahlia** roots stored in a cool place. Do not set them in the garden until next spring when the ground is warm and the danger of frost has passed. Store **Caladium** and **Elephant Ear** tubers in a warmer spot than **Canna** and **Dahlia** roots.

---

* See "Starting Seeds Inside," p.18
† See "How to Plant a Flower Bed," p. 62

** See "Southern Flowering Bulbs, Corms, Tubers, and Roots," p. 252
‡ See "Mulching: A Lesson from Nature," p. 243

VI. *Vegetables*

The vegetable garden is looking pretty bare this time of year. It is a hard decision whether to continue the walks out to see what is going on there. While there aren't any new insects to discover or ripening tomatoes to admire, it is still interesting to spot rabbit tracks, and maybe an occasional deer footprint in the bare earth.

Every year about this time the rabbits start nibbling at my Crimson Clover. They hop out into the middle of the plot and eat away a rounded circle in one specific area. While I could sprinkle human hair from the barber around the garden to scare them off like I did with my vegetables over the summer, there is plenty of Crimson Clover to go around, and I think

Crimson Clover is now growing well as it improves garden soil. It's too late to plant now but you can substitute Austrian Winter Peas with the same excellent results.

I'll let them nibble away. Maybe they need a little dessert since there is not much else green in the yard.

By November, it is too late to seed any new Crimson Clover as a cover crop. It needs a period of warm weather to establish itself, and you won't get the results you hope for this late in the season. Plant Austrian Winter Peas instead. They are a legume as well and will have the same beneficial effects as Crimson Clover.

VEGETABLE ACTIVITIES FOR NOVEMBER:

Plant

☞ Bare garden areas should be lightly tilled and sowed with a green-manure cover crop. With the cooler weather, **Austrian Winter Peas** should be used rather than **Crimson Clover**. Green-manure crops prevent washing, keep the soil loose through the winter, build nitrogen in the soil, and provide green-manure humus when you turn them under in the spring. Do not use cover crops, however, in areas where you are planning to plant in January.*

Prune

☞ Remove all dead vegetable plants or tops from the garden to prevent insects and diseases from overwintering.

Fertilize

☞ There is no need to fertilize hardy **onions**, **cabbages**, and **collards** which are growing for an early spring harvest.

☞ If your emerging **Crimson Clover** or **Austrian Winter Pea** cover crop is light green, it probably needs a light fertilizing. The nitrogen-fixing bacteria on its roots haven't yet begun producing enough nutrients to supply the plant. Don't worry; soon the bacteria will be producing an excess of nitrogen and fertilizing your garden for you.*

Other

☞ Dig fall **Irish potatoes** before hard freezes.†

* See "Planting Cover Crops," p. 205

* See "Planting Cover Crops," p. 205
† See "The Fall Vegetable Garden," p. 204

VII. *Houseplants*

November is one of my favorite times to garden indoors because of Paperwhites, hyacinths, and Giant Amaryllis. There is something unique and intriguing about growing these bulbs inside and having their delicate fragrances bless the house around Christmas. Although there are all kinds of kits available to grow bulbs which require little more than adding water, I like to start from scratch and fashion my own pots. Half of the fun is in the planting, and adding water just doesn't do it for me.

By November, most of our houseplants will have adjusted to the harsh, dry conditions they must endure over the winter. Your ferns might look horrible when compared to the memory of how they looked over the summer. Their once-full shape has thinned out, and they don't seem happy at all. Don't give up on them! Continue misting them as often as you remember. In the early spring, they can be cut back severely, so don't worry about whether or not you will be able to resuscitate their dilapidated winter fronds.

INDOOR FLOWERING PLANTS FOR THE HOLIDAYS

Plants with bright foliage or colorful flowers add tremendously to holiday decorations. They also scent our homes with the deliciously sweet fragrances of spring. Many of these plants are forced into bloom just for this season; others bloom naturally in December. All are tender plants and have to be indoors to flourish. Treat them in much the same way as you do tropical houseplants: watching their moisture level and misting frequently. Give special attention to the outdoor plants, like **azaleas** and **hyacinths**, which have been forced to blossom in the warm indoor environment.

Potted Plants

Poinsettia:

The **Poinsettia** is my favorite of all indoor blooming plants for Christmas. Their large red, pink, or white bracts have become a Christmas symbol throughout the world. Keep them away from heat and do not overwater. **Poinsettias** will continue to be attractive until spring if you give them good light, some fertilizer, and moderate water. They can be planted in a sunny bed in the garden where they will thrive until frost but will not bloom.

Some people carry over **Poinsettias** from year to year, but they are as tricky to force into bloom as **chrysanthemums** since they also require specific daylight procedures. I much prefer buying new plants each year than going through the hassle of covering my **Poinsettias** at sundown and uncovering them twelve hours later. This procedure has to be kept up from September 22 until you see their buds form in November.

Azaleas:

Azaleas are difficult for home gardeners to force correctly. It is best to purchase these as the buds begin to open so they will be colorful for several weeks.

Red and white **azaleas** are most often forced for the holidays. Keep these plants away from heating vents and out of direct sunlight. Keep them evenly moist but do not overwater. If the flowers begin to wilt or drop off, mist them with plain water.

Since **azaleas** are outdoor plants, they can be carried over to plant later. After Christmas, gradually acclimate them to winter by placing the pot where it is cold but will not freeze and where it receives plenty of light but not direct sun. Plant them outside in March after severe freezes are over.

Christmas Cactus:

Christmas Cactus can be forced into bloom for the holidays or purchased already blooming. These easy-to-grow succulents are a traditional holiday plant in the South. If you don't have one, purchase a plant whose buds are bright pink and just beginning to open. Carried-over plants should be kept in a semi-dormant state with little water and reduced light from September until early November, then brought into more light and lightly watered until pink buds appear. While blossoming, do not overwater them, but keep the soil slightly moist.

Also, keep them out of direct sunlight and mist them with plain water if the blossoms wilt or start to drop. **Christmas Cactus** may be held over after they bloom by keeping them in good light but no direct sun. After blooming, they start their growth stage and should be given more water and fertilized as new growth increases. Do not overwater. They will continue to grow until you harden them off in September. **Christmas Cactus** bloom best when slightly pot-bound. Repot them immediately after blooming in a larger pot, then do not repot for several years.

Begonias:

There are many **begonias** which can be purchased in bloom during the holidays. **Rex Begonia** have particularly attractive leaves. Remember to keep **begonias** away from heating vents and watered evenly. They all make good houseplants when given good light but no direct sun. Forcing growth will increase the amount of blossoms. **Begonia deliciosa** is a special favorite of mine (See picture, p. 166).

Chrysanthemums:

Much like **Poinsettias**, **chrysanthemums** require a very strict day-length treatment to produce blossoms at a specific time. Purchase flowers in bloom for the holidays rather than trying to force your own. Keep them in good light, evenly moist, and out of direct sun. After blossoming, put the pot in a cold place where it can harden up, but will not freeze. Cut off the top of the plants at soil level and keep the soil barely damp. In the spring you can separate the clump into many new plants and grow in full sun in the garden.

Jerusalem Cherry:

Jerusalem Cherry, a small tender perennial here but a medium shrub in the tropics, is used as a pot plant for its bright orange fruit and dark green foliage. The attractive fruit are somewhat poisonous, so keep plants away from small children.

Southerners often grow **Jerusalem Cherry** outside in pots where they set their colorful fruit before being brought inside prior to frost. You must keep them in bright light, well-misted, and fertilized for the fruits to remain colorful for the holidays. Flower shops and nurseries also have them available for the holidays.

Jerusalem Cherry may be kept over and planted in the garden after the danger of frost has passed in the spring or repotted and grown as a patio plant. Keep them evenly moist and fertilized well after they finish fruiting.

Shamrock:

This is a wonderful year-round flowering houseplant which grows and blossoms in cycles. I have never been able to time my plants to be in their blossoming period exactly when I want them to. For this reason, I prefer to see if mine are about to bloom during the holidays, and if not, I reluctantly buy a new one which *is* about to bloom.

This blooming **Shamrock** is **Oxalis acetosella** and not the true **Irish Shamrock**, which is **Trifolium procumbens**. Place them in medium light and water them just like your other houseplants. After a lengthy bloom, the plant will seem to die, but actually is going into a rest phase. Allow it to dry out a bit. After it has rested about a month, water and fertilize it, and it will sprout new growth and blossom again. There are white and pink cultivars.

Ornamental Peppers:

Ornamental peppers are sometimes used as an indoor holiday plant. The most attractive ones have small purple and white fruits. Keep them in good light, evenly watered, and misted if the fruits begin to wrinkle. Since they are a tender annual, carry them over inside. They grow well in a flower bed after frost and should set more colorful fruits. It is better to purchase new plants each year for your holiday decorations.

Forced Plants

Hyacinths:

Bulb growers specially treat some **hyacinth** bulbs to prepare them for early forcing. Use only prepared bulbs to force for Christmas, and be sure they have not been in a warm place (even at a nursery) all fall. There are special **hyacinth** glasses which hold the bulb properly for forcing in water. It takes about a month for forced **hyacinths** to bloom. You can also purchase already forced, blooming **hyacinths** at nurseries and flower shops.

Hyacinths are not only beautiful but have a pleas-

1 – Start Paperwhite Narcissus bulbs in early November for blossoms at Christmas.

2 – Place bulbs in containers with pebbles covering at least half the bulb. Then fill with water up to the top of the rocks.

3 – Keep Paperwhites in dim light until the first green shows, then put them in bright light.

ing fragrance. Once they are growing, it is important to keep them moist but not wet over the holiday season. Also keep them in a cool corner away from heating vents. **Hyacinths** thrive in good light but cannot take direct sun. Do not bother with them after they finish blooming.

Paperwhite Narcissus:

Paperwhite Narcissus is one of the most commonly forced holiday flowers. While normally used for the holidays, they are a wonderful breath of spring anytime during winter. It takes from four to six weeks from the time you plant until they are in full bloom, depending on the heat and light conditions of your home. I like to plant mine at the end of the first week in November so they will be flowering heavily for Christmas.

These days you can buy **Paperwhite** kits which only need to be watered. I prefer to buy the bulbs and plant them in a glass bowl filled with decorative rocks and water. The roots grow down through the rocks just as if it were soil. Keep **Paperwhites** in dim light until the first green shows, then put them in bright light to prevent their leaves and stems from becoming tall and falling over. They are useless after they blossom.

Giant Flowering Amaryllis:

These spectacular flowers are easily and quickly forced in only three or four weeks. You can buy them already potted, place them in a bright spot, water them, and let them develop into a beautiful blooming plant with two or three huge flowers. If you purchase already blooming **Giant Flowering Amaryllis**, they will continue blooming for a week or two.

HOUSEPLANT ACTIVITIES FOR NOVEMBER:

Plant

☛ Start **Paperwhites, hyacinths** and **Giant Amaryllis** in mid-November for blossoms at Christmas.*

* See "Indoor Flowering Plants for the Holidays," p. 256

☛ Check newly purchased houseplants for the need to repot. Repot if the roots have massed against the edge of the ball of soil and are dark in color. Always use a container which is at least two sizes larger. Also, check for sowbugs and pillbugs while the plants are out of the pot.†

☛ Pot cuttings of houseplants and tropicals as soon as they develop a root system. Use a peat-light potting mixture and begin applying a water-soluble fertilizer solution at one-half the recommended strength.‡

Prune

☛ Groom indoor plants whenever they need it. Remove weak branches or stems as well as off-color leaves.

Fertilize

☛ Continue fertilizing with half-strength applications of a water-soluble fertilizer solution like Peters every time you water. They will not need full-strength until the days begin to get longer next spring.**

Spray

☛ Check all indoor plants for insects such as spider mites, scale, and mealybug. Using a houseplant systemic insecticide to control them is easier and safer than spraying inside. If you do spray, remember to apply the insecticide to the undersides of the leaves.††

☛ Be careful when spraying **ferns**. Some insecticides are harmful to them. *Always read the label for warnings about **ferns** and other plants.*

† See "Repotting Houseplants," p. 67

‡ See "Propagating Herbaceous Houseplants and Garden Plants," p. 225

** See "Houseplant Care and Maintenance," p. 232

†† See "Common Houseplant Ailments," p. 280

Water

☛ During early November, gradually increase the water for **Christmas Cactus** and fertilize at half-strength when the pink buds first show. As soon as you see the buds, begin watering regularly just as you water tropical houseplants.*

☛ Continue to watch houseplants carefully during the winter. When they look limp, check for dry soil. If they are dry, water thoroughly in a sink or bathtub, letting the water drain completely, and don't water again until the surface is dry once more. Between waterings, mist with plain water on a regular basis. If the limp plants are in moist soil, do not water but allow the soil to dry a bit and mist frequently.**

☛ Tip-burn or edge-burn on leaves indicates that more water is being lost than is being absorbed by the roots. Check for dry soil, too much sunlight, or drafts from heating vents.**

☛ **Ferns** which have been brought inside are particularly troubled by low humidity. Mist them frequently and remove any dead fronds as soon as they occur.

Other

☛ A rule for **Poinsettias**: As soon as you see the flower bud from which the red bracts will grow, bring them into full light and water them with a water-soluble fertilizer solution like Peters.*

☛ Houseplants which become lighter in color or have very long intervals between branches or stems (internodes) may need more light.

☛ Newly purchased houseplants have been growing under ideal conditions at the nursery. When you bring them home, they may take a while to adjust to the drier conditions in your home. Water your new plants as prescribed above, but *do not overwater*! Mist them frequently and if they continue to do poorly, try placing a cool-air vaporizer near the plant for several days.**

* See "Indoor Flowering Plants for the Holidays," p. 256

** See "Houseplant Care and Maintenance," p. 232

* See "Indoor Flowering Plants for the Holidays," p. 256

** See "Houseplant Care and Maintenance," p. 232

NOTES

VIII. *Lawns*

With the arrival of the first hard freezes, most of us will put away the lawn mower for the season. The summer grasses like Bermuda Grass have long since browned, and the evergreen grasses like the fescues are slowing down to a crawl. The exception is Ryegrass which was seeded over Bermuda Grass lawns. This amazing grass grows straight through the winter with little care for 20-degree temperatures.

Other plants which unfortunately don't mind the cold weather are the winter weeds like chickweed and Annual Bluegrass. My personal nemesis is chickweed. It is an extremely tough weed which has managed to endure some of my most fervent spraying with a broadleaf weed killer. It has even managed to spread its seed into some shrubs I'm growing in pots 50 yards from my lawn!

Chickweed will really start to grow in late January. One way to control this troublesome weed is to apply pre-emergence weed killer this month, before it gets started. Although it won't kill the established plants, it will keep the seeds from germinating so that you can concentrate your efforts on dealing with the older plants.

LAWN ACTIVITIES FOR NOVEMBER:

Plant

☞ It is too late to plant evergreen and summer lawns. Wait until next spring.

Fertilize

☞ There is no need to fertilize your evergreen or summer grass lawn this month.

Spray

☞ Apply pre-emergence weed controls on lawns that had heavy infestations of winter weeds (chickweed, Annual Bluegrass) last winter and spring. This material will prevent winter weed seeds from germinating. Do not use on lawns to be reseeded with permanent grasses or annual Ryegrass.

Cut

☞ Cut lawns when the growth reaches the correct cutting height. Do not let newly seeded grasses become too tall before cutting.

☞ Cut evergreen lawns at the proper height:

EVERGREEN GRASSES	HEIGHT
Kentucky 31 Tall Fescue	3 to 3 $\frac{1}{2}$ inches
Turf-type Tall Fescues	3 inches
Fine Leaf Fescues	1 $\frac{1}{2}$ to 2 inches
Kentucky Bluegrass	2 to 2 $\frac{1}{2}$ inches

☞ If you have seeded **Ryegrass** over **Bermuda Grass,** keep the **Ryegrass** cut about an inch above the base lawn. If you let it grow tall in clumps, it will damage your permanent grass.

Other

☞ Keep leaves off grass. Heavy leaf fall can smother grass, even dormant grasses.

December

IN THE SOUTHERN GARDEN

December is a hectic month with the holidays taking more of our time than the garden. The Winter Solstice (shortest day of the year) usually falls on December 21 and marks the official start of winter, though most of us have already had plenty of cold weather by then. But our Southern winters are not so harsh as to keep us inside all the time, and our gardens still hold plants in flower like Camellia sasanqua, fall-blooming Camellia japonica, Meratia (Chimonanthus praecox), and pansies. Southern gardens never sleep in the winter; they blossom during warm spells and take naps during cold ones.

The holidays are filled with the old stand-bys passed down through the years — evergreen firs, hollies with their berries, and Poinsettias. In addition, the South has its own traditional plants—Camellia sasanqua, the sweet-scented Meratia, Christmas Cactus, heavily berried Pyracantha, Nandina, Aucuba, and Ground Cedar (Turkey Foot or Turkey Feather to most of us) for making swags and wreaths. Holiday plants bring cheer to our homes for the holidays, no matter what the weather is.

After Christmas, I'm always ready to do something energetic outdoors. Though December is an excellent planting month, it's hard to wade through the post-Christmas decorations sales at nurseries and find many plants I want. But there are dormant season activities like pruning and spraying which can fulfill the urge to start the long garden trek toward spring. Pretty soon January Jasmine and the first daffodils will be blooming, so late December is a great time to enjoy the mountains of catalogs which descend upon gardeners toward the end of the month. There is no finer way to spend the lull between Christmas and the New Year than sitting by the fire immersed in descriptions of new plants and new ideas for the year to come.

AT LEFT: *Heavily berried American Holly (Ilex opaca)*

I. *Shade and Flowering Trees*

With the holiday season upon us, we are busy buying presents, attending parties, and decorating the house. Since December is still a great time to plant a shade or flowering tree, why not give a tree as a Christmas present?

When thinking of a tree to give the man of the family, a utilitarian shade tree normally pops into mind. A Red Maple or slow-growing oak seems the most appropriate for husband or father. But there are alternatives. The Catalpa tree is perfect for the fisherman of the family (fishermen sometimes call it "Catawba"). Every year, a special caterpillar called a Catalpa worm shows up on the tree. These caterpillars make great fishing bait. The caterpillars eat the leaves off the tree which acts as a natural stimulus for the tree to grow vigorously. Remember to plant your Catalpa tree in an out-of-the-way spot, because when you walk under it in the summer, a few caterpillars are likely to drop on your shoulder. Men are also fond of fruit trees, especially the large-growing apple cultivars (rather than a dwarf).

Flowering cherries make beautiful gifts for your wife or mother. The Yoshino Cherry is renowned for its abundant white flowers in springtime. The Kwanzan Cherry has larger, fluffier pink-blushed blossoms (See picture, p. 78). They have numerous petals in wavy folds which look a lot like an old-fashioned rose blossom.

While children don't get quite as excited about receiving a tree as a present, one way to make it fun is to have a growing competition. Buy two similar types and let each child plant his own (with some help from Mom and Dad). My boys still get excited in judging whose apple tree is the biggest and best, 12 years after they planted them.

PLANTING TREES AND SHRUBS

My father, Donald Hastings, Sr., insisted that planting correctly was the most important step a gardener could take. His favorite saying was, "Plant a one-dollar plant in a ten-dollar hole rather than a ten-dollar plant in a one-dollar hole." My own experience has shown that a well-planted three-foot tree will be larger than a poorly planted six-foot tree in two years, and sometimes even within one year. The secret of the ten-dollar hole is in its size and how the soil is prepared.

This seems easy enough, but unfortunately preparing a good ten-dollar hole requires digging. As most Southern gardeners know, digging in Southern soils is no piece of cake. Sometimes there are rocks and pine tree roots nicely hidden in sticky clay. Other times there are boulders! More often than not, we leave the house, start digging, and throw in the towel when we have dug about a three-dollar hole. Then we plant the tree as quickly as possible because we're tired and it has already taken longer than we expected.

So this is the point where I am supposed to unveil my carefree, secret method of digging a hole. Sorry. There is no good, easy way to dig. Digging is digging, and it is never very easy. What I can suggest is to begin the project with the right perspective. Planting a tree is a huge deal. You are starting a project which won't end in 30 minutes, or six months, or even 20 years. That tree will continue to grow and expand every year, and it will affect your life. It might reduce your power bill, or make a new place for a hammock, or provide a beautiful show for everyone in the neighborhood each spring as it blooms. It will be an asset which enhances your life and the value of your home. With this perspective, enter the project slowly. Choose the spot one day, and then think about it again the next. When you have chosen your spot, decide on a day to dig. Then, return the next day, or a week later to finish the job. Before you know it, you might even be planting in a twelve-dollar hole.

There are two different methods of planting trees and shrubs. Spot planting is the basic method of planting one tree or shrub in a hole. Bed planting is used when planting a number of plants in a given area. Both require the same amount of soil preparation. Trees and shrubs which will stand alone as accents or for shade are most suited for spot planting while foundation plants, shrub borders, rose beds, and plant groupings are suitable for bed planting.

Spot Planting

Choose the location carefully. Most plants do badly in low, poorly drained locations. If the plant must be in such a place, dig a larger hole than normal, place gravel in the bottom, add chunks of bark on top of that, and then plant.

In normal areas, dig a hole larger and deeper than the ball of earth or, in the case of bare-root plants, larger and deeper than the root system. Prepare the soil removed from the hole by adding one-third finely ground bark or peat moss (not peat humus), one-third perlite or sand, and one-third soil from the hole. Mix this well. Feel the soil after mixing. If it still feels sticky, add more ground bark or peat moss. Place enough bark chunks in the bottom so that the top of the ball is about one inch above the surface of the surrounding soil. *Never plant woody plants with the top of the ball below the surface of the soil.* Trees and shrubs are very sensitive to the level at which they are planted.

Inspect the roots of container-grown and bare-root plants before setting them in the hole. The roots of container-grown plants may be matted heavily against the ball of earth. If so, loosen them by pulling them away from the ball. Check the roots of bare-root plants. Cut off any extremely long roots and all broken roots. Balled and burlapped (B&B) plants must be left in the burlap until after the plant is carefully set in the hole or the ball of earth will fall apart and likely damage many roots.

Set the plant in the hole and position it correctly before starting to pack the prepared soil around the roots. Again, the ball of earth should be at least one inch above the surface of the surrounding soil. Set bare-root trees with the soil level one inch above the top root. Planting too deeply can be disastrous, so always set plants at the correct level. With B&B trees and shrubs, cut the burlap off the top of the ball, leaving the rest to rot.

Now fill the hole with the prepared soil. When it is

1 – Dig a hole larger and deeper than the ball of earth.

2 – Prepare soil with 1/3 peat moss, 1/3 perlite or sand, and 1/3 soil from the hole.

3 – Plant woody plants with the top of the ball one inch above the surface of the soil.

4 – Tamp the soil as you fill the hole to remove air pockets around the roots.

half full, firm the fresh soil with the end of the shovel handle or with your fingers. Continue filling and tamping until the hole is full. Make a ring-shaped dam of soil on the surface around the outer edge of the hole to hold water and direct it toward the roots. Water the plant thoroughly to drive out all air pockets and to moisten the root system, even if the ground is wet.

Bed Planting

The principles are the same for bed planting as for spot planting except that you are preparing an area instead of a spot. Use a roto-tiller if the area is large, or a spading fork if it is for just a few plants. Mix in the same materials as above except that you won't need as many amendments if the soil is loose and fertile. Take a handful of the prepared soil and squeeze it into a ball in the palm of the hand. Try to break up the clod with your thumb. If it crumbles, the mixture is good; if it won't break up easily and feels slick, add more organic matter, perlite, and sand. Once the entire area has been prepared, plant each tree and shrub in its spot in the same way as described for spot planting. Bed planting benefits the plant by increasing the drainage in the area around it. It also helps by providing amended soil for the roots to grow into in future years.

A final step for newly planted shade and flowering trees is to stake them, especially if they were purchased bare-root. Attach three wires to the trunk about four to five feet off the ground and run them to wooden stakes driven at intervals around the tree. Make a collar of old watering hose to prevent the wire from cutting into the trunks. Staking will hold the tree in place until it develops enough roots to anchor itself.

With your new tree or shrub safely in the ground, you need to take only a few additional steps to ensure that your plant attains maximum growth. As new growth starts, spread a band of 15-15-15 fertilizer on top of the ground around the outer edge of the hole. Check with a local nursery to see if they have a special slow-release nitrogen tree fertilizer. Evergreen shrubs like **Camellia** and **Rhododendron** will need a special azalea/camellia acid fertilizer instead of 15-15-15. Use about 1/2 pound of fertilizer per three feet of height (check the specific instructions of your partic-

ular brand). An alternative is to use Osmocote slow-release fertilizer when planting. Water all your plants thoroughly after fertilizing.

As the plant begins to grow, check the surface of the soil for moisture. If it is dry, soak your newly planted tree or shrub thoroughly with a hose-end water breaker. Once warm weather arrives, water every week if there has been no significant rain.

While it is best not to plant in wet soil, sometimes we have no choice. A good way to remove moisture from your planting mixture is to add dry peat moss along with the perlite and soil. Dry peat moss will absorb excess water and allow you to plant your tree or shrub in a nice loamy mixture. If you plant in excessively wet soil, it will be difficult or impossible to settle the soil around the roots. The wet soil will clump together and later dry into hard chunks, never fully contacting the delicate root system.

CHOOSING A CHRISTMAS TREE

Decorating an evergreen tree with ornaments and lights is a major Christmas activity for most people. Part of the family tradition is the search for just the right tree. One of my jobs many years ago was to help find the best trees for our Christmas tree lot. This experience taught me a lot about buying trees for my own home.

Cut Trees

Of the Christmas trees available in the South, the **Fraser Fir** is my favorite. It is a "double balsam" with several layers of needles which are richly aromatic, and the tree tends to shed less than other balsams. While there are other "double balsams" grown in Canada, I prefer **Fraser Firs** from North Carolina since they are harvested closer to Christmas than the **Canadian Balsam** which is cut many months earlier. The foliage of all balsams holds well and will stay fresh and aromatic throughout the season.

While it is grown farther away and cut before the **Fraser Fir**, the **Canadian Balsam** is still a good choice. It also holds its needles well and has a rich aroma lasting through the holidays.

Another good tree is the **Virginia Pine**. These are locally grown and are usually fresher than **Scotch**

Pines, which are grown and cut in the North.

When you have decided which kind of tree to buy, try to find the freshest tree possible. Tamp the butt of the trunk on the ground to see if the needles shed badly. Also check the foliage to be sure it is not dry and brittle.

Once you get the tree home, keep it in a humid place until you are ready to bring it inside and decorate. Before placing the tree in its holder, cut off the butt of the trunk at least four inches to help the tree absorb water, and keep the holder filled with water at all times. It is also important to close all heating vents in the vicinity of the tree.

Living Trees

Many families use living plants for Christmas trees and plant them outside after the holidays as a reminder of happy Christmases of the past. The best for most of the South are **Norway Spruce**, **Virginia Pine**, **Japanese Black Pine**, and **Scotch Pine**.

Choosing the best plant is easy. Choose one just as you would any B&B or container-grown plant for planting outside. Container-grown trees are preferable. Be sure the plant is not loose in the container or ball of earth, for this shows it has been poorly handled by the grower.

Remember that living trees must remain healthy throughout the Christmas season. Drying out may damage them irreparably, so leave them inside for no more than one week. Before you take the tree inside, water it thoroughly. Place the tree in a cool spot away from heating vents, or close all nearby vents. Keep the soil moist as long as the tree is inside, and take it back outside as soon as possible after the holidays. Soak the tree thoroughly and let it sit outside several days before planting.

Remember that both cut and living Christmas trees are very flammable. Improperly wired lights and nearby candles can spell disaster. Use common sense with indoor foliage and never leave Christmas tree lights on when you are away from home. Finally, make sure your fire extinguisher is full and in an accessible location.

TREE ACTIVITIES FOR DECEMBER:

Plant

☛ Plant B&B, bare-root, and container-grown trees throughout the month when the ground is not frozen or likely to freeze soon. Make sure to plant trees at the correct depth in a well-prepared hole, and stake them to prevent swaying (especially bare-root trees). Never plant trees deeper than they were growing in the nursery. When planting B&B and container-grown trees, it is a good idea to leave the top of the root ball showing after planting. Plant bare-root trees with the soil level one inch above the top root.*

☛ Choose planting stock carefully. New shade trees should be straight with tight, smooth bark, have a dominant central shoot or leader, and should not be loose in the ball or container. Choose flowering trees carefully as well, making sure they are free from scars.

☛ Plant shade trees like **maples** and flowering trees like **dogwoods** dug from the wild only as a last resort and only if they are small. You are likely to cut their wide, sprangly roots drastically during digging, and then they will take forever to start growing vigorously again.

☛ Do not plant **Southern Magnolia** and **Cherry Laurel** until late February or March.

☛ When handling container or B&B trees, never pick them up by the stem; this will break the roots in the ball of earth.

☛ It is best to plant shade and flowering trees when the soil is not too wet. However, if planting is necessary before the soil dries out, use dry peat moss as the soil amendment. It will absorb excess moisture and allow you to make a better mixture to use in planting.

* See "Planting Trees and Shrubs," p. 264

Prune

☞ If necessary, begin pruning dormant, deciduous, and evergreen shade trees this month. Both light and heavy pruning are okay, but do not prune trees when the sap is frozen. Also, never remove the central shoot or leader of a shade tree; you will ruin its natural shape.†

☞ If necessary, prune spring-flowering trees like **Bradford Pear**, **flowering cherry**, **flowering peach**, and **flowering pear** but do so sparingly and selectively. Remove any crossed branches, damaged or diseased wood, and bad growth. Remember that buds for spring blossoms are already present on the branches and twigs grown last summer. Pruning them will reduce the number of flowers on the tree.†

☞ Summer-flowering trees like **Crape Myrtle** and **Chaste Tree (Vitex)** may be pruned severely to force new spring shoots on which the summer's blooms will develop. Prune selectively, however, to shape the tree and force new shoots in the direction you want them to grow.†

Fertilize

☞ It is still too soon to fertilize shade and flowering trees. When trees are dormant, they do not actively absorb nutrients from the soil. Fertilizer applied now will dissipate before the tree has a chance to use it.

† See "Pruning Shade and Flowering Trees," p. 4

Spray

☞ Control scale on evergreen plants. Use Cygon or Orthene on all except **hollies**. Use Orthene on **hollies**.‡

Water

☞ Water newly planted trees thoroughly, even if the ground is wet, in order to settle the soil around the roots.**

Other

☞ Mulch newly planted trees with pine straw or pine bark. Do not allow the mulch to pack against the tree's trunk.††

☞ Check mulch around older trees and replenish with fresh mulch if needed.††

☞ Stake newly planted shade and flowering trees, especially if they were purchased bare-root. Attach three wires to the trunk about four or five feet off the ground and run them to wooden stakes driven at intervals around the tree. Make a collar of old watering hose to prevent the wire from cutting into the trunks.

‡ See "Controlling Insects and Diseases," p. 80

** See "Proper Watering," p. 130

†† See "Mulching: A Lesson from Nature," p. 243

NOTES

II. *Shrubs and Vines*

With the arrival of the holiday season, we all want our lawn and garden to be in good shape. Many of us will begin pruning our evergreen and narrowleaf shrubs, trimming off some of last year's new growth which is shooting up from hedges. When trimming, remember that the top should be even with or narrower than the bottom. If you prune an evergreen shrub into the shape of a funnel, the bottom leaves won't get enough light and they will die. Watch out, though, because major structural pruning will remove a lot of leaf material which will not grow back until spring. Don't throw the baby out with the bath water! You might end up with no hedge to show your visitors.

As cold weather arrives in the South, there is no sadder sight than cold damage on shrubs and vines. The dead splotches which show up on shrubs and vines are unmistakable. The worst part is that there is nothing we can do after the fact. Insects can be controlled, diseases can be treated, poorly growing plants can be fertilized, but cold damage is a done deal. Prevention is the key to helping shrubs and vines in periods of extreme cold.

When trimming shrubs, the top should be even or narrower than the bottom.

Evergreen shrubs pruned like a funnel will lose lower leaves due to a lack of light.

HELPING PLANTS SURVIVE THE COLD

Remember how bad plants in your border looked after the first hard frost killed their flowers and foliage? We expect this, since annuals, biennials, and perennials die to the ground every year with the first "killing" frost. But cold can also be a problem for other plants in the Southern garden besides those which die when the growing season is over. Gardeners need to know how cold can affect their plants and how to help prevent serious or even fatal cold damage.

What about trees and shrubs in our landscape? Fortunately, most landscapers use plants which have cold resistance (hardiness) so there is not a great deal to worry about when the weather is normal. Plant hardiness is categorized by using a standard hardiness zone map. Zone 9 (20 to 30 degrees minimum) covers the lower South, including extreme South Texas, South Louisiana, South Alabama, North Florida, South Georgia, and the coastal regions of Georgia and South Carolina. Zone 8 (10 to 20

The best insurance against cold damage is to choose plants known to survive the winter in your area. Oleander is best suited for coastal areas.

degrees minimum) covers the mid-South, and Zone 7 (0 to 10 degrees minimum) includes Appalachia, Tennessee, Arkansas, Virginia and parts of northern Texas. However, gardeners in each zone often see temperatures *far* below what the hardiness map shows. Cold problems may occur when this happens. Other factors which may cause damage to normally hardy plants are if severe freezes come too early or too late in the season and how long the temperature stays very cold.

The best insurance against cold damage on permanent plants is to choose those known to survive best in your area. For example, while **Oleander** and **Gardenia** grow well in the lower South, they are subject to winter damage in the upper South and should be planted with caution and only in protected places.

The Effects of Cold

Cold damages plants in many ways. Plants unsuited to the depth of cold in an area may literally freeze. Ice crystals form in the sap moving through the plant and also in the intercellular spaces as well as inside cells. This type of freezing may burst the bark or freeze the cells of the plant, killing that part.

Flower damage is the most common type of cold damage in the South. Gardeners are disheartened when they see brown **Camellia** flowers, dead flowers on spring-flowering trees or early spring-flowering shrubs, beautiful **Oriental Magnolia** flowers suddenly turning brown, and spring-flowering bulbs which fail to come out. Unfortunately, this may happen because of our fickle winter weather. Flowers open during a warm spell, then are killed when a cold wave drops the temperature below freezing. There is no way to prevent flower damage when the temperature drops into the low twenties.

Cold can also damage plants by drying out leaves and tender stems when the ground is frozen and roots cannot absorb moisture as fast as it is being lost from the leaves. This results in "winter burning," which is most common on shallow-rooted, marginally hardy plants like **Gardenia, Loquat, Oleander, Banana Shrub**, and **Confederate Jasmine**. Plants exposed to direct sun or cold wind when the ground is very cold or frozen also lose moisture faster than the roots can replace it. I have had success with some of these plants here at Sweet Apple by planting them on the east side of the house where they are protected from cold west winds. A Southern exposure might seem to be the answer since it receives more sun in the winter and is usually a warmer location. However, when the temperature is in the low teens the ground may freeze for several days, preventing roots from obtaining moisture. Since the southern sun heats the leaves to a temperature higher than the surrounding air, severe burning may take place.

Though winter with its severe freezes is the most dangerous time for plants, less severe fall and spring freezes can also be destructive. Normally hardy plants may not be ready for such cold in the fall, or they may have started growing before the last heavy freeze in the spring. Actively growing plants are filled with less concentrated sap which freezes at a higher temperature than when the plants are dormant or growing extremely slowly.

Frost or freezing weather damages Camellia flowers. Unless it is extremely cold, tight buds will open when the weather warms up.

Winter "burn" on evergreens

Preventive Care

Reduce the danger of fall damage by helping plants slow down their growth and become dormant as the weather cools. Do not fertilize or prune after early August. You would be encouraging growth, especially on broadleaf evergreens like **azalea, Camellia, Pyracantha, Cleyera, Tea Olive**, and the marginally hardy plants mentioned above.

The only practical way to prevent dead blossoms on shrubs and trees in the winter and spring is to choose late-flowering cultivars. Even then, I'm afraid late freeze damage is always a possibility.

Protecting Plants From Cold

Protecting plants from cold is a way of life for Southern gardeners. I grew up seeing yards filled with plants wrapped in sheets, blankets, or plastic covers. Most of the time, plants still freeze since, unlike humans, plants manufacture very little heat to trap under the cover so it is almost as cold underneath as outside. Covers can be useful, however, in preventing wind-burning and frost damage, but only if they are of an insulating material like blankets, sheets, or burlap through which heat and air cannot easily travel.

Plastic can be useful to prevent wind-burning, but because heat travels easily through this non-insulating material, frost may still form on plants covered by plastic. Plastic is also dangerous to use because once the sun comes out, the "greenhouse" effect warms the plant excessively, creating conditions for "burning." And if the plastic is left too long, the plant may become more tender than before.

Even suitable covers must never be left on the plant too long because plants may get too warm during the day when the sun is shining brightly. When left on too long, heavy covers also can reduce photosynthesis in the plant's leaves, making the plant more tender than if left uncovered. The best way to cover a plant is to drive four stakes around it, attach sheets of burlap to the stakes to make a wall around the plant, and leave the top uncovered except when it is extremely cold. The side covers may be left for many weeks without damaging the plant.

There is another useful cover we have not yet mentioned: snow! While it's hard to believe, snow-covered leaves are less likely to be damaged by the cold than uncovered leaves because the snow acts as a barrier against bitter cold wind. Watch out, though; some shrubs like **boxwoods** cannot withstand the weight of the snow, and their limbs will break.

While protecting a plant's foliage from cold is important, don't forget that a sizeable portion of the plant is underground. Roots are affected by cold in much the same way as the foliage. Root cells die when the water inside them freezes, bursting the cell walls. It is especially important to protect shallow-rooted plants and shrubs like **boxwoods**, **azalea**, **Box Leaf Holly**, and **Gardenia**.

There are two methods of protecting roots from freezing temperatures. First, keep plants and shrubs well mulched over the winter months. Mulch insulates the soil and slows the loss of heat from the ground to the air above. Mulched soil may be several degrees warmer than unmulched soil. Mulching has other beneficial effects like preventing "heaving" which can break off feeder roots (see November, "Mulching: A Lesson from Nature").

Another way to insulate the soil and protect roots from cold is to water your plant or shrub when a hard freeze is announced. The roots will be more insulated if the soil is wet when the freeze comes than if it is dry. The wet soil will freeze and remain at about 31 degrees whereas dry soil could dip down to 15 degrees mimicking the temperature above.

DECK THE HALLS WITH BOUGHS OF HOLLY...

Though it may be winter outside, there are many cut evergreens which can be brought inside to add a natural touch to our decorations. Cut evergreens bring garden sights and scents into our homes, and are a wonderful tradition which dates back many hundreds of years. Here are a few suggestions which will make your home festive for the holidays.

Coniferous Evergreens

By far the best of the firs is the **Fraser Fir**, which comes from the Appalachian Mountains. This double balsam fir has several layers of needles which are richly aromatic and do not shed! **Arborvitae** is a departure from the norm. These plants make excellent

Our native Turkey Foot or Ground Cedar (Lycopodium tristachyum) makes great holiday wreaths and swags.

wreaths and swags but are not as commonly used as they were in the past. **Spruce** is another possibility, but is not preferable. The nature of the **spruce's** needles causes them to shed badly indoors. Of the cypress-type plants, the **Leyland Cypress** is most often found in Southern landscapes and is easily trimmed for evergreen boughs and decorations. And finally, the common **Red Cedar** can be used inside if you keep it away from open heating vents because it dries rapidly.

Broadleaf Evergreens

Some of my favorite broadleaf evergreens to cut and bring inside are the many different **hollies**. The **Burford Holly** is excellent to cut this time of year when it is loaded with large red berries. Keep the stems in water to prevent the berries from falling off too quickly. Other good hollies for bringing inside include **Foster's Holly** and **Nelly R. Stevens Holly**, provided you keep them in water.

Magnolia grandiflora is another broadleaf ever-green used in decorating. The huge leaves are a great inside addition at any time of the year, but they are especially nice during the holidays. Pound the cut ends with a hammer before immersing them in water so they will stay fresh longer.

While most broadleaf evergreens are a deep rich green, the variegated **Gold-Dust Aucuba** lends a little diversity. Cut branches work well inside provided they are kept in water. They will last longer than most evergreens and will even root if left long enough.

There is a broadleaf evergreen you can use in areas where you don't want to set a bowl of water. **Mahonia**, or **Holly Grape**, can be cut and arranged without water and will last a relatively long time. Unfortunately, its bright blue berries are usually gone by Christmas.

Remember that foliage brought indoors is very flammable. Keep your swags and wreaths away from candles. Also, check them frequently to see if the foliage is drying out and mist them with water if needed. Vases and urns holding greenery should be filled with water above the base of the stems at all times (your arrangements will smell fresher if you take off all foliage below the water level). And finally, make sure your fire extinquisher is full and in a handy location.

SHRUB AND VINE ACTIVITIES FOR DECEMBER:

Plant

☞ Plant all dormant container-grown, B&B, and bare-root shrubs like **Forsythia, Spiraea, Crape Myrtle, Camellia, azalea, Glossy Abelia, Aucuba,** and **Euonymus** whenever the ground is not frozen or likely to freeze soon. Prepare the holes as carefully as you do for shade trees.*

☞ Plant hardy woody vines like **Carolina Jessamine, Chinese Wisteria,** and **Confederate Jasmine** during periods of mild weather and when the ground is not frozen.*

☞ Plant hardy ground covers like **English Ivy, Liriope,** and **Spreading Juniper** whenever the ground is not frozen. Use only well-rooted plants, not sparsely rooted runners which seldom survive.*

☞ It is best to plant shrubs when the soil is not too wet. However, if planting is necessary before the soil dries out, use dry peat moss as the soil amendment. It will absorb excess moisture and make it easier to prepare a good mixture to use in planting.

Prune

☞ Heavy structural pruning of evergreen shrubs like **Burford Holly, Box Leaf Holly,** and **Ligustrum** may be done this month. If most of the leaf area is to be removed, I prefer to wait until mid-February to mid-March so I don't have to look at stubby plants so long.

☞ Prune broadleaf and narrowleaf evergreens like **boxwoods** and **Arborvitae** to shape any time this month. Always prune so the top is narrower than the bottom to keep plants from becoming top-heavy and unsightly.

☞ Prune summer-flowering shrubs (those which form their blossoms on the coming year's new growth) like **Althaea, Butterfly Bush,** and **Crape Myrtle** any time this month when the wood isn't frozen.†

☞ Do not prune spring-flowering shrubs (those which blossom on growth formed last year) like **deciduous azalea, Forsythia, Spiraea,** and **Viburnum** until after they blossom.†

☞ Wait to prune spring-flowering evergreen shrubs like **azalea, Camellia, Rhododendron,** and **Mountain Laurel** until after they have finished blooming. Fall and winter-blooming **Camellia japonica** and **Camellia sasanqua** cultivars can be pruned as soon as they finish blossoming.†

☞ Deciduous leafy shrubs like **Barberry** and deciduous **Euonymus** can be pruned this month.†

☞ Do not prune spring-flowering evergreen vines like **Carolina Jessamine** until after they bloom in the spring.†

☞ Giant hybrid **Clematis** can be pruned severely from now until new growth starts emerging in early spring.‡

☞ Other **Clematis** like **Sweet Autumn Clematis** should merely be thinned, leaving the main arms to develop shoots on which blossoms will form. A few like '**Duchess of Edinburgh**' and **Clematis montana** blossom on wood grown last summer. Prune them after they finish blossoming.‡

☞ Prune other deciduous spring-flowering vines like **Wisteria** after they have finished blooming.†

☞ Other deciduous summer-flowering vines like **Silver Lace Vine (Polygonum aubertii)** should be pruned now, before new growth starts in the spring.†

☞ Wait to prune cold-damaged stems until March or April after you can determine the true extent of cold damage.

† See "Pruning Flowering Shrubs and Vines," p. 31

‡ See "Growing Clematis and Other Southern Vines," p. 54

* See "Planting Trees and Shrubs," p. 264

☞ Cut back **Liriope** severely while the weather is cold and before new shoots emerge in early spring. If you wait too long, you will cut off new shoots or emerging buds and reduce the vigor of the clump.

Fertilize

☞ *Do not fertilize* shrubs and vines this month. Plants are dormant and are not actively absorbing nutrients. Summer-flowering and evergreen shrubs and vines like **Butterfly Bush**, **Burford Holly**, and **English Ivy** are fertilized in the early spring, and spring-flowering shrubs and vines like **azaleas** and **Wisteria** are fertilized in the spring after they bloom.**

Spray

☞ Control scale on evergreen plants. Use Cygon or Orthene except on **hollies**. Use Orthene on **hollies**.††

Water

☞ Water newly planted shrubs and vines thoroughly, even if the ground is wet, to settle the soil around the roots.

** See "How to Fertilize Shrubs and Vines," p. 30
†† See "Controlling Insects and Diseases," p. 80

Other

☞ Keep a constant check on mulches around evergreens, especially **azalea**, **Camellia**, **boxwood**, and **Box Leaf Holly**. Do not let mulch pack around lower stems and trunks. This causes roots to grow to the surface where they can be damaged easily by cold.‡‡

☞ During periods of extreme cold, protect broadleaf evergreens like **Gardenia, Banana Shrub, Loquat,** and **Indian Hawthorn (Raphiolepis indica)** by erecting a wind and sun screen made of burlap. This will prevent wind and sun damage to the leaves and stems when the ground is frozen.***

☞ Do not cover plants with plastic to protect them from extreme cold. The plants will be damaged by heat build-up when the sun is out. Use an old sheet or blanket but do not leave it on too long. Opaque material will stop photosynthesis in the leaves and make the plants more tender. ***

☞ During snowfalls, brush accumulated snow off limber evergreens like **boxwoods** with a broom to prevent spreading and breaking.***

☞ Snow on sturdy shrubs like **Camellia** and **Mahonia** should be left until it melts. Snow actually insulates plants and helps prevent cold damage.***

‡‡ See "Mulching: A Lesson from Nature," p. 243
*** See "Helping Plants Survive the Cold," p. 269

NOTES

III. *Fruits*

December continues to be a good time to plant fruits. If you find time to plant this month, it will ease some of the pressure next month when it is time to spray, prune, and buy fertilizer.

There are likely to be some cold snaps during December. Freezing weather followed by a quick thaw can cause November-planted strawberries to heave out of the ground. Keep them mulched heavily to regulate the soil temperature and prevent this problem.

If you just have to get out of the house later in the month, you can start pruning your fruit trees. Every year is a new chance to perfect your technique and produce the best harvest ever.

FRUIT ACTIVITIES FOR DECEMBER:

Plant

☛ Plant B&B, bare-root, and container-grown fruits all month. This includes fruit trees (**apples, cherries, peaches, pears,** etc.), bush fruits (**blueberries**), semi-bush fruits (**blackberries, raspberries,** etc.), and vine fruits (**grapes, muscadines**).*

☛ Do not plant **strawberries** and **figs** until February and March.

☛ Plant **Chinese Chestnut, pecan, walnut,** and other nut trees. (Always plant two or three **Chinese Chestnuts** so they can cross-pollinate. Otherwise, you will not have a good nut harvest.)

Prune

☛ Begin pruning fruit trees like **apples, nectarines, peaches,** and **pears** at the end of the month.†

☛ Do not prune **grapes** until January or early February, which is the best time.

☛ Remove any old canes of semi-bush fruits like **raspberries** and **blackberries** which bore fruit last summer if you have not done so already.‡

* See "Planting Trees and Shrubs," p. 264
† See "Pruning Fruit Trees," p. 13
‡ See "Secrets of the Berry Patch," p. 155

Fertilize

☛ Do not begin fertilizing fruit trees like **apples, peaches,** and **pears** until early spring when their buds begin to swell.

☛ **Grapes, blueberries, raspberries,** and **blackberries** are also fertilized in the spring.

Spray

☛ There is no need to spray fruits this month. The first spraying of the season will be in January/February with the application of a dormant spray.

Water

☛ Water newly planted fruits thoroughly, even if the ground is wet, to settle the soil around the roots.

Other

☛ Be careful when mowing in orchard areas not to hit the bark of fruit trees with the mower. Any damage to the bark will provide an entrance place for borers.

☛ Keep fruits mulched with pine straw to prevent weeds and grasses from competing for water and fertilizer. However, do not pile the mulch against the trunks of fruit trees. Remember to keep **strawberries** heavily mulched to prevent heaving out of the ground during freezing weather.**

** See "Mulching: A Lesson from Nature," p. 243

IV. *Roses*

The long rose season ended last month and planting time is already upon us. Many of us were burnt out by a season's worth of grooming, spraying, and fertilizing. Now that we've had a month to relax, finish up some old business by replacing any mulch from around roses which was there over the summer. This mulch is probably harboring overwintering insects and diseases.

It is still not the time to prune roses severely. While it may seem cold, pruning now will force growth during a sudden warm spell, growth which will be killed as soon as the temperature drops. If you haven't done so already, cut back tall roses by one-third so they aren't top-heavy and sway and loosen in the ground.

ROSE ACTIVITIES FOR DECEMBER:

Plant

☛ Continue to plant bare-root roses whenever the ground is not frozen. Before planting, trim long or broken roots and cut stems back to a healthy bud.*

Prune

☛ Lightly prune established plants if they are top-heavy to keep them from loosening in the ground. Do not prune heavily until early March.

Fertilize

☛ There is no need to fertilize this month. Roses are dormant and are not absorbing nutrients from the soil.

* See "Planting Bare-Root Roses," p. 250

Spray

☛ There is no need to spray roses this month. Spraying will begin next month with the application of lime sulfur as a dormant spray.

Water

☛ Water newly planted roses thoroughly, even if the ground is wet, in order to settle the soil around the roots.

Other

☛ Keep roses well mulched with a heavy layer, but do not pile mulch against the crown or lower stems. Many problems like cankers and botrytis occur when mulch covers the lower stems and keeps them damp.†

† See "Mulching: A Lesson from Nature," p. 243

NOTES

V. *Flowers and Colorful Garden Plants*

December is still a planting season for spring-flowering bulbs like tulips, hardy perennials like Astilbe, and hardy annuals like pansies. It is the truly dedicated gardener who makes it outside in December to brave the cold and work the soil. Most of us will be enjoying indoor flowering plants like Giant Flowering Amaryllis, hyacinths, and Paperwhite Narcissus. While these plants are beautiful over the holiday season, they won't last long enough to plant in the garden.

Poinsettia will continue growing after the holiday season.

One plant which we can save over from the holiday season is the Poinsettia. It will continue to sport its red leaves throughout the winter months if properly cared for and can be planted outside in the garden after the danger of frost. Outside, it will not last until next Christmas, but some people like to keep them going in the garden over the summer. I have personally attempted this many times over the years and have failed. By March I am so tired of seeing the Poinsettia's red leaves that I end up composting it before I ever plant it.

FLOWER ACTIVITIES FOR DECEMBER:

Plant

☛ Plant hardy annuals like **pansy** and **English Daisy** whenever it is warm.*

☛ Continue planting spring-flowering bulbs like **Narcissus, hyacinths,** and **tulips.** December is the last month to plant and have good success next spring.†

☛ Plant hardy perennials like **Hosta, Delphinium, Rudbeckia,** and **Shasta Daisy** whenever the ground can be worked.*

☛ Pot carry-over cuttings which have developed strong roots. Use a peat-light potting mixture.‡

Prune

☛ Finish removing the dead foliage of perennials and other garden plants. Compost them for humus next spring.

Fertilize

☛ There is no need to fertilize hardy annuals, hardy perennials, and other garden plants in December.

Other

☛ Remove and compost all dead plant material which makes a perfect harbor for overwintering insects and diseases.

☛ Keep **Canna** and **Dahlia** roots stored in a cool place. Do not set them in the garden until spring when the ground is warm and the danger of frost has passed. Store **Caladium** and **Elephant Ear** tubers in a warmer spot than **Canna** and **Dahlia** roots.

* See "How to Plant a Flower Bed," p. 62

† See "Southern Flowering Bulbs, Corms, Tubers, and Roots," p. 252

‡ See "Propagating Herbaceous Houseplants and Garden Plants," p. 225

VI. *Vegetables*

There is a reason that visions of fresh-cooked vegetables don't pop into mind when we think of Christmas. The vegetable garden is bare this time of year. Even the most ardent vegetable growers have little to do but watch their winter crop of onions, cabbages, and collards and hope there won't be a deep freeze.

It is also too late to plant green-manure crops in the vegetable garden. The weather is too cold this time of year for them to establish themselves. Besides, next month we will begin roto-tilling and preparing the garden for planting Asparagus, Jerusalem Artichoke, English peas, rhubarb, lettuce, broccoli, and cauliflower.

Since there is not much to do in the vegetable garden this month, go to the pantry, open up a jar of home-grown tomatoes, and dream about the season to come. There are not many moments like these in the Southern vegetable garden, so enjoy the rest while you can. Spring planting is on its way!

VEGETABLE ACTIVITIES FOR DECEMBER:

Plant

☛ It is too late to plant green-manure cover crops.

☛ Winter **lettuce** seeds can be started inside for planting in February.*

* See "Starting Seeds Inside," p. 18

Fertilize

☛ There is no need to fertilize hardy **onions, cabbages**, and **collards** which are being grown for an early spring harvest. In fact, hardy **onions, cabbage**, and **collards** which were planted in October for an early spring harvest should be left alone. There is nothing to do but hope the cold will not affect them too severely. Leave them in the garden when cold burns their foliage. They may still sprout from the stem or roots and produce earlier than February plantings.

NOTES

Paperwhite Narcissus can be forced inside for holiday blossoms.

VII. *Houseplants*

We have been talking all year about getting to know our houseplants. Discovering the ins and outs of a houseplant's peculiarities is what indoor gardening is all about.

By December, we have a good idea about how to keep certain plants happy. For a couple of months, we have been adjusting our watering practices and finding spots around the house with just the right exposure. Hopefully, careful tending has paid off with healthy plants.

One of the great things about houseplants is that they are dynamic. Every winter is different for houseplant gardeners, since plants continue to grow and their requirements change. A Ficus benjamina might have done well last winter in the southeast corner of the living room. This year it began losing leaves and must be moved. I think a limb on the Magnolia outside the window has grown too big and is stealing some of the Ficus's light. The leaves on the Heart-leaf Philodendron in the kitchen are also looking pale, and it could probably use a little more light. Moving houseplants and experimenting with growing conditions is what makes it gardening and not decorating.

Improper watering may cause leaves to look like they have been burned.

Scale is one of the "Big Three" houseplant insect problems.

COMMON HOUSEPLANT AILMENTS

Houseplants are seldom happy during the winter months. While the furnace may provide the warm temperatures that most indoor plants need, it also lowers the humidity more than they like. Most of our lush, green houseplants come from the tropics where the humidity is almost as high as the temperature. With the low humidity in our houses and the short and cloudy days of winter, houseplants often grow weak and spindly, if they grow at all. Indoor plants can be kept beautiful, though, by observing their growth and looking for signs that they need attention or some change in their environment. Plants can't tell us why they are doing poorly, but they do show us quite plainly. We have to look for the signs and take action to restore them to normal.

I find that well over half the problems of indoor plants result from improper watering. Unfortunately, this starts with the growing medium, which may be all right for a nursery but not all right for good growth in a home environment. The secret is to start with a light soil mixture, preferably one made up of peat moss and perlite or vermiculite. There are many of these peat-light mixtures, some of which may have other additives. Peat-light mixtures let excess water drain away, while holding enough to keep pots from becoming dry.

Water thoroughly each time so that the soil is completely damp with no dry parts. I like to do this in a sink or bathtub, where I can fill the pot with water several times and then allow it to drain out of the bottom for an hour or so. This prevents water from flooding the saucer underneath and ruining a table or carpet. Place the plant back where it belongs, then don't water it again until the soil surface begins to feel dry to the touch. There is no accurate way to say how often to water: once a day, once a week, or once a month. The only good way is to feel the soil. Never let the soil in the pot become so dry that it cracks away from the edge of the pot.

Overwatering and underwatering often produce similar symptoms of wilting, leaf-curling, brown edges (leaf- or tip-burn), and poor growth. Dry soil doesn't have enough moisture to support the water loss from a plant's leaves, while too wet soil causes poor root growth or even root rot. Both conditions keep otherwise healthy plants from taking up enough water. If you suspect overwatering is the problem, place the pot on its side and carefully pull out the ball of earth. Smell it. A sour smell indicates it has had too much water for too long a time (See October, "Houseplant Care and Maintenance").

Sometimes a plant will wilt or appear droopy even when the soil is damp. Check to see if the plant is close to an open heating vent or in a window where direct sun blazes through. These conditions can cause leaves to lose more water than the plant's roots can take up. Misting the plant with plain water will increase the humidity around its leaves and prevent excess evaporation.

If a houseplant does not respond to this treatment, it could be that it has been overwatered. Wilting is also a result of too much water. Try letting the soil dry out before watering again.

The majority of houseplant problems are watering problems, but there are others to watch out for. Spindly growth, especially in viney houseplants, indicates too little light or the lack of a balanced fertilizer. One sign of spindly growth is when a plant becomes lighter in color or has very long intervals between branches or stems (internodes). First use a complete houseplant fertilizer. Some of the best for houseplants are water-soluble fertilizer solutions like Peters. If it is too much trouble to fertilize every time you water, try using fertilizer spikes or Osmocote fertilizer, both of which last several months.

Plants which do not improve within several weeks of fertilizing should be moved to a location with more light. Remember, though, that plants are very sensitive to changes in light. Even if you think a plant is light-deprived, move it in stages, progressively introducing it to new lighter conditions.

Houseplants seldom have diseases since the humidity in our homes is so low. However, insects can be a serious problem. The "Big Three" insect problems are spider mites, scale, and mealybugs. Spider mites mottle both the undersides and tops of the leaves. If you think your plant has these almost microscopic pests, wipe the underside with a white tissue and you should see small streaks of red. You can also look at the underside with a strong magnifying glass. Scale is easy to identify by its crusty speckles on stems and foliage which can be scraped off with a fingernail. Mealybugs are found on the stem, usually where a leaf comes out. Since they may look like a white fungus, poke a sharp point into the white mass, and if it moves you have found a mealybug.

Treatment is about the same for all three insects. Take the plants outside on a warm day and spray with a chemical like Orthene which is supposed to control them. If you can't go outside, use a systemic insecticide which is safer than spraying inside. Systemic controls will also keep the problem from recurring.

By learning the characteristics of your plants and noticing quickly if they change, you can treat most houseplant ailments and in time have a happy plant.

HOUSEPLANT ACTIVITIES FOR DECEMBER:

Plant

☛ Check newly purchased houseplants for the need to repot. Repot if the roots have massed against the edge of the ball of soil and are dark in color. Always repot using a container which is at least two sizes larger. Check for sowbugs and pillbugs while the plants are out of the pot.*

☛ Pot any cuttings of houseplants and carry-over tropicals as soon as they develop a root system. Use a peat-light potting mixture and begin applying a water-soluble fertilizer solution at one-half the recommended strength.†

Prune

☛ Groom indoor plants whenever they need it. Remove weak branches or stems as well as off-color leaves.

Fertilize

☛ Continue fertilizing with half-strength applications of liquid fertilizer every time you water. They will not need full-strength until the days begin to get longer next spring.‡

Spray

☛ Check all indoor plants for insects such as spider mites, scale, and mealybug. I like to use a houseplant systemic insecticide to control them. It is easier and safer than spraying inside. If you do spray, remember to apply the insecticide to the undersides of the leaves.**

☛ Be careful when spraying **ferns**. Some insecticides are harmful to them. *Always read the label for warnings about **ferns** and other plants.*

* See "Repotting Houseplants," p. 67
† See "Propagating Herbaceous Houseplants and Garden Plants," p. 225
‡ See "Houseplant Care and Maintenance," p. 232
** See "Common Houseplant Ailments," p. 280

Water

☞ Watch houseplants carefully during the winter. When they look limp, check for dry soil. If it is dry, water thoroughly in a sink or bathtub, letting the water drain completely, and don't water again until the surface is dry again. Between waterings, mist with plain water on a regular basis. If the limp plants are in moist soil, do not water but allow the soil to dry a bit and mist frequently.‡

☞ Tip-burn or edge-burn on leaves indicates that more water is being lost through the leaves than is being absorbed by the roots. Check for dry soil, too much sunlight, or drafts from heating vents. Overwatering can also damage roots and cause a similar condition.‡

☞ Continue to watch **ferns** for signs of dead or dying foliage. Mist them frequently and remove any dead fronds as soon as they occur.

‡ See "Houseplant Care and Maintenance," p. 232

Other

☞ Houseplants which become lighter in color or have very long intervals between branches or stems (internodes) may need more light.‡

☞ Newly purchased houseplants have been growing under ideal conditions at the nursery. When you bring them home, they may take a while to adjust to the drier conditions in your home. Water your new plants as prescribed above, but *do not overwater*! Mist them frequently and if they continue to do poorly, try placing a cool-air vaporizer near the plant for several days.‡

☞ December 21 generally marks the Winter Solstice. This day has the fewest daylight hours of the year. After the Winter Solstice, the daylight hours will slowly increase until the Summer Solstice about June 21. Remember to check your houseplants periodically as the sun's position in the sky changes. Windows which currently receive enough light may lose some as the sun's position rises in the sky.

‡ See "Houseplant Care and Maintenance," p. 232

NOTES

VIII. *Lawns*

Winter is not an active time in the lawn world. Cloudy days and cold nights slow down the growth of all grasses. Summer grasses like Bermuda Grass and Centipede are brown. Evergreen grasses aren't growing and have lost their manicured look. Patches of brown have popped up here and there where an annual weed grew unnoticed in the green of summer. The winter weeds are still green and are on hiatus much like our fescue.

December is a slow month for lawn activities. It is best not to cut summer grasses because the foliage helps to protect the roots from bitter cold spells when they come. Established evergreen lawns and newly planted ones can be cut if they reach the recommended cutting height.

Weed control is often best left for spring. If you do decide to spray winter weeds like chickweed and wild garlic, it will take a while for the herbicide to penetrate the leaves and begin working. Try to choose a warm spell with no rain in sight to spray so the material won't be washed off before it is absorbed.

LAWN ACTIVITIES FOR DECEMBER:

Plant

☛ December is not the time to start a new evergreen or summer grass lawn.

Fertilize

☛ There is no need to fertilize evergreen or summer grass lawns this month.

Spray

☛ Control winter weeds like wild garlic (wild onions), chickweed, and Annual Bluegrass with a lawn formula broadleaf herbicide which is recommended for your type of grass. Spray on a warm day and be patient, because results are slow in the winter.

Cut

☛ Cut lawns when they reach the correct cutting height. Do not let newly seeded grasses become too tall before cutting.

☛ Cut evergreen lawns at the proper height:

EVERGREEN GRASSES	HEIGHT
Kentucky 31 Tall Fescue	3 to 3 ½ inches
Turf-type Tall Fescues	3 inches
Fine Leaf Fescues	1 ½ to 2 inches
Kentucky Bluegrass	2 to 2 ½ inches

☛ If you have seeded **Ryegrass** over **Bermuda Grass,** keep the **Ryegrass** cut about an inch above the base lawn. If you let it grow tall in clumps, it will damage your permanent grass.

Other

☛ Keep leaves off grass. Heavy leaf fall can smother grass, even those which are dormant.

Pests and Problems

IN THE SOUTHERN GARDEN

Gardening involves a series of steps, like planting, fertilizing, and cultivating, followed by a series of events like controlling pests and overcoming growth problems. You start by choosing what plant you want to grow inside your home or outside in your landscape or garden. Then you plant, grow, and nurture it with the best care you can give. The reward is a beautiful and productive plant.

Despite our hard work, however, plants sometimes don't live up to our expectations. The hardest part is deciphering what is wrong with a plant when it isn't growing the way it should. A gardener needs to be like Sherlock Holmes by searching for clues and solving the mystery.

A hole in a leaf might seem like the work of some wandering worm or Japanese Beetle. It could also be the result of a slug or snail's evening dinner. Then again, it could be caused by a shot hole fungus. Before you can mount your counterattack, you have to narrow your list of suspects and identify the culprit.

Look for clues. Most plant detective work starts with symptoms, like holes in a leaf. From them you begin to solve plant problems. With a pest like a slug, you may never actually see the culprit. He'll be hiding from the sun during the day while he rests from a busy night of leaf munching. Beside the holes, however, he has left a second clue: a trail of silvery mucus left behind as he moved across the leaf surface. With the two clues firmly in hand, you can be confident that a slug is your pest and take measures to control him.

The time of the crime is also important. The suspect cannot be a Japanese Beetle if the symptom shows up in March or April. Japanese Beetle larvae do not emerge from the ground as leaf-eating beetles until early summer. In the same way, you won't see aphids on your garden plants in January although you might see scale. The monthly checklists earlier in the book will help you narrow your list of suspects by identifying which pests might be active in your neighborhood.

This section is a good place to start solving plant problems. It contains a collection of some of our least favorite and most often seen pests as well as other plant problems. Hopefully, these photographs will help you identify the culprit before your plant is overwhelmed. If the guilty party doesn't hop off the page and say, "I did it," you might want to begin your detective work by reading the article, "Controlling Insects and Diseases" on pages 80-83.

LEFT: Aphids: *Aphids are a horrible menace in the garden and greenhouse. The tiny insects crowd on tender shoots and stems and literally suck the life out of your plant. The Viburnum on which these aphids were feeding had stunted shoot tips and wasn't growing at all. I usually control aphids with a systemic insecticidal spray like Orthene, although insecticidal soap works as well.*

SCALE INSECTS

Scale insects are some of the most exasperating, and hard to control, pests. They look like tiny brown oyster shells and are usually found encrusted along the leaf veins and smaller stems of houseplants, garden plants, shrubs, and even some trees. While there are insecticidal treatments that control scale outdoors, I have to admit that I usually throw away a scale-infested houseplant so it won't infect my other plants.

WHITEFLIES

Whiteflies usually arrive sporadically on succulent garden plants, vegetables, and young landscape plants. If you hang sticky yellow strips (available at garden centers) when you first see them, they usually don't get out of control. But beware, their population can grow extremely fast if left untreated and they can become almost impossible to control. If they start getting out of control, begin spraying with insecticidal soap and Neem, then move to insecticidal sprays.

MEALYBUGS

Mealybugs are most commonly found on houseplants and potted plants and look like tiny balls of cotton caught at the base of the leaf stem. Fortunately, Mealybugs seldom infest a plant in life-threatening numbers. While you can spray to control them, I usually poke them with a pin since they are easy to locate and move very slowly. Another way to kill them is to rub them with a cotton swab dipped in rubbing alcohol.

THRIPS

Thrips are tiny, fast moving, rod-shaped insects that infest flower petals and tender leaves. They love hot, dry weather and will multiply into a sizable population before you even notice them. Luckily, heavy rains naturally reduce their number. Even then, you will probably have to use a systemic insecticidal spray on flowers like roses where they can stay dry deep within the cluster of petals.

LEAF HOPPER

I find leaf hoppers every year on the flower stems of my Hosta. Before I discover the leaf hopper himself, I usually notice his white cotton candy up and down the stem. Searching through the fuzz with a pin, I'll usually come across him just before he flings himself off in some haphazard direction. Leaf hoppers never seem to cause much damage in my garden so I usually don't worry about them. There are several insecticidal sprays that will work, though, if needed.

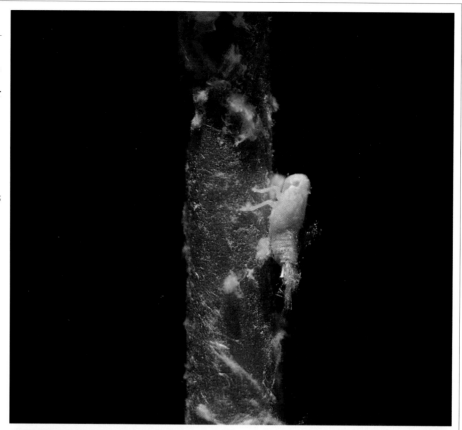

PILLBUGS

Pillbugs (roly-poly bugs) feed on the roots and crowns of houseplants and succulent garden plants. They especially love potted plants where they enter through the drain holes and feed happily on the contained root system. A good time to scout for pillbugs (and sowbugs) is when you repot. Dust the soil surface and root ball with Diazinon to control them.

SPIDER MITES

Spider mites are a pain. They are tiny (you can barely see them with a magnifying glass) and feed in droves on the underside of a plant's leaves. The top of the leaf will be off-color and appear to have been pricked countless times by a pin. Since spider mites can move from plant to plant, infected houseplants should be moved away from nearby plants while you control them with a recommended miticide/ovacide.

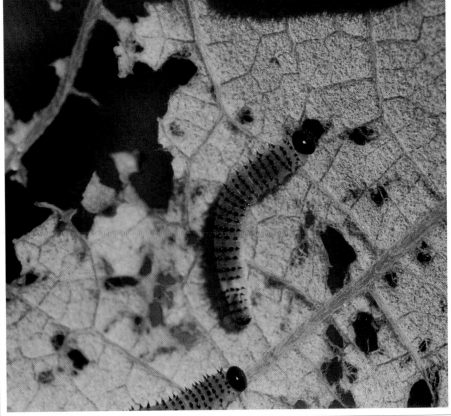

WORMS

There are numerous types of worms that feed on vegetables, fruits, and garden plants in the Southern garden. My least favorite are the ones that feed in droves along the edges of a leaf. Before you know it, your plant is almost defoliated (they get my grapes every year). As you know from numerous references in the book, a great way to control worms is by dusting or spraying with BT (*Bacillus thuringiensis*).

HOLLY LEAF MINER

Leaf miner larvae tunnel through the leaves of hollies, boxwood (see page 80), and various other garden plants, shrubs, and trees. The destruction on this American Holly began as a tiny pin-prick in the foliage marking the spot where the gnat-like adult laid its eggs. The larvae hatched and immediately began tunneling through the heart of the leaf. The best control is a systemic insecticide like Orthene.

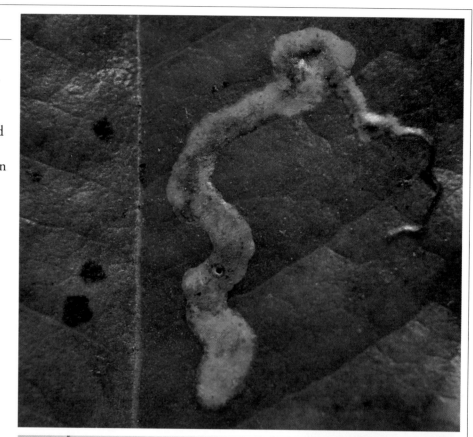

BAGWORMS

Bagworms are hideous creatures that commonly attack evergreen coniferous shrubs like juniper and arborvitae, although I have recently seen them on Leyland Cypress. The worm-like larvae spin 1-2 inch silken bags covered with bits of dead leaves/needles. The sneaky larvae poke their heads out, eat some of the plant, and then retreat down into the bag. The best way to control bagworms is to remove as many by hand as possible and then spray with Orthene.

JAPANESE BEETLE

Japanese Beetles lay their eggs in lawns and grass areas in mid to late summer. The eggs hatch and develop into grubs which begin feeding on grass roots. The best way to control Japanese Beetles is to treat your lawn with grub-control in late summer or early fall when the young grubs are feeding heavily. In winter the grubs burrow deep into the ground, but move to the surface again in the spring as the ground warms. They feed on grass roots to a lesser extent in April and May before emerging from the ground as a beetle in early summer.

TENT CATERPILLARS

Tent caterpillars are usually apparent in the summer when they spin silk tents in the crotches of trees and shrubs. They feed en masse at night and can defoliate a tree or shrub. If you can reach the silk tent, the best way to control them is to cut off the branch with the tent and seal it in a plastic bag. Otherwise, break the tent open with a stick and spray the tent and surrounding foliage with BT or another insecticidal spray.

CORN EARWORM

Since Corn Earworm populations explode in mid to late summer, the best way to protect your corn is to plant soon after the danger of frost has passed. That way, your harvest will be ready before the earworms become uncontrollable. Even then, a few will show up to decimate your harvest. A watchful eye and a dusting of Sevin and BT should keep them at bay.

FIRE BLIGHT

Fire blight is a bacterial disease that infects certain shrubs, fruits, and ornamental trees like pear, apple, and crabapple. It is spread in the spring by bees and other flower pollinators. The bacteria invades the flower and moves down twigs and branches, causing them to shrivel, turn brown, and die. While fire blight is difficult to control with sprays, an antiseptic method of pruning out the blight is described on page 86.

SNAILS

Although snails are slothful, slumbering creatures during the day, they feed energetically on garden plants at night. The tell-tale sign of a snail attack is the silver mucus trail he leaves along the leaf surface. The best way to control snails is to place a pie pan filled with beer in a shady nook of the garden. The snails will crawl in and die. Snail baits are also effective, but beware. They are often poisonous and can hurt dogs and friendly wild creatures living in the garden.

TAR SPOT

Tar Spot fungus often arrives on maple trees during the spring months. It is a benign fungus and does little more than mark the foliage. At first, the fungus appears as a circular spot with a reddish-purple halo. It persists into the summer and takes on a sooty appearance (pictured). Although it is harmless, it's good to know what it is so you won't worry about it.

POWDERY MILDEW

Powdery mildew seems to
have a mind of its own
since it shows up on gar-
den plants, vegetables, and
shrubs in both humid and
dry weather. The "mildew"
found coating the leaves is
actually a collection of
fungal spores. Although
not as visible as the spores,
the fungus is hard at
work feeding on the plant.
Powdery mildew can be
controlled by spraying with
a fungicide specifically
recommended for your
particular plant.

CAMELLIA LEAF GALL

There are few things as
shocking and grotesque as
a Camellia leaf attacked by
Camellia Leaf Gall. The
non-fatal condition is
caused by a fungus that
invades the leaf and causes
it to swell (a similar fungus
attacks Azaleas). Since
fungicidal sprays are ineffective, the best method of
control is to remove and
dispose of affected leaves.

GALL

There are numerous types of gall that affect garden plants, trees, and shrubs. They are caused when an insect, bacteria, virus, or other pest injects a chemical into the plant that causes a tumorous growth. Often, the gall becomes the short-term home of the pest or its young. In most cases, galls can be removed by careful pruning. If the problem is widespread or persistent, you might try a systemic insecticide.

MAPLE GALL MITES

Maple Gall Mites attack various species of maple including our native Red Maples. The microscopic mites bite the maple leaves and cause a tumorous growth to form. The mite takes up residence in the gall where it feeds and eventually lays its eggs. Despite their mottled foliage, maples are relatively unaffected by Gall Mites. This is lucky, since there is no practical way to stop them.

CHLOROSIS

Soil nutrients are absorbed by a plant's roots, travel up its stem or trunk, and move through veins into its leaves. This plant is suffering from a lack of available nutrients in the soil. There are still enough nutrients moving through the veins to supply nearby cells, but not enough to keep the entire leaf green. Fertilizing the plant and/or correcting improper pH will increase available nutrients in the soil and "green up" the leaves.

VOLE

The vole (a.k.a. pine mouse) is a sneaky little creature that crawls up through mulch, tall grass, or ground covers to chew on trees and shrubs. This Otto Luyken Laurel died after a vole chewed all the way around its trunk. Notice the white callous tissue that formed as the bush tried to heal itself. The best way to control voles is to keep mulch 3-4 inches away from the trunk or to buy a mean cat.

TOPPED TREE

There is nothing that will ruin a tree's shape more than pruning its central leader. This oak was "topped" by accident several years ago. Two shoots sprouted near the cut and the homeowners carefully removed one, trying to restore its natural top growth. Even then, the tree will always have a weak spot and ugly crook in its trunk.

SPLIT BRADFORD PEAR

Despite the spring beauty of the Bradford Pear, beware! Bradford Pears have the horrible habit of sprouting branches that grow upright rather than away from the central trunk. These branches are weakly connected to the tree and will peel like a banana in a wind or ice storm. The best solution is to buy a different tree (how about a Kwanzan or Yoshino Cherry?). If you must have a Bradford Pear, plan to judiciously prune upward growing branches each and every year.

HOUSEPLANT LEAF BURN

Leaf burn occurs when a plant's roots do not send enough water to the leaves. With houseplants, this usually happens when the potting soil dries completely or when some of the roots have died from overwatering. Dry plants should be watered immediately. Overwatered plants should be misted until the potting soil dries and the plant begins to grow new roots.

DRY AIR FROM HEATING VENTS

Air blowing from heating and air-conditioning vents can severely damage a houseplant. The dry air removes excessive amounts of moisture from the leaves to the point that they turn brown and fall off. The amazing thing, as seen with this Weeping Fig (*Ficus benjamina*), is that the column of dry air above a vent is extremely local. The only solution is to move the houseplant away from the vent.

HOUSEPLANT IN LOW LIGHT

In low light, houseplants often lose their natural form and beauty. They might stretch toward the light, drop their leaves, or begin to turn yellow. While some plants will adjust to low light, the majority will need to be moved closer to a window.

PLANTING IN JULY

Despite what your local landscape installer says, summer is not the time to plant a tree or shrub. The root systems of B&B trees and shrubs are severely pruned before they are wrapped with burlap. Even with daily watering, they may not be able to draw enough water from the soil to beat the summer heat. This $1000 tree died a week after its July planting. The others suffered a slow death over the following month. Wait until November!

GLOSSARY

Annual: A plant which grows from a germinated seed to a mature plant and then dies in one season.

Aphid: Soft, sap-sucking insect of many colors and shapes which multiplies rapidly and attacks plants in droves.

Artificial light: Light from man-made sources, not from the sun. Usually has a narrower spectrum than sunlight.

B&B: Balled and burlapped. Plants dug with a ball of soil around the roots, tightly covered with burlap.

Bare root: Plants dug without a ball of soil around the roots. Sometimes referred to as loose-rooted.

Basal cut: A cut made at the bottom of a trunk, stem, or limb.

Basal growth: Growth from the base of a trunk, stem, or limb.

Bed: A well-prepared garden area suitable for growing herbaceous plants or shrubs.

Bed, vegetable: A vegetable planting ridge which is higher than the middle which lies between the rows.

Biennial: A plant which grows from seed to maturity and then dies in two years, usually producing its flowers and seeds the second year.

Botrytis: A serious plant disease which attacks stems, crowns, and other plant parts.

Bract: A modified leaf associated with a flower which often looks like a part of the flower, as in dogwood and Poinsettia.

Broadcast: To sow seed evenly over an area rather than in rows.

Broadleaf evergreen: A plant which does not normally shed its foliage during the winter. The leaves are wider and more showy than found on needle-leaf plants.

BT: Short form for Bacillus thuringiensis, an effective natural, biological control of soft worms which attack plants.

Bud: An embryonic shoot or short growth-axis often concealed by the young leaves it bears.

Bud union: The point on a bud-grafted plant where the scion bud was inserted on the stock to produce a desired cultivar.

Bulb: A plant storage organ usually found underground which is a modified leaf bud consisting of a short thick stem and fleshy scales.

Cell trays: Trays which contain cells to start seed or plants in.

Cold frame: A partially buried, bottomless box-like structure covered with clear material which is used to propagate plants or grow plants early in the season.

Compost: Plant material which after being digested by bacteria, results in humus.

Container-grown: Plants which are grown from a small rooted cutting or seedling in a container and sold without disturbing their roots.

Cover crop: Plants grown to keep soil from washing during periods of high rainfall and to provide other benefits like green manure and nitrogen.

Crown: Usually the part of the plant where roots and stems meet, but can also be a part of a rhizome which can be propagated.

Cultivar: A plant which is horticulturally but not taxonomically different from the botanical species within which it falls.

Cutting: A section of a plant without roots which when placed in the proper medium will produce roots and a new plant.

Deciduous: A plant which naturally sheds all or most of its leaves each winter.

Divisions: A method of propagation in which an established plant is separated into several parts, each containing roots and foliage.

Dormant: A condition occurring when a plant stops its growth, usually indicated by shedding its leaves which are replaced when growth starts again.

Dormant cuttings: Woody cuttings made when a plant is dormant.

Dormant oil: A pest control material (usually very strong) sprayed on plants while they are dormant.

Drip Line: The circle on the ground under the outer extremities of the limbs of a shrub or tree.

Edge-burn: Browning of the edge of a leaf, generally caused by a water problem.

Espalier: A strict pruning method for fruits or other plants to make them flat-planed and suitable for fastening against a wall.

Evergreen: A plant which retains its leaves the entire year.

Evergreen lawn: Lawns containing grasses which do not go dormant but which remain green throughout the year.

Feeder roots: The small roots which, as they grow, actively take up water and nutrients from the soil.

Feeding a plant: The manufacture of food in a plant through the process of photosynthesis. Thus, a plant feeds itself. The term is often confused with fertilizing which means supplying fertilizer nutrients, not food, to the plant.

Fertilization: The union of two gametes resulting in a new cell which often results in a seed. This term is improperly used for applying fertilizer.

Fertilizer spike: Fertilizer molded into a spike suitable to drive in the ground.

Fertilizing: The act of applying nutrients of any type to a plant.

Foliar fertilizer: Soluble or liquid nutrients sprayed on a plant's foliage

Fruiting cane: The shoot of a fruiting plant like blackberries which produces fruit, often only once.

Fruiting spur: A small shoot on certain fruits like apples and pears on which flowers and fruits develop.

Graft union: The place on a plant's stem or trunk where the scion was inserted on the stock to produce a desired cultivar.

Green House: A heated glass or plastic covered structure used to grow plants.

Green manure crop: A plant which is grown on a bare area for large amounts of succulent green foliage which is later plowed into the ground to produce humus.

Grooming: Removal of unwanted or undesirable growth or matured flowers.

Hard freeze: Temperatures below 28-32 degrees Fahrenheit which last for many hours.

Half-Hardy (HH): Plants which can stand a frost but not a hard freeze.

Hardy (H): Plants which can withstand temperatures below 32 degrees Fahrenheit for many hours.

Herbaceous: Plants which are not woody and die to the ground each year.

Herbicide: Spray material used to control plant growth, usually herbaceous and woody weeds.

Hormodin: A brand of growth regulator used to induce roots to form on a cutting and to increase the number of roots.

Humus: Decomposed plant material which is useful in improving soils.

Hybrid: The result of a cross between two dissimilar but related plants.

Inorganic: A material not containing animal or plant matter.

Internode: The part of a stem or shoot between a single or a group of leaves or latent buds and the next single or group of leaves or latent buds.

Knife-cut shears: Pruning shears whose cutting blade passes behind a holding bar, acting somewhat like a knife.

Layering: Rooting a branch or piece of a plant while it is still attached to the mother plant.

Leader: A trunk or shoot which holds the terminal bud at the end. This bud generally takes precedence over the lateral or side buds.

Leaf burn: Browning of all or part of a leaf due to excessive water loss caused by wind, sun, or freezing.

Leaf Cutting: A leaf and petiole without roots which when placed in a proper medium will produce roots and a new plant.

Leaf scar: The identifiable point on the stem where a leaf developed and has fallen or been removed. A latent bud lies within the scar.

Maintenance pruning: Removal of unwanted or damaged stems or limbs which does not change the structure of the plant.

Narrowleaf evergreen: Evergreen plants with needle-like leaves which are often small. They seldom produce showy flowers.

Node: The place on a stem where a single or group of leaves arises.

Nutrients: Fertilizer compounds required by the plant to produce food through photosynthesis in its green area, and also required for growth. Nitrogen, Phosphorus, and Potassium compounds are the major ones.

Open Head/Basket method: A method of pruning which changes a tree's natural growth habit to open the fruiting or flowering area for more sun and air.

Organic: Refers to materials produced from plants or animals.

Overwintering diseases (spores): The dormant bodies of a disease which germinate in the spring, spreading to and infecting other plant parts.

Overwintering plants: Tender perennial outdoor plants which are kept where cold will not kill them during the winter.

Peat-light: Combination of sphagnum peat and perlite along with other additives to produce potting soil which drains well, yet holds sufficient moisture for good root development and plant growth.

Peat Moss: Decomposed sphagnum mosses which are usually found in bogs. It is the stage before complete decomposition into muck.

Perennial: A plant which grows for at least three years. In gardening, it is a herbaceous plant which dies to the ground each year, then resprouts from its roots or crown the following spring.

Perlite: A mined material which expands when heated into small pill-like particles. It is excellent as a soil amendment for drainage and the root of cuttings.

Petiole: The stalk which supports a leaf.

Pinching: Removing succulent shoots or buds with the fingers.

Pot-bound: When plants grown in pots become so compacted that new feeder roots are scarce and the plant's growth is restricted.

Propagation: Any method of increasing plants.

Root: The plant organ, usually underground, which absorbs moisture and nutrients from the soil and transports them to the food-producing areas of the plant. They also anchor the plant in the ground.

Rooting Bed: A special structure filled with a suitable medium in which cuttings are rooted.

Rooting medium: The material into which cuttings are inserted in order to develop roots.

Rootone: A brand of growth regulator used to induce roots to form on a cutting and to increase the number of roots.

Rose stem canker: A diseased area on a rose stem which can spread and eventually kill the entire cane.

Roto-Tiller: A power machine used to prepare, work, and cultivate soils.

Scaffold branches: The major branches of a tree which form the tree's structure and shape.

Scale: A serious and difficult-to-control insect which lives under a waxy coat while it sucks sap from plant sells.

Scion: A detached part of a desired plant containing two or more buds which is grafted upon root stock to produce a new plant.

Sealant: A material to seal wounds on trees and other plants, especially wounds caused by pruning.

Semi-bush fruit: Fruiting plants which regenerate canes from their roots and crowns on which fruit buds are set the first year, and produce blossoms and fruits the next year.

Semi-hardwood cutting: A cutting taken from a plant's new growth which has hardened sufficiently to root. These cuttings are usually made in the summer.

Shaping: Pruning a plant to a desired form.

Softwood cuttings: Green cuttings taken from herbaceous plants.

Soil auger: An implement used to bore holes in the ground. Often used to place fertilizer in the ground near the roots of trees.

Soluble fertilizer: Fertilizer which easily dissolves in water.

Spring-flowering shrub or tree: A woody plant which flowers in the winter, spring, or very early summer whose bloom buds were formed the previous season. Often but not always blooming before June 1.

Stem Cutting: A section of a plant's stem without roots which when placed in a proper medium will produce roots and a new plant.

Structural pruning: Major pruning of structural limbs of woody plants to improve their growth habit.

Sucker: A rapid growing unwanted shoot often arising from lower branches or on the trunk near the ground.

Suckering of grafted plants: Removal of shoots arising from the roots or remaining parts of the understock on which the desired cultivar was grafted.

Suckering of tomatoes: Removal of some or all shoots arising from the bud between a leaf and the stem.

Summer lawn grasses: Lawn grasses which turn brown with frosts and hard freezes and are dormant in the winter, starting new growth in the spring.

Summer-flowering shrub or tree: A woody shrub or tree which blossoms on new shoots set since the plant started new growth in the spring. Usually but not always blooming after June 1.

Tender plant: A plant which is killed by frosts or light freezes.

Terminal bud: The bud at the end of the main trunk or leader of a plant. This bud takes precedence over lateral buds.

Tip burn: Browning of the tips or edges at the end of a leaf caused by excessive water loss from the plant.

Tip-growth: Growth arising from the tip buds.

Training: The method of causing a plant to grow in a desired way

Transplanting: Moving a plant from one place to another. Also, moving seedlings from seedling trays to pots or cells for further development.

Understock: Vigorous plants, often seedlings, upon which a desired cultivar is grafted.

Variety: A taxonomic classification and subdivision of a species. Often incorrectly used to include horticultural cultivars.

Vermiculite: A mined mica material which, when heated to very high temperature, expands into a mineral mass which is highly absorbent. Excellent to increase water holding in soils.

Water breaker: A device which aerates water from a faucet or hose and makes the fall of water "soft."

Watering spike: A hollow probe which can be driven into the ground to deep-water roots of shrubs and trees. It attaches to a hose.